Insuring the Air Transport Industry Against Aviation War and Terrorism Risks and Allied Perils

Yaw Otu Mankata Nyampong

Insuring the Air Transport Industry Against Aviation War and Terrorism Risks and Allied Perils

Issues and Options in a Post-September 11, 2001 Environment

Springer

Yaw Otu Mankata Nyampong
Faculty of Law
McGill University
Montreal
Québec
Canada

ISBN 978-3-642-32432-1 ISBN 978-3-642-32433-8 (eBook)
DOI 10.1007/978-3-642-32433-8
Springer Heidelberg New York Dordrecht London

Library of Congress Control Number: 2012954862

Printed on acid-free paper

Springer is part of Springer Science+Business Media (www.springer.com)

Foreword

I am pleased to welcome the publication of this work by Dr. Nyampong, a colleague at the Institute of Air and Space Law at McGill University in Montreal.

This work provides a careful and detailed analysis of the insurance implications of the tragic events of September 11, 2001, involving the terrorist attack on the World Trade Center in New York. It includes discussion of the history, structure and workings of the international insurance market which provides cover against the risks of aviation war and terrorism, the impact of the events of September 11, 2001 on the aviation war and terrorism insurance market, and the response on the part of the insurers of said risks to September 11, including the forms and limits of coverage currently available in the market in respect of such risks.

September 11, 2001 brought to light certain fundamental problems inherent in the insurance of aviation war and terrorism risks. In the 11 years that have since elapsed, many initiatives have been proposed (some even implemented) at the national, regional and international levels to address these problems. Unfortunately, however, a permanent and sustainable solution to the problem has not been found as yet, and it is feared that the commercial aviation insurance market (which continues to provide primary insurance coverage for such risks) may not have the requisite capacity to bear the financial consequences of another large terrorist attack that involves the air transport system.

This work makes a significant contribution to the search for a permanent and sustainable solution to the problem by carefully analyzing and exploring the root causes thereof from a multidisciplinary perspective. In so doing, the book traces the rationale underlying the historical exclusion of war and terrorism risks from property/casualty and marine insurance contracts, and examines the manner in which these exclusionary practices were subsequently extended to, and have since evolved in, the aviation insurance market. Aside from insurance, this work also analyzes other different traditional and innovative mechanisms of risk transfer and risk management to determine whether they are perhaps better suited to provide permanent and sustainable coverage for aviation war and terrorism risks. The work concludes by identifying and proffering a number of recommendations on how to achieve permanent and sustainable coverage of aviation war and terrorism risks.

I commend this book to all who have a practical, legal or academic interest in aviation insurance, including particularly those with an interest or involvement in the insurance aspects of aviation war and terrorism risks.

Los Angeles
September 2012

Rod Margo

Preface

The saying that the terrorist events of September 11, 2001, changed the world forever is true not only in respect of how it changed the conduct of international relations between states but also in respect of the manner in which it affected the provision of insurance coverage for aviation war and terrorism risks. Although the quantum of loss and compensation that insurers had to pay as a result of the events of September 11, 2001, was unprecedented, events of such nature were not entirely new to the insurance market particularly the London aviation market where coverage of aviation war and terrorism risks was commonly provided. Indeed, the 1968 Israeli attack on Beirut airport is on record as the first major event of that nature that targeted the international air transport system. This marked the beginning of the exclusion of war and allied risks from aviation insurance policies issued in the London market, a practice that was successively expanded and developed as many more such events occurred over time. A few days after the fateful events of September 11, 2001, however, it became abundantly clear to everyone who had something to do with the air transport industry that the business-as-usual era in which airlines could obtain from commercial insurers as much insurance coverage for aviation war and terrorism risks as they desired was over and that the time had come to begin the difficult process of finding other reliable risk transfer mechanisms to serve as alternatives and/or complements to traditional insurance.

A review of the literature at the time indicated that the question of how to provide or ensure the provision of sustainable insurance (or other financial) coverage for aviation war and terrorism risks had not been addressed in a comprehensive manner by academicians, insurance practitioners, and government policymakers. What really complicated the issue is the fact that, in most countries, the law requires an air transport operator to maintain adequate insurance coverage (including coverage for war and terrorism risks) as a condition for the initial grant and continuing validity of an air operator's certificate. There being no mechanism to ensure that what the law requires as minimum insurance requirements would be available commercially or otherwise to airlines, events such as those of September 11, 2001, almost brought the global air transport industry to a halt. Proposals of all kind and manner were advanced, driven by the urgent desire to find a solution to the problem and the tendency to transpose solutions that have been successfully implemented in other areas of economic endeavor. Unfortunately, very little effort was directed toward determining what the root cause(s) of the problem were. As a result, most of the solutions that were implemented have either failed or remained stillborn.

In light of the foregoing, the rationale underlying my research and ultimately this book was to take a step back and look critically at the problem of how to provide sustainable insurance coverage for aviation war and terrorism risks, not only from a legal perspective but also taking into account various other nonlegal phenomena that could help delineate the exact boundaries of the problem before prescribing any solutions. In order to do so, it was important as a first step to provide readers with an overview of aviation insurance as practiced in the London market (and, subject to some marked differences in a few places, throughout the wider Common Law world). This is followed by a specific focus on how the commercial insurance market has addressed marine and subsequently aviation war and terrorism risks over the years. The book then analyzes the behavior of the commercial insurance markets to extreme events such as September 11, 2001, by resorting to a number of concepts and models propounded by eminent scholars in the fields of law and economics as well as behavioral law and economics. One of the major findings is that as a means of risk management, insurance works best under circumstances where the law of large numbers applies—large population size characterized by high frequency of occurrence of the risk concerned but a significantly low financial impact on each occurrence. Aviation war and terrorism risks on the other hand belong to the class of risks that are typically low frequency/high financial impact. As such, insurer appetite for those types of risks decreases as the size of the latest occurrence (payout) increases.

Clearly, if the commercial insurance markets alone cannot be expected to insure these risks at societally desirable levels and in a sustainable fashion, then it is imperative that alternatives and complementary solutions be found. The book therefore considers the extent to which capital markets, governments, and the international community of states (three of the many proposed solutions) may provide alternative or complementary mechanisms to the coverage of aviation war and terrorism risks by commercial insurers. Each of these raises peculiar issues which are discussed from a multidisciplinary perspective. Thus government-run insurance and guarantee schemes for air transport operators in a number of countries are analyzed along with the numerous issues associated therewith. For instance, it has been alleged that a domestic war and terrorism insurance market for air transport operations has not been able to develop due mainly to the federal government's continued provision of premium war risk insurance coverage to US airlines. At the international level, most states consider that aviation war and terrorism risks are a direct manifestation of each state's foreign policy. As such it has been difficult to develop an international mechanism that will address the insurance and financial aspects of such risks to the satisfaction of all (or at least a majority of) states. Capital market solutions on the other hand offer unique opportunities and deeper capital reserves for the insurance of such risks. However, it is important to tread with caution and to learn lessons from the recent economic crisis.

It is my hope that this exposition will enable policymakers, decision makers, government regulators, air transport operators, airlines, and their insurers to have a broader view of what aviation war and terrorism risk insurance really entails. It is intended to encourage and facilitate discussion and reflection about the way forward.

Montreal, QC, Canada Yaw Otu Mankata Nyampong

Acknowledgments

The manuscript that forms the basis of this book was written in partial fulfillment of the requirements of the Doctor of Civil Law degree program at the Institute of Air and Space Law, Faculty of Law, McGill University. I wish to express my deepest and most profound gratitude to Professor Paul Stephen Dempsey, Tomlinson Professor of Global Governance in Air and Space Law and Director of the Institute of Air and Space Law at McGill University for devoting his time, energy, and attention to the supervision of my dissertation and for providing me with invaluable guidance, encouragement, and support throughout my long years of research and writing at the Institute. I am also extremely grateful to him for employing me as the editor of the *Annals of Air and Space Law* since April 2007. This paid part-time position enabled me to provide for my family while studying full-time at McGill.

I also wish to express sincere gratitude to Professors Stephen Smith and H. Patrick Glenn, members of my advisory thesis committee. Their recommendations and suggestions during the earlier stages of my research provided me with broader insights and perspectives on the subject—perspectives which have heavily influenced the final shape of this book. I wish to thank Professor Ram Jakhu, Maria D'Amico, Mark Glynn, Ari Munisami, Kuan Wei (David) Chen, and indeed all my other colleagues at the Institute of Air and Space Law for their numerous (and at times unwelcome) distractions. These helped me maintain my sanity and prodded me on to finish this project.

I wish to acknowledge with appreciation the generous funding I received under doctoral fellowships awarded to me by the Social Sciences and Humanities Research Council of Canada (SSHRC) and the Quebec provincial *Fonds de recherche sur la société et la culture* (FQRSC) between May 2008 and September 2010. I am grateful to Air Transat Inc. and to George Petsikas, Director of Government and Industry Affairs, in particular for providing me with two complimentary air tickets for travel to Europe to conduct research on the London insurance market in 2007 and to present some of my research at a conference in Amsterdam in 2010, respectively. I am also grateful to Rod D. Margo, my mentor and role model, for agreeing to write a foreword to this book.

Finally, I wish to express my heartfelt appreciation and gratitude to my dear wife Emma Agyei-Dwarko for her support, patience, and understanding throughout my long years of graduate studies and to my children Yvonne, Yvette, and Fredo for their forbearance. I am also extremely grateful to my mother-in-law, Comfort Safoa Agyei, for enduring bitterly cold winters in Montreal for three consecutive years at my request and for providing indispensable babysitting services during that period.

I remain solely responsible for the views expressed in this book as well as any errors and omissions in the text.

This book is entirely dedicated to Emma, Yvonne, Yvette, and Fredo.

Yaw Otu Mankata Nyampong

Contents

1 Introduction 1
1.1 Conventional Insurance and Aviation Risks 1
1.2 The Insurance Aftermath of the Events of September 11, 2001 . . 4
1.3 The Nature of the Beast 8
1.4 Alternative Solutions for Insuring Aviation War and Terrorism Risks on a Sustainable Basis 9
1.5 Object, Approach and Structure of This Book 11
References 14

2 The Insurance of Aviation Risks by the Conventional Insurance Markets 17
2.1 Introduction 17
2.2 Conventional Insurance: A Means of Spreading Risks 20
2.2.1 The Premium 23
2.2.2 The Obligation of the Insurer 24
2.2.3 Payment of Money or Corresponding Benefit 24
2.2.4 The Special Uncertain Event 25
2.2.5 Loss and Indemnity 26
2.2.6 Transfer of Risk 27
2.2.7 The Subject-Matter of the Contract of Insurance 27
2.3 Legal Concepts and Principles Applicable to Insurance 28
2.3.1 The Utmost Good Faith: Uberrima Fides 29
2.3.2 Insurable Interest 30
2.3.3 Indemnity 33
2.3.4 Subrogation 36
2.3.5 Contribution 38
2.4 The Underwriting Practices of the Global Aviation Insurance Market 39
2.4.1 The Structure of the Global Aviation Risk Pool and the Law of Large Numbers 41
2.4.2 Direct Insurance: Placing the Risk 43

2.4.3 Reinsurance, Retrocession and Excess Insurance: Spreading the Risk Further 48
2.4.4 The Concept of Insurability and the Rating of Aviation Risks 51
2.4.5 Conditions, Warranties and Exclusions in Insurance Contracts: Methods for Trimming Underwriters' Exposure to Risks 55
2.4.6 The Role of Insurance in Aviation Litigation: The Duty of the Insurer to Defend Claims Brought Against the Insured 56
2.5 Compulsory Insurance Requirements in Domestic and International Air Transportation and the Question of "Adequate" Insurance Coverage 59
2.5.1 Insurance Requirements Relating to Air Passenger Liability 59
2.5.2 Insurance Requirements for Third-Party Liability 63
2.6 Conclusion 67
References 68

3 The Insurance of Aviation War and Terrorism Risks by Specialist War Insurance Markets 71
3.1 Introduction 71
3.2 The Historical Development of War Risk Insurance in the London Marine Market 71
3.3 The Evolution of War Risk Exclusions and Extended Coverage Endorsements in the Aviation Insurance Market 77
3.4 Judicial Interpretations of War Risk Exclusionary Terms Commonly Used in Aviation Insurance Policies 87
3.4.1 War, Invasion, Civil War, Warlike Operations, Hostilities, Insurrection, Rebellion, Revolution, Military or Usurped Power 90
3.4.2 Hostile Detonation or Use of Any Nuclear Weapon of War, Radioactive Force or Matter, Chemical, Biochemical or Biological Materials 95
3.4.3 Strikes, Riots, Civil Commotions or Labour Disturbances 96
3.4.4 Acts for Terrorist or Political Purposes 98
3.4.5 Malicious Acts and Acts of Sabotage 99
3.4.6 Confiscation, Nationalization, Seizure, Restraint, Detention, Appropriation, and Requisition for Title or Use 101
3.4.7 Hijacking or any Unlawful Seizure or Wrongful Control of the Aircraft or Crew 105
3.5 Aviation War Risk Insurance Market Reactions to the Occurrence of Catastrophic Events 106
3.6 Conclusion 111
References 112

4 Catastrophic Risks and Reflexes: Some Theoretical Perspectives on the Use of Insurance as a Risk Management Tool for Large Catastrophic Risks 115
4.1 Introduction 115
4.2 Market Failure Theory and Its Applicability to the Aviation War Risk Insurance Industry 117
4.2.1 Markets in Resource Allocation Theory 118
4.2.2 Early Market Failure Theories 120
4.2.3 The New Market Failure Arguments 121
4.2.4 How Market Failure Theories Explain the Behavior of Insurance Markets for Catastrophic Risks 129
4.2.5 Criticisms of the New Market Failure Arguments 134
4.3 Behavioural Explanations of the Post-Event Reactions of Extreme Event Insurance Markets 137
4.3.1 Ambiguity Aversion and Fairness 138
4.3.2 Irrational Abhorrence 140
4.4 The Systemic Nature of Aviation War and Terrorism Risks and Its Impact on Their Insurability 143
4.5 Conclusion 151
References 153

5 Enhancing the Insurance of Aviation War and Terrorism Risks Through the Use of Alternative Risk Transfer and Risk Financing Mechanisms 157
5.1 Introduction 157
5.2 Funding of Aviation War and Terrorism Risks Through Industry Captives, Risk Retention Groups (RRGs) and Other Mutualization Schemes 158
5.2.1 Equitime 160
5.2.2 Eurotime and New Eurotime 161
5.2.3 Globaltime 163
5.2.4 The Viability of the Risk Retention Concept in Relation to Aviation War and Terrorism Risks 167
5.3 Capital Market Solutions for Funding and/or Transferring Aviation War and Terrorism Risks Beyond the Insurance System 169
5.3.1 Capital Market Alternative Risk Financing Instruments 170
5.3.2 Capital Market Alternative Risk Transfer Instruments 175
5.3.3 The Viability of Capital Market ART Solutions Following the Global Credit Crisis of 2007–2009 190
5.4 Conclusion 200
References 200

6 The Insurability of Aviation War and Terrorism Risks Under ICAO's Unlawful Interference Convention of 2009 203
6.1 Introduction 203
6.2 The General Risks Convention of 2009 205
6.3 The Insurability of Aviation War and Terrorism Risks Under the Regime of Third-Party Liability and Compensation Established by the Unlawful Interference Compensation Convention of 2009 207
6.3.1 The First Tier of Compensation: Liability of the Operator 209
6.3.2 The Second Tier of Compensation: The International Civil Aviation Compensation Fund 217
6.3.3 The Third Tier of Compensation: Unlimited Liability of the Operator Based on Proof of Fault 223
6.4 Alternative Proposals for an International Liability Regime for Third-Party Damages Caused by Acts of Unlawful Interference Involving Aircraft 228
6.5 Conclusion 231
References 232

7 Governmental Involvement in the Insurance of Aviation War and Terrorism Risks 235
7.1 Introduction 235
7.2 Governmental Involvement in the Provision of Domestic Insurance Coverage for Large Catastrophic Risks in Property and Casualty Lines of Insurance 236
7.3 International Cooperation Between States in the Provision of Insurance Coverage for Large Catastrophic Risks 240
7.4 Existing Types of, and Modalities for, Governmental Involvement in the Provision of Insurance Coverage (or Other Support) for Aviation War and Terrorism Risks 245
7.4.1 The U.S. Federal Government's Aviation War Risk Insurance Program 247
7.4.2 The Federal Government of Canada's Aviation War Risk Indemnity Program 253
7.4.3 The Legality of European Governmental Schemes Providing Insurance Coverage/Guarantees to Air Transport Operators for Aviation War and Terrorism Risks Under EU State Aid Regulations 256
7.5 Rationale for Governmental Involvement in the Provision of Insurance Coverage for Aviation War and Terrorism Risks . . . 261
7.6 Limits and Drawbacks of Governmental Involvement in the Provision of Insurance Coverage for Aviation War and Terrorism Risks 263
7.7 Conclusion 265
References 266

8 Findings and Conclusions: Towards Sustainable Insurance of Aviation War and Terrorism Risks . . . 271
8.1 Can the Conventional Insurance Industry Be Expected to Provide Sustainable and Adequate Insurance Coverage to the Global Air Transport Industry for Aviation War and Terrorism Risks? . . . 271
8.2 Is It Possible to Enhance the Capacity of the Conventional Insurance Industry to Cover Aviation War and Terrorism Risks Through the Use of Alternative Risk Financing and Alternative Risk Transfer Mechanisms? . . . 273
8.3 Does the Unlawful Interference Compensation Convention of 2009 Provide a Viable, Sustainable and Insurable Solution? . . . 275
8.4 Do States and Their Governments Have a Role to Play in the Insurance of Aviation War and Terrorism Risks? . . . 276
References . . . 277

Appendix A Specimen FAA War Risk Insurance Policy . . . 279

Appendix B The Goverment of Canada's Undertaking with Respect to War Risk Insurance . . . 307

Appendix C Measures Planned or Taken by EU Member States to Assist Air Transport Operators Cover the Additional Costs of Insurance in the Immediate Aftermath of September 11, 2001 . . . 313

References . . . 317

Index . . . 319

List of Acronyms

9/11	September 11, 2001
ABS-CDOs	Asset-Backed Securities Collateralized Debt Obligations
AEA	Association of European Airlines
AICG	Aviation Insurance Clauses Group
AIGFP	AIG Financial Products
ARF	Alternative Risk Financing
ARM	Adjustable Rate Mortgages
ART	Alternative Risk Transfer
ATA	Air Transport Association of America
AVN 48	War, Hi-jacking and Other Perils Exclusion Clause (Aviation)
AVN 51	Extended Coverage Endorsement (Aircraft Hulls)
AVN 52	Extended Coverage Endorsement (Aviation Liabilities)
Cat-Bonds	Catastrophe bonds
CatEPut	Catastrophe Equity Put option
CDOs	Collateralized Debt Obligations
CDS	Credit Default Swap
CSFB	Credit Suisse First Boston
CWEC	Common North American Airline War Exclusion clause
EOL	Excess of Loss
EU	European Union
EUMS	EU Member States
FAA	Federal Aviation Administration of the US DOT
Fannie Mae	Federal National Mortgage Association (US)
FC & S	Free from Capture and Seizure clause
FIFA	Fédération Internationale de Football Association
FOR	Fire Offices Committee
Freddie Mac	Federal Home Loan Mortgage Corporation (US)
GRC	General Risks Convention
IAIS	International Association of Insurance Supervisors
ICAO	International Civil Aviation Organization
IOPC Fund	International Oil Pollution Compensation Fund

JTCC	Joint Technical and Clauses Committee
LSW 555	Aviation Hull (War and Allied Perils) Insurance Policy – London Special Wording
MTOM	Maximum certificated Take-Off Mass of aircraft
OECD	Organization for Economic Cooperation and Development
PFLP	Popular Front for the Liberation of Palestine
RCDI	Reverse Convertible Debt Instrument
RRG	Risk Retention Group
SG Policy	Lloyds Ship and Goods policy
SGMR	Special Group on the Modernization of the Rome Convention of 1952
SGWI	Special Group on War Risk Insurance
SPRV	Special Purpose Reinsurance Vehicle
SPV	Special Purpose Vehicle
UIC	Unlawful Interference Compensation Convention
US DOT	Department of Transportation of the Government of United States of America
WMD	Weapons of Mass Destruction
WTC	World Trade Center

Chapter 1
Introduction

1.1 Conventional Insurance and Aviation Risks

The core business of insurance is the undertaking of risk by insurers for reward in the form of premiums.[1] In the realm of aviation insurance, airlines, aviation products manufacturers and other service providers typically contract with insurance companies to cover the risks attendant to their operations by way of hull and liability policies. Hull policies usually provide for replacement or repair of the insured aircraft at the insurer's expense, whereas liability policies cover the insured's liability to third parties arising from the use of the aircraft or the air transport services provided. However, not all risks can be comprehensively insured by the conventional insurance market. Whereas some types of risk are generally considered to be outright uninsurable, other types may be insurable but only to some extent.

In order to provide insurance coverage for all kinds of risks, commercial insurers rely on a very finite amount of capital derived from investors (who usually require a return on their investments), and also from the premiums collected from their insureds, and the profits gained from investing them. For purposes of guaranteeing their own financial viability, and the sustainability of the insurance coverage they provide to their clients, one of the mechanisms commonly used by conventional insurers is to insert exclusion clauses into the insurance policies they underwrite. The effect of such exclusion clauses is to limit or cut down the risk(s) covered under the policy to manageable proportions "by excluding or excepting the insurer from liability for certain types of claims or for claims arising from certain types of risk".[2]

In the aviation insurance industry, the need to limit or cut down coverage of certain risks that are considered uninsurable or insurable only to a limited extent in conventional aviation insurance policies has provided an important subject for

---

[1] See [1999] Q.B.D. (Comm) 571 p. 587 per Langley J.

[2] Margo (2000) p. 185.

Y.O.M. Nyampong, *Insuring the Air Transport Industry Against Aviation War and Terrorism Risks and Allied Perils*, DOI 10.1007/978-3-642-32433-8_1,

standardization over the years, particularly in the London market.[3] One of the most significant results of this standardization effort has been the publication by the Aviation Insurance Clauses Group since 1968 of the *Aviation War, Hi-jacking* and *Other Allied Perils Exclusion Clause*, known in aviation insurance parlance as the AVN 48 series of model clauses,[4] and their subsequent wide usage on the global aviation insurance market.

The *Aviation War, Hi-jacking and Other Allied Perils Exclusion Clause* (AVN 48 series) is a non-binding standard clause which may be used at the discretion of individual aviation insurers. When inserted or adapted into an aviation insurance policy, it generally contains a declaration to the effect that the insured policyholder will not be reimbursed for claims arising out of *War*, *Nuclear weapons*, Strikes, *Pre-emption*, *Terrorist acts*, *Malicious acts or acts of sabotage*, *Confiscation*, and *Hijacking*.[5] Losses of this nature are rare and unpredictable and therefore difficult to evaluate and cost using actuarial methods. In effect, an insured airline or aviation operator whose hull or liability policy contains an original or modified version of the AVN 48 series of exclusion clauses will not be successful on a claim against the insurer that is based on any of the excluded risks. Thus, in spite of the insurance policy, the insured airline or aviation operator will continue to retain and bear primary responsibility for the risks excluded as a result of the operation of clause AVN 48.

An air transport operator has a few options if it desires not to bear financial responsibility for the risks excluded by clause AVN 48. With respect to *passenger* and *third party legal liability*,[6] an insured airline or aviation products manufacturer

[3] In this connection, the Aviation Insurance Clauses Group (AICG) and its predecessor, the erstwhile Joint Technical and Clauses Committee (JTCC), which holds the London market mandate to formulate and adopt non-binding standard wordings for specific clauses and endorsements bearing the prefix AVN, has over the years, published a number of such policies, clauses and endorsements, which are found in common use in the global aviation insurance industry. The AICG was established on 24th June 2005 by the International Underwriting Association of London (IUA) and the Lloyd's Market Association (LMA) acting jointly. Prior to the establishment of the AICG, standard clauses and endorsements for use in the London market were developed by the JTCC, a joint committee of the erstwhile Lloyd's Aviation Underwriters' Association (LAUA), (now replaced by the Lloyd's Market Association's Aviation Committee) and the former Aviation Insurance Offices Association (AOIA), (now replaced by the IUA Aviation Technical Committee). See International Underwriting Association (IUA) & Lloyd's Market Association (LMA) No. 015/0605 (2005). See also Caplan (2006). For the mandate of the AICG, see Aviation Insurance Clauses Group (2005).

[4] The current updated version of the clause was published by the AICG on August 4, 2006 and it is designated AVN 48D.

[5] For ease of reference, these risks are cumulatively referred to as "aviation war and terrorism risks" or simply "war risks" in subsequent sections of this book.

[6] *Passenger and third party legal liability* refers to the liability that an airline or other aviation operator may incur by reason of the operation of law should an accident or incident occur which causes its passengers or third parties to suffer death, bodily injury, wounding, loss of, or damage to their property, or delay of baggage and cargo. This usually takes the form of compensation and/or damages which the primary operator is called upon to pay, which is then transferred to the insurer.

could negotiate with the insurer to have some of the risks excluded by AVN 48 written back or reinstated into the existing liability policy by way of an extended coverage endorsement, the AICG's standardized version of which is designated as the AVN 52 series or endorsements.[7] With regard to coverage for *aircraft hulls*,[8] the airline or operator has two choices. It could negotiate with its existing hull insurer for an extended coverage endorsement for hulls, standardized by the AICG and designated as AVN 51 in the same manner as applies to AVN 52. Alternatively, or additionally, the airline could also take out an entirely separate aviation hull war and allied perils policy, designated as the LSW 555 series,[9] on the specialist hull war insurance market, also based in London. This market is separate and distinct from the mainline aviation insurance market. Each of the foregoing options has its own special characteristics and limitations.[10]

---

[7] Aviation Insurance Clauses Group (2006b), (AVN 52K). See also Aviation Insurance Clauses Group (2006a), (AVN 52P). As of this writing, the foregoing were the most current versions of the AVN 52 extended coverage endorsement series. They were published by the AICG on August 4, 2006.

[8] *Aircraft hull* refers to the cost of replacing or repairing a destroyed or damaged aircraft after it has been involved in an accident or incident. This is usually paid directly to the insured owner or operator of the aircraft.

[9] The *Aviation Hull "War and Allied Perils" Policy*, known as LSW 555B is the standard hull war wording generally used for major airlines on the hull war market. Following the events of September 11, 2001, the market introduced a new and very restrictive variant of the wording designated as LSW 555C. It sought to exclude claims arising from weapons of mass destruction (WMD). The most recent variant of the hull war wording, LSW 555D, was officially approved and designated by Lloyd's of London in April 2006. It provides for limited coverage of WMD claims only in specific circumstances. See JLT Risk Solutions (2006). See also A bigger bang for your buck (2006).

[10] The extended coverage endorsements (AVN 51 and 52 series) can only be issued in relation to existing policies containing an AVN 48 exclusion clause. Essentially, their purpose is to reverse some of the exclusions brought about by AVN 48. Such risks are considered to be very volatile thus their exclusion in the first place. As a result, they are typically written back into the policy subject to a 7-day cancellation clause and payment of an additional premium. The 7-day cancellation clause enables insurers to withdraw coverage at very short notice so as to re-assess the risk and the prices charged for covering them (usually after those risks have materialized). In effect, although aviation insurance policyholders may have the requisite war risk insurance cover provided by the respective write-back endorsements, this may be cancelled at the discretion of the insurers by giving 7-days notice. See Margo (2000) p. 329. In the specific case of AVN 52, an insurer may cancel coverage by giving 48 hours notice to the insured in the event of a hostile detonation. See Aviation Insurance Clauses Group (2006b), (AVN 52K), section 5(c). The LSW 555 series *hull war and allied perils policy* on the other hand amounts to a new contract of insurance in the first instance. A typical condition in LSW 555 series policies requires the insured to give immediate notice to the insurer of any material changes in the nature or area of the insured's operations, and no claim arising subsequent to any such material change over which the insured had control shall be recoverable unless the change had been previously notified to, and accepted by, the insurer. This provision, commonly known as the material change clause, also enables aviation hull war insurers to take a step back to reconsider and re-rate the risks covered under the policy in the event that the risks were to become materially different (usually after an occurrence).

In sum, conventional insurance coverage for aviation war and terrorism risks is less stable than it is for other traditional types of risks. Through the mechanism of exclusion clauses and write-back endorsements, insurers are able to unilaterally cancel coverage to policyholders at very short notice. This state of affairs is a direct consequence of the highly volatile nature of the underlying risks. Under normal circumstances, however (i.e., in the absence of any occurrences which materially change the nature of the risks covered), insurers engaged in these lines of business and their insureds usually manage to work out mutually acceptable levels and terms of coverage.

1.2 The Insurance Aftermath of the Events of September 11, 2001

The inherent instability of conventional insurance coverage for aviation war and terrorism risks inevitably manifests itself whenever a catastrophic event occurs. This is the exact situation in which the air transport industry found itself following the fateful events which occurred in the United States on September 11, 2001. Prior to that day, many insurers around the world were offering extended coverage endorsements for war risks (i.e., AVN 51 and 52) as well as LSW 555 policies to insured airlines and other aviation operators for practically little or no premium. Excessive competition between insurers in the market, coupled with the then prevailing and widely held perception that the probability of occurrence of those risks was extremely rare, accounted in part for this state of affairs. The events of September 11, however, turned the aviation insurance industry on its head. It marked the end of the era in which insurance coverage for aviation war and terrorism risks was taken for granted. Within 2 days of the attacks, almost all aviation insurers around the world had began handing out 7-day cancellation notices to their assureds, to expire at midnight on September 24, 2001, and thereby effectively reinstating clause AVN 48, and terminating insurance coverage for war and allied risks forthwith.

Naturally, the operations of several major airlines were about to be grounded, as full and/or adequate insurance coverage is not only a legal requirement for airlines and other aviation operators under national legislation and certain international treaties, but is also a pre-requisite for commercial airlines of any country to maintain their air operator's certificates for purposes of flying into or across the airspace of most other foreign countries. Cancellation of war risk coverage by the market following September 11, 2001 also meant that most airlines would be in automatic default under their aircraft leasing and financing arrangements which required them to maintain the prescribed minimum levels of insurance coverage, including war risk coverage.[11] As can be imagined, the results of these developments were rather chaotic. Indeed, they have been aptly described as the failure of the commercial aviation insurance markets.[12]

Before the 7-day notices could take effect, however, most aviation insurers in London and in other markets indicated their willingness to restore some level of coverage for passenger and third party liability war risks to their insured airlines. AVN 52C, then the applicable version of the write back endorsement, was re-drafted and re-issued as AVN 52D by the Joint Technical and Clauses Committee (JTCC).[13] In respect of coverage for *third party bodily injury* and *property damage*, AVN 52D introduced a sub-limit or cap of USD 50 million per occurrence and in the annual aggregate[14] for any of the named perils written back thereunder. AVN 52E was also introduced for general aviation operators,[15] and it established a sub-limit of up to USD 10 million per occurrence and in the annual aggregate.[16] With respect to *passenger liability coverage*, however, full policy limits[17] were retained under AVN 52C, D and E. The rationale underlying the different treatment of *passenger liability* and *hull war risk coverage* on the one hand and *third party liability war risk coverage* on the other hand was that, whereas insurers could quantify their exposure to liability under the former with a reasonable degree of certainty, the same could not be said of the latter.[18]

In addition to the introduction of sub-limits, and in spite of severe criticism and outcry from airlines, underwriters on the London aviation market introduced an additional premium of USD 1.25 per passenger carried for the limited *third party*

[11] Indeed, certain lessors and financiers of aircraft explicitly issued notices advising airlines operating aircraft financed by them that in view of the circumstances prevailing at the time, they would (for a limited period of time) not enforce their rights to require third-party liability war risk insurance coverage above that which was then available on the commercial markets. See e.g., Export Import Bank of the United States (2001).

[12] Fitzsimmons (2004) p. 81.

[13] The JTCC was the predecessor to the AICG.

[14] This meant that the maximum amount of money recoverable from the insurer for claims attributable to war risks during the effective period of the insurance was limited to USD 50 million. Also, this limit would apply irrespective of whether those war risk-related losses arose from one single occurrence or an aggregation of events. Prior to 9/11, there was no distinction between war risks and other risks so far as the limit of recovery was concerned. All risks were typically insured to full policy limits.

[15] General aviation refers to non-commercial, non-military civil aviation.

[16] Margo (2002) p. 389.

[17] Since AVN 52 is a write-back endorsement, it is typically subject to the maximum amount of insurance cover provided under the original policy. Writing back AVN 52 to "full policy limits" therefore means that, if for instance the amount of insurance provided under the original policy was $ 1 billion, then war risk coverage would also have been written back to the tune of $ 1 billion.

[18] Harding et al. (2000).

liability war risk cover provided under AVN 52D. Further, some underwriters on the London aviation market and from other markets began offering additional (excess) war risk cover in separate and distinct policies beyond the USD 50 million sub-limit: from USD 50 million to USD 150 million; and from USD 150 million to USD 1 billion. This two-layered excess cover was made available for an initial premium of USD 1.85 per passenger carried (i.e. in addition to the USD 1.25 referred to above), and was subject to a 30-day notice of cancellation.[19]

At present, the conventional aviation insurance market seems to have recovered from near failure although full pre-9/11 conditions have not been attained. Instead of coverage up to full policy limits, extended third party liability war risk coverage for airlines is now typically available up to a maximum per-occurrence and annual aggregate sub-limit of about US$ 150 million although higher limits of up to US$ 1 billion are selectively available from individual underwriters. There is no war risk insurance coverage available on the market for service providers in the air transport industry.[20] Premium rates for extended third party liability war risk coverage are still quite high as compared to pre-2001 levels, although they seem to be falling on a year-on-year aggregate basis. For war risk coverage only, some airlines are reported to have experienced premium rate increases in the order of up to 500 % in the immediate aftermath of 9/11.[21] Although the global aviation insurance industry is generally considered to have survived the impact of September 11, 2001, there are concerns that the industry may not be able to withstand another catastrophe of similar size and magnitude in the near future. Indeed, these concerns have significantly influenced recent industry discussions as to whether or not claims arising from weapons of mass destruction (WMD claims) should or should not be covered under aviation insurance policies.[22]

It has been said that "the importance of insurance, like many of life's essentials, is most evident when it is not available".[23] Accordingly, in response to the near failure of the conventional insurance markets, and in recognition of the indispensable role of air transportation within the global economy, numerous efforts have been made since September 11, 2001, to provide adequate[24] insurance coverage to operators in the air transport industry for their exposure to third-party war and

---

[19] Margo (2002) p. 389.

[20] Service providers are separate and distinct from airlines. They include airport operators, air navigation service providers, security screeners, ground handling service providers etc.

[21] Margo (2002) p. 390.

[22] See Marsh Inc. (2006).

[23] Laster and Schmidt (2005) p. 3.

[24] That is, coverage beyond the US$ 150 million limit that the commercial market is presently willing to offer.

terrorism risk liability. Governments around the world quickly established war risk insurance schemes in order to forestall the total grounding of both domestic and international air transport operations.[25]

At the international level, the International Civil Aviation Organization (ICAO) took the center stage in the effort to find a solution with its *Globaltime* proposal.[26] Following along the same lines, the Air Transport Association (ATA) in the United States also proposed a scheme to be known as *Equitime*,[27] and, in Europe, the Association of European Airlines (AEA) proposed a similar mechanism known as *Eurotime* as a means of providing coverage against war and terrorism risks in the air transport industry. This proposal failed to gather the needed support in the first instance, but it was re-introduced in 2004, captioned *New Eurotime*. Globaltime, Equitime and Eurotime were all designed as pure stop-gap solutions. They were intended as contingency mechanisms to be resorted to in the event of another market failure following the occurrence of a similar catastrophic event. For varied reasons, including the non-occurrence of another significant event since September 11, 2001, all of these schemes have not become operational as at the time of this writing.

---

[25] For example, In the United States, the federal government quickly enacted Pub. L. No. 107-42 (2001). This Act: extended the authority of the federal government to provide insurance and reinsurance to both domestic and foreign flag carriers if it was in the interest of air commerce and national security; authorized federal reimbursements to airlines for premium rate increases as a result of 9/11; and, limited the third-party liability of US air carriers for losses arising from future terrorist attacks to US$ 100 million, with the federal government assuming responsibility for any liability above the US$ 100 million limit. Pursuant to this Act (and subsequent renewals thereof), the US Department of Transportation (DOT), acting through the Federal Aviation Administration (FAA) has since September 22, 2001, continually offered premium-based war risk insurance to US flag carriers as part of the FAA Insurance Program. See Margo (2002) p. 393. The US government also enacted the Pub. L. No. 107-297 (2002), and thereby established the Federal Terrorism Insurance Program, a system of shared public/private compensation for insured losses resulting from acts of terrorism designed to protect consumers and to create a transitional period for the private insurance markets to stabilize. The original program was due to expire on December 31, 2005, but was extended till December 31, 2007, by Pub. L. No. 109-144 (2005). On September 19, 2007, the US House of Representatives passed Bill HR 2761 EH (2007), a Bill which sought to further extend the federal Terrorism Risk Insurance Program by 15 years. Subsequently, on November 19, 2007, the US Senate approved its own version of the Bill, Pub L 110-160, 121 Stat. 1839-1843 (2007), which sought to extend the program for an additional 7 years. In the United Kingdom, temporary war risk coverage was provided by a captive insurance company called *Troika* jointly established by the major aviation brokers: Marsh Inc., Aon Inc., and Willis Ltd., managed by Global Aerospace, and reinsured by Her Majesty's Treasury. See Atkins (2007) p. 132. See also Partridge (2001) p. B1, and Stewart (2001).

[26] The Globaltime mechanism entails the establishment of an international *contingency mechanism* to provide non-cancellable third-party aviation war risk cover to airlines, airport operators, air navigation service providers, ground handlers, manufacturers, aircraft lessors and financiers, refuellers, and general aviation operators, through a non-profit, special purpose Insuring Entity, with multilateral government backing for the initial years. To date, the scheme remains in abeyance partially because contracting States representing at least 51 % of ICAO contribution rates have not as yet declared their intention to participate in it as required.

[27] This scheme called for the establishment of a Vermont based, federally backed captive or Risk Retention Group (RRG) to insure its members against passenger and third party war risk liability for the first USD 300 million, while the federal government would reinsure the excess up to USD 2 billion per occurrence. See Airline group files to form vermont risk group (2002).

1.3 The Nature of the Beast

A look back into history reveals that September 11, 2001 was not the first instance in which a catastrophic occurrence caused the conventional insurance market to threaten to terminate or withdraw war risk cover to air transport operators. The Israeli attack on Beirut airport in 1968 was the first of such instances. It was only after the occurrence of that incident, in which more than a dozen aircraft were damaged or destroyed on the ground, that the London market began introducing the war and allied perils exclusion clause, (AVN 48) into aviation insurance policies.[28] The clause was amended and re-issued as AVN 48A on 12th August 1970. In September 1970, "a TWA Boeing 707, a Swissair DC-8, a Pan Am Boeing 747, and a BOAC VC-10 were all hijacked within a short time of each other. Three of the hijacked aircraft were flown to a desert airstrip at Dawson Field, Amman, Jordan, where they were destroyed. The Pan Am 747 was flown to Cairo, Egypt and blown up".[29] Again, in reaction to these occurrences, the JTCC replaced clause AVN 48A with clause AVN 48B and in so doing widened the scope of risks excluded from coverage. Following September 11, 2001, the AICG has published clauses AVN 48C and AVN 48D which seek to further broaden the scope and depth of the risks excluded from aviation insurance policies.

The above-described developments in the aviation war risk insurance arena clearly raise a number of issues which form the foundation upon which this book is built. It is an indisputable fact that the conventional insurance industry has its limits so far as coverage of aviation war and terrorism risks is concerned. The market has been progressively restricting the scope and depth of such coverage to insured air transport operators over the years, and, in spite of the widespread use of exclusions, the market is still vulnerable to failure whenever major catastrophic events occur.[30] The fundamental issue that remains unresolved in this regard is that,

[28] The original clause AVN 48 was issued on 12th November 1969. Prior to its introduction, standard aviation insurance policies in the London market contained a clause which excluded loss or damage which occurred as a direct or indirect consequence of war, invasion, acts of foreign enemies, hostilities (whether war be declared or not), civil war, rebellion, revolution, insurrection, military or usurped power, martial law, strikes, riots, civil commotions, confiscation, nationalization, requisition or destruction or damage to property by or under the order of any government or public or local authority. See Margo (2000) p. 325, n. 1.

[29] Margo (2002) pp. 386–387, n. 3.

[30] In the period following September 11, 2001, insurers in the commercial market have had the opportunity to make good money by charging relatively high premium rates for significantly restricted war risk coverage, without having to pay any claims. As a result, the market has become attractive to new capital providers who have successfully flooded it with excess capacity. The practice now is that some insurers are offering non-cancellable war risk coverage to insured operators for relatively small premiums in order to maintain a cash flow to cover their reinsurance costs. Denied of the opportunity to cancel coverage at short notice, those insurers engaged in practices such as these are exposed to the risk of financial ruin should another occurrence such as 9/11 materialize. This phenomenon has significant implications for the continued sustainability of the commercial insurance market.

having regard to past and recent developments in this field, can the conventional insurance industry be reasonably expected to provide full and adequate insurance coverage for aviation war and terrorism risks to operators in the air transport industry? If the answer is yes, what changes and/or enhancements would be required to facilitate this role? If the answer is negative, are there any viable alternatives?

1.4 Alternative Solutions for Insuring Aviation War and Terrorism Risks on a Sustainable Basis

It is generally agreed that governments have a role to play in the provision of war and terrorism risk insurance coverage (or such other financial equivalent) to operators in the air transport industry.[31] What needs to be addressed is the appropriate manner in which governments may perform this role both at the domestic and international levels.[32] Two potential remedies to this problem are particularly worthy of mention at this stage. Harold Caplan, a prominent commentator on the subject, proposes the adoption of an international convention on war and terrorism risk insurance not only for air transport operations but also for all other potentially vulnerable types of business endeavors.[33] In one of his many writings on the subject, Caplan proposes that States could pool their resources under the proposed convention to insure each other against war and terrorism risks, using the innovative concept of "sovereign risks", which he defines as "acts by or against a State which result in civilian casualties or damage to private property".[34]

The problem with aviation war and terrorism risks, according to Anthony Fitzsimmons, is their highly volatile nature and the difficulty insurers have in

[31] Theoretical justification for this has been provided by one commentator as follows: "Arguably, it is States (and of course terrorists) that ultimately cause and should therefore provide compensation for terrorism, since terrorism is the ultimate consequence of the failure of domestic policy or diplomacy at the highest levels". See Fitzsimmons (2004) p. 87.

[32] On one side of the argument, sustained governmental intervention in the war risk insurance market (as is presently the case in the US and in Canada) undoubtedly destroys the development of the commercial insurance markets by denying them the premiums which they could otherwise have earned. It also disrupts the functioning of the global air transport industry, as carriers that would have been bankrupt if they had to compete freely on the open market, end up being artificially resuscitated by government subsidies. On the other side of the argument, no government intervention at all is also not in the interest of the air transport industry and the economy at large (as was demonstrated in the immediate aftermath of 9/11, when air transportation was on the brink of grounding due to the collapse of the commercial insurance markets).

[33] Caplan (2004).

[34] Idem, p. 11.

assessing the potential loss exposure associated with them, especially during times of tension.[35] Fitzsimmons therefore proposes that, in order to maximize the insurability of aviation war and terrorism risks, governments, acting through ICAO, should borrow the concept of "channelling", as used in the Paris and Vienna Conventions on third-party liability in the nuclear energy sector and adapt it to create a regime to compensate third-parties for aviation war and terrorism losses.[36] This concept entails the limitation of liability arising from aviation war and terrorism risks at a level that would remain insurable in the long-term and exclusive channelling of the limited liability through specified operators. Beyond that level, the proposal calls upon governments to assume liability for excess losses on a national or international (i.e., treaty) basis.[37]

Indeed, several suggestions were advanced to the effect that ICAO should take advantage of then-ongoing efforts to modernize the 1952 Rome Convention[38] to develop a multilateral treaty that addresses the perennial problem of providing insurance coverage for aviation war and terrorism risks in a viable and sustainable manner, entailing some form of governmental involvement.[39] It is, however, important to note that, except for its singular provision requiring air carriers to maintain adequate insurance for the third-party liability to which they may be exposed thereunder, the 1952 Rome Convention does not primarily address the question of availability or sustainability of insurance coverage for third-party losses

---

[35] As such, war risks are typically considered to be less insurable than other traditional types of risk. Indeed, this is the rationale underlying the exclusion of war and terrorism risks from aviation insurance contracts in the first place. See Fitzsimmons (2004) pp. 87–88.

[36] Idem., pp. 87–88. Thus, by law, only those identified operators or entities would be liable to suit in respect of such claims even if someone else would, on normal legal principles such as negligence, be liable for the damage. The identified operators or entities would have no-fault liability for specified types of damages up to a certain limit, with the government assuming responsibility beyond that. The proposal envisages that the limitation of liability would bring about certainty in assessing the maximum possible loss arising from the identified entity's war risks, and this in turn would enhance the insurability of war risks.

[37] Idem.

[38] 310 UNTS 181, ICAO Doc. 7364 (1952). ICAO's recent efforts to update the 1952 Rome Convention predate the events of September 11, 2001. They commenced soon after (and were largely driven by) the adoption of the Montreal Convention of 1999 (on the unification of certain rules of international carriage by air). Sweden proposed that the subject be included in the work program of the ICAO Legal Committee in August–September 2000. The terrorist events of September 11, 2001 occurred only after the ICAO Legal Bureau had commenced work on the project by circulating a questionnaire to ICAO contracting States. See Jennison (2005) p. 786.

[39] It was said for instance that "[t]he potential of terrorist acts to cause such 'unbounded' losses as did occur on September 11 2001 [and the associated worldwide aviation insurance crisis that is still not fully resolved] has undoubtedly sharpened the need for a modernized [third-party liability] regime that accounts for both ordinary accidents and the results of unlawful interference with civil aviation". See idem p. 790.

attributable to aviation war and terrorism risks. In any event, ICAO's modernization efforts[40] culminated in the adoption in May 2009 of two new treaties addressing compensation of third-party victims for losses caused by general risks on the one hand and acts of unlawful interference with aircraft on the other. Only six States signed the conventions upon their adoption and there have been no ratifications to date.

1.5 Object, Approach and Structure of This Book

The object of this book is to take a step back from the various approaches that have been used or proposed as a means of finding a viable solution to the perennial problem of aviation war risk insurance, and instead, to explore the central issues underlying the problem in the hope of identifying the fundamental causes of the present state of affairs. Some of the issues to be addressed in this connection relate to the legal, economic and behavioural reasons underlying the failure of the conventional aviation insurance markets after the catastrophic events of September 11, 2001.

[40] Following the events of September 11, 2001, the ICAO Council established a Special Group on Aviation War Risk Insurance (SGWI) to develop recommendations contributing to the stabilization of the commercial insurance market. The SGWI recommended among other things "the expedited preparation of a new draft Convention on third-party liability and possibly other related mechanisms that would take into account and balance post-11 September 2001 economics, limitations of aviation industry liability for damages arising from war and allied perils, or similar unlawful interference and victim protection" as a long-term solution. See idem p. 790. The ICAO Council subsequently decided, on 4th March 2002, that this latter recommendation should be addressed as part of the work program of the ICAO Legal Committee dealing with the modernization of the 1952 Rome Convention. The entire 32nd Session of the ICAO Legal Committee held in March 2004 was devoted to the issue of modernization of the Rome Convention of 1952. At the end of the Session, a refined version of a draft new convention previously prepared by a secretariat study group to replace the 1952 Rome Convention had been produced. After considering the outcome of the work of the Legal Committee, the ICAO Council agreed that the draft convention was not yet mature for submission to a Diplomatic Conference, but required further study. Accordingly, the Council established a Special Group on the Modernization of the Rome Convention (SGMR) to further develop and refine the text produced by the Legal Committee, both on substantive legal issues and with respect to drafting and editorial concerns. The work of the SGMR culminated in the development of two draft Conventions: one to address the issues of liability and compensation arising from acts of "unlawful interference" with aircraft (referred to as the Unlawful Interference Compensation Convention); and, the other to provide a framework for compensating third party victims of aircraft accidents not caused by acts of unlawful interference (referred to as the General Risks Convention). Following final approval by the ICAO Council, these two draft conventions were considered and adopted at a Diplomatic Conference held in Montreal from April 20–May 2, 2009. See: Caplan (2007) pp. 11–12. See also ICAO (2002).

For instance, one commentator has attributed the failure of the conventional aviation insurance market to the presence of "systemic risk",[41] defined as "the danger that an event will trigger a loss of economic value and/or confidence in the financial system that has significant adverse effects on the real economy".[42] Similarly, another author has noted that "September 11 has ... reinforced the perception that due to the correlation of both insurance and financial risks, a sudden extreme event could set in motion a 'domino-like' collapse of a large segment of the insurance sector. This risk can be considered the systemic risk of the [insurance] industry".[43] Thus, if proof exists that systemic risk is one of the economic reasons underlying the inherent instability and eventual failure of the conventional aviation insurance market, this will be an extremely important consideration in determining what the most efficient remedies for the failure will be.[44] This book therefore explores this and such other relevant fundamental issues.

The book is divided into eight chapters. The first part (Chaps. 1–4) generally describes how conventional insurance operates as a risk management concept in connection with the provision of financial protection for the different types of risk inherent in air transport operations. After the general introduction presented in this chapter, Chap. 2 describes aviation insurance and the various legal principles and concepts that have shaped the development of that branch of law in the common law world to date. It explains the inner workings of the insurance industry, particularly how risks are placed and rated; how insurance companies assess risk and liability exposure, and set premiums; and, the role of the various actors on the market (e.g. brokers, direct insurers, reinsurers, and retrocessionaires).

---

[41] Mundy (2004) p. 30, where the author notes that in the wake of the insurance industry's biggest ever disaster (September 11 2001), although business continued "as usual" with very little impact on the global economy, there were clear signs of systemic risk underneath. He cites the fact that the aviation insurance industry had to substantially reduce the amount of cover available—reduce it below the level at which airlines could continue to operate; and also the fact that governments had to temporarily intervene to provide the limits of liability necessary to satisfy financiers and regulators as the clear signs of the presence of systemic risk.

[42] Idem., p. 29. See also Baur and Enz (2003) p. 7. It has been argued that systemic risk is a particular feature of the financial sector, a typical example being a situation in which the release of bad news about a financial institution or even its failure, or crash of a financial market leads in a sequential manner to considerable adverse effects on one or several other financial institutions or markets, e.g. their failure or crash. Essential is the "domino effect" from one institution to the other or from one market to the other emanating from the limited initial shock (even a rumour).

[43] De Mey (2003) p. 68. In the banking sector, the existence of systemic risk has provided the basis for continued financial regulation and prudential supervision of banking institutions all over the world. The global financial meltdown of 2008, precipitated by the unregulated sub-prime mortgage market in the United States underscores the foregoing. Indeed, "systemic risk is now widely accepted as the fundamental underlying concept for the study of financial instability and possible policy responses". On this, see De Bandt and Hartmann (2000) p. 8.

[44] For instance, in a 1997 study concerning the failure of crop insurance markets in America, it was recommended that if systemic risk was the primary cause of market failure, then cost efficient remedies may be available in the form of area yield reinsurance or exchange-traded area yield options. See Miranda and Glauber (1997).

With specific regard to the handling of aviation war and terrorism risks by the specialist war insurance markets, Chap. 3 provides a detailed outline of the evolution of coverage and/or exclusion of war risks in the different insurance markets. Beginning with the London marine market, where the practice of excluding war risks commenced historically, the Chapter traces the extension of war risk exclusions into the global aviation insurance market in an effort to provide some background to contemporary practices in that market. Chapter 3 also identifies how the markets have reacted to the occurrence of insured catastrophic events in the period leading up to and immediately following September 11, 2001. The chapter concludes by noting that the reactions of the commercial insurance markets in the immediate aftermath of an insured extreme event amount to market failure or, at the very least, a substantial market disruption.

Chapter 4 is mostly theoretical. It investigates the economic and behavioural underpinnings of the reactions of the conventional insurance industry to extreme events using theoretical principles derived from disciplines such as law and economics as well as behavioural law and economics. The chapter provides a review of the scholarly literature on market failure theory generally, and market failure in catastrophic insurance markets in particular, with the aim of establishing a theoretical framework for analyzing the specific market failure issues identified in the aviation war and terrorism risk market. It also discusses several psychological explanations that have been proffered to explain insurers' reactions during periods of heightened risk and uncertainty, including the concept of systemic risk. Chapter 4 concludes the first part of the book by identifying market failure and financial capacity constraints as the principal economic and behavioural reasons why as a risk management tool conventional insurance is not properly suited to fully and adequately provide coverage for catastrophic aviation war and terrorism risks.

The second part of the book examines the viability and repercussions of complementary/alternative mechanisms that have, since September 11, 2001, been proposed or implemented to adequately compensate third-party victims of acts of unlawful interference involving aircraft or otherwise to facilitate the provision of sustainable insurance coverage for aviation war and terrorism risks to the air transport industry. These principally include: alternative risk financing (ARF) and alternative risk transfer (ART) mechanisms such as captives, industry risk retention groups, and capital market instruments for raising contingent funding and for transferring top risks (Chap. 5); the adoption of an international treaty regime on third-party liability for damage resulting from acts of unlawful interference with aircraft and its impact on the insurability of aviation war and terrorism risks (Chap. 6); and, governmental involvement in the provision of aviation war risk insurance and the underlying policy/theoretical discussion concerning the proper role of national governments in the provision of compensation/insurance for victims of catastrophic unlawful acts (Chap. 7). A summary of the key findings and conclusions of the book is provided in Chap. 8.

References

2761 EH (2007) Terrorism Risk Insurance Revision and Extension Act of 2007. (U.S.)
310 UNTS 181, ICAO Doc. 7364 (1952) Convention on Damage Caused by Foreign Aircraft to Third Parties on the Surface
A bigger bang for your buck (2006). Airfinance Journal No. 289:24–26
Airline group files to form Vermont risk group (2002). Insurance Times, 11 June 2002
Atkins S (2007) State involvement in provision of terrorism insurance. In: Marangos H (ed) War risks and terrorism. Insurance Institute of London, London, pp 132–145
Aviation Insurance Clauses Group (2005) Terms of reference (17th March 2005). Available via http://www.aicg.co.uk/docimages/4982.pdf
Aviation Insurance Clauses Group (2006a) Aviation manufacturers products liabilities endorsement (AVN 52P, 27th February 2006). Available via http://www.aicg.co.uk/DocImages/6249.pdf
Aviation Insurance Clauses Group (2006b) Extended coverage endorsement (aviation liabilities) (AVN 52K, 4th August 2006). Available via http://www.aicg.co.uk/DocImages/6745.pdf
Baur P, Enz R (2003) Sigma no. 5/2003: reinsurance – a systemic risk? Swiss Reinsurance Company, Economic Research and Consulting, Zurich
Caplan H (2004) War and terrorism insurance: how to promote long-term international stability and affordability. Air Space Law XXIX(1):3
Caplan H (2006) The Aviation Insurance Clauses Group: a model for other markets. Air Space Law XXXI(4–5):254–290
Caplan H (2007) Who should pay for aerial terrorism? – challenges to ICAO policy initiatives. Air Space Law 21(3):11–16
De Bandt O, Hartmann P (2000) Systemic risk: a survey. ECB, Frankfurt
De Mey J (2003) The aftermath of September 11: the impact on and systemic risk to the insurance industry. Geneva Papers (Issues & Practice) 28(1):65–70
Export Import Bank of the United States (2001) Ex-Im Bank responds to airline insurance crisis in the wake of September 11 2001 terrorist attacks. September 24 2001. Available via http://www.exim.gov/pressrelease.cfm/B0BEB840-1032-5B0F-B332672F986C3E4F/
Fitzsimmons A (2004) Terrorism – maximizing the insurability of a catastrophe risk. Ann Air Space Law XXIX:67
Harding J, Hart D, Tippin P, Widdows J, Johnston C, Power R (2000) The aviation and space insurance market. Institute of Actuaries, Birmingham
ICAO (2002) Summary of decisions – assistance in the field of aviation war risk insurance (Subject No. 24.3). No. C-DEC 165/6
International Underwriting Association (IUA), Lloyd's Market Association (LMA) (2005) Aviation Insurance Clauses Group Established. No. 015/0605, 24 June 2005. Available via http://www.the-lma.com/DocImages/5305.rtf
Jennison M (2005) Rescuing the Rome convention of 1952: six decades of effort to make a workable regime for damage caused by foreign aircraft to third parties. Unif Law Rev 10 (4):785–824
Laster DS, Schmidt C (2005) Sigma no. 4/2005: innovating to insure the uninsurable. Swiss Reinsurance Company, Economic Research and Consulting, Zurich
Margo RD (2000) Aviation insurance: the law and practice of aviation insurance, including hovercraft and spacecraft insurance, 3rd edn. Butterworths, London
Margo RD (2002) 11 September 2001 – an aviation insurance perspective. Air Space Law XXVII (6):386–397
Marsh Inc. (2006) Marsh/IATA/AEA sponsored liability WMD write-back clauses now finalised by AICG. Marsh Aviation and Aerospace Practice Special Bulletin
Miranda MJ, Glauber JW (1997) Systematic risk, reinsurance, and the failure of crop insurance markets. Am J Agric Econ 79(1):206–215
Mundy C (2004) The nature of risk: the nature of systemic risk – trying to achieve a definition. Balance Sheet 12(5):29–31

Partridge J (2001) Ottawa flies to fill gap in air insurance. The Globe and Mail, 24 September 2001
Pub L 110-160, 121 Stat. 1839-1843 (2007) Terrorism Risk Insurance Program Reauthorization Act of 2007. (US)
Pub. L. No. 107-297 116 STAT. 2327 15 U.S.C. 6701 note (2002) Terrorism Risk Insurance Act of 2002. (US)
Pub. L. No. 107-42 115 STAT. 230 (2001) Air Transportation Safety and System Stabilization Act. (USA)
Pub. L. No. 109-144 119 STAT. 2660 15 U.S.C. 6701 note (2005) Terrorism Risk Insurance Extension Act of 2005. (US)
Q.B.D. (Comm) 571 Companhia de Seguros Imperio v. Heath (REBX) Ltd
JLT Risk Solutions (2006) The Hull War market. JLT risk solutions aerospace market update – plane talking 3
Stewart S (2001) Ottawa covers air Insurance: 90-day emergency aid: gives airlines, airports coverage against terrorism. National Post, 24 September 2001

Chapter 2
The Insurance of Aviation Risks by the Conventional Insurance Markets

2.1 Introduction

This chapter provides an overview of the concept of insurance as applied to all forms of human endeavor, especially air transportation. It discusses the concepts of direct insurance, reinsurance and retrocession, and the various legal principles that, to date, have shaped the evolution of the insurance industry in general, and the aviation insurance market in particular. It also defines and sets out the scope of aviation insurance and the types of risks typically covered under this branch of insurance. Further, this chapter explains the inner workings of the insurance industry, particularly how risks are placed with, and rated by, insurers; how insurance companies (i.e., direct underwriters, reinsurers and retrocessionaires) assess risk and liability exposure, and set premiums; and, the role of the various actors in the market (e.g., brokers, direct insurers, reinsurers and retrocessionaires). The object of this chapter is not to provide a detailed treatise on insurance and aviation insurance, for such an exercise would be beyond the scope of this book. Rather, the overview contained in this chapter is intended to provide an insight into the complexities of the law governing insurance in general and aviation insurance in particular in order to place the subject matter of this book—aviation war risk insurance—in its proper context.

From its very inception, mankind's attempts to overcome the forces of gravity by putting heavier-than-air craft into flight have been fraught with a very high level of risk. Although, over the years, there have been giant technological leaps in the use of aircraft as a means of transportation, there have also been numerous occasions when the results have been less than perfect. Notwithstanding the fact that civil aviation continues to be the safest means of transport in contemporary times, it is

---

A slightly modified version of this chapter has previously been published as a contribution under the author's name to Paul S. Dempsey's *Aviation Liability Law* (loose-leaf, published by LexisNexis Canada, 2010).

Y.O.M. Nyampong, *Insuring the Air Transport Industry Against Aviation War and Terrorism Risks and Allied Perils*, DOI 10.1007/978-3-642-32433-8_2,

still replete with enormous risks. Aviation disasters are usually large and tragic, involving the loss of multiple human lives and extensive damage to property. Apart from the risks naturally inherent in the conduct of civil aviation operations such as equipment failure, the industry is also exposed to perils which are external to, and beyond the control of, individual operators. In recent years, the use of civil aircraft by terrorists as weapons of mass destruction has been on the increase, and concerns are now being expressed in insurance circles about the magnitude of damage and loss of human lives should a nuclear or biological weapon be detonated on board a commercial aircraft or at a busy airport.

The risks incident to the conduct of air transport have very significant financial implications. In the commercial airline sector for example, airlines are continually exposed, among many other things, to the financial risks of: legal liability for death, wounding or bodily injury suffered by passengers if caused by an accident which takes place on board an aircraft operated by the airline or in the course of any of the operations of embarking and disembarking the aircraft;[1] legal liability for loss of, damage to, or delay of baggage and cargo;[2] and, legal liability for damage suffered by any person on the surface of the earth if such damage is caused by an aircraft in flight or by any person or thing falling therefrom.[3] In almost all the foregoing instances, the liability of the air carrier is strict or absolute and there is little or no opportunity for the air carrier to avoid or mitigate liability by way of defenses. As such, there have been numerous instances in which air carriers have been held liable to pay damages for loss of life or damage to property although they were not culpable but were indeed, victims of the event or occurrence which caused the said loss of lives or damage to property.

Absent insurance, if commercial airlines and other operators in the aviation industry (airport operators, air navigation service providers, security screeners, ground handling service providers etc.) were required to internalize the risks inherent in civil aviation operations, and to provide financial guarantees against them, no aircraft would be allowed to fly. This would require them to reserve billions of dollars in cash which, in turn, would typically mean that they would not be in a position to meet the financial requirements of their cash intensive day-to-day operations. The foregoing became apparent to the commercial air transport industry soon after its commencement in the early twentieth century. Thus, naturally, efforts were made to search for viable means of risk management so as to enable the conduct of commercial air transport operations to continue regardless of the individual operators' overwhelming exposure to risk.

Different risk management strategies[4] have been devised and implemented over the years by airlines and other operators in the air transport industry. These range

---

[1] 137 LNTS 11 (1929) art. 17. See also 2242 UNTS 350 ICAO Doc. 9740 (1999) art. 17.

[2] 137 LNTS 11 (1929) arts. 18–19; 2242 UNTS 350 ICAO Doc. 9740 (1999), arts. 18–19.

[3] 310 UNTS 181 ICAO Doc. 7364 (1952) art. 1.

[4] Leloudas and Haeck (2003) pp. 153–158 where the authors identify and discuss the following five stages of the risk management process: (a) risk identification; (b) risk measurement; (c) treatment of risk by: elimination, reduction, transfer, retention; (d) implementation of the selected treatments; and (e) the monitoring of results and consideration of changes in exposures.

from preventive methods such as safety and security programmes to alternative methods of risk transfer, such as captive insurance schemes, contingent capital, catastrophe bonds and derivatives.[5] However, these alternative strategies have not obviated the need for operators to seek insurance cover in the traditional aviation insurance market.[6] Today, one of the most significant and important elements of any aviation operator's risk management strategy is its traditional insurance programme. As demonstrated in the immediate aftermath of the events of September 11, 2001, the aviation industry cannot function effectively without a vibrant commercial insurance market. In an effort to demonstrate the true value of aviation insurance, Philip Chrystal describes insurance generally in the following words:

> [t]he textbook definition of insurance is as follows: "the individual can transfer the risk of a possibly large loss to the insurer by payment of a premium and so convert the uncertainty of a possible large loss into the certainty of a smaller but fixed annual cost". More than just that piece of paper, insurance is a promise by the insurers to reimburse the insureds for financial loss redeemable at some time in the future.[7]

"Aviation insurance is a specialized form of insurance written in a specialized insurance market,[8] although it has certain resemblances to other forms of insurance in which it has its origins".[9] It is generally agreed that the first aviation insurance policy was issued in Lloyds of London in 1911,[10] thereby commemorating the start of the aviation insurance industry. Since then, aviation insurance has grown rapidly, closely mirroring the development of the underlying aviation industry which it serves. Historically, London has also been the focal point of the international aviation insurance market, although other equally important aviation insurance markets have developed and are located in places such as the United States, France, Germany, Bermuda, Switzerland, Japan, Italy and Scandinavia.[11] Originally written in the London marine market in the early twentieth century, aviation insurance assumed significance as a separate form of insurance in the wake of the rapid development of the commercial aviation industry following the First World War.[12]

In the course of this evolution, certain fundamental concepts and principles of marine insurance have been adapted to the specialized field of aviation insurance. The bulk of common law insurance principles as we know them today derive from

---

[5] McClean et al. (2007) p. VIII-181-81A.

[6] Idem.

[7] Chrystal et al. (2004) p. 17.

[8] "The term 'insurance market' refers to a group of insurers in a particular area or a particular branch of insurance. In a global sense, the term 'aviation insurance market' or 'aviation market' refers to insurers worldwide who offer cover against aviation risks. The term also refers to aviation insurers located in a particular place or country who provide cover against such risks". See Margo (2000) p. 29.

[9] Idem, p. 12.

[10] Wells and Chadbourne (2000) p. 4. See also Margo (2000) p. 1, n1, where a concise description of the history of aviation insurance is provided. For a detailed history of the development of aviation insurance in the London market, See Insurance Institute of London (1968).

[11] Wells and Chadbourne (2000) idem.

[12] McClean et al. (2007) p. VIII–181.

the realm of marine insurance in England, where over the years, a considerable body of case law has grown up, representing interpretations, mostly by English courts, of terms and wordings of marine policies often handed down many years before the first aviation insurance policy was ever written.[13] The British *Marine Insurance Act of 1906*,[14] generally regarded as a codification of the principles of law applicable to marine and other branches of non-life insurance, introduces certain definitions and meanings to be attached to insurance policies which may not necessarily be relevant or appropriate to aviation policies. As part of its evolution, the aviation insurance industry has been in a position to adopt and/or adapt those principles and concepts of the marine market considered to be desirable in aviation insurance, and to reject those which are not.[15]

Further, the aviation insurance industry has been faced with unprecedented and constantly changing risks throughout its evolution, causing it to adapt its practices in order to be able to meet the new challenges posed to it. For instance, as summarized by the editors of *Shawcross and Beaumont*,

> [d]evelopments in the aviation industry, as well as political conditions in certain regions, including armed conflict, have sometimes required insurers to adjust their underwriting practices. Thus certain changes were required in the late 1950s with the introduction into service of jet transport aircraft, to deal with the risk of jet engine ingestion damage. Changes in the insurance of war and hijacking risks have been necessitated by the large number of hijackings of commercial aircraft, and acts of terrorism and sabotage which occurred in the late 1960s and early 1970s, and by the events of 11 September 2001, as well as by the enhanced threat of so-called Weapons of Mass Destruction (WMD). Changes have also been introduced as a result of difficulties which are sometimes experienced in determining whether a loss has been caused by a war risk or by a risk covered in an all risks policy.[16]

Thus, in order to gain a better appreciation of aviation insurance, it is essential first to have a broad understanding of the fundamental legal concepts which have been at its roots. Therefore, beginning with an effort to define the concept of insurance as understood in most common law jurisdictions around the world, the following sections of this chapter will generally attempt to demystify insurance in general and aviation insurance in particular by describing and exploring the various concepts and principles thereof.

2.2 Conventional Insurance: A Means of Spreading Risks

Insurance is a means of managing risks through pooling. Stated differently, "insurance is essentially a form of risk spreading which permits the risks of the few to be spread among the many so as to make them more manageable".[17] Indeed, as far

[13] Margo (2000) p. 10.
[14] 6 Edw. 7, c 41 (1906).
[15] Margo (2000) p. 13.
[16] McClean et al. (2007) p. VIII-181.
[17] Idem, p. 9.

back as 1601, the essence of the concept of insurance as a means of spreading and/ or managing risks through pooling was described in the often quoted preamble to the English *Policies of Assurance Act*[18] as having existed "*tyme out of mynde*", and as being:

> ... the means whereof it cometh to pass that upon the loss or perishing of any ship there followeth not the undoing of any man, but the loss lighteth rather easily upon many than heavy upon few, and rather upon them that adventure not than upon those who do adventure; whereby all merchants, specially those of the younger sort, are allured to venture more willingly and more freely.[19]

Elaborating on the purpose of insurance, the editors of the tenth edition of MacGillivray on insurance law agree that "[t]he purpose of a contract of insurance is to organize the sharing among a large number of persons of the cost of losses which are likely to happen only to some of them (or to happen at an earlier time to some other than to others)".[20] Another commentator has succinctly described what insurance does as follows:

> Fundamentally, insurance represents the delicate balance between the uncertainty and the predictability of future events associated with unfavorable consequences. ... Insurance is of value to the purchaser only because it allows for the sharing of risk across a pool of other similarly situated but widely distributed purchasers, guaranteeing for each purchaser protection against substantial but uncertain losses in exchange for the payment of premiums both certain and manageable.[21]

It is clear from the foregoing that, at one end of the spectrum, "[w]here there is no risk, there can be no insurance, and arrangements not involving risk which masquerade as insurance are more accurately understood as entitlement programs".[22] At the other end, in situations where the risk does exist, but cannot be estimated in accordance with traditional actuarial models, the use of insurance as a means of managing the risk is at best difficult and at worst impossible. Insurance can only be used as a meaningful means of risk management where the risk involved is real and can be assessed or quantified. As will be seen below, this is one of the major reasons why in the air transport sector, war, hijacking and terrorism risks are, to some extent, considered uninsurable and usually excluded from coverage in most traditional aviation insurance policies.[23]

---

[18] 43 Eliz. I, c. 12 (1901).

[19] Idem. See also Fitzsimmons (2004) p. 6.

[20] Leigh-Jones et al. (2003) pp. 913–914.

[21] Kendall (2002) p. 572.

[22] Idem.

[23] "Extremely catastrophic events are generally considered to be uninsurable in part because by nature, the do not conform to models based on the law of large numbers ... Past experience with events of such great magnitude is usually too sparse to accurately predict how often a similar event can be expected to occur. Further, where a particular loss is grossly disproportionate to other losses that can be anticipated to occur within the pool of policyholders, the catastrophic loss invalidates the calculation of rates and has the potential to create insolvency for the insurer". Idem, pp. 572–573, fn. 15.

Because insurance thrives on the pooling of the risks of the many, it is only feasible where conditions are in place for the "Law of Large Numbers"[24] to operate. The application of the law of large numbers enables insurers to predict losses with a reasonable level of accuracy enough to calculate premium rates which will not be excessively high but which will nonetheless produce reserves adequate to pay claims as and when the losses insured against occur without bankrupting the insurer.[25] "The cornerstone of the entire structure is the application of actuarial probability principles using complex statistical models based on data gathered from past experience. Discernment of a pattern that can be projected to forecast future losses is the sine qua non which, if lacking, eliminates the possibility of rational rate-setting".[26] Again, it will be noted later that in the realm of aviation insurance, the law of large numbers has limited applicability since the worldwide pool of potential assureds (i.e., airlines, manufacturers, ground handling service providers, airports and air navigation service providers,) is quite small when compared to the individual values at risk.

A contract of insurance has been defined as "one whereby one party (the "insurer") promises in return for a money consideration (the "premium") to pay to the other party (the "assured") a sum of money or provide him with some corresponding benefit upon the occurrence of one or more specified events".[27] It has also been defined in broad terms as "an agreement to confer upon the insured a contractual right which, prima facie, comes into existence immediately when loss is suffered by the happening of an event insured against, to be put by the insurer in the same position in which the insured would have been had the event not occurred, but in no better position".[28] In order to produce a mutually beneficial arrangement, the contract of insurance must relieve the assured of the burden of uncertainty associated with potential losses while allowing the insurer to profit from their reasonable calculability.[29] Perhaps the most authoritative and persuasive description of the concept of insurance is that found in the opinion of Judge Channell in the 1904 English case of *Prudential Insurance Company v. Internal Revenue Commissioners*:[30]

> When you insure a ship or a house you cannot insure that the ship shall not be lost or the house burnt, but what you do insure is that a sum of money shall be paid upon the happening of a certain event. That I think is the first requirement in a contract of insurance. It must be a contract whereby for some consideration, usually but not necessarily in periodical

---

[24] "The Law of Large Numbers is the statistical proposition that the more opportunities exist for an event to occur, the closer the actual relationship of occurrences to opportunities will be to the true probability. Once the true probability is estimated by observing a large sample of events, it must then be applied to a large number of exposures before the actual occurrences will approximate the true probability". Idem, p. 572, fn. 15.

[25] Idem.

[26] Idem, p. 573.

[27] Leigh-Jones et al. (2003) p. 3. See also Ivamy (1986) p. 3.

[28] Merkin (2006) at 4.

[29] Kendall (2002) p. 572.

[30] [1904] 2 KB 658.

> payments called premiums, you secure to yourself some benefit, usually but not necessarily the payment of a sum of money, upon the happening of some event. The next thing that is necessary is that the event should be one which involves some amount of uncertainty. There must be either uncertainty whether the event will ever happen or not, or if the event is one which must happen at some time, there must be uncertainty as to the time at which it will happen. The remaining essential [requirement] is ... that the insurance must be against something. A contract which would otherwise be a mere wager may become an insurance by reason of the assured having an interest in the subject matter – that is to say, the uncertain event which is necessary to make the contract amount to an insurance must be an event which is prima facie adverse to the interest of the assured.

The subject-matter of this case primarily concerned stamp duty and the Court's task was to determine whether or not a particular contract amounted to a policy of insurance depending on a life. However, it is agreed among leading authors on insurance law that the above-quoted statement by Judge Channell sets out the practical indicia of insurance as well as the substantive matters that go to make an insurance contract.[31] Consequently, one author has distilled three requirements for a valid contract of insurance from the statement of Judge Channell as follows: "[f]irst, it should provide some benefit for the assured on the occurrence of some event; secondly, the occurrence should involve some element of uncertainty; and thirdly, the uncertain event should be one which is *prima facie* adverse to the interest of the assured".[32] As acknowledged by Judge Channell himself, these requirements are by no means exhaustive.[33] In the following sections, we take a closer look at the various elements which distinguish a contract of insurance from all other types of contracts.

2.2.1 The Premium

Premium may be defined as the consideration paid by the assured in exchange for the promise from the insurer of a benefit upon the occurrence of a specified event.[34] Although premium is a very significant element of every contract of insurance, it is generally agreed that premium is in no respect a pre-requisite of a contract of insurance.[35] It is characteristic of a contract of insurance that "the amount of

---

[31] Merkin (2006) p. 4.

[32] Hodgin (2002) p. 2; see also Margo (2000) p. 9.

[33] [1904] 2 KB 658 p. 663.

[34] Margo (2000) p. 173; Merkin (2006); Leigh-Jones et al. (2003) p. 162.

[35] "In the majority of cases, a premium will be paid to the insurer, but this does not appear to be a prerequisite for the contract to qualify as one of insurance". See Margo (2000) p. 9. See also Merkin (2006) p. 280, where the author notes by way of example that, "after the event" insurance—the type of insurance which provides the assured with an indemnity for his own legal costs and for any costs order made against him in favour of a third party should the assured fail in an action brought against the third party—operates on the basis that the assured does not pay any premium at the outset and is liable for the premium only if his action succeeds and a costs order is made against the third party that encompasses the premium payable under the policy.

premium is not intended to be equivalent to the value of the insurer's actual performance (if any) but is calculated in relation to the likelihood that performance will be required (or will be required within a certain time)".[36] This is one of the characteristic features that distinguish insurance contracts from other types of contracts. The editors of the tenth edition of MacGillivray's treatise on Insurance Law provide the following scenarios by way of example:

> a contract by which an engineer undertakes to repair a machine whenever it breaks down is clearly not a contract of insurance if the engineer is to be remunerated in accordance with the amount of work done. If, however, the remuneration is fixed without regard to the amount of work done, it is a consideration of the type of an insurance premium and the contract may be one of insurance.[37]

2.2.2 *The Obligation of the Insurer*

For a contract to be regarded as one of insurance, it must contain or include a binding undertaking by the insurer to pay the assured or perform some other obligation upon the happening of the event insured against.[38] Accordingly, a contract in which the insurer has a discretion with regard to the performance of the obligation assumed thereunder upon the occurrence of the specified event does not amount to a contract of insurance.[39] According to MacGillivray, the rationale underlying this feature of insurance contracts is that "[a] contract of insurance is intended to convey security and certainty to the assured, and not merely an expectation of payment or performance, however well founded".[40]

2.2.3 *Payment of Money or Corresponding Benefit*

The binding obligation assumed by the insurer in a contract of insurance usually involves the payment of money or the performance of some other benefit upon the occurrence of an event specified in the contract. Previously, it was thought that the insurer's obligation was only limited to the payment of money. However, following the English decision in *Department of Trade and Industry v. St. Christopher Motorists Association Ltd.*,[41] the obligation of the insurer has been widened to include the provision of services for the benefit of the assured to be paid for by the insurer.

---

[36] Leigh-Jones et al. (2003) p. 3.

[37] Idem.

[38] Idem, pp. 3–4.

[39] Idem, pp. 3–4; Merkin (2006) pp. 6–7; Ivamy (1986) p. 4, where the author notes that: "where the payment of the money or other benefit is discretionary and not obligatory, the contract is not one of insurance".

[40] Leigh-Jones et al. (2003) p. 4.

[41] [1974] 1 All E.R. 395.

While payment of money appears to be the normal element of a contract of insurance, some doubts have been raised with regard to the issue of corresponding benefits; in particular as to how difficult it is to define the true limitations of this extension. In the English case of *Medical Defence Union Ltd. v. The Department of Trade*,[42] the Medical Defence Union regularly conducted legal proceedings on behalf of its members, mostly doctors and dentists, with a view to indemnifying them against claims for damages and costs arising from their professional work. The question arose as to whether or not the Medical Defence Union was carrying on an insurance business, and the resolution of that question turned partially on the determination as to whether the provision of legal defence services by the Union to its members amounted to "the payment of money or the provision of a corresponding benefit". In the specific circumstances of that case, it was held that the contract in question was not one of insurance.

This decision has however been criticized by a number of authors as portraying a rather restrictive approach to the issue.[43] The editor of Colinvaux's law of insurance expresses the view for instance that "it should suffice that some form of benefit is conferred".[44] Indeed, Judge Channell's above-quoted definition of the concept of insurance clearly envisages the possibility of the insurer providing some corresponding benefit to the assured in place of, or in addition to, the payment of cash.

2.2.4 *The Special Uncertain Event*

A contract of insurance must provide for the payment of money or the provision of the corresponding benefit by the insurer upon the occurrence of an event which is uncertain in terms of whether it will happen at all (indemnity insurance), or when it will happen if it is known that the event will happen at some point in time (life insurance).[45] In the words of Judge Channell, "there must be either uncertainty whether the event will ever happen or not, or if the event is one which must happen at some time, there must be uncertainty as to the time at which it will happen".[46] The need for an uncertain event precludes the possibility of insurance being placed after a loss has occurred to the knowledge of the assured.[47]

The element of uncertainty about the special event is also essential for purposes of distinguishing a contract of insurance from contracts of warranty and/or guarantee—"the express or implied undertaking of a contracting party to pay damages or

[42] [1979] 1 Lloyd's L.R. 499; [1979] 2 All E.R. 421.

[43] Merkin (2006) p. 6.

[44] Idem.

[45] Idem, pp. 6–7.

[46] [1904] 2 KB 658 p. 663.

[47] Merkin (2006) p. 7.

to perform some other secondary obligation, such as repair of a defective article, in the event of his own failure to perform a primary obligation".[48] To admit that a person may offer insurance against the possibility that he himself may commit some voluntary act or omission would be to risk confusing this necessary distinction between contracts of insurance and other similar types of contracts. Accordingly, there can be no contract of insurance if the assured has control over the occurrence of the event insured against.[49]

The foregoing statement must, however, be qualified. Some contracts of insurance (for instance, life or endowment insurance contracts) include the possibility of the assured surrendering the policy for its accrued surrender value before the occurrence of the event insured against. According to Colinvaux, "[t]he existence of this right to surrender does not convert the contract from one of insurance into something else, even in the exceptional contractual situation when the surrender value becomes equivalent to the amount payable under the policy in the event of death, as death remains the basis of the contract and it is irrelevant that the predominant purpose of the policy was investment and that other events could trigger payment".[50]

2.2.5 Loss and Indemnity

The event insured against must be of a character more or less adverse to the interest of the assured.[51] Stated differently, "the accident must be calculated, if it happens, to result in loss to the assured".[52] The *Prudential Assurance* case involved a contract in which the assured was to receive a certain sum of money if he lived to the age of 65. Judge Channell nevertheless insisted that loss was an essential element of a contract of insurance, and in applying that principle, he arrived at the artificial conclusion that the assured would indeed suffer loss by reaching 65 in that he would by that age be less able to provide for himself by earning his own living.[53] The English Court of Appeal rejected this conclusion and the analysis upon which it was based in the case of *Gould v. Curtis*,[54] where Lord Justice Buckley drew a distinction between contingency and indemnity insurance.[55]

In contingency insurance, the element of loss is not required. Instead, the contract involves an agreement to pay a specified amount of money on the happening of a specific event, irrespective of whether that event is adverse to the assured or

[48] Leigh-Jones et al. (2003) p. 5.

[49] Idem.

[50] Merkin (2006) p. 7, footnotes omitted.

[51] [1904] 2 KB 658 p. 663.

[52] Ivamy (1986) p. 4.

[53] Merkin (2006) pp. 7–8.

[54] [1913] 3 K.B. 84 p. 95.

[55] Merkin (2006) p. 8.

causes him loss.[56] Life and usually accident insurance policies fall within this category. Indemnity insurance on the other hand includes all forms of insurances in which loss forms an essential element. "[T]he assured's recovery [in indemnity insurance] is quantified by reference to the amount of his loss".[57] The concept of indemnity will be discussed in detail below as one of the general principles of insurance. For present purposes, however, it suffices to say that loss is an essential element of insurance insofar as indemnity insurance is concerned.

2.2.6 *Transfer of Risk*

As noted above, a contract of insurance deals with risk and must clearly involve the transfer of risk from the assured to the insurer. Accordingly, there can be no insurance where the contract does not involve a transfer of risk.[58] Intermediaries such as brokers play a very important role in the process of formation of the contract of insurance. However, as noted by Colinvaux, "a contract under which a broker is empowered to accept risks on behalf of an insurer by means of a binding authority is not a contract of insurance in its own right, as the contract of itself does not operate to transfer risks but merely provides a mechanism for the transfer under individual contracts to be made at a later date. The same analysis applies to reinsurance treaties".[59]

2.2.7 *The Subject-Matter of the Contract of Insurance*

According to Ivamy, in considering the various elements which portray the nature of the contract of insurance, it is extremely essential to distinguish between the *subject-matter of the contract of insurance* and the *subject-matter of the insurance*.[60] With respect to the former, he notes that:

> [t]he protection given by a contract of insurance is not protection against accident in that the contract can prevent an accident from happening. It merely secures for the assured, when the accident happens, the payment of a sum of money. The subject-matter of the contract of

---

[56] Idem.

[57] Idem.

[58] Idem, p. 9, footnotes omitted.

[59] Idem.

[60] Ivamy (1986) p. 11.

> insurance is, therefore, money [or a corresponding benefit], and it must be distinguished from the subject-matter of insurance, which exists independently of the contract.[61]

Turning to the latter—the subject-matter of insurance, Ivamy notes further that:

> [a] contract of insurance necessarily contemplates the existence of something to which an accident may happen, and anything, to which an accident may happen may therefore be the subject-matter of insurance. Strictly speaking, an accident can only happen to a physical object. There are, however, certain kinds of insurance intended to protect the assured in cases where he requires protection not against accidents to physical objects, but against the consequences to himself of such accidents. In these kinds of insurance, the interest of the assured which will be adversely affected by the happening of the accident insured against, and not the physical object to which the accident actually happens, is to be regarded as the subject-matter of the insurance.

As will be seen shortly, this distinction between the subject matter of the contract of insurance and the subject matter of the insurance is critical when it comes to determining whether an assured has an insurable interest or not. Certain conditions relating to the subject matter of insurance are implied in every contract of insurance. The subject matter of insurance must be in existence at the time when the policy is effective[62]; it must be described in the policy in such clear terms as to identify it and to define the risk undertaken by the insurers[63]; and, the assured must have an insurable interest in it.[64]

2.3 Legal Concepts and Principles Applicable to Insurance

A contract of insurance is a special type of contract. In addition to the above described features, there are a number of specific principles of law that apply to contracts of insurance independently (i.e., these principles do not derive from the contents of the contract). In the common law world, most of these principles of law have evolved through judicial precedents over the years; some have been codified in statutes, particularly in England; and they still apply today although, arguably, some of the foundations upon which these principles were originally based are no longer relevant. A discussion of the various legal principles applicable to insurance

---

[61] Idem. In support of this assertion, Ivamy quotes the dictum of Lord Justice Brett in (1881) 18 Ch. D 1 p. 9 as follows:

> Now, in my judgment, the subject-matter of the contract of insurance is money, and money only. The subject-matter of insurance is a different thing from the subject-matter of the contract of insurance... The only result in the policy, if an accident which is within the insurance happens is a payment of money. It is true that under certain circumstances in a fire policy there may be an option to spend the money in rebuilding the premises, but that does not alter the fact that the only liability of the insurance company is to pay money.

[62] Idem, p. 271.

[63] Idem, p. 272.

[64] Idem. See Sect. 2.3.2 below for a discussion of the concept of insurable interest.

generally follows in the following sections of this chapter. Where feasible, the applicability of these principles to the specialized area of aviation insurance is also demonstrated.

2.3.1 *The Utmost Good Faith: Uberrima Fides*

A fundamental principle of insurance law is that the utmost good faith must be observed by each party to a contract of insurance.[65] This is an exception to the general rule of contract law which, although requires parties to a contract not to mislead each other by positive misrepresentations, imposes no such positive duty upon the parties to make a full and frank disclosure of all material facts.[66] The principle of utmost good faith as applies in insurance law, and also known as the doctrine of *uberrima fides*, was stated by Lord Mansfield as far back as 1766 in the English case of *Carter v. Boehm*[67] as follows:

> Insurance is a contract upon speculation. The special facts, upon which the contingent chance is to be computed, lie more commonly in the knowledge of the insured only: the underwriter trusts to his representation, and proceeds upon confidence that he does not keep back any circumstance in his knowledge, to mislead the underwriter into a belief that the circumstance does not exist, and to induce him to estimate the risque as if it did not exist. The keeping back such a circumstance is a fraud, and, therefore, the policy is void. Although the suppression should happen through mistake, without any fraudulent intention; yet still, the underwriter is deceived, and the policy is void; because the risque run is really different from the risque understood and intended to be run at the time of the agreement. . . . The governing principle is applicable to all contracts and dealings. Good faith forbids either party by concealing what he privately knows, to draw the other into a bargain, from his ignorance of that fact, and his believing the contrary. . . .[68]

The principle applies to every contract of insurance,[69] be it a contract of indemnity or otherwise. Traditionally, the principle takes the form of an implied condition in the insurance contract,[70] and it imposes on both the prospective assured and the insurer the duty to disclose to each other all material facts and circumstances affecting the insurance at all material times. According to Ivamy, "[i]t is the duty of the parties to help each other to come to a right conclusion, and not to hold each other at arms length in defence of their conflicting interest[s]".[71] In practice, however, the duty of good faith usually refers to the assured's duty to disclose to the insurer facts within his actual or constructive knowledge which are

[65] Idem, p. 119.
[66] Merkin (2006) p. 133.
[67] (1766) 3 Burr. 1905.
[68] Idem, p. 1909, reproduced in Ivamy (1986) p. 119, footnotes omitted.
[69] Merkin (2006) p. 133, fn. 4.
[70] Ivamy (1986) p. 271. See Sect. 2.4.5 below for a discussion of conditions in insurance contracts.
[71] Idem, p. 120.

material to the risk and which enable the insurer to reach a rational decision as to whether or not to accept the risk and, if so, at what premium.[72]

The basis for this doctrine is that, during negotiations preceding the conclusion of insurance contracts, it is generally accepted that the insurer usually knows very little or absolutely nothing about the risk whereas the prospective assured on the other hand knows a great deal, if not everything.[73] This being the situation, the principle casts a duty upon the person who desires to be insured to make a full disclosure of all the material circumstances to the insurer without being asked,[74] so that the contract may be entered into on an equal footing. "Similarly, it is the duty of the insurers and their agents to disclose all material facts within their knowledge ... [to the assured]. All representations made by them during the negotiations with a view to inducing the assured to accept a policy must be true".[75]

The duty of good faith applies until the conclusion of the contract of insurance,[76] and non-compliance with it results in the contract being voidable at the option of the aggrieved party.[77] Prior to the conclusion of the contract, the principle obliges both parties and their agents "not only to be honest and straightforward, but also to make a full disclosure of all material facts. Further, all statements made by [both parties] during negotiations must be accurate".[78] As such, non-disclosure as well as misrepresentation of material facts amount to a breach of the duty and the result is the same irrespective of whether the non-disclosure or misrepresentation was innocent, negligent or fraudulent.[79] "Material facts", for the purposes of the principle, are those facts which would "influence the judgment of a prudent insurer in determining whether to accept the risk and in fixing the premium where the risk is accepted".[80]

2.3.2 *Insurable Interest*

Unlike other types of contracts, "[e]very contract of insurance requires an insurable interest to support it; otherwise it is invalid".[81] This means that whenever insurance is contracted for, the assured must stand in a legally recognized relationship to the

---

72 Achampong (1987).

73 Ivamy (1986) p. 120.

74 Idem.

75 Idem, at 120–121.

76 There has been long and intensive debate as to whether the doctrine of utmost good faith has extra-contractual effect. However, the generally accepted position would appear to be that the doctrine applies both before the contract is concluded (i.e., the pre-formation stage) and during the performance of the contract (i.e., the post-formation stage). See Leigh-Jones et al. (2003) p. 409. Several legal commentaries have also been written about the variety of duties it gives rise to before and after the formation of the contract of insurance; and the remedies for its breach. See generally Bennett (1999) and Soyer (2003).

77 Merkin (2006) p. 134.

78 Ivamy (1986) pp. 120–121.

79 Idem, p. 143.

80 Merkin (2006) p. 133.

81 Ivamy (1986) p. 22.

subject-matter of the insurance otherwise the contract may be declared void and unenforceable for being contrary to public policy.[82] The assured must be so situated that the happening of the event on which the insurance money is to become payable or the performance of the corresponding benefit is to become due, would as a proximate result, involve the assured in the loss or diminution of a right recognized by law or in legal liability.[83] The requirement that the assured must have an insurable interest in the subject matter of the insurance is an implied condition of every contract of insurance.[84] As such, insurable interest has been described as "the very warp and woof of the enforcibility [*sic*] of insurance contracts".[85] The mere conclusion of a contract of insurance does not entrust to the assured the right to recover thereunder when the insured event occurs. To be able to recover, the assured must demonstrate among many other things that he has an insurable interest in the subject-matter of the insurance.[86] Thus, the requirement of an insurable interest is the distinguishing element between a wagering contract and a contract of insurance.[87] Insurable interest usually functions as a defense employed by the insurer, justifying nonpayment after the insured event has materialized. If this defence is upheld, the contract no longer obliges the insurer to pay the promised sum of money to the assured.[88]

The classic definition of an insurable interest was pronounced by Judge Lawrence in the old English case of *Lucena v. Craufurd*[89] as follows:

> A man is interested in a thing to whom advantage may arise or prejudice happen from the circumstances which may attend it . . . and whom it importeth that its condition as to safety or other quality should continue: *interest does not necessarily imply a right to the whole or a part of a thing, nor necessarily and exclusively that which may be the subject of privation, but the having some relation to, or concern in the subject of the insurance, which relation or concern by the happening of the perils insured against may be so affected as to produce a damage, detriment, or prejudice to the person insuring*; and where a man so circumstanced with respect to matters exposed to certain risk or damages, or to have a *moral certainty* of

[82] Salah El Din (1971) p. 27.

[83] Idem.

[84] Ivamy (1986) p. 272. See Sect. 2.4.2 below for a discussion of conditions in insurance contracts.

[85] Harnett and Thornton (1948) p. 1163.

[86] There is a sharp conflict of authority across jurisdictions as to when the insurable interest must exist. Generally, however, it would appear to be the case that in life insurance matters, the assured must show that his insurable interest subsisted at the date of the contract and not at death, since the contract is not a contract of indemnity. See Leigh-Jones et al. (2003) p. 36. In all other types of insurance other than life insurance, the assured will only be required to show the existence of his insurable interest at the time of the loss. See Ivamy (1986) pp. 26–27.

[87] Fischer (1981) pp. 446–447. The author further distinguishes wagering contracts from insurance contracts as follows: "A wagering contract is founded upon chance, not upon the chance of an event; it creates its own risk – win all or lose all. An insurance contract is founded upon dispersion of a risk – the insured transfers a large risk for a small cost. He is not seeking a gain; he wants to avoid a possible future loss". See idem, at 446.

[88] Loshin (2007) p. 479.

[89] (1806) 2 Bos & Pul. (N.R.) 269 (HL) reproduced in Ivamy (1986) p. 19.

advantage or benefit, but for those risks or dangers, he may be said to be interested in the safety of the thing. To be interested in the preservation of a thing, is to be so circumstanced with respect to it as to have benefit from its existence, prejudice from its destruction. *The property of a thing and the interest devisable from it may be very different; of the first, the price is generally the measure, but by interest in a thing every benefit or advantage arising out of or depending on such thing may be considered as being comprehended.*[90]

A contract of insurance is null and void if it is concluded without an insurable interest on the part of the assured. It thereby becomes a gaming or a wagering contract, which, by statutory law in most countries, is illegal. Commenting on the significance of insurable interest, Colinvaux notes that:

> permitting a person to insure a subject-matter which he has no interest in preserving, and in which he has no interest other than the policy itself, gives rise to two dangers: [f]irst there is the possibility that the assured is doing no more than wagering with the insurer on the continued safety of the insured subject matter. . . . A second and probably more fundamental objection to insurance without interest is that an assured who stands to benefit from the early destruction of what has been insured will be tempted to take steps to bring about such early destruction.[91]

The insurable interest doctrine has been developed to address the concern of "moral hazard",[92] namely: "[i]f a policyholder does not have an interest in the continued life of a person covered by the policy, that person has the ill fortune of being worth more to the policyholder dead than alive; likewise, insured property is worth more destroyed than preserved".[93] Indeed, as Colinvaux notes further, even in situations where an insurable interest does exist, there may be a similar danger, particularly in life insurance, or in cases where insured property has been overvalued.[94]

Although the doctrine of insurable interest has been criticized as creating perverse incentives which undermine its own purpose of reducing moral hazard,[95] it nevertheless continues to apply to aviation insurance contracts in a number of

[90] (1806) 2 Bos & Pul. (N.R.) 269 (HL) idem, p. 302, emphasis added.

[91] Merkin (2006) p. 73.

[92] Loshin (2007) p. 480.

[93] Idem. The author notes further that: in the context of insurance law "moral hazard" describes situations in which the existence of insurance increases incentives for loss. Although moral hazard is often used to refer to a policyholder's tendency to take less care in safeguarding his/her own insured property, it also applies more broadly to situations where the policyholder has insured the property or person of another. In this latter situation, the existence of moral hazard increases the risk of loss to those third parties [or their property] insured by the policyholder. The concept of moral hazard will be discussed below as part of the means by which insurers assess risks.

[94] Merkin (2006) p. 73.

[95] See generally: Loshin (2007). In support of this criticism, the author argues that:

> when an insurance policy is invalidated for lack of insurable interest, the insurance company is relieved of its obligation to pay under the policy. The prospect of invalidation reduces the expected costs of a policy to an insurer and thereby encourages insurers to issue more such policies. Meanwhile, doctrinal uncertainty permits insurers to maintain the appearance of good faith for policies that are not clearly invalid when issued. Taken together, these dynamics create perverse incentives that work to subsidize moral hazard rather than to discourage it. See idem, p. 477.

different ways. With respect to aircraft hulls, the owner, lessee, operator or the person who has possession of the aircraft has an insurable interest in the hull up to his financial benefit therein.[96] Where there is a mortgage on the aircraft, the mortgagee's interest is limited to the sum of money he has advanced, and it is often the case that the mortgagee is named in the policy either as a co-insured or as a first loss payee up to the extent of the undischarged portion of the mortgage.[97] In all such hull policies, the subject-matter of the insurance is the aircraft hull itself. With respect to liabilities arising from aviation operations, aircraft operators, airport operators, air navigation service providers, ground handling service providers, and airframe, engine, spares and component parts manufacturers are all interested in the sums they may be called upon to pay to passengers and to third-parties as a result of accidents involving their aircraft or arising from the services they provide. Such potential liability derives either from domestic law or from the provisions of specific international treaties.[98] Where liability is concerned, the subject-matter of the insurance lies in the financial interest(s) of the assured which may be adversely affected when the insured peril occurs, and not the physical aircraft itself.

2.3.3 *Indemnity*

With the exception of life and personal accident insurance contracts,[99] all other contracts of insurance are classified as contracts of indemnity.[100] The essence of the principle of indemnity is that it permits the assured to recover from the insurer only that which he has actually lost, and no more. The underlying rationale is that insurance is not designed to enable the assured to realize a profit but to protect the assets that he already has. The contract of insurance, therefore, does not bring into existence any new risks, but offers protection against risk(s) that are already present.[101] The principle of indemnity enforces this concept by ensuring that when the assured suffers a loss, the insurer's obligation is limited only to placing the assured in the same financial position after the loss as he occupied before the happening of the insured peril.[102] The requirement that the assured be restored to

[96] Salah El Din (1971) p. 28.

[97] Idem.

[98] Idem. See e.g., 2242 UNTS 350 ICAO Doc. 9740 (1999); and 310 UNTS 181 ICAO Doc. 7364 (1952).

[99] Life insurance policies—agreements under which the insurer agrees to pay a specified sum on the death of the life assured or, in the case of endowment insurance, on the earlier of either a specified date or the death of the life assured—are for the most part not indemnity contracts because it is impossible to measure the value of a life or for that matter reinstate a dead person to the state in which he was before death. Accordingly, the assured under a life policy is entitled to insure for an unlimited amount. See Merkin (2006) p. 76.

[100] Salah El Din (1971) p. 32.

[101] Wells and Chadbourne (2000) p. 78.

[102] Salah El Din (1971) p. 32.

the exact financial position in which he was before the loss occurred (no better and no worse) explains why, as mentioned earlier, the element of loss is a critical factor in every contract of insurance based on indemnity.

The position is not the same where the contract is not one of indemnity but contingency, such as life insurance and accident insurance contracts. Under contingency contracts, the insured victim is allowed to accumulate recoveries from as many sources as he or she can.[103]

The doctrine of indemnity was defined by Lord Justice Brett in the nineteenth century English case of *Castellain v. Preston*[104] as follows:

> The very foundation, in my opinion, of every rule which has been applied to insurance law is this, namely, that the contract of insurance contained in a marine or fire policy is a contract of indemnity, and of indemnity only, and that this contract means that the insured, in case of a loss against which the policy has been made, shall be fully indemnified, but shall never be more than fully indemnified. That is the fundamental principle of insurance and if ever a proposition is brought forward which is at variance with it, that is to say, which either will prevent the insured from obtaining a full indemnity, or which will give the insured more than a full indemnity, that proposition must certainly be wrong.

The question arises as to whether or not the concept of indemnity applies with respect to valued insurance policies,—where "the value of the insured subject-matter is agreed between the parties at the outset and, on the happening of an insured event, the agreed sum is payable without the need for the assured to quantify his actual loss".[105] The specific question which arises is, as there is no guarantee that the pre-set value will be equal to the actual loss when it occurs, how does the concept of indemnity ensure that the assured will obtain a full indemnity from the insurer when he suffers a total loss? Conversely, where the subject-matter of the insurance has been overvalued and that value is accepted as the insured value under the policy, how does the principle of indemnity ensure that the insurer pays no more than the actual loss sustained by the assured when a total loss occurs?

In practice, agreed value policies are adopted because of their commercial utility; not because they provide a perfect indemnity. They are not contrary to the law.[106] Such contracts are considered to be contracts of indemnity, and indemnity only, the only difference being that the measure of indemnity is arranged or agreed upon at the inception of the contract rather than when the loss occurs.[107] In a valued

---

[103] Hasson (1985) p. 418. Serious criticism has been leveled against the decisions of the courts classifying life and accident insurance policies as not being contracts of indemnity. For instance, it has been argued that life and accident policies contain a considerable element of indemnity since it is clearly the intention of purchasers of such policies to indemnify either their families (in the event of death) or, in the event of accident, to compensate themselves for their lost earnings. Thus, there is no reason why the loss of property should be treated differently from the loss of an arm since both result in economic loss to the person who sustains them. See idem, p. 418.

[104] (1883) 11 Q.B.D. 380 (C.A.) p. 386, per Lord Justice Brett.

[105] Merkin (2006) p. 76.

[106] Salah El Din (1971) p. 32.

[107] Idem.

policy, the valuation is deemed to be conclusive as between the insurer and the assured, and the law would recognize the validity of the policy on the basis that the sum payable, while not necessarily a perfect indemnity, can be regarded as an indemnity by reference to the terms of the contract.[108] The effect of the valuation is merely to dispense with proof of the extent of the loss, as, in the event of total loss, the measure of indemnity is the fixed value of the policy. In the event of partial loss, the indemnity is represented by the actual loss of the assured up to the limit of the maximum agreed value set in the policy. The assured must still prove the fact that he has indeed sustained a loss.[109]

It would appear that the operation of the principle of indemnity and the requirement of an insurable interest in insurance contracts will often lead to one and the same conclusion. However, as Colinvaux points out, the two principles are distinct. He notes that:

> The question of indemnity only arises where a loss has occurred, for indemnity is concerned with the quantification of loss. By contrast, the rules of insurable interest are mainly concerned with ensuring that a person who has no prospect of suffering a loss is prevented from insuring in the first place. ... [Further,] where an assured is unable to satisfy the indemnity requirement by proving any loss, the position is quite simply that he cannot recover under the policy. ... Failure to demonstrate insurable interest is potentially more serious.[110]

It could lead to criminal sanctions when the agreement is declared to be one of gambling or wagering, or it could be declared illegal thereby preventing the parties from suing on it or claiming restitution of payments made under it.[111]

In the realm of aviation insurance, the principle of indemnity has very wide application as most aviation insurance contracts (i.e., aircraft hull, passenger legal liability, third-party legal liability, and products/services liability policies) are concluded on an agreed value basis. There are several methods of providing indemnity in aviation insurance. These include: cash settlements, replacement, repair and reinstatement.[112] Normally, liability insurance policies relating to aviation operations are subject to a per-occurrence and/or an annual aggregate limit for the period of time covered by the policy. This typically means that the expressed value is the maximum agreed value of the policy, and if it is exhausted before the end of the policy period, the policy lapses and no further claims can be made unless it is reinstated.[113]

---

[108] Merkin (2006) pp. 336–337.

[109] Ivamy (1986) p. 9. See also Salah El Din (1971) pp. 32–33.

[110] Merkin (2006) p. 77.

[111] Idem.

[112] Salah El Din (1971) p. 33.

[113] Idem.

2.3.4 Subrogation

The principle of subrogation flows from the operation of the principle of indemnity. In essence, the principle of subrogation ensures that when a loss occurs under a contract of indemnity, then the right to anything that would reduce or diminish that loss would belong to the person or entity originally paying for the loss (i.e., the insurer).[114] In consequence, the insurer, upon paying the loss, is entitled by virtue of the doctrine of subrogation to be placed in the position of the assured, and to succeed to all his rights and remedies against third parties in respect of the subject-matter of the insurance.[115] "While the effect of subrogation is to confer on the insurer the rights of the assured, it must be borne in mind from the outset that the proper claimant against the third-party is always the assured; as a result, the subrogation claim must be brought in the name of the assured".[116]

In the above-mentioned case of *Castellain v. Preston*, Lord Justice Brett commented on the role of the doctrine of subrogation as follows:

> That doctrine does not arise upon any terms of the contract of insurance; it is only another proposition which has been adopted for the purpose of carrying out the fundamental rule [i.e., indemnity] which I have mentioned, and it is a doctrine in favour of the underwriters or insurers in order to prevent the assured from recovering more than a full indemnity; it has been adopted solely for that reason.[117]

The right of subrogation therefore rests on the premise that the insurer's contract is a contract of indemnity and that he is therefore entitled, upon paying a claim for which others are primarily liable to the assured, to be proportionately subrogated to the right of action of the assured against them. The scope of the principle is so wide that it entitles the insurer to assume all the rights of the assured against the third-party responsible for the loss, whether in contract or tort, legal or equitable.[118] It also allows the insurer to take advantage of any benefit which accrues to the assured which has the effect of diminishing the loss. Most significantly, the principle permits the insurer to proceed against the assured for taking any action that prejudices or compromises the insurer's rights against the third-party.[119] If the third-party in question is also insured, then the effect of the principle of subrogation

---

[114] Idem, p. 34.

[115] Ivamy (1986) p. 465.

[116] Merkin (2006) p. 377, footnotes omitted.

[117] (1883) 11 Q.B.D. 380 (C.A.) p. 387, per Lord Justice Brett.

[118] Idem, where Lord Justice Brett stated that, as between themselves and the assured, the insurers are entitled

> to the advantage of every right of the assured, whether such right consists in contract, fulfilled or unfulfilled, or in remedy for tort capable of being insisted on or already insisted on, or in any other right, whether by way of condition or otherwise, legal or equitable, which can be, or has been exercised or has accrued, and whether such right could or could not be enforced by [them] in the name of the assured, by the exercise or acquiring of which right or condition the loss against which the insured is insured can be or has been diminished.

[119] Merkin (2006) p. 378.

is to shift the loss from one insurer to the other.[120] By these means, subrogation prevents the unjust enrichment of the assured,[121] although this is not always the case. The insurer is entitled to subrogate only to the extent of his payment.[122] As such, in instances where the insured property has been under-insured, and where the assured has been indemnified to the full extent of his policy, and yet the insurer is able to recover from a third-party more than what the insurer paid, the insurer would only be entitled to recoup what he actually paid and the insured would have the right to the balance of whatever was recovered.[123]

The continued application of the principle of subrogation in insurance contracts has been criticized on the ground that although it is intended to prevent unjust enrichment of the assured, it is unduly skewed in favour of the interests of the insurer. It is often said in support of subrogation that, after taking net subrogation recoveries into account, insurance companies are able to offer their assureds lower premiums.[124] This argument, however, loses sight of the fact that in assessing risks, insurance companies typically do not look to the prospect of possible subrogation claims as one of the factors that determine the rate of premium.[125] As noted by a commentator, if this was the case, then one would expect insurance companies to pursue subrogation recoveries more aggressively. Yet, this is precisely what they do not do.[126] Accordingly, it has been suggested that the real function of the doctrine of subrogation is to require overlapping insurance coverage (e.g., to require both a purchaser and a vendor, a tenant and a landlord, or a mortgagor and a mortgagee to take out two separate insurance policies to cover one and the same risk), and that "[t]his is the real attraction of subrogation for insurers".[127]

Irrespective of the foregoing criticisms, subrogation applies to aviation insurance contracts in the same way as it does in many other branches of indemnity insurance. Subrogation used to be the main reason why airframe, engine and component part manufacturers took out products liability insurance; insurers who paid claims arising from aviation accidents would usually seek to recoup their losses by proceeding against the manufacturer of the aircraft if it was established that the accident was caused by negligent or mal-manufacture of the aircraft.[128] In contemporary times, however, the trend has been to join the manufacturers directly in the primary action as co-defendants. Another ramification of the doctrine of

---

[120] Ivamy (1986) p. 467; see also Hasson (1985).

[121] Idem.

[122] Salah El Din (1971) p. 34.

[123] Idem.

[124] Horn (1964) p. 25.

[125] See Sect. 2.4.4 below (on Rating of Aviation Risks).

[126] Hasson (1985) p. 422. For instance, automobile insurers in England and Canada usually enter into what is known as "knock-for-knock" agreements, under which they agree that when two vehicles, respectively, covered by each of them are involved in a collision, there will be no subrogation as between them, and the damage sustained by each vehicle will be borne by its own insurer. See Ivamy (1986) p. 467.

[127] Hasson, idem., p. 425.

[128] Salah El Din (1971) p. 35.

subrogation in aviation insurance is that, if an insurer pays for a total loss with respect to an aircraft which is destroyed or declared a constructive total loss, it becomes automatically entitled to the salvage, if any.

2.3.5 Contribution

Occasionally, situations do arise in which an assured may have taken out more than one insurance policy from different insurers but with respect to the same subject-matter and the same insurable interest. In contemporary insurance parlance, when this happens, the assured is said to have taken out double insurance.[129] Although this is perfectly legitimate in most jurisdictions, the fact that there is double insurance does not necessarily mean that when the assured suffers an insured loss, he can recover separately under each policy. As noted above, the operation of the principle of indemnity will limit his recovery in the aggregate to his actual loss, or in the case of a valued policy, to his agreed loss.[130] The assured may recover from any one of the insurers and the insurer who has paid the claim may have the right to recoup a proportionate part of the amount paid from each of the other insurers.[131]

The right of contribution therefore derives from an equitable principle which does not rest on contract or statute. It "allows one insurer to recover from another by reason of having made a payment to the assured in respect of a sum for which the latter was also liable".[132] However, contribution must be distinguished from subrogation. Subrogation ultimately ensures that the assured receives no more than a full indemnity following a loss; contribution ensures that the insurers do not suffer injustice among themselves. Although, sometimes, both subrogation and contribution are applicable in the same case it should be noted that contribution will only apply when the following three conditions are met:

(a) There is double insurance i.e., the two policies cover the same assured, the same interest and the same period and are more or less of the same scope;
(b) Both policies respond to the loss; and,
(c) The paying insurer has paid under legal liability and not as a volunteer.[133]

---

[129] Merkin (2006) p. 407.

[130] Idem, p. 408.

[131] Idem, p. 414.

[132] Idem.

[133] Idem. See also Salah El Din (1971) where the author also identifies three similar pre-conditions for the application of the principle of contribution as:

(a) Where the same peril which caused the loss is covered by the policies concerned;
(b) Where the policies protect the same interest of the same insured and relate to the same subject matter; and,
(c) The policies must be in full force at the time of occurrence of such loss.

Presently, the predominantly marine insurance-derived principles discussed above also apply to a very large extent to aviation insurance, a relatively new class of non-life insurance. However, as previously mentioned, the evolutionary process through which aviation insurance has emerged made it possible for these principles to be adapted to suit the specific needs of the sector. The next section of this chapter assesses the manner in which the global aviation insurance industry typically handles large risks in reliance upon these and other basic principles.

2.4 The Underwriting Practices of the Global Aviation Insurance Market

Although a formal definition of aviation insurance is elusive,[134] the phrase generally refers to the insurance of risks associated with the manufacture, ownership, leasing, operation and maintenance of aircraft, as well as the operation of aviation facilities on the surface of the earth and in outer space in the not too distant future.[135] It is an important means by which operators in the aviation industry are able to transfer the financial burden of the risks attendant to their operations to other entities on the commercial insurance market (known as insurers), which are otherwise not primarily concerned with the conduct of air transport operations. As such, aviation insurance has been described as "an essential means of protecting the aviation industry against accidental loss or damage. It has also become an important means of enabling aircraft financiers and lessors to protect their property interests in financed and leased aircraft".[136]

The importance of insurance to the sustenance of the global air transport industry cannot be overemphasized. Without it, most operators in the industry will not dare engage in their daily operations, nor will lessors, lenders and government regulators allow aircraft to fly.[137] Yet, because insurers are willing to assume most of these enormous risks, and to provide the requisite financial guarantees for billions of dollars at risk in return only for the payment of relatively small premiums, air transport operations once again become financially feasible. On average, a typical airline's insurance costs are estimated to be less than 2 % of its overall annual

[134] Margo (2000) p. 10. See also Fortin and Haeck (2002).

[135] See ICAO (2004).

[136] McClean et al. (2007) p. VIII–181.

[137] Chrystal et al. (2004) p. 17, where it is reported for instance that in 2004, a low-budget airline had to ground a number of its jets owing to an administrative omission: the necessary insurance certificates were not on board the respective aircraft at the time of their scheduled departure.

budget,[138] a number sometimes larger than an airline's annual net profit margin. Aviation insurance is considered to be so indispensable to the air transport industry that it has been fittingly described as the lifeblood of the industry.[139] Several factors account for this. The potentially debilitating financial consequences aside, operating aircraft, airports, air navigation services, security screening, and ground handling services without any or adequate insurance cover is prohibited by domestic law in most countries[140] and also by certain international treaties.[141] Further, aircraft leasing corporations and financial institutions typically require lessees/airlines to maintain prescribed minimum insurance coverage over aircraft leased or financed by them, and failure to do so is usually deemed to be a breach of lease conditions.[142]

The scope of aviation insurance is broad. It embraces a wide spectrum of risks envisaged in air transportation, extending from the activities of aviation product manufacturers through those of aircraft operators to those of service providers in the aviation industry. Aviation risks are varied, and there are numerous criteria for classifying them.[143] Generally, however, aviation risks fall into the following classes:

- Airlines (hull and liability);
- Airlines (war risks);
- Service providers (airports, air navigation service providers, ground handling service providers, refuellers, security screeners, etc.);
- Products liability (manufacturers of aviation products, i.e., airframes, engines, component parts and spares);
- General aviation (charters, industrial aid, minor manufacturers, private business and pleasure);
- Workers compensation for aviation risks; and,
- Space insurance (satellites and launch services).[144]

[138] Idem. Philip Chrystal notes further that although insurance is an absolute prerequisite to an airline's operations, its actual total costs are relatively small and it is so incidental a cost factor that it is not specifically mentioned in most airlines' financial reports.

[139] Margo (2000) p. 1.

[140] See e.g., in the United States, 14 C.F.R. § 205 (2003); in Canada S.O.R./88-58 (1988); and, in Australia, (Cth.) Act No. 2 of 1959 (1959).

[141] For a comprehensive discussion of compulsory insurance requirements in international air transportation, See Margo (2000) pp. 15–27. See also, for example, article 50 of 2242 UNTS 350 ICAO Doc. 9740 (1999); and, article 4 of EC Regulation 785/2004 OJ L 1 (2004) both of which prescribe minimum insurance requirements for airlines operating in, into or over the territorial airspace of their respective member States.

[142] Margo (1996) p. 427.

[143] Leloudas and Haeck (2003) pp. 150–152.

[144] Ashenbrenner and Mrotek (2005).

Individual aviation insurance policies are thus tailored to provide coverage against the foregoing risks in accordance with the needs of the particular insured operator. "It is normal to insure aviation risks in comprehensive terms under a form of 'all risks' cover, which is cut down by exclusions. ... [Some] of the perils so excluded ... [may then] be covered by separate extension clauses or agreements".[145] For instance, an airline's *all risks insurance policy* will typically provide coverage against:

- Legal liability arising from: accidental death, bodily injury, wounding or delay to passengers; loss of, damage or delay to their baggage and/or cargo;
- Physical damage to and/or total loss of the aircraft (hull); and,
- Legal liability for death, bodily injury or damage to the property of third-parties on the surface of the earth.

Today, there are also in existence custom tailored insurance policies which provide coverage to airlines and other aviation operators against risks (whether stand-alone or in combination) such as:

- Hull total loss only;
- Aircraft spares;
- Passenger legal liability;
- Passenger baggage legal liability;
- Third-party and cargo legal liability;
- Passenger and crew personal accident liability;
- Motor vehicles airside; and,
- Employers and advertisers legal liability among others.[146]

In sum, "[t]he contents of aviation insurance policies vary according to the risks being covered, and in several instances, according to the insurer providing cover. Conventional policies contain an insuring clause which describes the risk(s) being insured against, exclusions, conditions, warranties, definitions of significant terms, and a policy schedule".[147]

2.4.1 The Structure of the Global Aviation Risk Pool and the Law of Large Numbers

Throughout the development of aviation insurance as a distinct branch of insurance, "the need to spread the high risks involved in the conduct of aviation as widely as possible resulted in the combination or pooling of aviation insurance interests,

[145] Leigh-Jones et al. (2003) p. 13.
[146] Chrystal et al. (2004) p. 17.
[147] Margo (2000) p. 183.

something which has remained a feature of this form of insurance to date".[148] In 2004, the global pool of insured western built aircraft in commercial service worldwide was estimated at 21,400, spread over some 400 commercial airlines, and representing an annual growth rate (in terms of values and units) of close to 5 % over the preceding decade.[149] In addition to this, there is at least one airport (international and/or domestic), and one air navigation services provider in each of the 191 countries which are presently members of the International Civil Aviation Organization, and there are also countless numbers of other service providers in the global aviation industry. Also, there are two major manufacturers of western built airframes which manufacture today's wide-bodied aircraft; two that manufacture smaller commercial jets, several aircraft engine manufacturers, and numerous component part manufacturers around the world. Since all these entities require insurance against possible loss or damage to their fleet and/or liability flowing from their operations or products, they constitute the global pool of aviation risks.

One should note that the global aviation risk pool as described above is relatively small when compared to risk pools in other lines of insurance. For instance, in the airline sector, although the accumulated hull insured value of the global fleet of western built aircraft in service was estimated to exceed USD 570 billion in 2004, "in terms of units, the number of aircraft insured worldwide roughly equals the number of vehicles registered in a medium sized European or North American city".[150] Further, it was estimated in 2002 that the total number of aviation insurance policyholders who insured against hull and/or liability risks was approximately 345,000, 200 of which were key airlines, with another 260 being major ancillary aviation related clients. Together, these 460 insureds accounted for roughly 50 % of the total direct aviation insurance premium collected that year.[151] These statistics point to one inevitable feature of the aviation insurance market: the global risk pool is small and heavily concentrated. "With additional cross-border mergers, [alliances and similar arrangements] anticipated between airlines in the future, [it is expected that] the concentration of insureds and their average exposure level will increase commensurately".[152] As a result of the relatively small number of insureds, the Law of Large Numbers, a statistical application employed by insurers to rate risks, is of very limited application in the field of aviation insurance.[153]

---

[148] McClean et al. (2007) p. VII–181.

[149] Chrystal et al. (2004) p. 8. In 2004, the accumulated hull insured value of the 21,400 western built aircraft in service was estimated as exceeding USD 570 billion. In addition, there were numerous Eastern built aircraft in commercial service in places like Eastern Europe, South America, Asia and Africa although it would appear that the insurance market has little or no appetite for insuring such aircraft.

[150] See idem. Further, on an individual basis, aircraft hull values range from USD 1 million per unit to USD 300 million for aircraft newly built and commissioned, and this reinforces the point that a smaller number of aircraft constitutes large single exposures.

[151] Idem.

[152] Idem.

[153] See Chrystal and LeBlanc (2002) p. 9. See Sect. 2.4.4 below for a discussion of the application of the Law of Large Numbers.

Subject to this limitation, however, the aviation insurance market essentially provides a mechanism which permits the collective pooling of the risks to which each of the individual operators are exposed, and their dissemination as widely as possible in order to make them more manageable for the individual entities. This mechanism comprises a global network of direct insurers, reinsurers and retrocessionaires whose operations naturally transcend national boundaries just as air transportation itself is inherently international in nature. The industry also includes intermediaries such as brokers and agents, who do not primarily underwrite aviation risks in the sense of placing their own capital at risk, but nevertheless play a very important overarching role in facilitating the execution of insurance contracts. In order to fully appreciate how this global mechanism works, the following sections describe the role played by each of the component parts thereof as well as the means by which aviation risks are initially placed and eventually spread throughout the market notwithstanding the limited applicability of the Law of Large Numbers.

2.4.2 *Direct Insurance: Placing the Risk*

Initially, aviation risks are placed on the aviation insurance market by way of direct insurance or direct business. Although referred to as direct business, the usual practice in most of the prominent markets around the world is that the placement of large aviation risks is arranged through intermediaries,[154] and not directly between the insured and the insurer(s). Thus, operating entities in the air transport industry desiring to have the risks attendant to their operations insured would typically approach brokers or agents, and instruct them to arrange for the desired coverage with insurers. In some countries, domestic laws require that direct insurance of national fleets (i.e. fleet operated by airlines of that country) must be placed and/or written locally, either by a national insurance company or by a local aviation pool.[155] Where such restrictions exist, direct insurance must be obtained locally.[156] Where there are no such limitations, on the other hand, brokers are free to place the risks with insurers wherever in the world they may be located.

"The manner in which the [London] market underwrites . . . risks and provides a service to its insured is, in general, accepted and followed throughout the world".[157]

---

[154] Most aviation insurance business is placed following the Lloyd's practice, whereby the prospective insured instructs a broker to act on his behalf in placing the insurance on the market. See McClean et al. (2007) pp. VII–212–220. However, there are instances in which the prospective insured deals directly with the prospective insurer without the involvement of a broker or an agent. In such instances, the insurer is known as a direct writer. See Margo (2000) pp. 135–136, fn. 195.

[155] McClean et al. (2007) p. VIII–188; Salah El Din (1971) p. 214.

[156] In most cases, these restrictions apply only to direct business and do not extend to reinsurance and retrocession. Accordingly, risks insured locally may be reinsured abroad. See McClean et al. (2007) p. VIII–188.

[157] Idem., p. VIII–191.

The practice in the London aviation market is that large aviation risks are usually placed by brokers. Brokers are independent intermediaries between insurers and insureds who hold themselves out for employment by the general public. Usually, they are specialized firms with a great deal of expertise and influence in the aviation insurance market.[158] "In addition to their specialised [*sic*] knowledge of prevailing market conditions, their ability to communicate simultaneously with insurers worldwide, and their expertise in advising clients on their specific insurance needs, brokers are also able to exercise certain leverage in negotiating premium levels and payment of claims".[159] Although brokers are independent intermediaries, they frequently represent the interests of the assured. Thus, in terms of the law, brokers generally act as agents of the insured, although occasionally, they may also act as agents of the insurer.[160]

When a prospective insured approaches a broker, an agent or an insurer for the placement of insurance, certain details of the risk must be provided.[161] The information provided may be recorded using one or more of several forms, depending on the market or the particular insurer concerned, and the type of coverage sought. The most commonly used forms are proposal forms,[162] slips,[163] and application

---

[158] Salah El Din (1971) p. 214.

[159] Margo (2000) p. 111.

[160] Idem., p. 81. It is a clearly established principle that in the placement of insurance, the broker acts exclusively as the agent of the insured. Notwithstanding the foregoing, the broker may also act as an agent of the insurer if the insurer holds the broker out as such, or if there is an express agreement creating a contract of agency. See generally: idem., Chap. 5. Typically, the broker will be deemed to be acting as agent of the insurer(s) when delivering the policy to the insured and also when collecting premiums from the insured. See McClean et al. (2007) pp. VII–212–220.

[161] These details relate to: (a) the description of the proposed assured; (b) the description of the risk proposed to be insured; (c) the description of circumstances affecting the risk; and, (d) the previous history of the proposed assured. See Ivamy (1986) p. 95. The principle of utmost good faith requires that all material information and circumstances affecting the risk must be disclosed.

[162] Proposal forms are most commonly used in the London market when prospective insureds approach insurance companies directly without engaging the services of a broker. "When completed and signed by the prospective insured, and lodged with the insurer, the proposal form constitutes an offer to the insurer to effect a contract of insurance. The proposal form indicates the basis upon which the proposer is prepared to contract and it is up to the insurer to decide whether to provide cover, and if so, at what premium". See Margo (2000) p. 123.

[163] Slips are heavily used by brokers in the placement of risks on the London market, particularly at Lloyds. It is a document prepared by the broker which sets out the cover sought by the prospective insured in abbreviated terms known to the broker and the insurers who specialize in aviation insurance. Frequently, it contains references to clauses published by the Aviation Insurance Clauses Group (AICG). See McClean et al. (2007) p. VII–221. The slip must contain sufficient information about the risk proposed therein to enable the insurer to whom it is offered to decide whether to offer cover, and if so, at what rate of premium. When a slip is used in negotiating for insurance, the contract is concluded as soon as the slip has been initialed or signed by the insurer. A slip may also be used for the purpose of obtaining a quotation for a risk. See Margo (2000) pp. 116–123. See also, Ivamy (1986) p. 92.

forms.[164] Irrespective of the form(s) used, when the information recorded is subsequently presented to, or lodged with, an insurer by or on behalf of a prospective insured for the purpose of effecting a contract of insurance, it amounts to an offer to enter into a contract of insurance.[165] In line with ordinary contract principles, the offer must be unconditionally accepted by the insurer before a contract of insurance will be deemed to have been concluded. Prior to his acceptance, if the insurer makes any modifications to the prospective insured's offer, this will amount to a counter-offer by the insurer, and it must in turn be accepted by the prospective insured for a contract of insurance to be deemed to have been concluded.[166] "Before the acceptance, neither party is bound, and either may withdraw at pleasure. After the acceptance, there is a contract from which neither party can withdraw, binding the assured to pay the premium and the insurers to accept the premium when tendered, to issue a policy, and to pay any sum that may become payable under the terms of the contract".[167]

The common procedure followed in the London market when a broker is involved in placing a large aviation risk is that a slip is prepared by the broker and submitted first to a leading underwriter with whom the broker negotiates the terms and premium rates for the coverage desired. If the terms and rates are acceptable to the leading insurer, he signs or initials the slip indicating alongside his signature or initials the percentage or proportion of the risk he intends to bear.[168] Once the leading insurer has initialed the slip with his line, the broker then offers the risk to the rest of the market by submitting the slip to selected insurers, and each insurer who is ready to follow the leading insurer's terms and rates signs the slip with his line.[169] The insurance cover is completed when the slip has been signed by insurers accepting 100 % of the risk. In cases where the slip is oversubscribed,[170]

---

[164] Applications, also sometimes called proposals, propositions or requests for insurance are commonly used in placing risks on the American insurance market, whether or not brokers are used in the process. As with proposals forms, the insurer must accept the application before any binding contract of insurance comes into effect. If prior to acceptance, the insurer modifies the terms of an application lodged with it, the changes amount to a counter offer which must in turn be accepted by the applicant before a binding contract of insurance is created. See Margo (2000) pp. 136–137.

[165] Ivamy (1986) p. 101.

[166] Margo (2000) p. 123, where the author notes: "While the proposal form is an offer to be insured under a policy in the ordinary form, and at the normal rate, it is open to the insurer to make a counter-offer to the proposer to effect the insurance at a different rate, or to subject the insurance to certain additional terms and conditions. In such a case, the proposer will be the one to decide whether to accept the counter-offer made by the insurer".

[167] Ivamy (1986) p. 92.

[168] This proportion is referred to as the insurer's line. See Margo (2000) pp. 112–113; See also Salah El Din (1971) p. 216.

[169] Margo (2000) idem. The insurers other than the leading insurer are known as the "following underwriters" or the "following market". All of the insurers on a slip are known collectively as "the security".

[170] A slip is oversubscribed when the total subscription exceeds 100 % of the security required to fully insure the risk.

the broker signs down the subscriptions by proportionately reducing the percentages signed by each insurer. "The initialing or signing of the slip by the insurer is the acceptance of the insured's proposal, and the insurer is bound by his line subject only to the contingency that it may fall to be written down on 'closing' to some extent if the slip turns out to have been oversubscribed".[171]

Another means by which risks are placed on the market is known as vertical placement. In such a placement, the broker will typically approach several insurers separately to obtain their quotes without determining in advance which one of them will be the leader. The broker will thus prepare several slips, one for each underwriter quoting for his own share, or group of underwriters on the same slip. "The essence of a vertical placement is that each insurer or set of insurers will apply a different premium rate in respect of the risk being insured".[172] This way, the broker is able to fill the slip with eager and/or new capacity at low premium rates and then approach the first one or two lead insurers and bargain for low lead terms on the basis of the already committed security. This is also known as the bottom-up approach to placing risks.[173]

In other markets,[174] brokers and insurance company agents typically use application forms instead of slips in placing aviation risks. A prospective insured will therefore be requested to complete an application for insurance and to provide therein full details of the risks for which coverage is sought. Once the application has been completed, the broker will approach those insurance companies or pools with good reputation and expertise in insuring the kinds of risks involved. Depending on the nature of the risks, the availability of capacity for the limits of coverage sought, and the specific needs of the applicant, the broker may place the insurance with one or more insurance companies or pools, either locally or in foreign markets. In any event, each of the insurers approached by the broker must accept the application before a binding contract of insurance will come into effect.

The foregoing procedures frequently result in situations where a single aviation risk is subscribed to by various insurers. In most jurisdictions, such arrangements are classified as co-insurance rather than joint insurance—each co-insurer who signs the slip with his line or otherwise participates in the risk enters into a separate contract of insurance with the insured.[175] "Thus, according to the practice in London, a policy consists of a bundle of contracts made between the insured and each individual underwriter according to the terms of the slip".[176] Consequently,

> as a general rule, the liability of each of the co-insurers is several and not joint. Thus in the event of a claim, the insured may only recover from each of the various insurers to the extent of the proportion which such insurer has underwritten. If one insurer is unable to

---

[171] Ivamy (1986) p. 117.

[172] Margo (2000) p. 114.

[173] Idem.

[174] Especially in the United States aviation market.

[175] Margo (2000) p. 112.

[176] Idem., p. 126.

meet his obligations to the insured, then, in the absence of language to the contrary, there is no authority for requiring any of the participating insurers to make up the shortfall.[177]

The operation of the principle of indemnity also ensures that the insured does not recover in excess of his losses in a typical co-insurance setting. Each insurer is obliged to pay only its proportion of the insured's actual losses.

Once a slip has been subscribed to the full extent of the risk, it is retained by the broker, who in due course prepares an insurance policy from the details contained therein for the approval of the insurer(s).[178] If the insurer(s) approve the wording of the policy, it is finalized, signed and issued. The policy contains the whole contract between the parties and replaces the slip, proposal or application form from which it was drawn.[179] "The contents of aviation policies vary according to the risks being covered, and, in several instances, according to the insurer providing cover. Conventional policies contain an insuring clause which describes the risk(s) being insured against, the exclusions, conditions, warranties, definitions of significant terms, and a policy schedule".[180] Various standardized policies have been adopted and published by the aviation insurance industry, particularly in the London market.[181] However, they are not commonly used in relation to the insurance of large aviation risks such as airlines and aircraft manufacturer's products liability. On the other hand, standardized clauses and endorsements, such as the *War and Allied Perils Exclusion Clause* (AVN 48) are common to find in all manner of aviation insurance policies.[182]

A time lapse is almost always interposed between the completion of the negotiations and the issuance of the policy. If the prospective insured requires some form of temporary coverage to protect his interests during the intervening time lapse, a cover note may be delivered to him by the broker.[183] A cover note sets out the essential details of the cover and usually incorporates the conditions of the insurer's policy. It may be issued by the insurer in which case it amounts to a

[177] Idem., p. 129.

[178] Idem.

[179] If either party considers that a mistake has been made, and that the policy does not truly reflect the contract that was made by the signing of the slip, then the remedy is to obtain rectification of the policy so that it truly reflects the terms of the agreement between the parties. See idem., p. 130.

[180] Idem., p. 183.

[181] An example is the standard London Aircraft Insurance Policy (AVN 1C), which offers comprehensive cover in respect of hull risks, passenger and third party legal liability. It is most commonly used in insuring risks associated with general aviation. See idem., p. 182.

[182] Brokers usually insert abbreviated references to standardized clauses and endorsements in slips used in placing insurance. Since the policy is eventually prepared from the details contained in the slip which have been agreed to by the underwriters, the policy will inevitably contain the clauses and endorsements referred to in the slip. The widespread practice of preparing insurance policies by skewering together various clauses gathered from various sources has been referred to by Margo as the "kebab" principle of policy drafting and has been criticized by Lord Justice Schiemann in [1997] 2 Lloyd's L.R. 687 (CA) [KAC v. KIC (CA)] at 701.

[183] Margo (2000) p. 129.

contract of insurance in itself, governing the rights and liabilities of the parties in the event of a loss materializing during its currency.[184] Pending the preparation of the policy, a broker may also issue a broker's cover note certifying that the insurance has been effected and setting out its terms. "By issuing the cover note, the broker does not incur liability on the insurance since he does not purport to be an insurer. But he is to be presumed to warrant to the prospective insured that his instructions have been properly carried out, and that the insurance has been effected. If, therefore, there is no insurance in fact, he will be liable for breach of the warranty. Such a cover note is not binding on the insurers".[185]

If a loss materializes during the pendency of the insurance, the insured must notify the insurer by filing a claim. If the loss is covered within the terms of the insurance and is otherwise not excluded from coverage by any applicable exclusions, then the insurer will be obliged to indemnify the insured by placing him in the same position as he occupied before the occurrence of the loss. In accordance with the terms of the insurance, the indemnification may be achieved by way of monetary payouts, by asset replacement or any combination thereof.

2.4.3 Reinsurance, Retrocession and Excess Insurance: Spreading the Risk Further

Once direct insurers have issued aviation insurance policies to insureds thereby assuming aviation risks as part of their portfolios, they must technically allocate the necessary capital reserves needed to back those risks. At the same time, direct insurers must also invest their capital so as to earn a return for their investors, pay claims and make some profit for themselves. An important means by which direct insurers obtain relief from the need to maintain capital reserves to back the risks they have assumed is reinsurance. "In its simplest form, reinsurance is insurance passed between insurance companies".[186] It is a mechanism which enables direct insurers to pass on to reinsurers a portion of the risks they have accepted in their capacity as direct insurers, thereby reducing the full extent of their exposure to risk.[187] A contract of reinsurance is therefore a contract of insurance for the benefit of an insurer. For instance, a direct insurer may accept a whole risk of say $100 million, and then reinsure a proportion of it (e.g., 25 %) with a reinsurer in order to reduce his/its net exposure in the event of loss. If a total loss should occur, the direct insurer will still be obliged to indemnify the assured $100 million. However, as the reinsured under a reinsurance contract, the direct insurer may in turn recoup up to

[184] Ivamy (1986) p. 107.
[185] Idem., p. 108.
[186] Phifer (1996) p. 2.
[187] Salah El Din (1971) p. 331.

$25 million of its losses from the reinsurer, thereby reducing its net loss to $75 million.[188]

In the reinsurance setting, the direct insurer who cedes part of the risk he has originally assumed to another insurer is known as the cedent or the reinsured, and that other insurer accepting the portion of the risk ceded by virtue of the contract of reinsurance is known as the reinsurer.[189] Depending on the terms of the agreement, any proportion of a risk may be reinsured, the remainder (if any) being retained by the reinsured.[190] The principles which apply to direct insurance are the same as those which apply to reinsurance.[191] The subject matter of reinsurance is also the same as that insured under the direct insurance. As such, the reinsurance contract is not an insurance of the direct insurer's potential liability to the insured, but an independent contract between reinsured and reinsurer in which the subject matter of the insurance is the same as that of the primary insurance.[192]

Reinsurance should be distinguished from excess insurance—a form of direct insurance which covers losses over and above a specified amount.[193] This specified amount is usually the agreed value in an agreed value policy, and it may not necessarily be equal to the actual value of the subject matter of the insurance (i.e., the aircraft or property in question), or the true extent of the liability exposure to which the insured is exposed. Excess insurance is therefore used to provide direct insurance coverage for the difference between the agreed value covered in an insurance policy and the actual value at risk.

The importance of reinsurance cannot be overemphasized. There are certain risks which would not be insurable but for the existence and availability of reinsurance.[194] Reinsurers help the industry to provide coverage and protection for a wide range of risks, including the largest and most complex risks covered by the insurance system.[195] According to aviation insurance expert Rod Margo, "[t]he ability of a direct insurer to reinsure its exposure allows the insurer to assume a larger percentage of any given risk. ... The availability of a strong and effective reinsurance market is critical to the existence of the aviation insurance market".[196] As such, reinsurance is an indispensable part of the insurance system that makes insurance more secure and less expensive.

---

188 Margo (2000) p. 491.

189 Idem.

190 "The portion of the risk retained by the reinsured is known as the retention. A reinsured may reinsure any proportion up to 100 % of the risk (in which case he would have a 'nil net retention')". See idem., p. 493.

191 Salah El Din (1971) p. 331.

192 Margo (2000) p. 492.

193 Idem.

194 Baur and Breutel-O'Donoghue (2004) p. 8.

195 Idem., p. 3.

196 Margo (2000) p. 491.

Traditionally, "[t]here are two basic ways of classifying reinsurance – proportional and non-proportional".[197] As the name implies, proportional reinsurance indicates that the portion of the risk (and accompanying premiums) ceded to the reinsurer, as well as the share of claims to be paid by the reinsurer, have been established according to a contractually pre-defined ratio (i.e., a specified percentage or proportion of each claim),[198] and "the reinsurer's share of the premiums is therefore directly proportionate to its obligation to pay any claims".[199] In non-proportional reinsurance, there is no proportionality between the portion of the risk ceded, the reinsurance premium and the portion of claims to be paid by the reinsurer.[200]

There are also two basic methods of effecting reinsurance—facultatively or through a reinsurance treaty.[201] Facultative reinsurance is a single reinsurance of a single directly insured risk, whereas treaty reinsurance comprises the reinsurance of a bundled up series or specified number of risks under and by virtue of a reinsurance treaty.[202] Facultative reinsurance implies that the direct insurer (cedent) is under no obligation to cede, and the reinsurer is under no obligation to accept the cession. The terms of the reinsurance agreement are negotiated and agreed upon between the parties on a case by case basis.[203] Facultative reinsurance encompasses mainly large scale risks that do not fit into the treaty portfolio and need to be individually evaluated and reinsured. As such, the bulk of aviation insurance business is reinsured facultatively.[204] Treaty reinsurance, on the other hand, is based on a pre-existing obligatory arrangement, binding both the direct insurer (as reinsured) and the reinsurer, respectively, to cede and to accept certain specified risks or portions thereof up to certain limits.[205]

Reinsurers may wish to transfer some of the risks they have absorbed from direct insurers outside their company. For this, reinsurers can either use traditional retrocession agreements or capital market techniques such as securitization.[206] Retrocession is the transfer of ceded risks and premiums to other reinsurers or

[197] Idem., p. 493.

[198] Patrik (2004) p. 1. The reinsured must cede a fixed portion of the risk and the applicable premiums to the reinsurer who is then obliged to pay the same portion of all claims.

[199] Baur and Breutel-O'Donoghue (2004) p. 16.

[200] In non-proportional reinsurance, the portion of the risk ceded and the share of claims to be paid by the reinsurer is typically defined on an excess-of-loss basis—the part of each claim or aggregation of claims above a specified dollar amount. See Patrik (2004) p. 1. If the claims do not exceed the specified amount, the reinsured retains them. If they do exceed the specified amount, the reinsurer is obliged to pay the excess up to the upper limit of the reinsurance policy.

[201] Margo (2000) p. 493.

[202] Idem., pp. 493–494. A reinsurance treaty is a pre-existing agreement pursuant to which all of the reinsured's risks of a particular class are automatically ceded to and reinsured by the reinsurer.

[203] Salah El Din (1971) p. 332.

[204] Idem.

[205] Idem.

[206] Baur and Breutel-O'Donoghue (2004) p. 13.

insurers. A retrocession agreement is therefore different from a reinsurance contract; it is a contract under which a reinsurer, in turn, insures his own exposure with another underwriter.[207] "The reinsurer who cedes his business, or a portion or part thereof, is known as the 'retrocedant', while the reinsurer who accepts the business ceded to him is known as a 'retrocessionaire'".[208] Retrocession therefore provides a means for reinsurers to spread risks even more broadly.

An alternative to retrocession is securitization—a means by which peak risks are transferred to the capital markets in the form of securities.[209] Through securitization, reinsurers are able to repackage insurance risks and sell them on the capital markets in the form of insurance-linked securities (ILS) either as catastrophe (cat) or non-catastrophe (non-cat) bonds.[210] In the broader market, securitization has traditionally been used for natural catastrophe exposures such as hurricanes, windstorms and earthquakes, or extreme mortality risks such as lethal epidemics; but not for catastrophic aviation risks such as war risks and terrorism. As such, one of the key objectives of this book will be to assess the extent to which securitization may be used in the aviation insurance market to enhance the provision of sustainable cover for such risks.

2.4.4 The Concept of Insurability and the Rating of Aviation Risks

In determining whether to accept a risk or the level of premium to charge, insurers consider several factors,[211] the most fundamental of which are the insurability[212] of the risk in question and the physical and moral hazards associated with it. "While it is theoretically possible to insure all possibilities of loss, some risks are not insurable at [all or at] a reasonable price. For practical reasons, insurers are not willing to accept all the risks that ... [the market] may wish to transfer to them. To be considered a proper subject for insurance, there are certain characteristics that should be present"[213] in any risk. The risk must be measurable in the sense that its likelihood is known or can be estimated with a reasonable degree of certainty; it

---

[207] Margo (2000) p. 492.

[208] Idem., p. 492, fn. 8.

[209] Baur and Breutel-O'Donoghue (2004) p. 13.

[210] "In a typical ILS transaction, a Special Purpose Vehicle (SPV) enters into a reinsurance contract with a cedent and simultaneously issues cat bonds to investors. The reinsurance is usually an excess of loss contract. If no loss event occurs, investors receive a return of principal and a stream of coupon payments that compensate them for the use of their funds and their risk exposure. If, however, a pre-defined catastrophic event does occur, investors suffer a loss of interest, principal, or both. These funds are transferred to the protection buyer or cedent, in fulfillment of the reinsurance contract". See Helfenstein and Holzheu (2006) p. 4.

[211] McClean et al. (2007) p. VIII–211.

[212] For a general overview on the insurability of risks, See Faure and Hartlief (2003) pp. 81–120.

[213] Vaughan (1982) p. 28.

should not be overly correlated with any other risks in the insurer's portfolio; the total loss potential associated with any single event must be manageable for the insurer; and, the risk profile must have events of sufficiently high frequency and low severity.[214] The insurability of war and terrorism risks in aviation, for instance, is limited since the risk profile usually comprises events of low probability (frequency) and high loss (severity).[215] In addition to the foregoing actuarial characteristics, which are by no means exhaustive,[216] there are other market-driven or societal criteria that the risk must also meet in order to be insurable.

Although it is difficult to create a precise formula or checklist to differentiate between what is and what is not insurable, Table 2.1[217] below summarizes the criteria of insurability as is generally accepted in the insurance industry.

As important determinants of insurability, the physical and moral hazards associated with the risk in question must be assessed. It is not entirely possible to exclude either type of hazard—consequently, a combination of both must be considered when assessing the underlying risk. Physical hazards consist of those physical properties that increase the chances of loss from the risk or peril.[218] They relate to the subject-matter of the insurance in question and, generally, can be ascertained by a physical study of the risk involved. "In general, physical hazards can be assessed and therefore can be rated; therefore, except when dealing with a risk which is literally uninsurable, a fair premium can be arrived at".[219] Moral hazard, on the other hand, refers to the increase in the probability of loss which results from evil or dishonest tendencies in the character of the insured.[220] In the words of Lord Justice Slesser,

> It is elementary that one of the matters to be considered by an insurance company entering into contractual relations with a proposed assured is the question of the moral integrity of the proposer – what has been called the moral hazard.[221]

---

[214] Source: Laster and Schmidt (2005) p. 5.

[215] Jaffee and Russell (2003) p. 35. The authors refer to such low probability/high loss events as extreme events.

[216] Vaughan also lists the following prerequisites as representing the four ideal elements of an insurable risk:

- There must be a sufficiently large number of homogeneous exposure units to make the losses reasonably predictable;
- The loss produced by the risk must be definite and measurable;
- The loss must be fortuitous or accidental; it must be the result of a contingency; and,
- The loss must not be catastrophic.

See Vaughan (1982) p. 29.

[217] Laster and Schmidt (2005) p. 5.

[218] Vaughan (1982) p. 6.

[219] Salah El Din (1971) p. 60.

[220] Vaughan (1982) p. 6.

[221] [1936] 1 K.B. 408 at 414.

Table 2.1 Criteria of insurability of risks

	Category	Criterion	Characteristic
1	Actuarial	Risk/uncertainty	Measurable
2		Loss occurrences	Independent
3		Maximum loss	Manageable
4		Average loss	Moderate
5		Loss frequency	High
6		Moral Hazard, adverse selection	Not excessive
7	Market-determined	Insurance premium	Adequate, affordable
8		Insurance cover limits	Acceptable
9		Industry capacity	Sufficient
10	Societal	Public policy	Consistent with cover
11		Legal system	Permits the cover

In the sense of fraud or misrepresentation, moral hazard cannot be assessed and dealt with by a premium scale. As such they cannot be insured, "for when dealing with such moral hazards, no premium loading would alter the risk and no additional premium would be adequate for covering such a risk".[222] This provides continued justification for strict adherence to the principle of utmost good faith in insurance contracts.[223] However, moral hazard in the sense of carelessness or irresponsibility[224] can be effectively dealt with by making the insurance subject to restrictive conditions such as deductibles, conditions, warranties and exclusions. Failure to comply with such restrictive conditions renders the insurance void or voidable.[225]

Once it has been determined that a risk is insurable, it must be rated. The object of rating is to produce a premium rate adequate to cover the risk concerned, based on the theoretical probability of the occurrence of events which may cause loss and having in mind the insurer's expenses, the need to accumulate reserves against the future, and the need to make a profit for investors.[226] "To arrive at an actuarially based evaluation or rating, insurers generally categorise insureds or clients collectively. The criterion for this allocation is that each member of the group is exposed to the same type of risk. The larger the group or sample size, the closer the average loss will approach a statistically valid number".[227] This statistical application is

[222] Salah El Din (1971) p. 61.

[223] Non-disclosure of material information or misrepresentation by the insured amounting to breach of the duty of utmost good faith usually results in the contract of insurance being voidable at the option of the insurer.

[224] Vaughan (1982) p. 6. Morale hazard refers to a careless attitude on the part of the insured toward the occurrence of losses. The purchase of insurance, for instance, may create a morale hazard since the realization that the insurance company will bear the loss may lead the insured to exercise less care than if forced to bear the loss alone.

[225] Salah El Din (1971) pp. 60–61.

[226] Spurway (1991) p. 36.

[227] Chrystal and LeBlanc (2002) p. 9.

known as the "Law of Large Numbers" and it is a very effective rating tool in lines of insurance where the sample size is relatively large.

With respect to other lines of insurance such as aviation, where sample sizes are relatively small, risks are normally rated on the basis of *an estimate* of the population mean, with an allowance being made for a margin of error.[228] The extent of the margin of error depends on the concentration of the individual values at risk that make up the mean and the size of the sample.[229] In aviation insurance, "[t]he inability to obtain a statistically acceptable margin of error because of the small sample size [and the high concentration of large single exposures] means that a more technically accurate rating is difficult to ascertain".[230] As such, insurers have had to rely extensively on their historical experiences in rating aviation risks.

Rating of risks becomes a difficult task in situations where there is a lack of precise information concerning the predictability of occurrence of the risk concerned and/or the magnitude of losses associated therewith if it should occur. This phenomenon has been described by Howard Kunreuther and his collaborators as "insurer ambiguity".[231] They argue that an insurer can respond to this uncertainty by charging a so-called risk premium (or ambiguity premium) to account for this unpredictability.[232] Although, theoretically, an additional risk premium is the answer to insurer ambiguity, in practice, the insurer will at least require some information to make more than an educated guess concerning the risk premium he has to charge.[233]

Moreover, given the fact that insurers often find themselves in competitive environments, market forces may well drive them to engage in certain lines of insurance business involving a high degree of uncertainty even when an appropriate risk premium cannot be charged.[234] Again, the option of charging an additional risk premium will obviously work if there is a reciprocal willingness on the part of the insured to pay. To a very large extent, this willingness to pay depends on the extent to which the insured perceives that there are, albeit uncertain, additional risks for which additional cover needs to be extended. If, as a result of informational deficiencies, the potential insured does not recognize that there are additional risks, they will not be willing to pay for the additional risk premium and insurance cover will not take place.[235]

[228] Vaughan (1982) p. 24.

[229] Idem.

[230] Chrystal and LeBlanc (2002) p. 9.

[231] Kunreuther et al. (1993).

[232] Idem., p. 75. See also Faure and Hartlief (2003) p. 86.

[233] Kunreuther et al. (1993).

[234] Idem.

[235] Idem.

2.4.5 *Conditions, Warranties and Exclusions in Insurance Contracts: Methods for Trimming Underwriters' Exposure to Risks*

The rating of risks and the charging of premiums alone do not fully address the problems posed to insurers by moral hazard, adverse selection and non-insurability. Whereas some risks are considered to be outright uninsurable, there are other risks that are insurable, but only to some extent. The practice of insurers who underwrite such risks is to describe the risk in the insuring section of the policy in general terms and then introduce into the policy a variety of mechanisms aimed at qualifying their undertaking.[236] "Language which limits coverage in aviation insurance policies may take one of several forms – exclusions, conditions or warranties. There are significant differences in legal effect between these three types of limitations".[237] This section provides a brief overview of the means by which insurers normally attempt to reduce or limit their exposure to risk within the insurance policies they have underwritten.

Conditions are those terms of an insurance contract "on the fulfillment of which the validity of the policy or the liability of the insurer depends".[238] They may be express or implied,[239] precedent to the validity of the policy or the liability of the insurer, or subsequent to the formation of the contract of insurance.[240] Depending on the nature of the condition broken, a breach of condition will either avoid the policy (*ab initio* or from the date of the breach onwards), or preclude the insured from recovery thereunder.[241] A warranty is a promise by the insured that appears in

[236] Ivamy (1986) p. 257. These mechanisms include: exclusions (also known as exceptions), conditions and warranties.

[237] Hagglund and Arthur (1973) p. 8.

[238] Ivamy (1986) p. 271.

[239] Idem., pp. 271–272. Implied conditions are those implied by law which govern the validity of every contract of insurance unless it clearly appears to have been the intention of the parties to exclude them or to modify their operation. It is therefore unnecessary for them to be expressed in the policy. Express conditions are those expressly inserted into the contract upon the agreement of the parties thereto. They may extend or restrict the scope of the implied conditions.

[240] Hagglund and Arthur (1973) p. 8 where the authors differentiate between conditions precedent and conditions subsequent as follows:

> Conditions precedent are those which relate to the attachment of the risk; in other words, they call for the performance of some event after the terms of the contract have been agreed upon, but before the contract shall take effect. The insured has the burden of proving [that] he has complied with these conditions. Conditions subsequent are those which pertain to the contract of insurance after its issuance and during its existence; that is, they provide that a policy shall become void or its operation suspended, or the insurer wholly or partially relieved from the liability upon the happening of some event or omission to do some act. The insurer has the burden of proving [that] the condition avoiding coverage has occurred.

[241] Ivamy (1986) pp. 290–292.

the contract and relates to the risks it insures against.[242] It has been held that "any statement of a fact bearing upon the risk introduced into the written policy is, by whatever words and in whatever place, to be construed as a warranty".[243] "A breach of warranty, whether it is material or insignificant will void an insurance contract completely. Significantly, a breach of a warranty prevents recovery by the insured even if the breach is not material to the cause giving rise to the dispute".[244]

Exclusions limit the risks insured in a contract of insurance by excluding or excepting the insurers from liability for certain types of claims or for claims arising from certain types of risk.[245] The exclusions section of an aviation insurance contract allows the insurer to explicitly set forth those risks which are not covered as part of the bargain.[246] Exclusions may be "formulated in such a way as to qualify the whole of the insurance undertaking, or ... [they may] simply exclude from the operation of the insurance undertaking particular classes of cases which, but for the exclusion, would fall within it, leaving some part of the general scope of the undertaking unqualified".[247] The insurer's duty to defend or indemnify the assured may be suspended in the event of loss being caused by any of the excluded events.[248] In other words, "a loss which falls within an exclusion entitles the insurers to deny liability for the loss but not to treat the coverage under the policy as void".[249]

2.4.6 *The Role of Insurance in Aviation Litigation: The Duty of the Insurer to Defend Claims Brought Against the Insured*

As noted above, aviation insurance policies typically cover property losses (e.g., loss or damage to the hull of the aircraft) as well as the liability that the insured may be exposed to as a result of its air transport operations (e.g., liability for death, injury or bodily harm to passengers; destruction, loss of or damage to baggage and cargo; damages arising from delay to passengers and goods; and, liability for damage to third-parties). Generally, liability insurers have a duty to defend their insureds regardless of the merits of the claim or the damage claimed. Most aviation insurance policies covering the liability of the insured therefore provide that the insurer will defray any legal costs and expenses incurred by the insured with its written consent in defending any action for compensatory damages

[242] Libby (1995) p. 621.
[243] (1884) 9 App. Cas. 671 p. 684, per Lord Blackburn.
[244] Libby (1995) p. 621.
[245] Margo (2000) p. 185.
[246] Libby (1995) p. 621.
[247] Margo (2000) p. 185.
[248] Caban (2003)at 429.
[249] Margo (2000) p. 185.

covered by the policy.[250] Such provisions create a contractual obligation on the part of the insurer to defend claims brought against the insured, or alternatively, to pay for any legal costs and expenses incurred by the insured in defending such claims. The defence obligation is therefore contractual, and it is defined by the terms of the policy.[251]

"In most liability policies, the duty to defend is dependent on the duty to indemnify".[252] This means that although the duty to defend is much broader than the duty to indemnify,[253] it will only arise when there is a potential for indemnity under the terms of the policy. The important distinction, however, is that whereas "the duty to defend arises where there is any potential for indemnity under the insurance contract, the duty to indemnify only arises when it is ultimately determined that a covered event has occurred".[254] Thus, theoretically, it is possible for an insurer to be obliged to defend a claim brought against an insured although ultimately, the claim in question may be determined not to be covered under the policy.[255]

In most instances, insurers fulfill the duty to defend by retaining lawyers to represent the insured in the defence of the liability claim.[256] Although, as a practical matter, the nomination of lawyers in this manner is frequently done in collaboration with the insured, the question arises as to whether the duty to defend requires that the insurer must always provide the insured with independent counsel. This question arises because there is an inherent conflict of interests as between the insurer and the insured: "the insurer's primary concern is demonstrating non-coverage;

[250] See for example sections II(3) and III(3) of the London Aircraft Insurance Policy (reproduced in the Appendix to Margo (2000) idem., pp. 559–577), which provide as follows:

> The liability of the Insurers under this Section shall not exceed the amount stated in Part . . . of the Schedule, less any amounts under Part . . . The Insurer will defray in addition any legal costs and expenses incurred with their written consent in defending any action which may be brought against the Insured in respect of any claim for compensatory damages covered by this Section, but should the amount paid or awarded in settlement of such claim exceed the Limit of Indemnity then the liability of the Insurers in respect of such legal costs and expenses shall be limited to such proportion of the said legal costs and expenses as the Limit of Indemnity bears to the amount paid for compensatory damages.

[251] King and Benas (1994–1995) p. 248.

[252] Idem.

[253] See 65 Cal. 2d 263, 419 P.2d 168, 54 Cal. Rptr. 104 (1966).

[254] See King and Benas (1994–1995).

[255] In most jurisdictions in the US, an insurer faced with such a situation may file a declaratory action in court to determine whether the claim concerned falls within the coverage contracted under the policy. In the absence of such a declaratory judgment, the insurer must defend even where it believes that there is no coverage under the policy or risk being held in breach of contract.

[256] According to Rod Margo, the practice with larger insurance firms is to "nominate a particular law firm, or a series of law firms if the insured is active in several jurisdictions, to represent the insured in relation to the liability claims". See Margo (2000) p. 394.

[whereas] the insured's interest lies in avoiding liability, or at least limiting it to a covered item".[257]

It would appear that where such a conflict of interest exists, the duty to defend simply becomes an obligation on the part of the insurer to pay for the reasonable value of the services of defence counsel retained by the insured. In *Executive Aviation Inc. v. National Insurance Underwriters*,[258] the court stated *obiter* that, in such a conflict of interest situation, the insured should select defence counsel and the insurer should pay for the reasonable value of that counsel's services. In *San Diego Navy Federal Credit Union v. Cumis Insurance Society*,[259] the court addressed the conflict of interest created in such a situation in detail and outlined the duty of the insurer to pay for counsel independently selected by the insured.[260] In any event, the duty to defend exemplifies a significant aspect of the role played by lawyers in the aviation insurance industry.[261]

---

[257] Randall (1996–1997) p. 223. Rod Margo's view of the conflict of interest is as follows:

> In the United States, it is clearly established that counsel appointed to defend the interests of the insured have an attorney-client relationship with the insured. Communications between the parties are therefore protected by the attorney-client privilege. Thus an insurer who wants to pay the fees of a lawyer appointed to represent its insured must ensure that there is no interference with the lawyer's independent professional judgment or with the attorney-client relationship. It follows that defence counsel appointed to represent the insured are prevented from commenting on coverage aspects in the course of their representation of the insured.

See Margo (2000) p. 394.

[258] (1971) 16 Cal. App. 3d 799, 94 Cal. Rptr. 347.

[259] (1984) 162 Cal. App. 3d 358, 208 Cal. Rptr. 484.

[260] Rod Margo agrees with the foregoing. In his opinion: "[w]here defence counsel is appointed to represent an insured, and there are questions of coverage which result in a conflict of interest between the insurers and the insured, some jurisdictions permit the insured to appoint independent defence counsel of his choosing at the expense of the insurers". See Margo (2000) p. 394.

[261] See generally idem., pp. 392–393. Lawyers play a variety of significant roles in resolving claims involving aviation insurance policies. Whenever notice of a claim is brought to the attention of an insurer, the usual (if not prudent) practice is to instruct lawyers—either in-house counsel or external counsel—to assess the extent of the insurer's exposure to liability and report same to the insurer. The kinds of matters which lawyers will report on will include the available evidence on liability, evidence of injuries and damages sustained by passengers or their survivors, the regime of liability under which claimants are to be compensated and the likelihood of enforcing any limitation of liability in favour of the insured, the exposure of the insured to an adverse finding if claims are pursued to trial, the extent of the liability reserves that should be maintained for the payment of judgments and lawyer's fees, and the amount for which claims could be settled before the trial. Lawyers may also advise on such matters as policy compliance, prospects of repudiation of the claim, and the possibility of pursuing subrogated actions against third parties in relation to the claim(s). They may also be called upon to assist in: resolving complex hull claims such as those involving a structured financing where numerous parties have an interest in the insured aircraft; negotiating settlements for claims; and, drafting or reviewing insurance policies and/or particular clauses thereof.

2.5 Compulsory Insurance Requirements in Domestic and International Air Transportation and the Question of "Adequate" Insurance Coverage

As mentioned above, the eagerness with which operators in the air transport industry purchase insurance in respect of their operations derives not only from prudential financial management but also from the fact that they are required to do so by law. At the international level, states parties to a number of treaties have voluntarily assumed obligations thereunder to require their air transport operators to maintain adequate insurance covering their liability under those treaties. Within the European Union, a number of EU regulations prescribe mandatory insurance requirements applicable to air transport operators operating within, into and out of the territories of European states. For most air carriers and air transport operators licensed in Europe or using aircraft registered in member states of the European Union, the dictates of these regulations must be met in order to be eligible for the necessary authorization (e.g., Air Operators Certificates) to commence or continue commercial operations. At the national level, most countries have domestic laws which prohibit the operation of aircraft, airports, air navigation services, airport security screening services, ground handling facilities, refueling facilities and the like without any or adequate insurance coverage.

Interestingly, however, although most of these regimes insist on air transport operators maintaining adequate insurance coverage, they do not define exactly what adequate insurance means in practical terms. It would also appear, particularly at the international level that, these regimes levy compulsory insurance requirements almost exclusively against air carriers and air transport operators much to the exclusion of other equally important entities in the air transport industry. Also, a cursory look at the compulsory insurance requirements indicates that they tend to focus on the legal liability owed by air carriers to passengers, cargo shippers/consignees and third-parties, and to a large extent fail to address insurance requirements for any property loss that air carriers may face. Following broadly along the lines of the types of insurance coverage air carriers must maintain, this section provides a brief survey of the compulsory insurance requirements prescribed under domestic laws and various international agreements affecting air transportation, and the ongoing debate as to what constitutes adequate insurance coverage under the terms of those treaties.

2.5.1 Insurance Requirements Relating to Air Passenger Liability

The Convention for the Unification of Certain Rules Relating to International Carriage by Air, signed at Warsaw, 12 October 1929 (the Warsaw Convention of 1929 as subsequently amended)[262] and the Convention for the Unification of

[262] 137 LNTS 11 (1929).

Certain Rules for International Carriage by Air, signed at Montreal, 28 May 1999 (the Montreal Convention of 1999)[263] are the two major international treaty regimes that address air carrier liability for passengers, baggage and cargo in those states that are party to them. In essence, both conventions ascribe liability to the carrier for: damage sustained in the event of the death, wounding or other bodily injury suffered by a passenger if the accident which caused the damage so sustained took place on board the aircraft or in the course of any of the operations of embarking or disembarking the aircraft;[264] damage sustained in the event of destruction or loss of, or damage to any registered luggage or goods if the event or occurrence which caused the damage took place during the carriage by air;[265] and, damage occasioned by delay in the carriage by air of passengers, luggage or goods.[266]

Under the Warsaw regime, the liability of the carrier under each of the foregoing heads was limited to a specified amount, and the claimant could only claim damages exceeding those specified limits upon proof either that the documents of carriage required by the convention had not been delivered or were deficient in some respect or that the carrier had engaged in willful misconduct. The Warsaw regime did not contain a compulsory insurance requirement with regard to the air carrier liability arising thereunder. As such, it is not discussed any further in this section.

The Montreal Convention was negotiated and adopted as a replacement for the Warsaw regime. However, as yet, not all states parties to the Warsaw regime have ratified the Montreal Convention. As a result, both regimes currently exist side by side. On its part, the Montreal Convention does not limit passenger liability *per se*. Instead, it establishes a first tier of claims of up to 113,100 SDRs[267] per passenger in which the carrier is prohibited from excluding or limiting its liability by any means.[268] Beyond this first tier, the liability of the carrier is unlimited, and there is a presumption of negligence with a reversed burden of proof placed on the carrier. Thus, to avoid liability in this tier, the carrier must prove that the damage was not due to its negligence or other wrongful act, or that the damage was solely due to the negligence of a third party.[269] For damage occasioned by destruction or loss of, or delay to baggage and cargo, and delay to passengers, the Montreal

[263] 2242 UNTS 350 ICAO Doc. 9740 (1999).

[264] 137 LNTS 11 (1929) art. 17; 2242 UNTS 350 ICAO Doc. 9740 (1999), art. 17.

[265] 137 LNTS 11 (1929) art. 18; 2242 UNTS 350 ICAO Doc. 9740 (1999) art. 18.

[266] 137 LNTS 11 (1929) art. 19; 2242 UNTS 350 ICAO Doc. 9740 (1999) art. 19.

[267] Originally, the upper limit of the first tier was set at 100,000 SDRs. However, following the first review of limits of the convention carried out by ICAO in 2009, it was determined that the amount should be raised to 113,100 SDRs with effect from December 30, 2009 on account of a 13.1 % inflation rate recorded since the entry into force of the convention.

[268] 2242 UNTS 350 ICAO Doc. 9740 (1999) art. 21(1), except upon proof of contributory negligence as provided for in art. 20.

[269] Idem., art. 21(2).

Convention retains the specified limits model of the Warsaw regime, albeit with higher specified limits than the Warsaw regime.

As a matter of direct relevance for present purposes, article 50 of the Montreal Convention provides as follows:

> States Parties shall require their carriers to maintain adequate insurance covering their liability under this Convention. A carrier may be required by the State Party into which it operates to furnish evidence that it maintains adequate insurance covering its liability under this Convention.[270]

Unfortunately, however, the Montreal Convention does not contain a definition of what amounts to adequate insurance; neither does it provide any guidance for computing same except for the fact that it limits the required adequate insurance coverage to liability arising under the convention (i.e., damage sustained due to passenger death, wounding, bodily injury or delay; and, destruction or loss of, or delay to baggage and goods). Thus, under the Montreal Convention, there is no doubt concerning the *type* of insurance coverage compulsorily required. However, considering the fact that carrier liability for passenger death, wounding or other bodily injury is technically unlimited under the Montreal Convention, the question as to what constitutes adequate insurance coverage remains unanswered. What remains in doubt under the Montreal Convention is the *quantum* of insurance coverage a carrier needs to maintain in order to be considered adequately insured. In the absence of any pointers in the negotiating history of the Montreal Convention identifying the intention behind the insertion of this provision by the drafters, it has been suggested by one commentator that recourse may need to be had to current insurance requirements established by national law at least in the major commercial aviation stakeholder countries in order to properly determine what level of insurance coverage meets the standard of adequate insurance coverage as prescribed by the Montreal Convention.[271]

In April 2004, the European Parliament and the Council of the European Union adopted Regulation (EC) No. 758/2004 on Insurance requirements for air carriers and aircraft operators.[272] This regulation generally applies to all air carriers[273] and aircraft operators[274] operating within, into or out of the territory of the member states of the European Union.[275] It requires that such air carriers and aircraft operators must be insured as regards their aviation-specific liability in respect of baggage, cargo and

---

[270] Idem., art. 50.

[271] Fernandez-Peña (2009) p. 369.

[272] EC Regulation 785/2004 OJ L 1 (2004).

[273] An air carrier is defined as an air transport undertaking with a valid operating license. Idem. art. 3(a).

[274] Aircraft operator is defined as the person or entity, not being an air carrier, who has continual effective disposal of the use or operation of the aircraft; the natural or legal person in whose name the aircraft is registered shall be presumed to be the operator, unless that person can prove that another person is the operator. See idem., art. 3(c).

[275] Idem., art. 2.

third parties. The insured risks are to include acts of war, terrorism, hijacking, acts of sabotage, unlawful seizure of aircraft and civil commotion.[276] Most significantly, the Regulation sets the *minimum insurance requirements* to be maintained by the air carriers and aircraft operators affected by it.

With regard to air carrier liability in respect of passengers, article 6(1) of the Regulation prescribes the minimum insurance coverage required to be maintained by air carriers and aircraft operators at 250,000 SDRs per passenger. Article 6(2) as subsequently amended[277] sets the minimum insurance coverage for liability in respect of baggage at 1,131 SDRs per passenger, whereas for liability in respect of cargo, the minimum required insurance coverage is set at 19 SDRs per kilogram.[278] These minimum insurance requirements do not apply to flights over the territory of the member states carried out by non-Community air carriers and by aircraft operators using aircraft registered outside the European Community which do not involve a landing on, or take-off from, such territory.[279] Although these mandatory insurance requirements set a minimum threshold for those air carriers and aircraft operators operating within, to or from the European Union, they do not provide any guidance as to what exactly amounts to adequate insurance. Indeed the question of adequate insurance does not arise in the context of the Regulation—this is a matter which is left entirely within the discretion of individual air carriers and aircraft operators.

In the United States, minimum insurance requirements applicable to domestic and foreign direct air carriers (including commuter air carriers) as well as US air taxi and Canadian charter air taxi operators are prescribed in Federal Regulations promulgated by the Department of Transportation (DOT).[280] In connection with passenger liability, the regulations provide that any domestic and foreign direct air carrier providing passenger transportation shall maintain aircraft accident liability insurance coverage for bodily injury to, or death of, aircraft passengers with minimum limits of (1) US$300,000 for any one passenger; and, (2) a total per-involved aircraft per-occurrence of US$300,000 multiplied by 75 % of the number of passenger seats installed in the aircraft.[281] For US air taxi operators and Canadian charter air taxi operators engaging in passenger transportation, the minimum insurance requirements for bodily injury to, or death of, aircraft passengers are: (1) US$75,000 for any one passenger; and, (2) a total per involved aircraft for each occurrence of US$75,000 multiplied by 75 % of the total number of passenger seats installed in the aircraft.[282]

---

[276] These risks are typically excluded from coverage under most commercial aviation liability insurance policies usually by the insertion of some variant of clause AVN 48. An air carrier or aircraft operator may however negotiate with his insurer to have those risks written back into the policy. Alternatively, an air carrier or operator may take out a stand-alone war and allied risks policy to cover some or all of the excluded risks.

[277] See EC Regulation 285/2010 OJ L 19 (2010) art. 1.

[278] Idem.

[279] EC Regulation 785/2004 OJ L 1 (2004) art. 6(4).

[280] See 14 C.F.R. § 205 (2003).

[281] Idem., § 205.5(b)(2).

[282] Idem., §§ 205.5(c)(2) & (d)(2).

2.5.2 Insurance Requirements for Third-Party Liability

Until April 2009, the relevant international treaty with respect to third-party liability was the Convention on Damage Caused by Foreign Aircraft to Third Parties on the Surface[283] (the Rome Convention of 1952) as subsequently amended by the Montreal Protocol of 1978.[284] The original Rome Convention dealt with damage caused to persons and property on the surface in a contracting state by foreign aircraft registered in another contracting state, and the amending Protocol sought to extend it to damage caused in the territory of a contracting state by an aircraft registered anywhere so long as the operator thereof had a principal place of business or a permanent residence in a contracting state. The liability of the aircraft operator for damage giving a right to compensation under the convention was limited to specified amounts for each aircraft and each incident, based on the maximum certificated take-off weight of the aircraft.[285]Further, with regard to loss of life or personal injury, the liability of the operator was limited to an absolute maximum of 500,000 francs per person killed or injured.[286]

Under article 15 of the Rome Convention, a contracting state may require an operator registered in another contracting state to be insured in respect of the operator's liability for damage sustained in its territory for which a right to compensation exists under the convention, and there are provisions enabling a contracting state to refuse to allow an aircraft to overfly its territory if the insurance is unsatisfactory.[287] Aside conventional insurance coverage, the minimum insurance requirements of the Rome Convention could also be satisfactorily fulfilled by operators could if they procured any of the following as security to cover their liability: (1) "a cash deposit in a depositary maintained by the Contracting State where the aircraft is registered or with a bank authorised to act as a depositary by that State"; (2) "a guarantee given by a bank authorised to do so by the Contracting

[283] 310 UNTS 181 ICAO Doc. 7364 (1952).

[284] 2195 UNTS 370 ICAO Doc. 9527 (1978).

[285] Idem., art. 11(1). In this regard, the Rome Convention established five categories of aircraft weight and their corresponding limits as follows:

Weight of aircraft	Limit of liability (francs)
1,000 kg or less	500,000
More than 1,000 kg but not exceeding 6,000 kg	500,000 plus 400 francs per kg
More than 6000 kg but not exceeding 20,000 kg	2,500,000 plus 250 francs per kg
More than 20,000 kg but not exceeding 50,000 kg	6,000,000 plus 150 francs per kg
More than 50,000 kg	10,500,000 plus 100 francs per kg

The amounts mentioned in francs referred to a currency unit consisting of 65½ milligrammes of gold of millesimal fineness 900. These amounts were to be converted into national currencies using the gold value of such currencies at the date of such conversion.

[286] Idem., art.11(2).

[287] Idem., art.15.

State where the aircraft is registered, and whose financial responsibility has been verified by that State"; and, (3) "a guarantee given by the Contracting State where the aircraft is registered, if that State undertakes that it will not claim immunity from suit in respect of that guarantee".[288]

In April 2009, two new treaties aimed at modernizing the Rome Convention were adopted in Montreal under the auspices of the International Civil Aviation Organization. They are the *Convention on Compensation for Damage Caused by Aircraft to Third Parties* (The General Risks Convention)[289] and the *Convention on Compensation for Damage to Third Parties, Resulting from Acts of Unlawful Interference Involving Aircraft* (The Unlawful Interference Compensation Convention).[290] The General Risks Convention applies to damage to third parties which occurs in the territory of a state party caused by an aircraft in flight on an international flight[291] other than as a result of an act of unlawful interference[292] whereas the Unlawful Interference Compensation Convention applies to such third party damage caused by an act of unlawful interference. These treaties are discussed in greater detail in Chap. 5. Here, we only refer to the insurance requirements prescribed thereunder.

Both conventions ascribe strict liability to the operator of the aircraft for third party damage due to death, bodily injury, mental injury and property damage sustained as a direct consequence of the event giving rise thereto.[293] The liability of the operator of the aircraft is limited to 700 million SDRs per event, and this is calibrated on a scale according to the maximum certificated take-off mass (MTOM) of the aircraft.[294] For claims exceeding 700 million SDRs, the Unlawful Interference Compensation Convention establishes an International Civil Aviation Compensation Fund to pay compensation of an additional 3 billion SDRs to third parties. The fund will be financed by mandatory contributions levied against departing passengers, cargo shippers and general aviation operators in amounts subsequently to be determined. For damages exceeding the total compensation available in the first two tiers (i.e., 3.7 billion SDRs), claims may be brought against the operator upon proof of fault. Beyond the 700 million SDRs, the General Risks Convention does not provide for recovery of additional third party compensation.

[288] Idem., art.15(4).

[289] ICAO Doc. 9919 (2009) (not yet in force).

[290] ICAO Doc. 9920 (2009) (not yet in force).

[291] If a state party so declares to the depositary, both Conventions shall also apply to damage to third parties caused by an aircraft in flight other than on an international flight. See idem., art. 2(2); ICAO Doc. 9919 (2009), art. 2(2).

[292] An act of unlawful interference is defined in both conventions as: an act which is defined as an offence in the Convention for the Suppression of Unlawful Seizure of Aircraft, Signed at The Hague on 16 December 1970, or the Convention for the Suppression of Unlawful Acts Against the Safety of Civil Aviation, signed at Montréal on 23 September 1971, and any amendment in force at the time of the event. See ICAO Doc. 9920 (2009), art. 1(a); ICAO Doc. 9919 (2009), art. 1(a).

[293] ICAO Doc. 9919 (2009), art. 3; ICAO Doc. 9920 (2009), art. 3.

[294] ICAO Doc. 9919 (2009), art. 4; ICAO Doc. 9920 (2009), art. 4.

In striking similarity to the mandatory insurance requirements of the Montreal Convention described above, article 9(1) of the General Risks Convention and article 7(1) of the Unlawful Interference Compensation Convention both provide that: "[h]aving regard to Article 4, [i.e., the provision that limits operator liability to 700 million SDRs in each convention] States parties shall require their operators to maintain adequate insurance or guarantee covering their liability under this Convention".[295] Article 7(1) of the UIC Convention provides further that: "[i]f such insurance or guarantee is not available to an operator on a per event basis, the operator may satisfy this obligation by insuring on an aggregate basis. . . .".[296] Under both conventions, an operator may be required by a State Party into which it operates to furnish evidence that it maintains adequate insurance or guarantee.[297]

Here also, although the conventions oblige states parties to require their operators to maintain adequate insurance or guarantee covering their respective liabilities thereunder, there is neither a definition nor any guidance as to what amounts to adequate insurance coverage. As such, the concerns expressed above in relation to article 50 of the Montreal Convention apply here with equal force. There is no doubt regarding the *type* of insurance coverage or guarantee required—third party liability coverage. What remains unresolved is the *quantum*—how much coverage is adequate coverage.

Moreover, the language used in article 7(1) of the UIC Convention is very vague and ambiguous; it provides no clues as to what the intention of the drafters was. Article 7(1) of the UIC Convention begins with the phrase: "Having regard to Article 4", and as noted above, article 4 of the UIC Convention is the provision that limits the operator's liability in the first tier to 700 million SDRs per event. This means that the mandatory insurance or guarantee required to be maintained by operators is limited exclusively to their liability under article 4 of the convention—a maximum of 700 million SDRs. In the result, although the UIC Convention envisages the possibility of an operator being exposed to additional liability in the third tier (i.e., for those claims exceeding the total compensation available in the first two tiers—3.7 billion SDRs per event), the mandatory insurance provision does not require operators to maintain adequate insurance or guarantee in respect of such additional liability. Had the drafters intended to require operators to maintain insurance for their liability beyond that provided for in article 4, they would have omitted the phrase in question from article 7(1). Thus, since the international fund is responsible to pay compensation in the second tier, it would appear from the language of article 7(1) that, for liability exceeding 700 million SDRs per event, the operator has no obligation under the convention to maintain adequate insurance or guarantee.

European insurance requirements with respect to third-party liability are slightly different although they are based upon the same classification of exposure to liability according to the MTOM of aircraft that appears in the General Risks

[295] ICAO Doc. 9919 (2009), art. 9(1); ICAO Doc. 9920 (2009), art. 7(1).

[296] ICAO Doc. 9920 (2009).

[297] Idem., art 7(2); ICAO Doc. 9919 (2009), art. 9(2).

Convention and the Unlawful Interference Compensation Convention. The scheme established by the EU Regulation 785/2004 does not require that air carriers and air transport operators maintain adequate insurance coverage. Rather, it establishes a minimum threshold of compulsory insurance on the basis of the weight of the aircraft, and leaves the upper limit of coverage to the discretion of the air carrier or air transport operator.[298] Thus, subject to meeting the minimum insurance requirements, the question as to what level of insurance coverage is adequate does not arise under the Regulation.

It is also significant to note that the minimum insurance coverage required under the EU Regulation is specified on a *per-aircraft per-accident* basis, instead of an *aggregate basis*.[299] This means, for instance, that where an operator falling within the scope of application of the Regulation operates ten aircraft, each weighing more than 500,000 kg, the *minimum* third-party liability insurance coverage required for the entire fleet would be 7 billion SDRs (i.e., each of those 10 aircraft must be covered for at least 700 million SDRs per-accident). In contrast, if coverage were to be allowed on an aggregate basis, the operator could negotiate for a significantly lower amount of coverage (say 4 or 5 billion SDRs) based on an aggregate of

[298] In essence, article 7(1) of EC Regulation 785/2004 OJ L 1 (2004) provides that, in respect of liability for third parties, the minimum insurance cover per accident for each aircraft shall be as follows:

Category	MTOM (kg)	Minimum insurance (million SDRs)
1	<500	0.75
2	<1,000	1.5
3	<2,700	3
4	<6,000	7
5	<12,000	18
6	<25,000	80
7	<50,000	150
8	<200,000	300
9	<500,000	500
10	≥500,000	700

[299] A liability insurance policy may be written on a per-event basis, on an aggregate basis or on a combination of the two bases. In a per-event policy, the insurer is obliged to indemnify the insured for losses arising from any number of insured events so long as the losses from each single event does not exceed the specified per-event limit. On the contrary, in an aggregate loss policy, losses arising from all events which occur during the policy period are added up and the total may not exceed the aggregate limit stated in the policy. If the aggregate limit is exhausted before the end of the policy period the policy lapses and no further claims can be made on it unless and until it has been reinstated by the insurer. Normally, liability insurance policies relating to aviation operations are written subject to a per-occurrence or per-event limit, as well as an aggregate policy limit known as a combined single limit for the period of time covered by the policy. This typically means that such policies may be exhausted by one large single claim or a culmination of several small claims which occur during the policy period. The type of insurance coverage required under the EU Regulation is a per-event type of coverage.

expected claims. The only circumstances under which it would be possible to insure the fleet on an aggregate basis is when a determination has been made by the EU Commission to the effect that conventional insurance coverage for third-party liability due to war and terrorism risks is not available on a per-accident basis.[300]

In the United States, the above-mentioned Federal Regulations also prescribe minimum insurance requirements for the third-party liability exposure of air transport operators. For US and foreign direct carriers, the required minimum insurance coverage for bodily injury to, or death of, persons other than passengers and for damage to property is set at US$300,000 for any one person in any one occurrence, and a total of US$20 million per involved aircraft for each occurrence.[301] For aircraft of not more than 60 seats or 18,000 pounds maximum payload capacity, carriers need only maintain coverage of US$2 million per involved aircraft for each occurrence.[302] For US air taxi operators, the minimum insurance requirements for third-party liability are US$75,000 for any one person in any one occurrence and a total of US$300,000 per-involved aircraft per-occurrence for injury and death, and at least US$100,000 per-occurrence for loss of, or damage to, property.[303] For Canadian Charter air taxi operators, the requirements are US$75,000 per-person per-occurrence and a total of US$2 million per-involved aircraft per-occurrence.[304]

2.6 Conclusion

As clearly demonstrated in this chapter, although conventional insurance is an indispensable risk management tool critical for the financial survival of the air transport industry, not all risks inherent in, or related to, air transport operations are considered insurable by conventional insurance techniques. Historically, the market has been reluctant to provide the desired level of insurance coverage for aviation war and terrorism risks to the air transport industry. The next chapter therefore takes a closer look at the insurability or otherwise of aviation war and terrorism risks, and the manner in which the conventional insurance industry has provided and/or excluded coverage for those special types of risks to date.

---

[300] Under article 7(2) of EC Regulation 785/2004 OJ L 1 (2004), a carrier may satisfy the minimum insurance requirements by insuring on an aggregate basis if at any time, insurance cover for damage to third parties due to risks of war or terrorism is not available on a per-accident basis. Even under those circumstances, provision is made for the EU Commission to closely monitor the application of the Regulation in order to ensure that any such insurance contracted on an aggregate basis is at least equivalent to the relevant amount set in the table. This provision addresses the insurance aftermath of major events such as September 11, 2001, in which the insurance markets typically withdraw coverage for war and terrorism related risks.

[301] See 14 C.F.R. § 205 (2003) § 205.5(b)(1).

[302] Idem.

[303] Idem., § 205.5(c)(1).

[304] Canadian charter air taxi operators operating aircraft of more than 30 seats or 7,500 pounds maximum cargo payload capacity and a MTOM greater than 35,000 pounds are required to maintain third-party coverage of US$20 million per-involved aircraft per-occurrence. See idem.,§ 205.5(d)(1).

References

(1806) 2 Bos & Pul. (N.R.) 269 (HL) Lucena v. Craufurd
(1881) 18 Ch. D 1 Rayner v. Preston
(1883) 11 Q.B.D. 380 (C.A.) Castellain v. Preston
(1884) 9 App. Cas. 671 Thomson v. Weems
[1904] 2 KB 658 Prudential Insurance Company v. Internal Revenue Commissioners
[1913] 3 K.B. 84 Gould v. Curtis
[1936] 1 K.B. 408 Locker and Woolf Ltd. v. Western Australian Insurance Co. Ltd.
(1971) 16 Cal. App. 3d 799, 94 Cal. Rptr. 347 Executive Aviation Inc. v. National Insurance Underwriters
[1974] 1 All E.R. 395 Department of Trade and Industry v. St. Christopher Motorists Association Ltd.
[1979] 1 Lloyd's L.R. 499; [1979] 2 All E.R. 421 Medical Defence Union Ltd. v. The Department of Trade
(1984) 162 Cal. App. 3d 358, 208 Cal. Rptr. 484 San Diego Navy Federal Credit Union v. Cumis Insurance Society
[1997] 2 Lloyd's L.R. 687 (CA) [KAC v. KIC (CA)] Kuwait Airways Corporation v. Kuwait Insurance Co.
(1766) 3 Burr. 1905 Carter v. Boehm
(Cth.) Act No. 2 of 1959 (1959) Civil Aviation (Carrier's Liability) Act (including amendments up to Act No. 21 of 2007). (Australia)
137 LNTS 11, (1929) Convention for the Unification of Certain Rules Relating to International Carriage by Air
14 C.F.R. § 205 (2003) Aircraft Accident Liability Insurance Regulations. (US)
2195 UNTS 370, ICAO Doc. 9527 (1978) Protocol to amend the Convention on Damage caused by Foreign Aircraft to Third Parties on the Surface, signed at Rome on 7 October 1952
2242 UNTS 350, ICAO Doc. 9740 (1999) Convention for the Unification of Certain Rules for International Carriage by Air
310 UNTS 181, ICAO Doc. 7364 (1952) Convention on Damage Caused by Foreign Aircraft to Third Parties on the Surface
43 Eliz. I, c. 12 (1901) Policies of Assurance Act (UK)
6 Edw. 7, c 41 (1906) Marine Insurance Act. (UK)
65 Cal. 2d 263, 419 P.2d 168, 54 Cal. Rptr. 104 (1966) Gray v. Zurich Insurance Co.
Achampong F (1987) *Uberrima fides* in English and American Insurance Law – a comparative analysis. Int Comp Law Q 36:329–347
Ashenbrenner CX, Mrotek K (2005) Taming the turbulent cycle of aviation insurance. Milliman Global Insur Newsl 7–12
Baur P, Breutel-O'Donoghue A (2004) Understanding reinsurance: how reinsurers create value and manage risk. Swiss Re Econ Res Consult, Zurich
Bennett HN (1999) Mapping the doctrine of utmost good faith in Insurance Contract Law. Lloyds Marit Commercial Law Q 165–222
Caban EE (2003) War-Risk, hijacking & terrorism exclusions in aviation insurance: carrier liability in the wake of September 11, 2001 . J Air Law Commerce 68:421
Chrystal P, LeBlanc S (2002) Flight to quality – financial security in the aviation insurance market. Swiss Reinsurance Company, Zurich
Chrystal P, Fok M, Martino F, Peter A, Shirai S (2004) The true value of aviation insurance. Swiss Reinsurance Company, Zurich
EC Regulation 285/2010 (2010) Commission Regulation (EU) No. 285/2010 of 6 April 2010 amending Regulation (EC) No. 785/2004 of the European Parliament and of the Council on Insurance Requirements for Air Carriers and Aircraft operators. OJ, L 87/19
EC Regulation 785/2004 (2004) Parliament and Council Regulation (EC) 785/2004 of 21 April 2004 on insurance requirements for air carriers and aircraft operators. OJ, L 138/1

Faure MG, Hartlief T (2003) Policy issues in insurance no. 5: insurance and expanding systemic risks. Organisation for Economic Cooperation and Development (OECD), Paris
Fernandez-Peña S (2009) Defining insurance coverage adequacy under the Montreal Convention of 1999 . Ann Air Space Law XXXIV:343
Fischer E (1981) The rule of insurable interest and the principle of indemnity: are they measures of damages in property insurance? Indiana Law J 56:445–472
Fitzsimmons A (2004) Terrorism – maximizing the insurability of a catastrophe risk. Ann Air Space Law XXIX:67
Fortin P, Haeck L (2002) Aviation insurance and risk management. Assurances 69(4):533–543
Hagglund CE, Arthur LG (1973) Coverage problems in aviation insurance policies. Federation Insur Couns Q 23(4):4
Harnett B, Thornton JV (1948) Insurable interest in property: a socio-economic reevaluation of a legal concept. Colum Law Rev 48(8):1162–1188
Hasson R (1985) Subrogation in insurance law – a critical evaluation. Oxford J Legal Stud 5(3):416–438
Helfenstein R, Holzheu T (2006) Sigma No. 7/2006: securitization: new opportunities for insurers and investors. Swiss Reinsurance Company, Economic Research and Consulting, Zurich
Hodgin R (2002) Insurance law: text and materials, 2dth edn. Cavendish, London
Horn RC (1964) Subrogation in insurance theory and practice. Irwin, Homewood
ICAO (2004) A Practical Way Forward on Legal and Institutional Aspects of Communications, Navigation, Surveillance/Air Traffic Management (CNS/ATM) Systems. No. A. Res. A35-3
ICAO Doc. 9919 (2009) Convention on Compensation for Damage Caused by Aircraft to Third Parties
ICAO Doc. 9920 (2009) Convention on Compensation for Damage Caused to Third Parties, Resulting from Acts of Unlawful Interference involving Aircraft
Insurance Institute of London (1968) A short history of aviation insurance in the United Kingdom: Report H.R.10 by an historic records working party of the Insurance Institute of London, 2dth edn. Insurance Institute of London, London
Ivamy ERH (1986) General principles of insurance law, 5th edn. Butterworths, London
Jaffee D, Russell T (2003) Markets under stress: the case of extreme event insurance. In: Arnott R, Greenwald B, Kanbur R, Nalebuff B (eds) Economics for an imperfect world – essays in Honour of Joseph E. Stiglitz. MIT Press, Cambridge
Kendall J (2002) The incalculable risk: how the World Trade Center disaster accelerated the evolution of insurance terrorism exclusions. Univ Rich Law Rev 36:569
King LH, Benas HL (1994–1995) The duty to defend: when does it exist and what damages are recoverable for its breach? Univ San Francisco Marit Law J 7(1):245–269
Kunreuther H, Hogarth R, Meszaros J (1993) Insurer ambiguity and market failure. J Risk Uncertain 7:71–87
Laster DS, Schmidt C (2005) Sigma No. 4/2005: innovating to insure the uninsurable. Swiss Reinsurance Company, Economic Research and Consulting, Zurich
Leigh-Jones N, Birds J, Owen D (eds) (2003) MacGillivray on insurance law relating to all risks other than marine, 10th edn. Sweet and Maxwell, London
Leloudas G, Haeck L (2003) Legal aspects of aviation risk management. Ann Air Space Law XXVIII:149
Libby JB (1995) War risk aviation exclusions. J Air Law Commerce 60:605
Loshin J (2007) Insurance law's hapless busybody: a case against the insurable interest requirement. Yale Law J 117(3):474–509
Margo RD (1996) Aspects of insurance in aviation finance. J Air Law Commerce 62:423
Margo RD (2000) Aviation insurance: the law and practice of aviation insurance, including hovercraft and spacecraft insurance, 3dth edn. Butterworths, London
McClean JD, Balfour JM, Gardiner RK, Goh J, Margo RD, Martin P, EdM M (eds) (2007) Shawcross and Beaumont air law, Issue 109, 4th edn. Butterworths, London
Merkin R (ed) (2006) Colinvaux's law of insurance, 8th edn. Sweet and Maxwell, London

Patrik G (2004) Reinsurance. In: Teugels JL, Sundt B (eds) Encyclopedia of actuarial science. Wiley, Chichester
Phifer R (1996) Reinsurance fundamentals: treaty and facultative. Wiley, New York
Randall S (1996–1997) Redefining the insurer's duty to defend. Conn Insur Law J 3:221
S.O.R./88-58 (1988) Air Transportation Regulations. (Canada)
Salah El Din A (1971) Aviation insurance practice, law and reinsurance. Clowes, London
Soyer B (2003) Continuing duty of utmost good faith in insurance contracts: still alive? Lloyds Marit Commercial Law Q 39–79
Spurway MJ (1991) Aviation insurance, the market and underwriting practice. Witherby & Co. Ltd., London
Vaughan EJ (1982) Fundamentals of risk and insurance, 3rd edn. Wiley, New York
Wells AT, Chadbourne BD (2000) Introduction to aviation insurance and risk management, 2nd edn. Krieger, Florida

Chapter 3
The Insurance of Aviation War and Terrorism Risks by Specialist War Insurance Markets

3.1 Introduction

This chapter focuses on the manner in which insurance coverage for aviation war and terrorism risks and such other closely related perils (referred to altogether for the sake of convenience as aviation war risks) has been provided and/or excluded by the different insurance markets in the period before and after the fateful events of September 11, 2001. In order to provide a broader perspective of the subject, this chapter begins by tracing the historical development of insurance coverage and/or exclusion of war, terrorism and related risks in the London marine market, and the extent to which the practices of the London marine market have been extended and adapted to, or implemented in, other relevant insurance markets, particularly the aviation market. A survey of the judicial interpretations that have been ascribed to some of the specific perils cumulatively described as war and terrorism risks in aviation then follows. The chapter concludes by establishing a consistent trend of aviation war risk insurance market failure each time an extreme insured event materializes. In support of the foregoing, the chapter particularly focuses on documenting the reactions of the air transport industry, national governments as well as other stakeholders to the most recent war risk insurance market failure: that which occurred in the immediate aftermath of September 11, 2001.

3.2 The Historical Development of War Risk Insurance in the London Marine Market

The bulk of insurance as we know and understand it in the common law world today evolved from marine insurance as practiced in London from the sixteenth century. As such, it is not possible to recount the historical development of war and terrorism

Y.O.M. Nyampong, *Insuring the Air Transport Industry Against Aviation War and Terrorism Risks and Allied Perils*, DOI 10.1007/978-3-642-32433-8_3,

insurance without referring to the general history of marine insurance.[1] As far back as the seventeenth century, when marine underwriters in Lloyds of London started using the well-known S.G. Form,[2] marine risks and war risks were typically combined and insured in the same policy. As noted by one source, "[n]o less than 12 (some would say more) of the perils we would today describe as war risks were insured by the same policy which also insured such marine risks as 'perils of the seas'".[3] It was rare to exclude war risks from the policy as these were the very risks which the assured wished most to cover.[4] Occasionally, however, underwriters wished to exclude war risks from the policy, particularly following periods of heightened political tension between Britain and foreign countries. For example, in 1739, following one such period of increased political tension between Britain and France, underwriters in London began excluding "capture and seizure" from the perils insured by the Lloyd's S.G. policy.[5]

Several wars fought between the eighteenth and nineteenth centuries shaped the development of war risk insurance in the marine market. They amply demonstrated to underwriters that a real distinction had to be made between the coverage of marine risks and war risks.[6] These wars were fought as much on the seas as they were on land, and the enemy's seaborne trade was a special target. Although, back then, the British Empire and its influence around the globe was extensive, "the Royal Navy was never able entirely to obviate the depredations of skilled,

---

[1] O'May and Hill (1993) p. 250.

[2] S.G. is said to stand for "Ships, Goods". See Fitzsimmons (2004) p. 70, n. 6. The S.G. Form is an old insurance policy used for the insurance of marine risks at Lloyds until 1983. It had its origins in the bond or document by which seventeenth century merchants and ship owners meeting together in Edward Lloyds' Coffee House bound themselves one to another to make good any loss which any of them might suffer. The S.G. Form was never a planned document. Risks and exceptions were added on an ad-hoc basis as the demands of the insured ship owners, the practices of the market, and the decisions of the courts indicated were necessary. It was issued with the relevant clauses attached, usually by no more than a paperclip. See Miller (2005) p. 1.

[3] Miller (2005) p. 3. See also Marangos (2007) p. 16.

[4] O'May and Hill (1993) p. 251.

[5] Miller (2005) p. 3. See also Marangos (2007) p. 16. This marked the informal beginnings of the F.C. & S. Clause discussed below.

[6] In the words of O'May and Hill:

> Marine insurance war risk cases make a fascinating study, tracing as they do the history of the Western world from the Napoleonic Wars, the American War of Independence, the Bolshevik Revolution, the war between Greece and Turkey in 1922, Italy's invasion of Abyssinia in 1935, and the Spanish Civil War in the following year. The First and Second World Wars both made an important impact on the development of war risk insurance. So also did the more limited conflicts, such as those between India and Pakistan, the closure of the Suez Canal as a result of the Six-Day War and the war between Iran and Iraq which entrapped a large number of vessels in the Shatt-al-Arab. Modern manifestations of violence on a smaller scale, involving terrorism in its many forms, 'hijacking', covert attacks and political demonstrations by groups of dissidents throughout the world, have had to be considered in the context of traditional war risk insurance wordings.

See O'May and Hill (1993) p. 250.

determined and powerful enemy seafarers",[7] and thereby protect British ships engaged in foreign commerce. As such, the marine insurance community considered it prudent to exclude coverage for war risks by introducing a variety of exclusions such as the F.C. & S. (Free from Capture and Seizure) Clause, which did not form part of the original S.G. policy, but were added thereon by way of endorsement.[8]

"The exclusion of war risks gave rise to a corresponding demand for the excluded cover which various pioneering London underwriters were prepared to offer".[9] It would appear that around this time, the London market became informally divided into the "marine" and the "marine war risks" segments, and the latter segment somehow came to be looked upon with some disfavour by the broader market.[10] Towards the end of the nineteenth century, however, there was growing awareness among underwriters regarding their increasing exposure to war.[11] These

---

[7] Miller (2005) p. 3.

[8] According to Miller, "[a] particularly favoured exclusion, which seems to have been directed at excepting risks to ships at European ports which may have been affected by Napoleon's Continental system read: 'Free of capture and seizure in the ship's port of discharge'... This can be said to have been the beginnings of the F.C. & S. Clause as it later appeared". See idem.

[9] Marangos (2007) p. 16. See Miller (2005) p. 3 where the author notes: "The perils thus excepted could be insured by underwriters willing to write war risks. They seem to have found the business very profitable, although several were ruined by the disaster in 1780, when only eight British ships out of a convoy of 63 escaped capture". The Historic Records Committee of the Insurance Institute of London provides perhaps the most succinct description of the growth of war risk insurance during the period of the Napoleonic Wars as follows:

> Although in 1780 a disaster to a British convoy resulting in only eight of sixty-three vessels escaping capture led to the failure of a number of Lloyd's Underwriters, nevertheless the covering of war risk proved, during the years of British naval supremacy, distinctly profitable; many Underwriters made fortunes from doing so during the Napoleonic wars and Lloyd's grew greatly in wealth, power and prestige. However, it was during these wars that the practice of excluding war risks became common. Most Baltic and Western European ports were in a state of intermittent hostility to Britain (however sympathetically disposed towards Britain the inhabitants might be). Trade with Europe continued, but was hazardous – not on the high seas, where the British Navy was ubiquitous – but in the Continental ports where the writ of Napoleon and his allies ran.

See Insurance Institute of London, *Report H.R. 3 of the Historic Records Committee*, at 122, reproduced in O'May and Hill (1993) p. 251.

[10] Miller (2005) p. 3.

[11] See O'May and Hill (1993) pp. 251–252 where the authors note:

> The French navy launched its first submarine in 1893, and this together with the invention of the torpedo, heralded the advent of underwater naval warfare, against which there was no known protection. Two international incidents contributed to the growing unease of underwriters. A minor frontier dispute between Venezuela and British Guiana in 1895 threatened to escalate into war between Britain and the United States. Three years later in 1898 there was a danger of a confrontation between the British and French which threatened to spark off naval warfare between the two countries. ... A French expedition to Fashoda in the Sudan challenged British claims to that area. At the time it seemed likely that the fleets of Great Britain and France would become embroiled in global naval warfare, with modern weapons which differed greatly from those of the Napoleonic Wars. This presented a potential exposure which underwriters felt they might not be able to face.

developments led to calls for changes to create an organized and uniform method to be used by the entire market in dealing with war risks. In response, the Institute of London Underwriters produced the first set of Institute Time Clauses in 1889, which included in the body of the policy, an exceptive F.C. & S. Clause to the effect that the coverage provided under the policy was:

> warranted free from capture, seizure and detention, the consequences thereof, or of any attempt thereat, piracy excepted, and also from all consequences of hostilities, or warlike operations, whether before or after declaration of war.[12]

At a general meeting held in 1898, Lloyd's of London also responded to these developments by passing a resolution to the effect that marine risks and war risks should be rated separately and insured by separate policies unless a special agreement was reached that war risks should be included in the standard policy.[13] In line with the foregoing, Lloyd's also introduced the requirement that all standard marine covers were to include in the body of the policy the following F.C. & S. Clause:

> Warranted nevertheless free of capture, seizure and detention, and the consequences thereof, or any attempt thereat, piracy excepted, and also from all the consequences of hostilities or warlike operations.[14]

The F.C. & S. exclusion was couched as a statement bearing on the risk insured and was construed as a warranty on the part of the assured.[15] Over the years, these exclusion clauses were continually amended in response to the many armed conflicts of the time, and also in response to judicial interpretations which had the effect of disturbing the delicate balance between insurers and insureds established by the existing versions of the exclusions.[16] By 1937, the Lloyd's version of the F.C. & S. Clause, for instance, had been extended to read: "... whether there be a

---

[12] Idem., p. 252. In earlier versions of the F.C. & S. Clause, "riots or commotions" had been used instead of "warlike operations". The substitution of "warlike operations" for "riots or commotions" occurred in 1883, a year after the Royal Navy had heavily bombarded Alexandria. Technically, there was no state of war as the Royal Navy was merely aiding a friendly State to put down a rebellion. However, underwriters at the time found it necessary to expand the scope of the F.C. & S. Clause to exclude cover for losses sustained during such dangerous operations. See Miller (2005) p. 3.

[13] It is generally agreed that this resolution was in response to developments at the time, in particular: heightened tensions between all of the Great Powers, including the still-emerging United States; fuelled by the scramble for control in Africa and in particular, a naval arms race. Underwriters seemed to have been especially concerned about the Fashoda Incident referred to above. See Marangos (2007) p. 16.

[14] Idem.

[15] (1884) 9 App. Cas. 671 per Lord Blackburn at 684: "In policies of marine insurance, I think it is settled by authority that any statement of a fact bearing upon the risk introduced into the written policy is, by whatever words and in whatever place, to be construed as a warranty ...." Also reproduced in: Ivamy (1986) p. 282, fn. 6.

[16] O'May and Hill (1993) p. 253.

declaration of war or not, civil war, rebellion, insurrection or civil strife arising therefrom, or piracy".[17]

With time, the F.C. & S. Clause came to be printed in italics in the body of the S.G. policy then in common use.[18] If, by agreement of the underwriter and the insured, war risks were not to be excluded from coverage under the standard policy, the clause was deleted from the policy. However, whenever the clause was not deleted, it overrode the perils enumerated in the policy which were inconsistent with its terms, thereby excluding them from coverage.[19] In such instances, the assured had to take out a separate war risk policy from a war risks underwriter in order to obtain coverage for the perils excluded from the marine policy by the F.C. & S. Clause.

The problem was that, as a result of the mechanics of the then-applicable traditional method of insuring war risks, the assured did not always obtain the desired protection from the positive cover provided by the war risk policy. Instead of naming the specific perils covered, the traditional method of underwriting war risks was to simply state in the war risks policy that the insurance provided thereunder covered *only* "the risks excluded from the Standard Form of English Marine Policy by the F.C. & S. Clause…".[20] This meant that for a loss to be covered under the war risk policy, it must have first been positively covered in the marine policy, and then excluded from coverage by the F.C. & S. Clause contained therein.[21] In the words of a prominent author, one had to carry out the following inquiry to determine if a loss was covered under the war risks policy:

> First, did the loss fall within the positive cover in the marine policy? Secondly, if it did, was the loss taken out of the marine cover by the F.C. & S. exclusion? The inquiry was the more difficult because the words of the F.C. & S. exception were not identical with the words of the positive marine cover, so that claims under this part of the war risk cover could involve applying two different sets of words in the same factual situation.[22]

This method of insuring marine war risks was described as cumbersome, convoluted, tortuous and complex in the extreme.[23] Following long years of adverse criticism from the market, the judiciary and international bodies, Lloyds in 1983 abolished the S.G. Form and the F.C. & S. Clause, along with the above described formula they generated for insuring war risks, replacing them with the

---

[17] According to Marangos, "[t]he new wording was a response to the massive upheavals, not just the First World War itself, of course a war in the formal sense, but also, to the Sino-Japanese War and the Russian Revolution, neither of which were formally declared 'wars' but nevertheless posed a massive threat to insured property". Marangos (2007) pp. 16–17.

[18] This meant that the F.C. & S. Clause had paramountcy over all other coverage wordings of the policy. See O'May and Hill (1993) p. 252.

[19] Idem.

[20] Idem., p. 254.

[21] In other words, a loss was recoverable under the war risks policy if it would have been recoverable under the marine policy if the marine policy had not included the F.C. & S. clause.

[22] O'May and Hill (1993) p. 254.

[23] (1970) 2 Lloyd's L.R. 355 per Justice Mocatta, [reproduced in O'May and Hill (1993) p. 254].

Lloyd's Marine Insurance Policy (the MAR Form).[24] The new method of insuring war risks thereby established is simple and proceeds on the premise that marine and war risk insurances complement each other. Specifically named war risks are excluded from the marine policy by clauses such as the War Exclusion, the Strikes Exclusion, the Malicious Acts Exclusion and the Nuclear Exclusion. Separate policies such as the War and Strikes insurance policies are then available to provide coverage for the excluded risks in terms almost identical to the exclusion clauses.[25] By positively setting out the marine insured perils and the war insured perils in separate policies, it is no longer necessary to refer to another document (i.e., the marine policy) before determining whether a peril is insured by the war risks policy.[26]

Although no longer in use, the Lloyd's S.G. Form and the F.C. & S. Clause heralded the formal introduction of war risk exclusions into insurance policies by underwriters in London. Following its establishment in the marine market, the practice of excluding war risks was extended to other branches of non-marine insurance both in London and elsewhere. For instance, following the Spanish Civil War of 1936 in which insurance markets in London and the United States[27] suffered heavy losses from war risks,[28] non-marine underwriters in the London market, including Lloyd's underwriters, entered into the *War and Civil War Risks Exclusion Agreement* in 1936.[29] The agreement, which is still in effect and has attained worldwide application,[30] essentially provides that underwriters would exclude from all insurances and reinsurances loss, damage or liabilities resulting directly or indirectly from war and civil war.[31] As a result of its implementation, all

---

[24] Marangos (2007) p. 17.

[25] Miller (2005) p. 8.

[26] Idem.

[27] Caban (2003) p. 431. See also Libby (1995) p. 622.

[28] "In 1914, underwriters at Lloyd's had made great profits from their new insurance policies for bomb damage, since the damage had not been as extensive as many predicted. After the war many underwriters began to insure war risks on property such as buildings (land-based war risks) around the world, based on that earlier experience. ... The insurance market willingly sold insurance against the possibility of losses from the 'civil commotion' in Spain beginning in 1936, for both land- and sea-based war risks ... In 1937, news reports began to tell of high losses and mounting claims on war risk policies, both marine and land-based. Many underwriters had insured ships trading with Spain against war risks, counting on military protection from British naval vessels stationed in the Mediterranean. The insured ships ... suffered damage and loss in the conflict when the British navy did not intervene. ... The land-based war risks policies led to the most bruising losses for insurers. The Spanish Civil War was notable for innovations in warfare that led to massive aerial bombardment of cities and towns and destroyed lives and property that would not have been at such great risk in earlier wars". See Haufler (1997) pp. 78–80.

[29] This was an inter-underwriter (or market) agreement which resulted in a near total ban on land war risks insurance implemented and enforced by the London insurance market. With the experiences of the Spanish Civil War freshly in mind, the agreement was based on the premise that the potential liability of insurers arising from accumulation of valuable property exposed to war risks on land was too formidable to be handled in the insurance markets, and therefore such risks were just not insurable. See idem., p. 81.

[30] For instance, the insurance market in the United States has signed on to it. See Caban (2003) p. 431. See also Libby (1995) p. 622.

[31] Thompson and Sloane (2001) pp. 2–3.

non-marine policies issued around the world must (and usually do) include a War and Civil War Exclusion Clause.[32]

Following these developments in the non-marine market, the marine market came to the realization that although the same likelihood of concentration of value as pertains to land war risks did not exist in marine insurance, that possibility could arise when many ships carrying valuable cargo were in a congested port of loading or discharge at the same time.[33] It was also realized that if marine underwriters were prepared to grant unlimited war risk cover, it might seriously prejudice the universal agreement between the non-marine underwriters.[34] The *War Risks Waterborne Agreement*[35] was therefore introduced whereby marine underwriters agreed not to insure goods against war risks whilst on land unless the goods were at a port of transshipment and, even then, only for a limited period. A similar agreement, the *War Risks Airborne Agreement*, was also introduced in respect of goods carried by air.[36] These agreements have since been implemented by insurers in different segments of the global insurance market. The next section of this chapter discusses the manner in which they have been implemented in the aviation insurance market.

3.3 The Evolution of War Risk Exclusions and Extended Coverage Endorsements in the Aviation Insurance Market

As noted above, the heavy war risk losses sustained by insurers during the Spanish Civil War of 1936 spawned a number of market agreements the implementation of which has effectively extended the practice of excluding war risks beyond the London marine market to other insurance markets. In this section, we assess how the global aviation insurance market has responded to these developments over the years.

In North America, the implementation of these market agreements generally meant that, "exclusive of the United States and Canada, no underwriter will insure against damages due to war, including civil war".[37] Up until the 1973 decision of the U.S. Federal Court for the Southern District of New York in *Pan Am World Airways, Inc. v. Aetna Casualty and Surety Co., et al.*,[38] aviation insurers in the United States traditionally implemented the market agreements by accepting standard war risk exclusionary language drafted by the Fire Offices Committee

[32] O'May and Hill (1993) pp. 296–297. Standardized versions of this clause have been published by the London Non-Marine Association, and they are preceded by the prefix NMA. They are commonly used in property and casualty (P&C) insurance policies.

[33] Idem., p. 297.

[34] Idem.

[35] The current (1982) version of the Agreement is reproduced in idem., at pp. 297–298.

[36] Idem., p. 298.

[37] Libby (1995) p. 622; Caban (2003) p. 431.

[38] 368 F. Supp. 1098 (S.D.N.Y. 1973). This decision is discussed in detail in Sect. 3.4 below.

(FOR).[39] This landmark decision demonstrated to the aviation insurance market in the United States that there was the need to devise and insert into insurance policies clear and unambiguous language which excluded from coverage those specific perils they did not intend to insure.[40] Prior to the decision, all-risk aviation insurers in the United States were faced with a practical dilemma. The wording of the then existing war risk exclusions did not afford them the opportunity to distinguish between, and retain in their policies non-warlike hijacking (which they preferred to insure), and exclude warlike hijacking (which they desired to exclude). Wary of the possibility that if they were to exclude all hijacking losses from their all-risk policies, their clients—U.S. carriers—would turn to the London market to obtain coverage for non-warlike hijackings,[41]

---

[39] According to Jason Libby, the standard war risk aviation exclusion clause drafted by the Fire Offices Committee, which has since become the grandfather of modern aviation war risk exclusions, was probably similar to the following:

> THIS POLICY DOES NOT APPLY:
>
> (10) To loss or damage or any liability of the Insured directly or indirectly occasioned by, happening through or in consequence of military, naval or usurped power whether in time of peace or war and whether lawful or unlawful, war, invasion, civil war, revolution, rebellion, insurrection or warlike operation, whether there be a declaration of war or not.

See Libby (1995) p. 622.

[40] Generally, all-risk insurers in the US at the time did not want to treat hijacking as a unitary risk, but instead, desired to divide hijacking risks by excluding from all-risk coverage those hijackings which fell within the general application of the war and related risks exclusions (warlike hijacking), and covering other types of hijacking (non-warlike hijacking). For instance, all-risk insurers were willing to cover hijacking by say an individual who is demented or seeking personal gain because, as the aircraft was usually returned in such instances with little or no liability incurred, there appeared to be little risk of substantial property loss from such non-warlike hijackings. Conversely, all risk insurers desired to exclude warlike hijacking from coverage because of the possibility of incurring extensive liability when the aircraft was totally or substantially destroyed. See Bidinger and Bninski (1974) p. 1192.

[41] Idem., pp. 1192–1193. The decision not to write a hijacking exclusion into the all-risk coverage prior to the *Pan Am* decision was supported by several facts and considerations. U.S. all-risk insurers were very much aware that by excluding warlike hijacking from coverage, the U.S. carriers who they insured would go to other markets to seek coverage for those risks, and this would cause the U.S. insurers to lose premium volume and competitive position. Further, although international airlines had the greatest need for hijacking coverage at the time, all U.S. air carriers, including the domestic trunk airlines, needed and desired insurance coverage for non-warlike hijacking and non-warlike intentional damage. Since there was no specific market where merely non-warlike hijacking coverage could be purchased, the exclusion of hijacking by U.S. all-risk insurers would have forced domestic trunk carriers to purchase complete war risk coverage—which would provide coverage for all hijackings—from the London market, even though they had no need for coverage for warlike hijackings. Since domestic trunk carriers constituted the largest source of premiums written and earned by the U.S. all-risk insurers, the fear was that if these airlines were forced to go to the London market to supplement a reduced all-risk coverage that excluded all hijacking losses, they might be inclined to acquire all their insurance from the London market in one package, thereby resulting in a loss of business for the U.S. insurers. Again, the all risk insurers in the U.S. feared that those carriers which continued to be insured in the U.S. would demand a reduction in premium corresponding to the reduction in coverage brought about by the exclusion of hijacking, thereby resulting in a loss of earnings. This is why the all risk policies kept silent about excluding hijacking.

all-risk aviation insurers in the U.S. simply decided not to write a hijacking exclusion into their policies.[42]

The *Pan Am* case arose from the destruction of a Boeing 747 aircraft belonging to Pan American World Airways, which was hijacked on September 6, 1970, by two armed terrorists belonging to the Popular Front for the Liberation of Palestine (PFLP) during a flight from Brussels to New York City. It was taken to Beirut, Lebanon, where it was laced with explosives, and then finally to Cairo, Egypt, where it was blown up after the passengers had been evacuated. Pan American Airlines had taken out three types of insurance coverage over the aircraft: (1) all-risk insurance;[43] (2) private sector war risk insurance;[44] and, (3) a war risk insurance policy provided by the Secretary of Transportation of the United States.[45] The main question which had to be determined by the court was whether the loss of the aircraft would be borne by the all risk insurers or by the war risk carriers.[46] All three groups of all risk insurers sought to avoid liability by asserting

---

[42] Idem., pp. 1194–1195, where the authors describe the situation of the US all risk carriers as follows:

> Unable to select the appropriate words to exclude only warlike hijacking, and, yet desiring to maintain their coverage and premiums while not desiring to enter the war-risk market, the all-risk insurers did not insert a hijacking exclusion into their policies prior to the *Pan American* case. In effect, they assumed the risk that their policies would cover all aircraft hull losses resulting from hijackings, apparently to continue to offer a full range of all-risk insurance coverage as well as to maintain the premium volume paid by the U.S. domestic trunk air carriers.

[43] All risk insurance covers all losses except those resulting from perils or risks specifically excluded from the particular policy. In this case, three groups of insurers had written the all-risk coverage for Pan American World Airways under identical policies—the United States Aviation Insurance Group (U.S.A.I.G.) for one-third of the aircraft's value, a Lloyd's of London underwriting syndicate for one-sixth of the aircraft's value, and the Associated Aviation Underwriters (A.A.U.) for one-half of the value of the aircraft. These three groups included all the underwriters in the world at the time who supplied aviation all-risk insurance to American air carriers. See Vinciguerra (1974–1975) fn. 3. See also Caban (2003) p. 435.

[44] Because United States aviation insurers did not provide private war risk insurance, Pan American had purchased a war risk policy from the London market. This policy was underwritten by a Lloyd's of London war risk syndicate, and it covered the aircraft in question for up to $14.2 million. See Caban (2003) p. 435. The actual value of the aircraft was $20 million.

[45] The U.S. Federal Government (acting through the Secretary of Transportation—the FAA) issued the second war risk policy covering the remainder of the value of the aircraft, i.e., $9.8 million.

[46] Caban (2003) p. 435.

a war risk exclusion appearing in their identical all risk policies.[47] After a rather protracted trial, the court held that the all risk insurers could not escape liability since the war risk exclusions upon which they relied did not clearly exclude losses arising from hijackings.

Following this decision, which was subsequently affirmed on appeal,[48] all-risk aviation insurers in the United States adopted the *Common North American Airline War Exclusion Clause* (CWEC).[49] In an outstanding commentary on the subject, the features of the CWEC have been described in the following words:

> This exclusion clause has several distinguishing characteristics. Section A, dealing with various standard war and warlike risks as well as irregular warfare, and section B,

---

[47] Idem., fn. 120. The exclusions in the all-risk policies read:

> C. This policy does not cover anything herein to the contrary notwithstanding loss or damage due to or resulting from:
>
> capture, seizure, arrest, restraint or detention or the consequences thereof or of any attempt thereat, or any taking of the property insured or damage to or destruction thereof by any Government or governmental authority or agent (whether secret or otherwise) or by any military, naval or usurped power, whether any of the foregoing be done by way of requisition or otherwise and whether in time of peace or war and whether lawful or unlawful (this subdivision 1. shall not apply, however, to any such action by a foreign government or foreign governmental authority following the forceful diversion to a foreign country by any person not in lawful possession or custody of such insured aircraft and who is not an agent or representative, secret or otherwise, of any foreign government or governmental authority);
>
> war, invasion, civil war, revolution, rebellion, insurrection or warlike operations, whether there be a declaration of war or not;
>
> strikes, riots civil commotion.

See Bidinger and Bninski (1974) p. 1196, fn. 195.

[48] 505 F.2d 989 (2d Cir. 1974) In affirming the decision of the District Court, the United States Court of Appeals for the Second Circuit held that a war risk exclusion clause does not bar recovery under an all risk policy for damages resulting from terrorist activities, unless such activities are clearly excluded from the coverage of the policy. See Vinciguerra (1974–1975) p. 924, fn. 7, where the author adds that "[i]n accordance with the canon of *contra proferentem*, an ambiguous insurance term will be construed against the drafter".

[49] The Common North American Airline War Exclusion Clause [CWEC] excludes any losses arising from:

> War, invasion, acts of foreign enemies, hostilities (whether war be declared or not), civil war, rebellion, revolution or insurrection, military or usurped power or confiscation and/or nationalization or requisition or destruction by any government or public or local authority or by any independent unit or individual engaged in activities in furtherance of a program of irregular warfare. ANY OR ALL OF THE ABOVE APPLYING HOWSOEVER AND WHERESOEVER OCCURRING.
>
> Any hostile detonation of any weapon of war employing atomic or nuclear fission and/or fusion or other like reaction or radioactive force or matter.
>
> Other than excluded in paragraph (a) hereinabove, any unlawful seizure, diversion or exercise of control of the aircraft, or attempt thereat, by force or threat thereof or by any other form of intimidation, by any person or persons whether on board aircraft or otherwise.
>
> Other than as excluded in paragraph (a) hereinabove, strikes, lockouts, disturbances, riots, civil commotion.
>
> Other than as excluded in paragraph (a) hereinabove, vandalism, sabotage, malicious act or other act intended to cause loss or damage.

concerning loss from nuclear weapons and radioactive materials, are mandatory exclusions in the aircraft hull insurance policy – the insured cannot purchase coverage for these risks under an all-risk policy that includes the CWEC. The exclusions found in sections C (hijacking), D (strikes, riots, and civil commotion), and E (intentional damage) contain a "buy-back" provision. For an additional premium, the insured, under an all-risk policy, can purchase coverage for any one or more of these exclusions.[50]

Today, all-risk aviation insurers in the United States still exclude losses from war and civil risks by subscribing to the CWEC.[51]

Similar developments occurred in the London aviation market, where efforts have been made to formulate and standardize the wordings of commonly used aviation insurance clauses and endorsements. In this connection, the erstwhile Joint Technical and Clauses Committee (JTCC),[52] which held the London market mandate[53] to formulate and adopt non-binding standard wordings for specific clauses and endorsements bearing the prefix AVN (an acronym for Aviation), had, over the years, published a number of such clauses and endorsements, which were found in common use in the global aviation insurance industry. Naturally, the need to limit, cut down or exclude war risks in aviation insurance policies in compliance with the requirements of the market agreements discussed above had served as an important area of work for the JTCC over the years, and one of its most significant achievements has been the publication of the *War, Hijacking and Other Perils Exclusion Clause (Aviation)*, (AVN 48)[54] series of model clauses, and their subsequent wide acceptance and usage in the global aviation insurance market.

The original clause AVN 48 was issued on November 12, 1969, after the 1968 Israeli attack on Beirut airport, an incident in which more than a dozen aircraft were

---

[50] Bidinger and Bninski (1974) pp. 1195–1196.

[51] Caban (2003) p. 431.

[52] The Joint Technical and Clauses Committee (JTCC) was established jointly by the erstwhile Lloyd's Aviation Underwriters' Association (LAUA), and the former Aviation Insurance Offices Association (AIOA). The Committee was abolished on 24th June 2005, and replaced by the Aviation Insurance Clauses Group (AICG). The AICG, which now holds the market mandate to formulate and publish model aviation clauses and endorsements, was established jointly by the Lloyd's Market Association (LMA) which replaced the LAUA, and the International Underwriting Association of London (IUA) which replaced the AIOA. See International Underwriting Association (IUA) & Lloyd's Market Association (LMA) No. 015/0605 (2005). See also Caplan (2006).

[53] This mandate has now been entrusted to the AICG. See Aviation Insurance Clauses Group (2005).

[54] The most current version of the clause was published by the AICG on August 4th 2006, and it is designated AVN 48D.

damaged or destroyed on the ground.[55] Prior to its introduction, standard aviation insurance policies issued in the London market contained a "war and allied perils" clause.[56] Clause AVN 48 was subsequently amended and re-issued as AVN 48A[57] on August 12, 1970. In the following month, (i.e., September, 1970), "a TWA Boeing 707, a Swissair DC-8, a Pan Am Boeing 747, and a BOAC VC-10 were all hijacked within a short time of each other. Three of the hijacked aircraft were flown to a desert airstrip at Dawson Field, Amman, Jordan, where they were destroyed".[58] The fourth aircraft was the Pan Am Boeing 747 which was destroyed in Cairo. Again, in reaction to these occurrences, the JTCC amended clause AVN 48A and re-issued it as clause AVN 48B. In so doing, the scope of risks excluded from

---

[55] Caban (2003) p. 432. The original AVN 48 provided as follows:

> This Policy does not cover claims directly or indirectly arising from anyone or any combination of any of the following causes or any consequences thereof:
>
> *War.* War, invasion, acts of foreign enemies, hostilities (whether war be declared or not), civil war, rebellion, revolution or insurrection, including malicious acts in furtherance of any of the foregoing.
>
> *Nuclear weapons.* Any hostile detonation of any weapon of war employing atomic or nuclear fission and/or fusion or other like reaction or radioactive force or matter.
>
> *Strikes.* Strikes, riots, civil commotions, or labour disturbances.
>
> *Pre-emption.* Pre-emption.
>
> *Confiscation.* Confiscation, seizure, restraint, detention, appropriation or requisition for title or use by any authority or Government (whether civil, military or de facto) for any reason whatsoever.
>
> *Hi-jacking.* Unlawful seizure or wrongful exercise of control of the Aircraft or crew in flight (including any attempt at such seizure or control) made by any person or persons on board the Aircraft acting without the consent of the Insured.
>
> Furthermore, this Policy does not cover claims arising whilst the Aircraft is outside the control of the Insured by reason of a peril listed in (d), (e) or (f).

See Margo (2000) p. 325, fn. 1.

[56] This war and allied perils clause was narrower in scope than the original AVN 48. It excluded loss or damage which occurred "(a)s a direct or indirect consequence of war, invasion, acts of foreign enemies, hostilities (whether war be declared or not), civil war, rebellion, revolution, insurrection, military or usurped power, martial law, strikes, riots, civil commotions, confiscation, nationalization, requisition or destruction or damage to property by or under the order of any government or public or local authority". See Margo (2000) p. 325, fn. 1. In addition to excluding the war and civil risks set out above, AVN 48 was adapted to exclude claims caused by perils unique to the aviation industry, such as hijacking. See Thompson and Sloane (2001) p. 3.

[57] AVN 48A amended and updated AVN 48 by:

- Removing the reference to "malicious acts" in section *(a)* and placing it in a section of its own [section *(e)*] and including a reference to "any act of sabotage";
- Deleting section *(d)* relating to pre-emption;
- Including a new section *(d)* relating to "Any act of one or more persons, whether or not agents of a sovereign power, for political or terrorist purposes and whether the loss or damage resulting therefrom is accidental or intentional"; and,
- The inclusion of "nationalisation" as an excluded risk between "confiscation" and "seizure".

See Margo (2000) p. 325, fn. 1.

[58] Margo (2002) pp. 386–387, fn. 3.

coverage was widened. AVN 48B was in wide usage around the world when the events of September 11, 2001, occurred.

As model clauses, both the CWEC and the AVN 48 series of clauses are non-binding in nature, and individual aviation insurers are at liberty to insert them, as published or in any variation they may prefer, into the aviation insurance policies they underwrite. When so inserted, however, the clauses generally provide a declaration to the effect that the policy will not cover claims arising out of all or any combination of the following perils: War; Nuclear weapons; Strikes; Pre-emption; Terrorist acts; Malicious acts or acts of sabotage; Confiscation; and, Hijacking.[59] In effect, an insured airline or aviation operator whose insurance policy contains the CWEC and/or an AVN 48 exclusion clause will not be successful on a claim against the insurer based on any of the specifically excluded risks. As a result, the insured airline or aviation operator will continue to retain and bear financial responsibility for the risks excluded from coverage under the policy. Although the wording of clause AVN 48B was slightly different from that of the CWEC, they both excluded essentially the same risks.[60] However, AVN 48B was wider in scope than the CWEC in the sense that it did not attempt to exclude hijackings by persons not aboard the aircraft, whereas the CWEC did.[61]

Before September 11, 2001, a few options were available to an aviation insurance policyholder who desired not to bear financial responsibility for any of the perils excluded by the insertion of either CWEC or AVN 48B into their insurance policies. An airline or other insured operator wishing to obtain coverage for any of the excluded perils "could do so either by means of a write-back endorsement to an All Risks Policy, or by purchasing a separate War Risks Policy".[62] Comparing the two means of obtaining coverage for some of the excluded risks, Margo and Posner note as follows:

> The write-back method was advantageous for an insured. In most cases, the insured would be indemnified for a loss without delay because it would not be faced with a protracted coverage dispute over whether the All Risks Policy or the War Risks Policy covered the loss since the distinction would be largely irrelevant. If a separate war-risk policy was issued and there was doubt as to whether the war risk exclusion had been triggered, the burden would be on the all risks carrier to establish that the loss or damage is excluded before the insured could look to the war risks carrier for coverage.[63]

---

[59] As will be seen below (see Sect. 3.5 below for discussion of judicial interpretations of terms used in war risk exclusions), each of the terms used in these exclusion clauses has been subject to rather extensive litigation. See Margo and Posner (2008) p. 473. Throughout this book, however, these perils are cumulatively referred to as "war risks" or "war and allied risks" for ease of reference.

[60] Margo (1996) p. 446.

[61] Caban (2003) pp. 431–432.

[62] Margo and Posner (2008) p. 473. The authors note further that, "[w]hile some U.S. insurers offer write-back coverage, the specialist market in London is the only private market for full war risks coverage". Idem., fn. 50.

[63] Idem., pp. 473–474. The authors cite the *Pan Am* case (discussed above) in support of this assertion. See also Margo (1996) p. 447.

With respect to *passenger* and *third party legal liability*,[64] an insured airline or aviation products manufacturer could negotiate with its all risks insurer to have some of the risks excluded by AVN 48 or CWEC written back or reinstated into the existing all risks liability policy by way of an extended coverage or write back endorsement. The AICG's standardized version of this write back endorsement is designated as the AVN 52 series.[65] By this means, all the risks excluded, with the exception of the risk of hostile detonation or explosion of a nuclear weapon, could be written back into an existing liability all-risks policy in return for an increased or an additional premium.[66] Coverage for the insured's liability to third parties for damage to property on the ground caused by any of the war and allied risks written back was also typically limited to those arising from the use of the aircraft.[67] With regard to coverage for *aircraft hulls*,[68] the airline or operator could negotiate with its existing all-risks hull insurer for an extended coverage or write-back endorsement for hulls, standardized by the AICG and designated as AVN 51, in the same manner as applies to AVN 52. The risks that could be written back into the all risks hull policy using AVN 51 include strikes, riots, civil commotions, acts of sabotage, and hijacking.[69]

The extended coverage or write-back endorsements (AVN 51 and 52 series) could only be issued in relation to existing hull or liability all-risks policies containing the AVN 48 or CWEC exclusion. Essentially, "they gave back to the insured the coverage which had been excluded, in whole or in part, by AVN 48B".[70] Those risks which were originally excluded by AVN 48B/CWEC and then written back by AVN 51 and 52 are considered to be very volatile; this is why they are excluded in the first place. As a result, they are typically written back subject to a 7-day cancellation clause and payment of an additional premium. The 7-day cancellation clause gives insurers the opportunity to withdraw coverage at very

---

[64] *Passenger and third party legal liability* refers to the liability that an airline or other aviation operator may incur by reason of the operation of law should an accident or incident occur which causes its passengers or third parties to suffer death, bodily injury, wounding, loss of, or damage to their property, or delay of baggage and cargo. This usually takes the form of compensation and/or damages which the primary operator is called upon to pay, which is then transferred to the insurer.

[65] As of this writing, the most current versions of the AVN 52 extended coverage endorsement series published by the AICG were: Aviation Insurance Clauses Group (2006b), (AVN 52K) and: Aviation Insurance Clauses Group (2006a), (AVN 52P).

[66] Margo (1996) pp. 446–447.

[67] Idem., p. 447.

[68] *Aircraft hull* refers to the cost of replacing or repairing a destroyed or damaged aircraft after it has been involved in an accident or incident. This is usually paid directly to the insured owner or operator of the aircraft.

[69] Margo (1996) p. 446.

[70] Margo and Posner (2008) p. 473.

short notice and to re-assess the risk and the prices charged for covering them (usually after those risks have materialized).[71] In effect, although the aviation insurance policyholder may have obtained the requisite war risk insurance cover provided by the respective write-back endorsements, this could be cancelled at the option of the insurers by giving notice effective at the expiration of 7-days from the day on which the notice is issued.[72] Also, in the specific case of AVN 52, an insurer could cancel coverage by giving 48 hours notice to the insured in the event of a hostile detonation.[73]

As all risks insurers in the global aviation market are only willing to write back some and not all of the risks excluded by CWEC or AVN 48 in relation to aircraft hulls, additional hull war risks may be insured in the specialist hull war insurance market based in London.[74] This hull war market is separate and distinct from the global aviation insurance market. Indeed it is part of the British marine insurance market.[75] The wording normally used for this type of coverage is the *Aviation Hull "War and Allied Perils" Policy,* designated as the LSW 555 series.[76] Prior to September 11, 2001, the *Aviation Hull "War and Allied Perils" Policy*, (LSW 555B) was the standard hull war wording generally used in providing war risk cover for major airlines on the hull war market.[77] It provided coverage for

> loss of or damage to aircraft caused by, *inter alia*, war, invasion, acts of foreign enemies, hostilities, civil war, rebellion, revolution, insurrection, martial law, strikes, riots, civil commotions, labor disturbances, acts committed for political or terrorist purposes, malicious acts, acts of sabotage, confiscation, nationalization, seizure, restraint, detention, appropriation, requisition for title or use, and hijacking or any unlawful seizure or wrongful control of aircraft.[78]

---

[71] Idem.

[72] Margo (2000) p. 329.

[73] Aviation Insurance Clauses Group (2007), section 5(c).

[74] Margo (1996) p. 447.

[75] As the specialist hull war market in London remains an integral part of the marine market, it would appear that those distinctive marine market practices discussed in Sect. 3.2 above are applied in issuing aviation hull war policies. As such, in determining whether a particular peril is covered under a hull war policy, one has to determine whether it has first been excluded in the insured's all risk policy. In practice, however, this does not present much of a difficulty as the language of the hull war policy (LSW 555) in most cases amounts to a mirror reflection of the exclusionary language used in the all risks policy (AVN 48).

[76] See JLT Risk Solutions (2006). See also A bigger bang for your buck (2006) p. 26.

[77] Lloyds Market Association (1994), (LSW 555B), reproduced in Margo (2000) at p. 681.

[78] Margo (1996) p. 448. "The policy also provided coverage, up to policy limits, for ninety percent of any payments made because of threats against any insured aircraft, its passengers, or crew and for extra expenses incurred following confiscation, nationalization, seizure, hijacking of an insured aircraft, and related risks". See Lloyds Market Association (1994), (LSW 555B), section 2.

Among other things, however, the LSW 555B policy usually excluded loss damage or expense caused by war between the five major powers (whether declared or not);[79] confiscation, nationalization, seizure, restraint, detention, appropriation, and requisition for title or use by any government named in the policy schedule or any public or local authority acting thereunder;[80] and, loss or damage arising directly or indirectly out of any detonation of any nuclear or radioactive weapon of war.[81]

An LSW 555 policy amounts to a new contract of insurance in the first instance on the hull war market, since it does not write back into an existing policy risks which were previously excluded. "The policy is expressed to be subject to the same warranties, terms and conditions as are contained in the insured's hull all risks policy".[82] As there may be sudden changes in domestic and international political situations, LSW 555 insurers may, at any time, upon short notice to the insured (usually 7 days), cancel coverage, or review premium rates and/or the geographical limits applicable to the insurance.[83] If notice is given, and the insured accepts the new rate of premium, the conditions, or the geographical limits proposed by the insurer before the expiration of the notice, the existing policy may be reinstated by the insurer.[84] The policy is subject to automatic review of the premium, conditions, or geographical limits upon hostile detonation of any nuclear weapon,[85] and coverage may automatically terminate upon an outbreak of war between any of the major powers.[86]

A typical condition in most LSW 555 policies, commonly known as the material change clause, requires the insured to give immediate notification to the insurer of any material changes in the nature or area of the insured's operations, and no claim arising after the occurrence of any such material change over which the insured had control shall be recoverable unless the change had been previously notified to, and

---

[79] These are: United States, Russian Federation, People's Republic of China, United Kingdom and France. See Lloyds Market Association (1994), (LSW 555B), section 3(i)(a).

[80] These risks were otherwise covered by the policy except when they were carried out by certain governments specifically named in the policy schedule. See idem., sections 1(e) and 3(i)(b).

[81] Idem., section 3(ii).

[82] Margo (2000) p. 329.

[83] Lloyds Market Association (1994), (LSW 555B), section 5(1). See also Margo (2000) p. 329, fn. 24, where the author notes that: "This right was exercised by the war risk insurers of Kuwait Airways when the armed forces of Iraq overran Kuwait on 2nd August 1990. The airline's insurance brokers agreed with the insurers that the war risk cover could be cancelled from midnight on 9 August". See [1996] 1 Lloyd's L.R. 664 [KAC v. KIC, (Comm.)].

[84] Margo (1996) p. 448.

[85] Lloyds Market Association (1994), (LSW 555B), section 5(1)(b). If the revised terms are not acceptable to the insured, the policy will be cancelled 7 days after the time of the detonation which triggered the review. See Margo (1996) p. 449.

[86] Lloyds Market Association (1994), (LSW 555B), section 5(2). However, if the aircraft is in the air when such an outbreak of war occurs, the policy will continue in effect until the insured aircraft has completed its first landing thereafter. See Margo (1996) p. 449.

accepted by, the insurer.[87] Flowing from this condition, however, there is the tendency on the part of LSW 555 insurers to frequently classify changes in circumstances over which the insured operator has absolutely no control as material changes affecting the nature of the risk, and to seek a review of the policy under such instances.[88]

Together, these provisions in the AVN 51 and 52 write back endorsements and LSW 555 policies which allow automatic or short notice cancellation or review of policy terms enable insurers to take a step back to reconsider and re-rate the risks covered under the policy in the event that the risks were to become materially different as a result of changed circumstances or the occurrence of an insured peril. Although they inure to the benefit of insurers, from the perspective of the insured—the global aviation industry—these features cumulatively make private insurance coverage for aviation war risks extremely unstable, vulnerable and susceptible to market failure. However, before considering the phenomenon of market failure in war risk insurance markets following the occurrence of extreme insured events, it is useful at this stage to survey the judicial interpretations and meanings that have been ascribed to the various war risk exclusionary terms commonly used in aviation insurance policies.

3.4 Judicial Interpretations of War Risk Exclusionary Terms Commonly Used in Aviation Insurance Policies

So far, the discussion in this chapter has focused on the evolution of war risk exclusions in insurance generally, and in aviation insurance in particular. Primarily, exclusion clauses are intended to protect insurance companies from extraordinarily hazardous risks.[89] The exclusions section of an aviation insurance contract therefore allows the insurer to explicitly set forth those risks which are not covered in the contract.[90] Exclusion clauses often result in litigation when a policyholder is denied coverage after he has sustained loss from an aviation accident. Although courts recognize the legality of war risk exclusion clauses as well as the insurer's right to

[87] Lloyds Market Association (1994), (LSW 555B), section 4(2). For the purposes of the policy, "material change" means any change in the operation of the insured which might reasonably be regarded by the insurers as increasing their risk in degree or frequency, or reducing possibilities of recovery or subrogation. See Margo (1996) p. 329, fn. 23.

[88] For instance, where an airline's core operations remain unchanged despite the outbreak of hostilities (i.e. the airline has neither increased nor decreased frequencies, is not ferrying troops or ammunitions and is not in any other way involved in the hostilities), it cannot be said that there has been a material change in the nature of the risk which justifies re-assessment and re-pricing.

[89] Simon (1991).

[90] Libby (1995) p. 622.

limit its liability, in almost all such instances, the dispute between the insured and the insurer centers around the meaning of the exclusion, and the question as to what was excluded and what was not.[91]

In construing an insurance policy, the duty of the court is to determine the true meaning and intent of the contracting parties from the four corners of the policy.[92] As such, a court of law would usually avoid re-writing an insurance contract for the parties, and would enforce a war risk exclusion if it is properly drafted.[93] Courts normally apply fundamental principles in the construction of insurance policies when analyzing claims by an insured (e.g., that an all-risks policy with a war exclusion clause covers a loss), or to the contrary claims by an insurer (e.g., that a war risk policy does not cover a loss).[94] These fundamental principles include the common meaning doctrine, which requires that words used in an insurance policy must be construed in their plain, ordinary, common and popular sense, except when it is apparent from the face, scope and purpose of the contract that the words were intended by the parties to have some special meaning. Where such is the case, the court will ascribe the technical or special meaning intended by the parties to the words.[95] On the other hand, in line with the doctrine of *contra proferentem*,[96] courts will normally construe ambiguities in an insurance contract against the party that drafted the contract—usually the insurer—and in favour of the other party, the insured, irrespective of whether the insured is an individual or a large corporation.[97] In this section, an attempt is made to decipher the essential meanings of the various terms commonly used in aviation war risk exclusion clauses by surveying interpretations ascribed to those terms by English and American Courts over the years.

At the outset, a few caveats must be sounded. It must be emphasized that although "[e]ach of the terms used in the war risk exclusion to describe actions that fall within the exclusion has been subject to rather extensive litigation",[98] some of the resulting judicial decisions were either based on, or heavily influenced by, the particular facts of the case. Where practicable in the ensuing discussion, such decisions are distinguished since they did not establish judicial precedents which

[91] Idem., pp. 622–623.

[92] Idem., p. 626.

[93] Idem.

[94] See Caban (2003) p. 434.

[95] Libby (1995) pp. 624–645.

[96] This is a rule commonly used in the construction of contracts generally, and in the construction of contracts of insurance in particular. The import of the rule is that any ambiguous or uncertain language will be construed against the party who drafted it. Although the insurer is often the party who drafts the wording of the policy, there are occasions in which the insured, through his broker, proffers a form of wording to the insurer for his acceptance. In such cases, the operation of the doctrine will ensure that the wording is construed as having that meaning least favorable to the insured. The rule applies only in cases of real ambiguity or uncertainty, and may not be used to create an ambiguity or uncertainty where none exists. See Margo (2000) pp. 454–455.

[97] See 368 F. Supp. 1098 (S.D.N.Y. 1973) p. 1122. See also: Bidinger and Bninski (1974) p. 1175.

[98] Margo and Posner (2008) p. 473.

are of direct relevance to the war risk exclusions found in commercial aviation insurance policies. Margo, for instance, recognizes limitations in the usefulness of some judicial precedents in this area when he notes:

> [m]ost of the reported cases in the English courts relate to losses occurring during the two World Wars in the context of marine insurance policies. Prior to the decision in *Pan Am World Airways, Inc. v. Aetna Casualty and Surety Co., et al.* . . . there was only a handful of reported cases which dealt with war risks in the aviation insurance context. Those cases, which were decided in the United States, dealt mostly with the question of whether a particular air crew member or passenger had been killed in, or as a result of, war, for the purpose of determining the application or otherwise of a war risk exclusion in a life insurance policy. . . . There have been no similar cases reported in the English courts.[99]

As noted above,[100] one of the leading cases in terms of the construction of war risk exclusions in the context of aviation insurance policies is the U.S. District Court decision of *Pan Am World Airways, Inc. v. Aetna Casualty and Surety Co., et al.*[101] Recall that Pan American World Airways Inc., whose Boeing 747 aircraft had been hijacked and destroyed in Cairo by members of the PFLP had taken out, among other insurances, all-risks hull insurance policies containing an identical war exclusion clause, and "the principal question facing the court was whether to construe the war risk exclusion clause in a manner that precluded recovery for the loss of the . . . aircraft under the all-risk policies. Under the terms of the war risk clause, losses stemming from the following risks were not insured: (a) insurrection, rebellion, revolution, civil war; (b) capture, seizure, taking, or destruction by a military or usurped power; (c) war or warlike operations whether there be a declaration of war or not; and (d) riots or civil commotion".[102] In answering the question, the court critically analyzed the circumstances leading to the destruction of the aircraft—the hijacking by members of the PFLP—in the light of each of the foregoing exclusions, and eventually concluded that those circumstances did not fall within the ambit of any of the exclusions.

In spite of the fact that the all-risks insurers in the Pan Am case were familiar with notions of hijacking and terrorism prevailing at the time, and the fact that specific exclusionary terms reasonably apt and precise to describe risks arising therefrom were readily available and in wide usage in other markets,[103] they simply failed to incorporate such terms specifically to exclude those risks from the all risks policies issued to Pan American. The all-risks insurers argued that the hijacking

[99] Margo (2000) p. 334, fn. 58 [citations omitted]. See also Libby (1995) pp. 622–642, where the author analyzes American judicial decisions relating to war risk aviation insurance exclusions in the context of life insurance policies.

[100] See Sect. 3.4 above for a brief statement of the facts of this case.

[101] 368 F. Supp. 1098 (S.D.N.Y. 1973).

[102] Bidinger and Bninski (1974) p. 1174.

[103] The District Court in Pan Am made specific reference to, and took judicial notice of, clause AVN 48 which, at the time, was in wide circulation and use on the London and U.S. markets, and which was contemporaneously vivid to the American all-risk insurers. See 368 F. Supp. 1098 (S.D.N.Y. 1973) pp. 1119–1120.

could be characterized as a riot, and also that the use of a range of exclusionary terms from "war" down to "riot" exhausted all conceivable possibilities so the loss must be caught by at least one of them.[104] The U.S. Court of Appeals rejected these contentions made by the all-risks insurers, affirming the decision of the District Court to the effect that:

> Where the risk [of hijacking] is well known and there are terms reasonably apt and precise to describe it, the use of substantially less certain phraseology, upon which dictionaries and common understanding may fairly differ, is likely to result in interpretations favouring coverage rather than exclusion. ... As reflected by their array of alternative proposals in this case, the words of exclusion upon which these defendants rely are not in any instance applicable with a comfortable degree of aptness to the circumstances of the disputed loss.[105]

The U.S. Court of Appeals explained further that:

> ... each of the exclusionary terms has dimensions besides the level of violence ... The doctrine of *contra proferentem* shrinks the all risk 'overlapping areas' to mere points on a line of violence. The lacunae between these points include the vast number of nameless causes [such as hijacking] that are not precisely described by the terms actually employed.[106]

Flowing from this, it becomes immediately necessary and extremely important that all parties to an insurance contract, especially insurers and reinsurers, understand both the particular meanings of each of the exclusionary terms they employ, and also appreciate the fact that "such terms will be of varying efficacy depending on several factors including the burden of proof, whether they appear in an 'all risks' or traditional 'named peril' context, and indeed, the law governing the contract [of insurance]".[107]

3.4.1 *War, Invasion, Civil War, Warlike Operations, Hostilities, Insurrection, Rebellion, Revolution, Military or Usurped Power*

A common practice of the insurance markets is to cluster together those excluded risks that are similar or closely related to each other. It is also common practice for a court of law to look at how an exclusion clause is structured in an effort to construe the meaning of the words appearing therein. The exclusion clauses in the Pan American case were no exception. In determining whether the loss of the aircraft was due to or resulted from

---

[104] Marangos and Tobin (2007a) p. 24.

[105] 368 F. Supp. 1098 (S.D.N.Y. 1973) p. 1118.

[106] 505 F.2d 989 (2d Cir. 1974) p. 1005. Mustill J expressed similar concerns in [1980] 1 Lloyd's L.R. 406 at 428, when he stated that he was "not convinced that all the listed perils lie in a straight line with riot at the bottom and civil war at the top. Some appear to stand to one side".

[107] Marangos and Tobin (2007a) p. 25.

the risks of *civil war, revolution, rebellion or insurrection*, the District Court in the Pan Am case set about to consider: (1) whether an insurrection or rebellion existed at all times material to the destruction of the aircraft; and, (2) whether the loss was one due to or resulting therefrom.

Relying upon a 1954 decision of the First Circuit U.S. Court of Appeals in *Home Insurance Co. v. Davila*,[108] in which an "insurrection" had been defined to mean "a violent uprising by a group or movement acting for the specific purpose of overthrowing the constituted government and seizing its powers",[109] the court concluded that the concepts of civil war, revolution, rebellion and insurrection involved, or at least envisaged, some element of an attack against a government, with "insurrection" being "a somewhat less august (more embryonic, smaller scale) attack upon a government than 'rebellion', and a less momentous and organized conflict than a 'civil war'."[110] The Court of Appeals affirmed this decision holding that "rebellion, revolution and civil war are progressive stages in the development of civil unrest the most rudimentary form of which is insurrection".[111] As such, if no insurrection had occurred, then a rebellion or civil war could not have existed contemporaneously.[112] Both courts concluded that neither an insurrection nor a rebellion existed at all times material to the destruction of the aircraft.

Having decided that there was neither an insurrection nor a rebellion in existence at all times relevant to the destruction of the aircraft, there was no need for the District Court to determine whether the loss was due to, or resulted from, any of those perils. However, by holding in the alternative that there must have been a direct link between the destruction of the aircraft in question and the alleged insurrection for the war risk exclusion to apply, the court impliedly resorted to

---

[108] 212 F.2d 731 (1st Cir. 1954). The court in this case decided that an intention to violently overthrow the government was an essential element of an insurrection. The court, however, distinguished the intent to cause the violent overthrow of the government (which it held to be the hallmark of an insurrection) from the intent to fire a shot heard around the world for propaganda purposes. The *Pan Am* court did not fully accept this inclusion of intent as an element of insurrection, noting that while it was a necessary condition, in and of itself, intent was not sufficient. See Bidinger and Bninski (1974) p. 1176.

[109] 368 F. Supp. 1098 (S.D.N.Y. 1973) p. 1124.

[110] Idem., pp. 1123–1124; Bidinger and Bninski (1974) p. 1176. See also [1991] 2 Lloyd's L.R. 281 where Saville J held, concerning Renamo rebel activities in Mozambique in the 1980s, that:

> 'Rebellion' and 'insurrection' have somewhat similar meanings to each other. To my mind, each means an organized and violent internal uprising in a country with, as a main purpose, the object of trying to overthrow or supplant the government of that country, though 'insurrection' denotes a lesser degree of organisation and size than 'rebellion'.

[111] 505 F.2d 989 (2d Cir. 1974) p. 1017. However, Mustill J in [1980] 1 Lloyd's L.R. 406 did not find the practice of ranking such phenomena especially helpful.

[112] It had been held previously in 67 U.S. (2 Black) 635 (1862) p. 666 that: "Insurrection against a government may or may not culminate in an organized rebellion, but a civil war always begins by insurrection against the lawful authority of the Government".

the theory of proximate cause in construing the exclusion.[113] According to one commentary, "[r]elevant precedents, when applied to the peculiar facts of the *Pan American* case, appear to support the court's interpretation and application of the theory of proximate cause. Under accepted insurance principles, if an insured ship or airplane is taken or seized as a result of a war risk, including an insurrection, but is subsequently destroyed due to a nonwar peril, ... the loss is covered by war-risk insurance".[114] It would therefore appear from the foregoing that where the exclusionary language used in an aviation insurance policy excludes losses "due to or resulting from" certain specified risks, those losses will be held excluded by a court of law only if they are proximately caused by the specified risks.

Although the Pan Am court declined to rule directly on the question as to what constitutes a *military or usurped power*, it nevertheless agreed that "occupation of ground by sufferance of the *de jure* government is surely insufficient"[115] to establish the existence of a military or usurped power. There has been some debate in the jurisprudence and literature regarding the status in which a belligerent must be in order to be capable of exercising military or usurped power. For instance, it has been said in one commentary that, by merely stating that the PFLP was not such a power, the District Court in the *Pan Am* case followed over 100 years of judicial precedent, since no U.S. court had previously ruled that for a group to be a military or usurped power for insurance purposes, it must also be a *de facto* government.[116]

On the contrary, other courts and commentators have expressed the view that to give rise to a military or usurped power, it is absolutely necessary that the belligerents attain the status of a *de facto* government.[117] In supporting the latter view, the Second Circuit Court of Appeals in the *Pan Am* case authoritatively held that "in order to constitute a military or usurped power, the power must be at least that of a *de facto* government".[118] A few years later, an English court politely rejected the above mentioned decision of the U.S. Court of Appeal and confirmed that under English law, there was no such need for a *de facto* government to exist.[119]

---

113 Bidinger and Bninski (1974) p. 1178.

114 This principle was set forth by the U.S. Supreme Court in 267 U.S. 76 (1925), where the Court stated: [I]f a vessel should be taken from an owner's hands without his consent and should be lost while thus held by a paramount power, obviously a company that had insured against such taking could not look beyond and attribute the loss to a peril of the sea. Whatever happens while the taking insured against continues fairly may be attributed to the taking. See Bidinger and Bninski (1974) p. 1179.

115 368 F. Supp. 1098 (S.D.N.Y. 1973) p. 1129.

116 See Bidinger and Bninski (1974) p. 1182.

117 See Vinciguerra (1974–1975) pp. 925–926. This commentator cites the American case of 95 U.S. (5 Otto) 117 (1877) as well as the English case of 95 E.R. 863 (K.B. 1767) in support of this assertion.

118 505 F.2d 989 (2d Cir. 1974) p. 1009. Margo, however, is of the view that this is not the law in England, as none of the English cases places the test as high as this. He refers to Mustill J's decision in [1980] 1 Lloyd's L.R. 406 p. 435.

119 [1980] 1 Lloyd's L.R. 406.

As the authorities on this issue are at best unsettled, it would appear that in the U.S., a military or usurped power would be construed as involving "an invasion by a foreign power or an internal rebellion in which the insurgent force or foreign power assumes the reins of government [*de facto*] by making laws and by punishing for failure to obey those laws".[120] Accordingly, the District Court in the *Pan Am* case correctly held that "[i]f the phrase [military or usurped power] meant anything, it refers to action by a 'power' within or near or related to the controlled territory".[121] Margo adds that "military or usurped power includes not only the acts of foreign enemies engaged in warfare within the realm or of subjects of the Crown engaged in external rebellion but also acts done by forces of the Crown in repelling foreign enemies or suppressing the rebellion".[122] On the other hand, English courts are more likely to recognize the exercise of military or usurped power by an entity that has not yet attained the status of a *de facto* government.

With respect to *war*, the District Court in the *Pan Am* case found that the term "... has been defined almost always as the employment of force between governments or entities essentially like governments, at least *de facto*".[123] In affirming this finding, the Second Circuit Court of Appeals noted, when the *Pan Am* case came before it on appeal, that "war is a course of hostility engaged in by entities that have at least significant attributes of sovereignty. Under international law, war is waged by state-like entities".[124] Thus, a conflict will be considered to be a war for insurance exclusion purposes only if the belligerents involved therein have at least the significant attributes of sovereignty. In *Kawasaki Kisen Kabushiki Kaisha of Kobe v. Bantham Steamship Co. Ltd (No. 2)*,[125] a case primarily concerning the cancellation of a charterparty on the grounds of war, the English Court of Appeals rejected the submission that the term "war" had a technical meaning based on principles of public international law; namely that it had to be declared to be a war. Instead, the court held that "... in the particular context in which the word war is found ... that word must be construed, having regard to the general tenor and purpose of the document, in what may be called a common sense way".[126]

---

[120] Vinciguerra (1974–1975) p. 924.

[121] 368 F. Supp. 1098 (S.D.N.Y. 1973) 1130. In the present case, since the scene of the loss—Cairo—was far removed from Jordan, where the PFLP had taken control of a small portion of territory under sufferance of the Jordanian government, it was held that the PFLP was not a military or usurped power.

[122] Margo (2000) p. 343.

[123] 368 F. Supp. 1098 (S.D.N.Y. 1973) 1130. In support, the court cites the case of 67 U.S. (2 Black) 635 (1862) pp. 666–667.

[124] 505 F.2d 989 (2d Cir. 1974) 1012. The court was quick to add however that the international law definition of war does not necessarily govern the insurance meaning of the term, but it provides a starting place for enquiry. See idem., fn. 12.

[125] [1939] 2 K.B. 544.

[126] Idem., pp. 558–559, per Sir Wilfrid Greene M.R.

In the same vein, English courts interpreting the term *civil war* in insurance contracts have indicated that the term refers to a war with a special characteristic of being civil—i.e., internal rather than external.[127] In *Spinney's Case*, Judge Mustill went on to specify the particular characteristics of a civil war, succinctly summarized in one commentary as follows:

> (a) There must be opposing 'sides' in the sense that it is possible to 'say of each fighting man that he owes allegiance to one side or another, and it must also be possible to identify each side by reference to a community of objective, leadership and administration'; ...
>
> (b) The objectives of the warring sides must be of a certain scale, including (i) to seize all or part of a state, or if not, (ii) to 'force changes in the way in which power is exercised without fundamentally changing the existing political structure', or (iii) to be motivated by tribal, racial or ethnic animosities.
>
> ...[128]

Judge Mustill hastened to add that "[n]evertheless a civil war is still a war. The words do not simply denote a violent internal conflict on a large scale",[129] thereby distinguishing a civil war from a civil commotion. The U.K. House of Lords has also confirmed the position held by most English courts that the term "war" includes civil war unless a contrary intention can be discerned.[130] In the United States, however, a district court has held that civil war implies the element of a specific intent to overthrow the government.[131]

With regard to *warlike operations*, the District Court in the *Pan Am* case wholeheartedly adopted the definition of the term as had been previously stated by Lord Atkinson in the 1921 English case of *Britain Steamship Co., Ltd. v. The King*,[132]

> The term '*hostilities*' refers to acts or operations of war committed by belligerents; it presupposes an existing state of war ... There seems no reason to doubt that the [term] applies to acts committed in the course of a civil war; and perhaps also to an organized armed rebellion... '*Warlike operations*' have a much wider reach, and not only include 'hostilities,' but cover, even where a state of war does not exist, operations of such a general kind or character as belligerents have recourse to in war, as for instance where combative operations are undertaken to suppress a rebellion against an allied or friendly power .... The transfer of the combative forces of a power from one area of war to another, or from one part of an area of war to another part, for combative purposes, would ... be a 'warlike operation' ... as would be also the patrolling by the ships of war ... for the purpose of

[127] [1980] 1 Lloyd's L.R. 406 p. 429 per Mustill J.; [1991] 2 Lloyd's L.R. 281.

[128] [1980] 1 Lloyd's L.R. 406 pp. 429–430; Marangos and Tobin (2007a) p. 30.

[129] [1980] 1 Lloyd's L.R. 406 429.

[130] (1949) 82 Lloyd's L.R. 501 p. 513, where Lord Morton stated:

> ... the word 'war' in a policy of insurance includes civil war unless the context makes it clear that a different meaning should be given to the word... I can see no good reason for giving to the word 'war' a meaning which excludes one type of 'war'.

[131] 571 F. Supp. 1460 (S.D.N.Y., 1983) pp. 1494–1498; See also Marangos and Tobin (2007a) p. 30.

[132] [1921] A.C. 99.

> preventing invasion, or even for the purpose of protecting from hostile attack by enemy vessels the lives and property of the inhabitants of its seaboard towns.[133]

Although the term *warlike operations* has been held to be a much broader concept than the term *war*, a court of law construing a warlike operations exclusion clause in an insurance policy will, in all likelihood, "characterize warlike operations as involving actions identical to those taken by military or naval forces in connection with an actual war".[134] In other words, by their very nature, *warlike operations* are restricted in scope only to those "perils due directly to some hostile action, military maneuver or operational war danger, and ... [do] not include the aggravation or increase of [an existing] ... risk because of war operations".[135] The District Court in the *Pan Am* case alluded to this point when it expressed the view that:

> There is no warrant in general understanding of English, in history, or in precedent for reading the phrase 'warlike operations' to encompass the infliction of intentional violence by political groups (neither employed by nor representing governments) upon civilian citizens of non-belligerent powers and their property at places far removed from the locale or the subject of any warfare. This conclusion is merely reinforced when the evident and avowed purpose of the destructive action is not coercion or conquest in any sense, but the striking of spectacular blows for propaganda effects.[136]

3.4.2 Hostile Detonation or Use of Any Nuclear Weapon of War, Radioactive Force or Matter, Chemical, Biochemical or Biological Materials

As exclusions, the terms: hostile detonation or use of any nuclear weapon of war, radioactive force or matter, chemical, biochemical or biological materials have not been interpreted by the courts as yet. However, it is not difficult to foresee disputes arising from the interpretation of the word hostile. Does the term refer to the intentions of the person or entity causing the detonation or to the effect of the detonation upon third parties? A detonation may not be intended to be hostile by those causing it, but its effect upon an insured might in fact be hostile. For instance, if an insured airline suffers damage or loss as a result of a detonation of a nuclear

---

[133] Idem., p. 114 per Lord Atkinson, reproduced in: Bidinger and Bninski (1974) p. 1185. See also [1980] 1 Lloyd's L.R. 406 p. 437 where Mustill J held:

> The term "hostilities" refers to acts or operations of war committed by belligerents; it presupposes an existing state of war ... There seems no reason to doubt that the [term] applies to acts committed in the course of a civil war; and perhaps also to an armed organized rebellion ... "Warlike operations" has a wider meaning and includes such operations as belligerents have recourse to in war, even though no state of war exists ... Nevertheless, the acts must be done in the context of a war ...

[134] Bidinger and Bninski (1974) p. 1184.

[135] See178 F.2d 488 (1949), aff'd 340 U.S. 54 (1950).

[136] 368 F. Supp. 1098 (S.D.N.Y. 1973) p. 1130.

weapon and it alleges that the detonation was not hostile, but fails to establish the non-hostile intentions of those who caused it, would the damage or loss be covered or excluded under an insurance policy that excludes losses arising from hostile detonation of such weapons? Having regard to the fact that a court of law will likely resolve ambiguities in an insurance contract in favour of the insured under the doctrine of contra proferentem, it behoves on insurers to draft such clauses in such a manner as to clearly demonstrate the exact meaning they intend when they use words such as "hostile detonation or use".

3.4.3 Strikes, Riots, Civil Commotions or Labour Disturbances

As pointed out by the Second Circuit Court of Appeals in the *Pan Am* case, the existing legal authorities as to the insurance meaning of *riot* was in some considerable disarray at the time the matter was pending before the District Court.[137] There was one body of authority that nominally supported a technical definition of riot.[138] There was also a second body of authority which suggested that a common law riot must, as a matter of necessity, be accompanied by a tumult or commotion. There was yet a third body of authority to the effect that, in insurance, the term *riot* takes its meaning from common speech, namely a tumultuous assembly of a multitude of people.[139]

Faced with these conflicting interpretations of the term, the District Court applied the doctrine of *contra proferentem*, the effect of which was to cast upon the proponents of the riot exclusion—the all-risk insurers—the burden of showing that the technical definition of "riot", which they sought to rely upon, was the only reasonable formulation.[140] Such proof not forthcoming, the court determined that the popular and usual meaning of the term would govern, as, on the face of the policy, this was the meaning intended by the parties.[141] According to the court, the ordinary meaning of riot evoked images of such wild disorders as "draft riots", "prison riots", "bread riots", and "student riots"; uproar, tumult and violent mobs.[142] The Court of Appeal upheld the common meaning approach relied upon

---

[137] 505 F.2d 989 (2d Cir. 1974) p. 1021.

[138] See e.g., [1907] 2 K.B. 853 p. 860, where the following technical criteria for establishing a riot was set out: (1) there must have been at least three participants; (2) they must have had a common purpose; (3) there must have been execution or inception of the common purpose; (4) the persons concerned must have intended to help one another, by force if necessary, in the execution of the common purpose; and, (5) force or violence must have been displayed in such manner as to alarm at least one person of reasonable firmness and courage.

[139] 505 F.2d 989 (2d Cir. 1974) p. 1021.

[140] Idem.

[141] On the contrary, it had been clearly established that the two non-technical definitions of riot requiring tumult were at least reasonable. See idem.

[142] 368 F. Supp. 1098 (S.D.N.Y. 1973) p. 1132.

by the District Court, holding that: "... under this formula, a riot occurs when some multitude of individuals gathers and creates a tumult".[143]

In the same manner, *civil commotion* was held by the District Court in the *Pan Am* case to denote, in its ordinary sense, "encounters 'such as occur among fellow-citizens or within the limits of one community', disturbance, disorder, turbulent crowds, and tumult having some extension in time or space".[144] Elaborating further, the District Court noted that "civil commotion occurs in a locale – a city, a county, perhaps a country, or an area. It is essentially a domestic disturbance ....."[145] Perhaps the most comprehensive description of what amounts to a civil commotion was that provided by the Privy Council in its ruling in the case of *Levy v. Assicurazione Generali*:[146]

> The phrase 'civil commotion' is used to indicate a stage between a riot and a civil war. It has been defined to mean an insurrection of the people for general purposes, though not amounting to rebellion; but it is probably not capable of any very precise definition. The element of turbulence or tumult is essential; an organised conspiracy to commit criminal acts, where there is no tumult or disturbance until after the acts, does not amount to civil commotion. It is not, however, necessary to show the existence of any outside organisation at whose instigation the acts were done.[147]

The District Court in the *Pan Am* case justified its use of the ordinary meaning approach in construing the terms *riot* and *civil commotion* on the basis of the language of the insurance policy itself. As some able commentators have succinctly pointed out, "[b]y placing civil commotion in the exclusion clause with strikes and riots, which are considered local disturbances, a category was created [in the policy] that the court held could be 'fairly characterized as 'domestic disturbances''".[148] Thus, not only did the court rely upon the ordinary meaning approach in construing the exclusions; it also looked at the words surrounding the terms being construed for purposes of determining what the parties intended those words to mean. In so doing, the court paid allegiance to the established age old common law canon of construction that: "[i]f it is found that things described by particular words have some common characteristic which constitutes them a genus, the general words that follow ought to be limited to things of that genus".[149] In essence, the effect of this canon, also known as the *ejusdem generis* rule, is that words will be construed in the light of the color they derive from other surrounding words.

---

[143] 505 F.2d 989 (2d Cir. 1974) p. 1021.

[144] 368 F. Supp. 1098 (S.D.N.Y. 1973) pp. 1132–1133.

[145] Idem., p. 1137.

[146] [1940] 67 Lloyd's L.R. 174.

[147] Idem., p. 179.

[148] Bidinger and Bninski (1974) p. 1191.

[149] See Lewison (2004) p. 224.

3.4.4 *Acts for Terrorist or Political Purposes*

In the immediate aftermath of September 11, 2001, insurers and reinsurers were in general agreement concerning the necessity of limiting their exposures to terrorism. However, there was no universal consensus as to precisely what "terrorists", "terrorism", "acts of terror" or "acts for terrorist purposes" actually meant for insurance purposes.[150] Insurance law had previously tackled some important aspects of risks arising from terrorism,[151] yet unlike other typical terms such as "war" or "riot", there was no clear settled meaning of the term "terrorism" in judge-made common law.[152] It will be recalled that the aviation insurance exclusions dealing with acts for terrorist and political purposes were introduced as part of clause AVN 48B in or about 1968, following the increased incidence of aircraft hijacking and terrorism in that period. Being relatively new, these exclusionary terms have also not been considered by English courts in any detail.[153]

A U.S. court had a clear opportunity to consider the meaning of what constitutes a terrorist act for insurance purposes in 1991 in the case of *New Market Investment Corp. v. Fireman's Fund Insurance Co.*[154] At issue was whether the poisoning with cyanide of two grapes within a shipment of grapes imported from Chile amounted to a terrorist act. However, the judge did not provide a definition of terrorist purpose for the jury but left them to decide on the facts whether terrorism had taken place. The jury found that an act of terrorism had in fact taken place although the identity of the perpetrators was unknown. Faced with a dearth of judicial precedent as to what amounts to a terrorist act or terrorism for insurance purposes, the insurance industry has relied upon several general definitions of the terms found in criminal and other statutes.[155] However, these statutory definitions do not provide much guidance on the issue since, at best, they are inconsistent from one jurisdiction to the other and, at worst, they are ambiguous.[156]

Following the events of September 11, 2001, the attention of OECD Ministers was drawn to the lack of a standard definition of terrorism for compensation purposes both within OECD countries and the wider global community. The Ministers therefore commissioned a task force to assist the OECD Insurance

[150] Marangos and Tobin (2007b).

[151] For instance, in the Pan Am case, the destruction of the aircraft by the PFLP was classified as a terrorist act. So also was the destruction of three other aircraft by members of the PFLP at Dawson's Field in Jordan a few days earlier.

[152] Marangos and Tobin (2007b) p. 51.

[153] Thompson and Sloane (2001) p. 6.

[154] 774 F. Supp. 909 (1991).

[155] See e.g., the definition of "terrorism" in the U.K. Terrorism Act, 2000; the U.S. Terrorism Risk Insurance Act, etc.

[156] See Margo (2000) p. 348 where the author notes that the English statutory definition of terrorism as "any use of violence for the purpose of putting the public or any section of the public in fear", or "the use of violence for political ends" is clearly ambiguous and not capable of any precise definition for all purposes.

Committee to develop policy analysis and recommendations on the subject. As a result of this effort, the OECD published in December 2004 a *Checklist of Criteria to Define Terrorism for the Purpose of Compensation*.[157] The checklist provides a non-binding list of key elements for OECD and non-OECD countries to consider, which can be adapted to meet the needs of their specific market and regulatory frameworks as well as their policy objectives. These elements include the intention behind and the means and effect of an attack, the criteria required for the risk to be insurable (including economic, legal and regulatory factors), and the potential for compensation by the state or via other forms of financial protection, such as bonds.[158] According to the OECD, the Checklist which highlights the difficulties of defining terrorism and also surveys in tabular form the meanings ascribed to terrorism across different jurisdictions, is only illustrative and not intended to be binding.

What the insurance community needs is a clear and dry definition "that should, in theory at least, enable anyone examining the wording [of a terrorism exclusion clause] and the incident in question to arrive at more or less the same conclusions as to whether a 'terrorist' act has occurred, regardless of subjective factors, such as the examiner[']s own political outlook or environment".[159] For such a definition to be effective, it must be incorporated into the wording of the policy. The Lloyd's market definition of terrorism which has remained unchanged since immediately after 2001 is a good starting point. Under that definition, a terrorist act means:

> an act, including the use of force or violence, of any person or group(s) of persons whether acting alone or on behalf of or in connection with any organisation(s), committed for political, religious or ideological purposes including the intention to influence any government and/or put the public in fear for such purposes.[160]

3.4.5 Malicious Acts and Acts of Sabotage

In *Nishina Trading Co. Ltd., v. Chiyoda Fire and Marine Insurance Co. Ltd., (The Mandarin Star)*,[161] the English Court of Appeal held that an act which is performed maliciously is one which is done with "spite, or ill will, or the like".[162] *Maliciously*, according to Margo, "implies an intention to do an act which is wrongful to the detriment of another".[163] The question which usually arises is whether the malice (i.e., the spite or ill will) must be directed against the insured

[157] OECD (2004).

[158] DLA Piper Inc. (2005).

[159] Marangos and Tobin (2007b) p. 51.

[160] DLA Piper Inc. (2005) p. 2.

[161] [1969] 1 Lloyd's L.R. 293.

[162] Idem., p. 298, per Lord Denning.

[163] Margo (2000) p. 349.

victim for the exclusion to apply. It was held in *Strive Shipping Corp. v. Hellenic Mutual War Risks Association (The Grecia Express)*,[164] that "[t]he words [persons acting maliciously] ... cover causal or random vandalism and do not require proof that the person concerned had the purpose of injuring the assured or even knew the identity of the assured".[165] *Sabotage*, on the other hand, has been defined as the "malicious destruction of or damage to property, so as to injure e.g., a business or the military potential of a state".[166]

Another significant issue which arises in relation to the meaning and scope of the malicious acts exclusion is the question as to whether or not malicious acts include acts of terrorism. On a literal reading, terrorist acts are clearly malicious, and so would be encompassed within the scope of the malicious acts exclusion. However, as suggested in one commentary, the malicious acts exclusion "has a qualitative flavour that does not seem appropriate to describe terrorist acts".[167] This issue arose directly before the U.S. District Court for the Southern District of New York in the case of *SR International Business Insurance Co. Ltd., v. World Trade Center Properties LLC*.[168] The applicable contracts of insurance in this case were "per occurrence" policies which defined "occurrence" as "[a]ny one loss, disaster or casualty, or series of losses disasters or casualties arising out of one event. *When the word applies to loss or losses from the perils of ... vandalism and malicious mischief one event shall be construed to be all losses arising during a continuous period of seventy-two (72) hours*".[169] The insurers sought to limit their liability to the insured by arguing that the destruction of the World Trade Center buildings by two aircraft hijacked and eventually crashed into each of the two towers 16 minutes apart was one occurrence since the terrorist attacks were the result of vandalism and malicious mischief arising during a continuous period of 72 hours.

Applying New York canons of construction to the problem,[170] the court construed the meaning of the policy from the standpoint of a reasonably intelligent ordinary businessman and held that:

> while it can be argued that the attack on the World Trade Center fits within dictionary definitions of "malicious mischief" and "vandalism," it is doubtful that anyone familiar with the events of that day would describe what occurred as an act of malicious mischief or

---

[164] [2002] 2 Lloyd's L.R. 88.

[165] Idem., p. 96.

[166] Margo (2000) p. 349.

[167] Marangos and Tobin (2007a) p. 48.

[168] 2003 U.S. Dist. LEXIS 1103, 01 Civ. 9291 (JSM).

[169] Idem., pp. 15–16 [emphasis added].

[170] Under New York law, the terms of an insurance policy are interpreted from the vantage point of the "average person on the street". When interpreting a "specialized business policy", however, the average person is not the housewife purchasing flight insurance but the average purchaser of broad business liability insurance. Complex comprehensive general liability policies issued to large corporate manufacturers should be viewed as if by a reasonably intelligent business person who is familiar with the agreement and with the industry in question. Accordingly, the court applied tests of "common speech" and the "reasonable expectation and purpose of the ordinary businessman" in this case. See idem., pp. 19–20.

> vandalism ... it cannot be said that the ordinary businessman would consider an act of wanton terrorism such as the attack on the World Trade Center to be an act of malicious mischief or vandalism. One could argue that the Japanese attack on Pearl Harbor fits within the dictionary definition of "malicious mischief" or "vandalism". But if one searched all of the contemporaneous or historical accounts of that attack, it is doubtful that even one account would be found which described it as an act of malicious mischief or vandalism. Since the attack on the World Trade Center resulted in an even greater loss of life and property damage than the raid on Pearl Harbor, it is equally inappropriate to describe that attack as an act of malicious mischief or vandalism.[171]

This decision has been hailed as a "manifestly sensible ruling, to which an English Court would no doubt now have regard".[172] However, it would appear from the excerpts quoted above that the sheer magnitude of property damage and loss of life that occurred on September 11 (as compared to Pearl Harbor) weighed heavily on the court's decision not to characterize the terrorist attacks as acts of malicious mischief. It therefore remains to be seen whether the distinction between malicious acts and acts of terrorism will be upheld in a case involving terrorist damage on a smaller scale.

3.4.6 Confiscation, Nationalization, Seizure, Restraint, Detention, Appropriation, and Requisition for Title or Use

The various terms appearing in this exclusion namely: *confiscation; nationalization*; *seizure*; *restraint*; *detention*; *appropriation*; and, *requisition for title or use* are similar in meaning, although each one of them has a distinctive trait.[173] *Confiscation* has been held by an English court to mean the removal or seizure of property by the government of the country in which the property is situated.[174] It had previously been held in an earlier case that "confiscation must be an act done in some way on the part of the government of the country where it takes place and in some way beneficial to the government; though the proceeds may not, strictly speaking, be brought into its treasury".[175]

In 1976, the English Court of Appeal interpreted the meaning of *nationalization* in the context of a 1971 agreement under which the Egyptian government paid compensation for British property rights affected by the actions of the Egyptian government. Lord Denning expressed the view that, as used in the agreement, nationalization had a wide sense which "embraced all property which had been brought under the control of the State.... Such bringing under control may be done by its being taken over by a government department, or by a nationalised corporation, or by the government obtaining the shares in a company, or in any other way.

---

[171] Idem., pp. 21–22 [citations omitted].

[172] Marangos and Tobin (2007a) p. 48.

[173] Idem., p. 44.

[174] (1922) Lloyd's L.R. 7 pp. 12–13 per Bankes LJ. See also Margo (2000) p. 349.

[175] 15 East 267 (1812) p. 269 per Ellenborough CJ.

So long as it is taken under government control, it is nationalised".[176] Although the case did not primarily concern an insurance exclusion, the decision nevertheless provides some guidance as to how a court of law might construe the term in an insurance policy or insurance exclusion setting.

The case of *Kuwait Airways Corporation v. Kuwait Insurance Corporation*[177] is very instructive as to the meaning of the term *seizure* when it appears in an aviation insurance policy or exclusion clause. Fifteen aircraft and large quantities of spares and equipment belonging to Kuwait Airways were appropriated and removed from the Kuwait Airport by the government of Iraq after the invasion of Kuwait on August 2, 1990. Kuwait Airways had taken out war risks insurance policies which provided cover inter alia in respect of:

(a) War, invasion, acts of foreign enemies, hostilities ... civil war, rebellion, revolution, insurrection, martial law, military or usurped power or attempts at usurpation of power...

(e) Confiscation, nationalization, seizure, restraint, detention, appropriation, requisition for title or use by or under the order of any governmental ... or public or local authority.

By a separate endorsement, the policy was extended to cover loss or damage to aircraft spares and equipment belonging to Kuwait Airways resulting from any of the perils listed in the policy except those specified in clause (a).[178] The policy nevertheless provided cover for the said aircraft spares and equipment in respect of clause (a) perils whilst in transit by sea or air. It was not disputed that the cause of the loss of the aircraft and spares was an event falling within paragraph (a), i.e., *invasion* of Kuwait by Iraq and the *acts of foreign enemies* (Iraq). However, Kuwait Airways argued that the spares were also lost as a result of "seizure" by the Iraqi government so that the loss would be covered under paragraph (e) of the policy. The insurers argued that there was not intended to be any overlap between paragraphs (a) and (e), and that the seizure in paragraph (e) was only intended to be restricted to non-belligerent seizures by governments which were performed under the colour of law. The trial judge accepted the insurer's argument.[179] On appeal, the Court of Appeal unanimously rejected the trial judge's findings on this question. Lord Justice Otton stated:

> I see no reason to construe the word [seizure] narrowly, or to deprive the relevant peril of its usual meaning; the peril of seizure within this policy has no different meaning from that which would normally be ascribed to it. The word has a well accepted commercial usage in the context of insurance.... I am unable to accept that paragraph (e) perils are limited to the acts of governments or other public authority within their own territories. The assets of an international corporation can be situated in many countries throughout the world. They are not necessarily all fixed assets. Thus one sovereign government might confiscate a fixed asset or restrain an aircraft of another national Airline lying within the territory and make a demand (usually in money) which must be satisfied before the aircraft will be released.[180]

[176] [1976] Q.B. 297 p. 309 per Lord Denning MR [emphasis added].

[177] [1999] 1 Lloyd's L.R. 803 (HL) [KAC v. KIC (HL)].

[178] Idem., p. 811.

[179] [1996] 1 Lloyd's L.R. 664 [KAC v. KIC, (Comm.)], per Rix J.

[180] [1997] 2 Lloyd's L.R. 687 (CA) [KAC v. KIC (CA)] p 700, per Otton L.J.

This finding was subsequently affirmed by a majority decision in the House of Lords. Delivering the opinion of the majority, Lord Hobhouse cited the old English case of *Cory v. Burr*,[181] in which it had been held that "the ordinary meaning of the word 'seizure' is 'the act of taking forcible possession either by lawful authority or overpowering force' and *this is its ordinary meaning in an insurance policy*".[182] This ordinary meaning of the term, according to the learned law lord, is inclusive; "it includes both belligerent and non-belligerent forceable dispossession".[183] Lord Hobhouse noted further that: "Were the ordinary meaning of the word seizure confined to peaceful seizures, it could certainly be said that the context was not clear enough to widen that meaning so as to refer also to all forcible seizures. But where, as here, the ordinary meaning of the word is any forcible seizure, the context does not suffice to show that the word must have been used in some special or restricted sense".[184] This suggests that in construing an insurance policy, a court of law would likely reject arguments based on inferences drawn from the context which seek to restrict the clear ordinary meaning of the word. On the other hand, a court would be open to widening the ordinary meaning of words where the context in which they have been used is not clear.

In his dissenting opinion in the *Kuwait Airways* case, however, Lord Browne-Wilkinson disagreed with the foregoing method of construction. He was of the view that "[t]he word seizure does not have one meaning that it bears in all normal circumstances",[185] and that the context in which it is used always influences its intended meaning. He pointed out that Lord FitzGerald's definition of the term in *Cory v. Burr*[186] relied upon by the majority did not categorically state that the normal and usual meaning of seizure included forcible capture, but that it *may* include, or is capable of including, such behaviour.[187] Accordingly, in his judgment, a determination as to whether or not "seizure" as used in an insurance policy includes forcible capture must, as a matter of necessity, depend on the context in which the word is used. Examining the context in which the word appeared in the Kuwait Airways policy, Lord Browne-Wilkinson held that it was

[181] 8 App. Cas. 393 (1883). This was a case concerning the ordinary meaning of seizure as used in marine policies. The House of Lords rejected the argument that the word seizure was confined to belligerent seizure and held instead that:

"'Seizure' seems to be a larger term than 'capture' and goes beyond it, and may be reasonably interpreted to embrace every act of taking forcible possession either by a lawful authority or by overpowering force". See idem., p. 405 per Lord FitzGerald.

[182] [1999] 1 Lloyd's L.R. 803 (HL) [KAC v. KIC (HL)] p. 814 [emphasis added].

[183] Idem.

[184] Idem., p. 815.

[185] Idem., p. 807, per Lord Browne-Wilkinson.

[186] 8 App. Cas. 393 (1883).

[187] [1999] 1 Lloyd's L.R. 803 (HL) [KAC v. KIC (HL)] 807, per Lord Browne-Wilkinson.

clear that each of the paragraphs (a)–(f) of the policy was designed to deal with one particular type of peril, exclusively of perils dealt with by other paragraphs.[188]

As such, "[t]o take a risk of a kind which is plainly a war risk and say that it is not only covered by the war risk clause (paragraph (a)), but also by another clause is ... to give a false and unnatural meaning to the policy".[189] In his view, such an approach would also mean that "almost any event which occurs in a war (and therefore covered by paragraph (a)) is also a 'malicious act' within paragraph (d)".[190] This would mean that the exclusion from cover of risks under paragraph (a) would be wholly ineffective. Lord Browne-Wilkinson's dissenting opinion appears to be the preferred view; it is in line with the later decision of the US District Court for the Southern District of New York in *SR International Business Insurance Co. Ltd., v. World Trade Center Properties LLC*,[191] discussed in Sect. 3.4.5 above.

Lord Hobhouse also had the following to say in the Kuwait Airways case about the meaning of *requisition for title or use*:

> The phrase 'requisition for title or use' is strongly supportive of the normal meaning of the word seizure. Requisition is typically something which occurs in the time of war or hostilities involving an exercise of executive or military power. ... From the point of view of the assured it would make no difference whether the aircraft (or spares) were requisitioned to assist the war effort of the foreign government, as, for example, by providing transport for their armed forces, or by way of outright seizure. The situations are directly analogous as are the consequences.[192]

There is a dearth of modern judicial authority on the meaning of the following terms: *restraint*, *detention*, and *appropriation*. Margo, however, states that restraint is the action of restraining or checking a thing or operation;[193] that detention involves a taking with intent to return the property taken,[194] whereas appropriation

---

[188] In this regard, his Lordship found that: "[p]aragraph (a) deals with belligerent risks; paragraph (b) with risks caused by civilian gatherings and commotions; paragraph (c) with acts of terrorism and political unrest; paragraph (d) with deliberate damage to property not covered by any other paragraphs; paragraph (e) losses from the assumption of control over the property by the local government whether national or at a lower rank". See idem., 807, per Lord Browne-Wilkinson.

[189] Idem.

[190] Idem.

[191] 2003 U.S. Dist. LEXIS 1103, 01 Civ. 9291 (JSM) where it was held that although acts of terrorism are malicious in nature, they do not fall within the malicious acts exclusion.

[192] [1999] 1 Lloyd's L.R. 803 (HL) [KAC v. KIC (HL)] p. 815.

[193] Margo (2000) p. 352. In support, Margo cites the dictum of Chief Justice Bovill in (1873) LR 8 CP 649 as follows:

> What then according to common understanding is the meaning of the term restraint? Does it imply that the limitation, restriction, or confinement must be imposed by those who are in possession of the person or thing which is limited, restricted or confined? Or is the term satisfied by a restriction by the application of external force? If for example a town be besieged and the inhabitants confined within its walls by the besieging army, if, in attempting to come out, they are forced back, would it be inaccurate to say that they are restrained within those limits. The court believes it would not.

[194] Margo (2000) p. 353 where he cites the dictum of Justice Vaughan Williams in [1903] 1 K.B. 712 p. 719.

is the act of making a thing the property of a person.[195] He notes further that, appropriation is presumably intended to cover any manner in which goods are made the property of a person to the extent that this is not already covered by the other exclusionary terms discussed above.

3.4.7 Hijacking or any Unlawful Seizure or Wrongful Control of the Aircraft or Crew

The construction of the meaning of aircraft hijacking when characterized as an excluded risk in an aviation insurance policy does not present too much of a challenge. *Hijacking*, which is also a specific criminal offence in most jurisdictions, occurs when a person (or group of people) unlawfully, by the use or threat of use of force or violence of any kind seizes, exercises control over, or attempts to seize or exercise control over an aircraft or its crew.[196] Early definitions of hijacking both for insurance and criminal law purposes restricted its scope to acts committed by persons on board the aircraft and to acts committed while the aircraft was in flight.[197] However, following the Pan Am decision in which it was held that the risk of hijacking had not been excluded under the relevant all-risks policies, the US aviation market adopted the CWEC, paragraph (c) of which seeks to exclude hijackings and attempts thereat by persons not necessarily on board the aircraft.[198]

Thus, at least in North America, the hijacking exclusion has a far-reaching meaning that extends to the acts of people on the ground. In the London market, however, it is still the general understanding that hijacking is relevant only when the aircraft is "in flight".[199] As will be recalled, one of the central points of controversy in the recent London hull war market debate regarding the new LSW 555 wording has been focused on when an aircraft is considered to be "in flight" for hijacking purposes, rather than on the definition of hijacking as a whole.[200]

---

[195] Margo (2000) p. 353.

[196] Idem., pp. 352–354.

[197] See e.g., 354 F. Supp. 369; 1973 U.S. Dist. LEXIS 15191. The defendant in this case boarded an aircraft armed with two sticks of dynamite and a pistol. Federal Marshals at the airport evacuated the aircraft when they learned that the defendant planned to hijack it. The defendant was arrested and her weapons seized. At no point did the aircraft leave the airport terminal gate or start its engines. When a charge of aircraft piracy was brought against her under federal criminal legislation, she was acquitted on the ground that the legislature did not intend the statute creating the offence of aircraft piracy to apply when the aircraft was on the ground.

[198] CWEC; See also Margo (2000) p. 355.

[199] Aviation Insurance Clauses Group (2006d), (AVN 48C) clause (g); QBE Insurance (Australia) Ltd 2007, (LSW 555D) section 1(f). According to Margo, these London market definitions make it clear that persons who are not on board the aircraft do not fall within the ambit of hijacking. Depending on the facts, persons on the ground who participate in the hijacking of an aircraft could be found to have committed a malicious act or, if damage is caused to the aircraft, an act of sabotage. See Margo (2000) p. 354; fn. 234.

[200] Adams et al. (2007) p. 112.

The next section of this chapter outlines the reactions of the relevant insurance markets to the occurrence of catastrophic insured events in an effort to establish a consistent trend of market failure in those markets. Particular attention will be focused on aviation war risk insurance market reactions to the events of September 11, 2001.

3.5 Aviation War Risk Insurance Market Reactions to the Occurrence of Catastrophic Events

The inherent instability of aviation war risks and allied perils coverage on the commercial markets inevitably manifests itself whenever a major event occurs. It will be recalled that, in the United States, all-risks aviation insurers introduced the Common North American War Exclusion Clause (CWEC) after the Pan American incident.[201] In the London market, clause AVN 48 started appearing in all risk hull and liability insurance policies in November 1969, after the Israeli raid of Beirut airport had resulted in huge insurance payouts.[202] During the terrorist campaign waged by the Popular Front for the Liberation of Palestine (PFLP) in the 1970s, which involved the widespread hijacking and destruction of several commercial aircraft, clause AVN 48 was progressively amended and reissued by the London market, the scope of exclusions being ever widened on each occasion.[203] As a result of the conflict in the Persian Gulf in the early 1990s,[204] the London hull war market introduced maximum aggregate limits applicable to LSW 555 policies.[205] These maximum aggregate limits permitted insurers to limit the amount they will pay to an insured with respect to hull war risks in any specified period.[206]

Immediately after the Persian Gulf conflict began on August 2, 1990, there were increased requests in the United States for both premium and non-premium

---

[201] See discussion in Sect. 3.3 above.

[202] Idem.

[203] Idem.

[204] On 2nd August 1990, Iraqi forces invaded the state of Kuwait and effectively occupied its territory, including its airport. 15 aircraft on the ground belonging to Kuwait Airways Corporation and a substantial quantity of aircraft spares altogether valued at US$ 692 million were taken over by the Iraqi troops and removed to Iraq. The airline carried a war risks policy underwritten by a number of Kuwaiti insurance companies and reinsured on the London market. The insurers paid US$ 300 million to the airline contending that this was their maximum liability under the contracts. The airline sued the insurers in London. The matter traveled all the way to the U.K. House of Lords which made a final pronouncement on it in March 1999. See [1999] 1 Lloyd's L.R. 803 (HL) [KAC v. KIC (HL)], discussed in Sect. 3.5 below. This incidence led to the introduction of aggregate limits into hull war policies issued on the London market.

[205] Margo (1996) p. 449. Some war policies provide for reinstatement at an agreed premium in the event that the aggregate limit is exhausted before the policy expires. However, reinstatement does not increase the policy limits for any one loss.

[206] Excess aggregate war risk coverage is available to deal with this situation. See idem.

insurance under the FAA Aviation Insurance Program.[207] This was because commercial insurers had canceled or dramatically increased premiums for war-risk insurance, and had imposed surcharges on insurance for all flights to the Middle East. In addition, many commercial insurers simply refused to provide war-risk liability coverage for any flights carrying troops, and increased their liability rates for non-military passengers to very high levels. For example, the commercial insurance premiums for one airline's war-risk coverage increased from $210 per flight before the conflict to over $54,000 per flight after the conflict began.[208]

Soon after the fateful events which occurred in the United States on September 11, 2001, the global aviation insurance industry found itself in the exact situation described above. Prior to that incident, many insurers around the world were offering extended war risk insurance endorsements (i.e. AVN 51 and 52) to insured airlines and other aviation operators for little or no premium. For instance, commercial aviation insurers were providing US airlines and "critical subcontractors" such as airport security companies, ground handlers, refuelers and caterers up to US $ 1.5 billion of war risk liability coverage for no additional premium.[209] This state of affairs in the commercial markets was caused in part by excessive competition between insurers, coupled with the then-prevailing and widely held perception that the possibility of materialization of those catastrophic risks was extremely rare.

The events of September 11, however, turned the aviation insurance industry on its head. It marked the end of the era in which aviation war risk coverage was to be taken for granted. Within two days of the attacks, almost all hull and liability all-risk insurers around the world had began handing out 7-day cancellation notices to their assureds, to expire at midnight on September 24, 2001, and thereby effectively reinstating the CWEC or AVN 48B, and terminating insurance coverage for war and terrorism risks forthwith.

Naturally, the operations of several major airlines were about to be grounded, as full and/or adequate insurance coverage is not only a legal requirement for airlines and other aviation operators under national legislation and certain international treaties, but is also a pre-requisite for commercial airlines of any country to maintain their air operator's certificates for purposes of flying into or across the airspace of most other foreign countries. It is also a common requirement under aircraft lease and loan agreements. Impending cancellation of war risk coverage by the conventional insurance market following September 11, 2001, therefore meant that most airlines would be in automatic default under their aircraft leasing and financing arrangements, which required them to maintain the prescribed minimum levels of insurance coverage, including war risk coverage.[210] As can be imagined,

[207] The FAA Aviation Insurance Program is discussed in detail in Chap. 7 of this book.

[208] Government Accountability Office (1994) p. 4.

[209] Warfel (2003) p. 4.

[210] Indeed, certain lessors and financiers of aircraft explicitly issued notices advising airlines operating aircraft financed by them that in view of the circumstances prevailing at the time, they would (for a limited period of time) not enforce their rights to require third-party liability war risk insurance coverage above that which was then available on the commercial markets. See for example: Export Import Bank of the United States (2001).

the results of these developments were rather chaotic. Indeed, they have been aptly described as the *failure* of the commercial aviation insurance markets.[211]

Before the 7-day notices could take effect, however, most all risks insurers in London and in other markets indicated their willingness to restore some level of passenger and third party liability war risk coverage to their insured airlines. The then-existing version of the applicable write back endorsement, AVN 52C was re-drafted and re-issued by the Joint Technical and Clauses Committee (JTCC) as AVN 52D,[212] thereby introducing in respect of third party bodily injury and property damage, a sub-limit or cap of US$ 50 million per-occurrence and in the annual aggregate[213] for any of the named perils written back thereunder. AVN 52E was also introduced for general aviation operators,[214] and it established a sub-limit of up to US$ 10 million per-occurrence and in the annual aggregate.[215] For passenger liability, full policy limits[216] were retained under AVN 52C, D and E. In addition to the introduction of sub-limits, and in spite of severe criticism and outcry from airlines, all-risk underwriters on the London aviation market introduced an additional premium of USD 1.25 per passenger carried for the limited *third party liability* war risk cover provided under AVN 52D. "The US$ 50 million sublimit, however, did not conform to the minimum limit (i.e., [US]$ 500 million) typically required by bank lenders and aircraft leasing companies".[217]

Further, some underwriters on the London aviation market and from other markets began offering additional (excess) war risk cover for third party liability in separate and distinct policies beyond the US$ 50 million sub-limit: from US$ 50 million to US$ 150 million; and from US$ 150 million to US$ 1 billion. This two-layered excess cover was made available for an initial premium of USD 1.85 per passenger carried (i.e. in addition to the USD 1.25 referred to above), and was subject to a 30-day cancellation clause.[218] The rationale underlying the different treatment accorded by all risk insurers to *passenger liability* and *hull war risk*

---

[211] Fitzsimmons (2004) p. 81 [emphasis added]. See Chap. 4 below for a detailed discussion of the theory of market failure.

[212] The JTCC was the predecessor to the AICG.

[213] This meant that the maximum amount of money recoverable from the insurer for claims attributable to war risks during the effective period of the insurance was limited to USD 50 million. Also, this limit would apply irrespective of whether those war risk-related losses arose from one single occurrence or an aggregation of events. Prior to 9/11, there was no distinction between war risks and other risks so far as the limit of recovery was concerned. All risks were typically insured to full policy limits.

[214] General aviation refers to non-commercial, non-military civil aviation.

[215] Margo (2002) p. 389.

[216] Since AVN 52 is a write-back endorsement, it is typically subject to the maximum amount of insurance cover provided under the original policy. Writing back AVN 52 to "full policy limits" therefore means that, if for instance the amount of insurance provided under the original policy was $ 1 billion, then war risk coverage would also have been written back to the tune of $ 1 billion.

[217] See Warfel (2003) p. 4.

[218] Margo (2002) p. 389.

coverage on the one hand, and *third party liability war risk coverage* on the other hand was that, whereas insurers could quantify their exposure to liability under the former with a reasonable degree of certainty, the same could not be said of the latter.[219]

At present, although the market is still a distance away from pre-September 11, 2001, conditions, all-risks liability insurers appear to be slowly easing the restrictions established immediately after September 11. Instead of coverage up to full policy limits, extended third party liability war risk coverage for airlines is now typically available up to a maximum per-occurrence and annual aggregate sub-limit of about US$ 150 million although higher limits of up to US$ 1 billion are selectively available from individual underwriters.[220] There is no war risk insurance coverage available on the conventional market for service providers in the air transport industry.[221] Premium rates for extended third party liability war risk coverage are still quite high as compared to pre-2001 levels, although they seem to be falling on a year-over-year aggregate basis. For war risk coverage only, some airlines are reported to have experienced premium rate increases in the order of up to 500 % in the immediate aftermath of 9/11.[222] The insurance of Chicago airports offers a practical illustration of the foregoing. Prior to September 11, 2001, Chicago carried US$ 750 million of terrorist insurance for an annual premium of US$ 125,000. Post-September 11, their insurers would only offer US$ 150 million of coverage for a new premium of US$ 6.9 million.[223] Not only had premiums been significantly increased; the upper limit of coverage had also been severely reduced.

Although the global aviation insurance industry is generally considered to have survived the impact of September 11, 2001, it has since not fully returned to pre-September 11 levels, and there are concerns that the industry may not be able to withstand another catastrophe of the same size and magnitude as September 11, 2001, in the near future. Indeed, these concerns have significantly influenced recent industry discussions as to whether or not claims arising from the use of weapons of mass destruction (WMD claims) should or should not be covered under aviation insurance policies.[224] Accordingly, on August 4, 2006, the AICG published two new model exclusion clauses: AVN 48C[225] and AVN 48D.[226] These new clauses seek to further broaden the scope and depth of the risks excluded from aviation insurance policies by introducing a revised and expanded section (b) to replace that same section of AVN 48B, which excluded cover for claims caused by

---

219 Harding et al. (2002).

220 Information obtained from personal interview with Ken Coombes, Marsh Inc, London, UK (November 2007).

221 Service providers are separate and distinct from airlines. They include airport operators, air navigation service providers, security screeners, ground handling service providers etc.

222 Margo (2002) p. 390. See also Margo and Posner (2008) p. 474.

223 Jaffee and Russell (2003) p. 36.

224 See Marsh Inc. (2006). See also idem.

225 Aviation Insurance Clauses Group (2006d), (AVN 48C).

226 Idem.

"[a]ny hostile detonation of any weapon of war employing atomic or nuclear fission and/or fusion or other like reaction or radioactive force or matter".[227] Margo and Posner summarize the features of the new clauses by noting that:

> ... they expressly exclude coverage for damage caused by a broad range of weapons of mass destruction, including electromagnetic pulse, and the hostile 'emission, discharge or release of chemical or biological materials that are poisonous or pathogenic'. AVN 48D excludes all hostile release of such substances whereas AVN 48C limits its exclusion of the use of chemical or biological materials that are poisonous or pathogenic to those arising from war or other specified types of hostilities. Both of the new exclusions also define when an aircraft is deemed 'in flight' for purposes of determining application of the exclusion for hijacking.[228]

For the relevant part, under both AVN 48C and AVN 48D, "an aircraft is considered to be in flight at any time from the moment when all its external doors are closed following embarkation until the moment when any such door is opened for disembarkation, or when the aircraft is in motion".[229]

The reaction on the specialist hull war market in London was similar. While the amended versions of AVN 48B (i.e. AVN 48C and AVN 48D) were under review awaiting ratification and approval by some of the world's leading aviation regulatory bodies,[230] a series of new and very restrictive wordings of the *Hull War and Allied Perils Policy (Aviation)* (LSW 555), which sought to exclude all claims arising from weapons of mass destruction (WMD), was written and implemented by hull war insurers.[231] However, the market was not able to achieve consensus on the new wording, as each version focused on excluding losses on the basis of the method of causation.[232] As a result, there were some considerable variations and inconsistencies between different versions of the new LSW 555C wording proffered by different segments of the hull war market.[233]

---

[227] Joint Technical and Clauses Group (JTCC) 1996, (AVN 48B 1.10.96).

[228] Margo and Posner (2008) p. 476.

[229] Aviation Insurance Clauses Group (2006d), (AVN 48C), clause (g). See also Adams et al. (2007) p. 111.

[230] The insurance market, working through market associations such as the Aviation Insurance Clauses Group (AICG), had to seek regulatory approval prior to the use of the new clauses from the relevant regulatory agencies (such as the EC Competition Directorate, and the EC Transportation Directorate) in order to avoid charges of collusion and anticompetitive behavior being brought against them.

[231] Adams et al. (2007) p. 112.

[232] Idem., p. 112, 118.

[233] For instance, one version of the new wording sponsored by R.J. Kiln underwriters and designated as LSW 555C, amended the definition of "in flight" in relation to the external doors as set out in AVN 48C and AVN 48D, and also excluded cover for loss or damage caused by the emission, discharge, release or escape of chemical/biological materials, except within the normal definitions of hijacking. Another variant of LSW 555C sponsored by ACE underwriters was generally understood to exclude loss caused by the "use", rather than the "emission, discharge, release or escape" of chemical, biological or biochemical materials. Yet another variation of the new wording sponsored by Talbot underwriters and designated as LSW 556 contained a different definition of "in flight" which referred to contact between the aircraft and the ground rather than when the doors are closed or opened. See idem., p. 112.

On the basis of feedback obtained from interested parties and, in particular, in conjunction with Marsh Insurance Brokers, the aviation war underwriters at R.J. Kiln developed LSW 555D,[234] a toned-down variant of the new hull war wording to provide elements of cover previously excluded from earlier versions of the wording. Instead of focusing on excluding losses arising from the method of causation, the market's attention was drawn to the issue of "quantum and its [the market's] response to non-catastrophic losses arising from chemical, biological, biochemical, electromagnetic pulse, and radioactive contamination, the preface being that the commercial insurance market could and should be able to respond to limited, single aircraft incidents, almost regardless of the nature of the cause (subject to normal insurance practice)".[235]

Accordingly, LSW 555D contains language designed to address these issues. In order to avoid catastrophe aggregation at airports from WMD attacks, LSW 555D provides certain elements of war risk cover to the aircraft while the wheels are no longer in contact with the ground.[236] It also provides for limited coverage of WMD claims (including while the aircraft is on the ground) only in specific circumstances: the WMD attack must have originated solely and directly on board the aircraft.[237] Notwithstanding the foregoing, LSW 555D retains the nuclear exclusion and as such does not cover any claims caused by nuclear weapons. LSW 555D was officially approved and designated for use by underwriters at Lloyds of London in April 2006.[238]

3.6 Conclusion

This object of this chapter has been to provide a detailed description and analysis of: the evolution of war risk exclusions in insurance generally, and in the field of aviation insurance in particular; the meanings of the specific exclusionary terms commonly found in aviation insurance policies; and, the reactions of commercial aviation war risk insurance markets to the occurrence of extreme insured events. It has been established that whenever a catastrophic insured peril materializes and causes large scale losses, this is always followed by severe reductions in the upper limits of war risk insurance coverage offered by the commercial markets and steep increases in premium rates. In the aftermath of September 11, 2001, the most recent of such occurrences, aviation war risk insurance coverage on the commercial markets was

---

[234] Idem.

[235] Idem.

[236] QBE Insurance (Australia) Ltd 2007, (LSW 555D), section 3(g). See also Adams et al. (2007) p. 112.

[237] QBE Insurance (Australia) Ltd 2007, (LSW 555D), section 3(c)(ii). See also Adams et al. (2007) p. 112.

[238] JLT Risk Solutions (2006) p. 3.

completely unavailable initially, and subsequently, when some limited coverage was restored, it was relatively unaffordable. This trend has been characterized by some commentators as an *insurance market failure*[239] necessitating governmental intervention both at the national and international levels. Another commentator has referred to this phenomenon as a *substantial disruption in insurance markets* which underscores the need for a permanent solution.[240] Other writers have also suggested that this trend occurs due to the existence of *systemic risk* in the relevant markets.[241]

Against this backdrop, and particularly in view of the current international geopolitical climate including the American war on terror, there are fears that history will repeat itself in the future and, if nothing is done, the commercial insurance markets will not be able to withstand another catastrophic loss the size of September 11, 2001, should one occur again. Accordingly, several measures[242] have been proposed for adoption at the national and international levels, all aimed at preventing disruptions in, and/or failure of, the commercial war risk insurance markets in the event that another catastrophic loss occurs. In an effort to establish a theoretical framework for analyzing the viability of the various proposed measures, the next chapter of this book will focus on the economic and psychological underpinnings of insurance market failures and/or disruptions, paying particular attention to the aviation war risk insurance industry.

References

(1873) LR 8 CP 649 Rodocanachi v. Elliott
(1884) 9 App. Cas. 671 Thomson v. Weems
[1903] 1 K.B. 712 Miller v. Law Accident Insurance Co.
[1907] 2 K.B. 853 Field v. Receiver of Metropolitan Police
[1921] A.C. 99 Britain Steamship Co., Ltd. v. The King
(1922) Lloyd's L.R. 7 White, Child & Beney v. Simmons
[1939] 2 K.B. 544 Kawasaki Kisen Kabushiki Kaisha of Kobe v. Bantham Steamship Co. Ltd (No. 2)
[1940] 67 Lloyd's L.R. 174 Levy v. Assicurazione Generali
(1949) 82 Lloyd's L.R. 501 Pesquerias y Secaderos de Bacalao de Espana S.A. v. Beer
[1969] 1 Lloyd's L.R. 293 Nishina Trading Co. Ltd., v. Chiyoda Fire and Marine Insurance Co. Ltd., (The Mandarin Star)
(1970) 2 Lloyd's L.R. 355 Panamanian Oriental Steamship Corporation v. Wright (The Anita)
[1976] Q.B. 297 Benin v. Whimster
[1991] 2 Lloyd's L.R. 281 National Oil Company of Zimbabwe and Others v. Sturge
[1996] 1 Lloyd's L.R. 664 [KAC v. KIC, (Comm.)] Kuwait Airways Corporation v. Kuwait Insurance Co.

239 See Fitzsimmons (2004) p. 81; Jaffee and Russell (2003) p. 35.

240 See Warfel (2003) p. 1.

241 See e.g., De Mey (2003) p. 68; Mundy (2004); and, Miranda and Glauber (1997)where the authors argue that systemic risk and not asymmetric information problems pose a more serious obstacle to the emergence of an independent private crop insurance industry.

242 These measures are discussed in detail in subsequent chapters of this book.

[1997] 2 Lloyd's L.R. 687 (CA) [KAC v. KIC (CA)] Kuwait Airways Corporation v. Kuwait Insurance Co.
[1999] 1 Lloyd's L.R. 803 (HL) [KAC v. KIC (HL)] Kuwait Airways Corporation v. Kuwait Insurance Corporation et al.
[2002] 2 Lloyd's L.R. 88 Strive Shipping Corp. v. Hellenic Mutual War Risks Association (The Grecia Express)
[1980] 1 Lloyd's L.R. 406 Spinney's (1948) Ltd. v. Royal Ins. Co. Ltd.
15 East 267 (1812) Levin v. Alnutt
178 F.2d 488 (1949), aff'd 340 U.S. 54 (1950) United States v. Standard Oil Co., (New Jersey)
2003 U.S. Dist. LEXIS 1103, 01 Civ. 9291 (JSM) SR International Business Insurance Co. Ltd., v. World Trade Center Properties LLC, et al.
212 F.2d 731 (1st Cir. 1954) Home Insurance Co. v. Davila
267 U.S. 76 (1925) Standard Oil Co. v. United States
354 F. Supp. 369; 1973 U.S. Dist. LEXIS 15191 United States v. Pliskow
368 F. Supp. 1098 (S.D.N.Y. 1973) Pan Am World Airways, Inc. v. Aetna Casualty and Surety Co., et al.
505 F.2d 989 (2d Cir. 1974) Pan Am World Airways, Inc. v. Aetna Casualty and Surety Co.
571 F. Supp. 1460 (S.D.N.Y., 1983) Holiday Inns Inc., v. Aetna Insurance Co.
67 U.S. (2 Black) 635 (1862) The Brig Amy Warwick (The Prize Cases)
774 F. Supp. 909 (1991) New Market Investment Corp. v. Fireman's Fund Insurance Co.
8 App. Cas. 393 (1883) Cory v. Burr
95 E.R. 863 (K.B. 1767) Drinkwater v. The Corporation of London
95 U.S. (5 Otto) 117 (1877) Insurance Co. v. Boon
A bigger bang for your buck (2006). Airfinance Journal No. 289:24–26
Adams M, Leslie K, Marangos H (2007) War, terrorism and associated perils in aviation insurance. In: Marangos H (ed) War risks and terrorism. Insurance Institute of London, London, pp 105–118
Aviation Insurance Clauses Group (2005) Terms of Reference 17th March 2005. Available via http://www.aicg.co.uk/docimages/4982.pdf
Aviation Insurance Clauses Group (2006a) Aviation manufacturers products liabilities endorsement. (AVN 52P, 27th February 2006). Available via http://www.aicg.co.uk/DocImages/6249.pdf
Aviation Insurance Clauses Group (2006b) Extended coverage endorsement (aviation liabilities). (AVN 52K, 4th August 2006). Available via http://www.aicg.co.uk/DocImages/6745.pdf
Aviation Insurance Clauses Group (2006c) War, hi-jacking and other perils exclusion clause (aviation). (AVN 48D, 4th August 2006). Available via http://www.aicg.co.uk/DocImages/6740.pdf
Aviation Insurance Clauses Group (2006d) War, hi-jacking and other perils exclusion clause (aviation). (AVN 48C, 4th August 2006). Available via http://www.aicg.co.uk/DocImages/6738.pdf
Aviation Insurance Clauses Group (2007) Guidance note: extended coverage endorsement (aviation liabilities). (AVN 52K. 2nd July 2007). Available via http://www.aicg.co.uk/DocImages/7466.pdf
Bidinger JR, Bninski RA (1974) Comment: a legal response to terrorist hijacking and insurance liability. Law Policy Int Bus 6:1167–1210
Caban EE (2003) War-risk, hijacking & terrorism exclusions in aviation insurance: carrier liability in the wake of September 11, 2001. J Air Law Com 68:421
Caplan H (2006) The Aviation Insurance Clauses Group: a model for other markets. Air Space Law XXXI(4–5):254–290
De Mey J (2003) The aftermath of September 11: the impact on and systemic risk to the insurance industry. Geneva Papers (Issues & Practice) 28(1):65–70
DLA Piper Inc. (2005) Defining Terrorism. DLA Piper's Insurance Group Bulletin
Export Import Bank of the United States (2001) Ex-Im Bank responds to airline insurance crisis in the wake of September 11 2001 terrorist attacks. September 24 2001. Available via http://www.exim.gov/pressrelease.cfm/B0BEB840-1032-5B0F-B332672F986C3E4F/
Fitzsimmons A (2004) Terrorism – maximizing the insurability of a catastrophe risk. Ann Air Space Law XXIX:67
Government Accountability Office (1994) Aviation insurance: federal insurance program needs improvements to ensure success. GAO/RCED-94-151
Harding J, Maddocks M, Moss G, Pryde A (2002) Aviation insurance. Institute of Actuaries, Paris

Haufler V (1997) Dangerous commerce: insurance and the management of international risk. Cornell University Press, Ithaca
International Underwriting Association (IUA), Lloyd's Market Association (LMA) (2005) Aviation Insurance Clauses Group Established. No. 015/0605, 24 June 2005. Available via http://www.the-lma.com/DocImages/5305.rtf
Ivamy ERH (1986) General principles of insurance law, 5th edn. Butterworths, London
Jaffee D, Russell T (2003) Markets under stress: the case of extreme event insurance. In: Arnott R, Greenwald B, Kanbur R, Nalebuff B (eds) Economics for an imperfect world – essays in honour of Joseph E. Stiglitz. MIT Press, Cambridge
Joint Technical and Clauses Group (JTCC) (1996) War, hi-jacking and other perils exclusion clause (aviation),. (AVN 48B 1.10.96, 1st October 1996)
Lewison K (2004) The interpretation of contracts, 3rd edn. Sweet & Maxwell, London
Libby JB (1995) War risk aviation exclusions. J Air Law Com 60:605
Lloyds Market Association (1994) Aviation Hull "War and Allied Perils" Policy, (LSW 555B, November 1994)
QBE Insurance (Australia) Ltd (2007) Aviation hull (war and allied perils) insurance policy. (LSW 555D, 2007). Available via http://www.intermediary.qbe.com.au/content/idcplg?IdcService=GET_FILE&dID=6912&dDocName=PRODCT006854&allowInterrupt=1
Marangos H (2007) Historical overview of the insurance and exclusion of 'War Risks' and Associated Perils. In: Marangos H (ed) War risks and terrorism. Insurance Institute of London, London, pp 15–22
Marangos H, Tobin A (2007a) Legal and technical definition of terms: (1) terms other than 'Terrorism' – 'War', 'Civil War', 'Rebellion' and others. In: Marangos H (ed) War risks and terrorism. Insurance Institute of London, London, pp 23–48
Marangos H, Tobin A (2007b) Legal and technical definition of terms: (2) 'Terrorism'. In: Marangos H (ed) War risks and terrorism. Insurance Institute of London, London, pp 49–61
Margo RD (1996) Aspects of insurance in aviation finance. J Air Law Com 62:423
Margo RD (2000) Aviation insurance: the law and practice of aviation insurance, including Hovercraft and Spacecraft Insurance, 3dth edn. Butterworths, London
Margo RD (2002) 11 September 2001 – an aviation insurance perspective. Air Space Law XXVII (6):386–397
Margo RD, Posner KB (2008) An aviation insurance primer – an overview for the aviation practitioner. In: Harakas AJ (ed) Litigating the aviation case: from pre-trial to closing argument, 3rd edn. American Bar Association, Tort Trial and Insurance Practice Section, Chicago
Marsh Inc. (2006) Marsh/IATA/AEA sponsored liability WMD write-back clauses now finalised by AICG. Aviation and Aerospace Practice Special Bulletin
Miller MD (2005) Marine war risks, 3dth edn. LLP, London
Miranda MJ, Glauber JW (1997) Systematic risk, reinsurance, and the failure of crop insurance markets. Am J Agric Econ 79(1):206–215
Mundy C (2004) The nature of risk: the nature of systemic risk – trying to achieve a definition. Balance Sheet 12(5):29–31
O'May D, Hill J (1993) Marine insurance: law and policy. Sweet & Maxwell, London
OECD (2004) OECD check-list of criteria to define terrorism for the purpose of compensation http://www.oecd.org/daf/financialmarketsinsuranceandpensions/insurance/34065606.pdf
JLT Risk Solutions (2006) The Hull War Market. JLT Risk Solutions Aerospace Market Update – Plane Talking 3
Simon SI (1991) The dilemma of war and military exclusion clauses in insurance contracts. Am Bus Law J 19(1):31–45
Thompson J, Sloane S (2001) War and terrorism – exclusions, extensions and issues of aggregation in the non-marine markets. Holman Fenwick & Willan, London
Vinciguerra R (1974–1975) Recent decisions: insurance – war risk exclusion clause does not bar recovery under an all risk policy for damages resulting from terrorist activities. Vand J Transnatl Law 8:923–233
Warfel WJ (2003) Terrorism and disruption in insurance markets:the need for a permanent solution. CPC Underwriters J 56(6):1–13

Chapter 4
Catastrophic Risks and Reflexes: Some Theoretical Perspectives on the Use of Insurance as a Risk Management Tool for Large Catastrophic Risks

4.1 Introduction

This chapter investigates the economic and behavioural reasons underlying the reactions of extreme event insurance markets such as the aviation war risk insurance market following the occurrence of an extreme insured event. Two broad areas of legal scholarship are conscripted to provide a theoretical basis for this investigation: the traditional law and economics movement on the one hand;[1] and, the behavioural law and economics movement on the other.[2] Both schools of thought involve economic analysis of law, a concept which has been used both in an effort to explain the legal system as it is (*i.e.*, positive or descriptive analysis) and also to

[1] The discipline of law and economics deals with the economic analysis of legal rules through verbal, mathematical and/or graphical models in order to distill the essence of the relationships being studied. The traditional law and economics approach posits that legal rules are best analyzed and understood in the light of standard economic principles. See generally: Polinsky (2003) pp. xv–xvii; 3. Central to the use of models in the analytical process is the introduction of various assumptions. Economists make assumptions for the obvious reason that the world, viewed economically, is too complicated to understand without some abstraction. A typical account of the assumptions usually made in such analysis is as follows: "all human behavior can be viewed as involving participants who [1] maximize their utility [2] from a stable set of preferences and [3] accumulate an optimal amount of information and other inputs in a variety of markets". See Jolls et al. (1998) p. 1476.

[2] As a discipline, behavioral law and economics builds upon and sometimes challenges some of the central concepts of traditional law and economics mainly by exploring the implications of actual human behavior (as opposed to hypothesized behavior) on the economic analysis of law. It involves both the development and incorporation within traditional law and economics of behavioral insights drawn from various fields of psychology. According to proponents, some of the foundational assumptions of traditional law and economics (e.g.: utility maximization; stable preferences; rational expectations; and, optimal processing of information) reflect an unrealistic picture of human behavior, and models built on those assumptions sometimes yield erroneous predictions. Behavioral law and economics therefore attempts to improve the predictive power of traditional law and economics by building in more realistic accounts of actors' behavior. See Jolls (2007). See also Jolls et al. (1998) p. 1476.

Y.O.M. Nyampong, *Insuring the Air Transport Industry Against Aviation War and Terrorism Risks and Allied Perils*, DOI 10.1007/978-3-642-32433-8_4,

recommend changes that might improve it (*i.e.*, normative or prescriptive analysis).[3] The difference between the two schools lies only in the nature and scope of the underlying assumptions which drive their respective analyses and conclusions.[4]

For clarity of presentation, the focus of this chapter is necessarily descriptive or positive—it taps a number of analytical tools used within both schools of legal scholarship to explain the post-event behaviour of the aviation war risk insurance market as it operates under the existing legal regime(s) governing the industry (as described in previous chapters). Subsequent chapters of this book will focus on the normative or prescriptive aspects of the analysis—they will analyze alternative and/or complementary proposals for enhancing the provision of insurance coverage for aviation war and terrorism risks.

In the last 50 years, the scope of economics as a discipline has expanded dramatically beyond its traditional domain of explaining explicit market transactions.[5] "Today, there is an economic theory of property rights, of corporate governance and other organizations, of government and politics, of education, of the family, of crime and punishment ... and, overlapping all these ... of law".[6] Contemporary economic theory provides several useful insights into the behaviour of extreme event insurance markets in the period after an extreme insured event has materialized. These include: the theory of market failure which has been, and

---

[3] Polinsky (2003) p. xvii.

[4] A fundamental assumption within the law and economics movement is that individuals are rational maximizers of their satisfactions in their non-market as well as their market behavior. This assumption of perfect rationality is drawn from neoclassical microeconomic theory and is refutable as an empirical matter because empirical studies often find participants whose behavior systematically deviates from economic definitions of rationality. Proponents of law and economics acknowledge this descriptive inaccuracy but retain the assumption for a lack of a better alternative for prediction and policy analysis. In contrast, a fundamental assumption of the behavioral law and economics movement is that individuals systematically fall prey to a host of cognitive illusions that lead to predictable non-rational behaviors both inside and outside traditional markets. This assumption is drawn from behavioral studies of judgment and decision-making which suggest that human judgment and decision-making necessarily rely on imperfect psychological mechanisms that cause departures from rationality. Because these irrational tendencies are supposedly uniform, pervasive and predictable, they can be incorporated into behavioral models and used in policy analysis. Thus, whereas law and economics treats all legal actors in all situations as if they were perfectly rational, behavioral law and economics treats all legal actors in all situations as if they were equally predisposed to commit errors of judgment and choice. See Mitchell (2002–2003) pp. 68–71.

[5] Posner (1987). The author, a long time Judge of the United States Court of Appeals for the Seventh Circuit and a Senior Lecturer at the University of Chicago Law School, wrote this article in reaction to the opposition raised by some economists to the extension of economics from the study of market to non-market behavior. In refuting the claims made by these economists, he noted *inter alia* that: "The economics of law is the set of economic studies that build on a detailed knowledge of some area of law; whether the study is done by a 'lawyer', an 'economist' or someone with both degrees, or a lawyer-economist team has little significance". See idem., p. 4. As evidenced by the title of this article, Judge Richard Posner has been given credit as helping start the traditional law and economics movement.

[6] Idem., p. 1.

continues to be, frequently used as justification for governmental intervention in the private competitive market mechanism; and, the concept of systemic risk the existence of which has been identified as another possible cause of instability/ disruptions in extreme event insurance markets. In order to determine the appropriateness and suitability of the various measures proposed at different levels to forestall the future occurrence of disruptions in the private aviation war risk insurance markets, it is essential to first have a firm grasp and appreciation of the economic and behavioural causes of those disruptions.

To put the issue in perspective and also to justify the resort to economic and behavioural theory in this chapter, it is instructive to briefly refer to the suggestion that has been made by several scholars that the events of September 11, 2001, led to a complete breakdown of the commercial insurance markets and, as such, there is a need for governments to step in and either assist the market in one way or the other, or provide the insurance coverage themselves.[7] Suggestions of this kind necessarily assume that the institutional framework for the private provision of insurance coverage by commercial entities (i.e., the open competitive market mechanism) can no longer function efficiently and thus needs to be replaced by another institutional framework—public (or governmental) provision of insurance. Contemporary economic theory suggests, however, that such a conclusion cannot be reached without first carrying out a comparative institutional analysis to determine the failings of the current institutional framework and the strengths of the proposed remedial institutional framework.

In other words, we can prescribe effective institutional treatments for insurance market disruptions only when we know enough to enable us to diagnose the institutional causes of those market disruptions. Merely proposing that governments should provide or assist the commercial market in the provision of war risk insurance does not solve any problems. The question that needs to be specifically addressed is: are the conventional insurance markets imperfect? If they are, to what extent can governments (and other stakeholders) improve market performance or provide alternatives? The object of this chapter is precisely to address the first part of the question with respect to the conventional aviation war risk insurance market. The second part of the question—what governments and other stakeholders can do to enhance market performance or provide alternatives—are addressed in the second part of this book.

4.2 Market Failure Theory and Its Applicability to the Aviation War Risk Insurance Industry

At the outset, it is essential to provide a brief recap of the phenomena that this chapter seeks to explain by resorting to economic and behavioural theories. Commercial insurers rate risks (for purposes of determining whether they will

[7] See e.g., Wolf (1979).

provide coverage and, if so, what premium to charge) on the basis of several factors including: the perceived probability that the event will occur; the magnitude of losses; the need to accumulate reserves against future claims; and the state of competition in the market. Over the course of time, accumulated reserves are driven down by competition and the payment of dividends to capital providers. Most commercial insurers are prudent in this regard as they set aside enough reserves not only to meet regulatory requirements but also to cater for envisaged payouts. However, when catastrophic events occur, they effectively wipe out reserves accumulated over several years as the reserves are usually inadequate to cover payments to insureds. Long periods between catastrophic losses therefore result in the accumulation of inadequate reserves to cover them, creating panic among insurers.

In an effort to restore depleted reserves following the occurrence of a catastrophic event, insurers raise premiums sharply and sometimes withdraw coverage completely or substantially. When this happens, it is classified as a failure or a substantial disruption of the market. As reserves improve, premiums are lowered; coverage is restored albeit subject to new restrictions; and, the cycle begins again. Those economic and psychological considerations that drive conventional insurers to behave the way they do under circumstances of heightened uncertainty are the subject matter of this chapter. To provide the foundation for the market failure discussion, the next section assesses how competitive markets operate to efficiently allocate production resources in an economy.

4.2.1 Markets in Resource Allocation Theory

Generally, in order for *microeconomic efficiency*[8] to occur in any economy, a number of conditions must be met:

- A particular good or service should be *produced efficiently*—a given quantity of a good of a given quality should be produced at the lowest possible cost;
- A good or service should be *used efficiently*—everyone who values a good or service more than its cost of production, should consume the good or use the service; and,
- *All* goods or services that customers value more than they cost to supply should be produced.

[8] Microeconomic efficiency, also referred to as Pareto optimality, is the degree to which an economic system meets the material wants, as measured by quantity and quality, of its members. It is achieved when it is impossible to make one person better off without making someone else worse off. See Winston (2006) p. 2.

According to the neo-classical theory, economically efficient outcomes are generally produced by competitive markets.[9] In a competitive market, the price of a good and the quantity of a good supplied are set by equating supply and demand. At this point, known as the equilibrium, there are no potential customers who would be willing to pay more for the product or service than it would cost to produce additional units of the good (*i.e.*, the marginal cost). In addition, the value to society of consuming an additional unit of the good is equal to the value to the individual who purchases the good, and the social and individual values of producing the good are also equal. Thus, in an efficient market, the interests of the firm and society exactly coincide. Under assumptions of perfect competition (*i.e.*, perfect information, freely exchangeable property rights, no market power, rational behavior, absence of externalities and zero transactions costs), this phenomenon is known as the competitive general equilibrium model. Because of the assumptions of perfect competition, the model foresees no shocks or unanticipated events. One author describes the model as follows: "At the beginning of time, the full equilibrium was solved – [determined simply by the interaction of supply and demand, and Adam Smith's invisible hand] – and everything from then on was an unfolding over time of what had been planned in each of the contingencies".[10]

As an extension of the competitive general equilibrium model, the standard economic model of risk exchanges also predicts that competition in insurance markets leads to microeconomic efficiency in the allocation of risks in the economy.[11] In particular, under assumptions of perfect competition,[12] the model states that: "all diversifiable risks in the economy will be washed away through mutual risk sharing arrangements";[13] "all risks will be pooled in financial and insurance markets";[14] "the residual systematic risk in the economy will be borne by the agents who have a comparative advantage in risk management as insurers and investors";[15] and, "in short, all individual risks will be insured".[16] However, as will be demonstrated below, this prediction of the general competitive equilibrium model is contradicted

---

[9] The argument that free markets lead to efficient outcomes "as if by an invisible hand" was first made by Adam Smith in 1776. See Smith (1977, first published in 1776).

[10] Stiglitz (2003) p. 580.

[11] Chiappori and Gollier (2006) p. 2.

[12] Idem., p. 3 where the authors state:

> ... it is assumed that all agents [market participants] share the same information about the likelihood of the various states. This allows for heterogeneous populations as long as the characteristics of the risk borne by each participant is [*sic*] common knowledge. For example, the fact that young women are safer drivers than young men is compatible with full insurance of every driver at the competitive equilibrium with a risk neutral insurance industry. The premium rate for every category of risk will be fair (hence gender specific), thereby inducing every individual to purchase full insurance at the optimum.

[13] Idem., p. 2.

[14] Idem.

[15] Idem.

[16] Idem.

by casual observations in the real world. Information is not always perfect, and even when it appears to be so, it is usually distributed unevenly in the market. Transactions costs and externalities are always present. In the risk exchanges sector (including the insurance sector), many diversifiable risks end up being borne by individuals.

While the market generally functions well for allocating normal "private" goods,[17] it does not do so for all goods. Once the economic conditions required for a free market fail to hold, market forces will no longer guarantee an efficient outcome and "market failure" will occur. Under the competitive general equilibrium theory, a market failure occurs whenever a system of price-market institutions produce too little of socially desirable goods, or too much of goods that are socially undesirable.[18] Accordingly, market failure is defined under that theory as an equilibrium allocation of resources that does not enhance microeconomic efficiency or is not Pareto-optimal.[19]

4.2.2 *Early Market Failure Theories*

From its early beginnings in the mid-twentieth century, most of the market failure arguments were expounded by economists in relation to theories of public goods[20] and externalities.[21] These theories of public goods and externalities suggested that market participants will fail to produce certain mutually beneficial goods and services as a result of pricing inefficiencies.[22] The classic example given is that of a lighthouse: "[e]ach shipping company owner knows that if a lighthouse is erected by another shipping company, it will effectively serve his ships as well. Thus, each ship owner will likely try to shirk paying his share of the costs [of erecting the lighthouse] and thereby "free ride" off the efforts of others".[23]

[17] See footnote 20 below for a distinction between "private" and "public" goods.

[18] See Bator (1958) where the author states that market failure refers to the failure of a more or less idealized system of price-market institutions to sustain "desirable" activities and estop "undesirable" activities.

[19] See footnote 8 above for a definition of Pareto optimality (also known as microeconomic efficiency).

[20] A public good involves two elements: non-excludability and non-rivalrous consumption. Non-excludability refers to the impossibility of preventing non-paying individuals from enjoying the benefits of a good or service, whereas non-rivalrous consumption refers to cases where an individual's ability to consume a good or service is not diminished by allowing additional individuals to consume it. All other goods are private goods. See Cowen (1988). See also Cowen and Crampton (2003a) pp. 3–4.

[21] An externality exists whenever an individual's actions affect the utility of another individual. Positive externalities are those that benefit others; negative externalities are those that make others worse off. See Cowen (1988) p. 2.

[22] Cowen and Crampton (2003a) p. 3.

[23] Cowen (1988) p. 3.

As a result, even if the benefits of the lighthouse would exceed the costs, the market may not provide it, as there is no way of excluding non-payers from enjoying the benefits. Thus, if left to the market, the provision of public goods will not be socially optimal: markets will underproduce goods and services whose provision would entail positive externalities and overproduce those whose provision would entail negative externalities.[24]

Although aspects of the public goods and externalities theories of market failure can be traced back to the very beginnings of economics, the modern formulations were laid down by Paul Samuelson,[25] James Meade, Francis Bator,[26] and other economists in the 1950s.[27] Since that time, and despite some significant differences, a general consensus developed that governments should provide at least a few basic public goods that were vulnerable to market failure, such as national defence, but that markets do the best job of providing most goods and services. Many proponents of the public goods and externalities theories of market failure argued that the pricing inefficiencies inherent in certain sectors of the economy could be alleviated by having the government supply the goods and services at marginal cost and financing them through taxation.[28] However, this consensus fell apart in the 1970s and 1980s, as new market failure arguments were constructed, largely driven by the work of Joseph Stiglitz and George Akerlof.[29]

4.2.3 The New Market Failure Arguments

In his criticism of the competitive equilibrium analysis and the market failure models derived therefrom, Joseph Stiglitz has noted for instance that:

> The underlying *mathematics* required assumptions of convexity and continuity, and with these assumptions, one could prove the existence of equilibrium and its (Pareto) efficiency.... The standard proofs of these fundamental theorems of welfare economics did not even list in their enumerated assumptions those concerning information: the perfect information assumption was so ingrained it did not have to be explicitly stated. The *economic* assumptions to which the proofs of efficiency called attention concerned the absence of externalities and public goods. The market failures approach to the economics of the public sector (Bator 1958) discussed alternative approaches by which these market failures could be corrected, but these market failures were highly circumscribed by assumption.[30]

---

[24] Idem.

[25] Samuelson (1954).

[26] Bator (1958).

[27] Cowen and Crampton (2003a) p. 3.

[28] Cowen (1988) p. 4.

[29] These two leading economists were awarded the 2001 Nobel Prize in Economics for their groundbreaking work on the economics of information.

[30] Stiglitz (2003) pp. 579–580.

In a brief talk delivered to a Teachers' Conference organized by the UK's Institute of Economic Affairs in June 2008 and subsequently published as a discussion paper,[31] Philip Booth cited the following example which vividly illustrates the shortcomings of the competitive general equilibrium model of market failure and also demonstrates the illusory nature of perfect competition:

> If I were to give you an engineering lecture and I were to start by saying, correctly I believe, that the maximum theoretical speed of a perfect car was the speed of light and that a car that travelled at any speed lower than that was a 'failed car' or suffered from 'car failure', you would probably think that it was a pretty useless lecture. And you would be right.
>
> Yet, a common approach in economics teaching is to teach the preconditions of a so-called perfect market – full information, no transaction costs, no externalities and so on – and then look at how markets, in practice, deviate from that textbook model. We then call those deviations 'market failures'. This is despite the fact that it is as impossible to have a perfect market as it is to have a perfect car.[32]

These new market failure arguments were based on the idea of information and informational imperfections. Proponents have pointed to the existence of information problems in virtually every sector of the economy (including insurance) which show for instance that, "in equilibrium, firms may charge a price in excess of their marginal costs, or workers may be paid a wage in excess of their reservation wage so that the incentive to maintain a reputation is maintained".[33] If these arguments are correct, more than just a few markets are bound to fail. We can expect market failure whenever information is imperfect or distributed asymmetrically.

According to the classical model (*i.e.*, the competitive general equilibrium model), prices create and communicate information about resource scarcity and help markets economize on information. A price, according to this theory, clears the market and tells distant buyers and sellers about the relative scarcity of differing goods and services.[34] On the contrary, proponents of the new market failure arguments argue that when prices are used to signal or guarantee the quality of goods and services, they cannot also clear the market, and will not properly measure the relative scarcities of goods and services. They demonstrate that in the real world, information is imperfect (incomplete) and is unevenly distributed in the market: "different people know different things. Workers know more about their own abilities than the firm does; the person buying insurance knows more about his health, for example, whether he smokes and drinks immoderately, than the insurance firm. . . ."[35] They argue further that the "information asymmetry in the market cannot be overcome by exchange precisely because the unequal distribution of information interferes with mutually beneficial exchange".[36] In their view, the

---

[31] Booth (2008).

[32] Idem., p. 1.

[33] Stiglitz (2003) p. 581.

[34] Cowen and Crampton (2003a) p. 6.

[35] Stiglitz (2003) pp. 584–585.

[36] Cowen and Crampton (2003a) p. 5.

existence and pervasiveness of information imperfections in the market is the cause of market failure.

As one commentary rightly put it, "[i]t is hard to think of any area where these new market failure arguments would not apply. Indeed the work of Joseph Stiglitz suggests that market failure will occur whenever the price system is used".[37] Accordingly, proponents of the new market failure arguments have not restricted themselves to explaining economic phenomena in abstract markets. The theory of imperfect information has been used, for instance, to explain credit rationing in the banking sector and efficiency wages in the labour market.[38] However, of direct relevance for our present purposes is the fact that these theories have also offered some explanations of the behaviour of insurance markets in general[39] and extreme event insurance markets in particular[40] when faced with real world situations in which information is neither perfect nor evenly distributed. With respect to insurance market failures, the standard explanations that have been offered by many proponents of the information-based market failure theories are the problems caused by asymmetric information; in particular, the problems of *moral hazard* and *adverse selection*.[41] These phenomena are discussed in detail below.

4.2.3.1 Moral Hazard

As noted above, in the context of insurance, moral hazard refers to the tendency of insurance protection to alter an insured individual's or entity's motive to prevent loss.[42] Stated differently, moral hazard refers to the detrimental effect that insurance has on an individual's incentives to avoid losses.[43] The occurrence of an insured event "may not be completely avoidable but the probability or size of the loss is almost always influenced by an individual's actions".[44] Moral hazard arises

---

[37] Idem., p. 4. See also Stiglitz (2003) p. 582 where the author notes: "Perhaps most importantly, under the standard paradigm, markets are Pareto efficient, except when one of a limited number of market failures occurs. Under the imperfect information paradigm, markets are almost never Pareto efficient".

[38] In a number of his writings on the subject, Joseph Stiglitz presented credit rationing and efficiency wages—both based on imperfect information—as two clear examples of how markets may misfire. See Cowen and Crampton (2003a) p. 6.

[39] See e.g., Rothschild and Stiglitz (1976), Arnott and Stiglitz (1991) and Wilson (1977).

[40] See Jaffee and Russell (2003).

[41] See Chiappori and Gollier (2006) p. 3. The authors claim that asymmetric information is a central reason why competition in insurance markets may fail to guarantee that all mutually advantageous risk exchanges are realized in our economies. They specifically identify *moral hazard* and *adverse selection* as two phenomena derived from asymmetric information that can explain why competitive insurance markets fail to provide an efficient level of insurance, and why public interventions are required to cure the problem. See also Jaffee and Russell (2003) p. 36.

[42] Shavell (1992).

[43] Winter (1992).

[44] Idem., pp. 61–62.

in insurance contracts under two conditions. The first is that the insured risk will be influenced by decisions taken by the insured individual after the contract is signed.[45] It has long been recognized that individuals and entities who are better covered by insurance invest less in risk prevention *ex ante* and risk mitigation *ex post*, particularly if the investments in risk prevention/mitigation have little or no bearing on the premium rate charged by the insurer.[46] Therefore, "[a]nyone who is insured against a risk will not capture the full benefits of efforts to reduce [or mitigate] the risk".[47]

The expenditure or effort taken by the insured individual to reduce risks or mitigate losses is referred to as the individual's care.[48] For instance, in the case of terrorism insurance in relation to air transport operations, it is clear that enhanced airport security can lower the possibility of a terrorist attack on an airport or on board an aircraft.[49] A distinction is often made in the economics literature between care and activity levels. In automobile insurance for example, care refers to driving at lower speeds and with greater diligence, whereas the level of activity refers to the amount of driving. However, decisions on *ex ante* care, *ex post* care and activity levels are all potentially distorted by insurance.[50] In the enhanced airport security example above, the issuance of a terrorism insurance policy to the airport or airline concerned may blunt the incentive to take such measures since the latter usually involves some large capital outlays.[51]

The second condition under which moral hazard arises in an insurance contract is that the care and activity levels cannot be costlessly specified in the insurance contract and enforced by the insurer.[52] To be amenable to specification and enforcement in the contract, the care and activity levels of the insured must be observable, *i.e.*, it should be possible for the insurer to easily monitor those phenomena. At this point, it is instructive to recall that under the assumptions of perfect competition/information underlying the competitive general equilibrium model of risk and insurance exchanges, the states of nature which occur with exogenous probabilities are assumed to be observable in that model, and insurance therefore has no adverse incentive or substitution effects.[53] In most typical real world situations, however, not much is observable beyond the fact that a particular accident has occurred or not.[54] The insurer is neither in a position to observe the states of nature nor the actions of the insured (*e.g.*, the investments in risk

---

[45] Idem., p. 62.

[46] Chiappori and Gollier (2006) pp. 4-5.

[47] Winter (1992) p. 62.

[48] Idem. It is also referred to as "effort" in the economics literature.

[49] Jaffee and Russell (2003) p. 36.

[50] Winter (1992) p. 62.

[51] Jaffee and Russell (2003) p. 36.

[52] Winter (1992) p. 62.

[53] Arnott (1992) p. 327.

[54] Idem., p. 326.

prevention made by the insured; the insured's vulnerability to the insured event; etc.).[55] In these circumstances, there is no mechanism by which the insurer can induce an insured individual to truthfully reveal either the state of nature or the care he has taken.[56] "Moral hazard arises because of [this] particular form of informational asymmetry – the insured's actions are unobservable by the insurer".[57]

"Moral hazard arises when neither the states of nature nor the actions of individuals are observable to an insurer. ... Thus, the insured-against events are accidents of varying degrees of severity not conditioned upon either the state of nature or the insured's actions. The provision of insurance against these events will generally affect the individual's incentives to take precautions, i.e., [it] has adverse incentive or substitution effects".[58] The resulting inverse relationship between risk prevention and insurance coverage leads to an inefficiently low level of risk prevention, as the incentives to avoid or to mitigate losses are compromised by insurance. Insurers anticipate this effect (*i.e.*, the low degree of prevention and the higher frequency of losses that it entails), and, in response, they raise insurance premiums. Insurers also employ partial solutions to the problem of moral hazard and these include providing incomplete coverage against loss through the use of deductibles, coinsurance, etc. Insurers assume that incomplete coverage gives an insured individual or entity a motive to prevent loss by exposing him directly to some of the financial risk.[59]

Economic analysis has established that "as the cost of taking care falls from very high levels (at which full [insurance] coverage is best), partial coverage becomes desirable; but at no point is the optimal level of coverage zero – *moral hazard cannot entirely eliminate the possibilities for insurance*; and as the cost of taking care approaches zero, the optimal coverage, although partial, approaches full coverage".[60] Building upon this finding, proponents of the new market failure theories have forcefully argued that the presence of moral hazard radically alters the nature of competitive equilibrium.[61] Specifically, it has been concluded that: in the presence of moral hazard, equilibrium may or may not exist;[62] when equilibrium exists, *some insurance markets may be inactive even though there is demand for insurance*;[63] and, in those insurance markets that are active, equilibrium may be characterized by positive profits, *rationing of insurance* and/or random premia and payouts.[64] In essence, these conclusions suggest, contrary to what the competitive general

[55] Winter (1992) p. 62.

[56] Arnott (1992) p. 326.

[57] Idem.

[58] Idem.

[59] Shavell (1992) p. 280.

[60] Idem., [emphasis added].

[61] Arnott (1992) p. 326.

[62] Idem.

[63] Idem., [emphasis added].

[64] Idem., at 327 [emphasis added].

equilibrium model suggests, that, there cannot be full insurance coverage for all individuals in each class of risk (and therefore an optimal equilibrium allocation of resources) if moral hazard is present in any economy. Most significantly, the new market failure theorists have also asserted with regard to moral hazard and insurance that "market prices do not reflect social opportunity costs. As a result, *the potential scope for efficiency-improving government intervention is considerable*".[65]

4.2.3.2 Adverse Selection and Imperfect Information

Adverse selection is conceptually distinct from moral hazard although, in real world insurance contexts, both phenomena are ubiquitous and occur simultaneously.[66] It is an insurance-related phenomena caused by another form of informational asymmetry—the insurer's inability to identify the specific risk types of individuals.[67] Normally, the potential buyer of insurance has prior knowledge about the risk (*i.e.*, his own health, living habits, driving behaviour, quality of maintenance of equipment, etc.) that the insurer does not have.[68] According to the theory, this situation is due to the fact that although the population may be heterogeneous, the observable characteristics of individual market participants may not perfectly reveal their risk.[69] Because it is impossible or prohibitively expensive for an insurer to overcome this informational asymmetry and thereby distinguish between high (bad) and low (good) risks, the price charged for covering the risk is fixed at an average value which attracts only those who are worse than average risks.[70] Adverse selection therefore occurs when, as a result of asymmetric information, a voluntary market mechanism tends to attract the wrong buyers and sellers,[71] *i.e.*, when high-risk individuals/entities purchase more insurance than low-risk individuals/entities.

The first explicit exposition of this phenomenon was made by Nobel Laureate Economist George Akerlof in his 1970 article titled "The Market for 'Lemons': Quality Uncertainty and the Market Mechanism".[72] George Akerlof used the second-hand car market as a possible example of this phenomenon. Akerlof's

[65] Idem. [emphasis added]. The issue of governmental intervention in private insurance markets is discussed in detail below.

[66] Idem. See also Winter (1992) p. 65 where the author notes that the contractual implications of adverse selection and moral hazard are identical. He cites the following example in support: "under both moral hazard and adverse selection, partial coverage for at least some individuals is optimal".

[67] Arnott (1992). See also Winter (1992) p. 64.

[68] Outreville (1998) p. 152.

[69] Chiappori and Gollier (2006) p. 3.

[70] Outreville (1998) p. 152.

[71] Cowen and Crampton (2003a) p. 7.

[72] Akerlof (1970).

market for lemons[73] theory has been succinctly summarized by one commentator as follows:

> The model assumes that sellers know the quality of the used car they are selling, but the buyers do not know the quality of what they are getting. Buyers, then, will only be willing to pay a price conditioned on the probability of receiving a lemon – a price that will necessarily be lower than the value of a good used car. This makes potential sellers of good used cars more reluctant to offer them for sale, lowering average quality in the marketplace even further. In equilibrium, only the lemons are sold, making it impossible to get a good used car simply by paying a higher price.[74]

In his groundbreaking work based on the economics of information, Nobel Laureate Economist Joseph Stiglitz extended the application of the concept of adverse selection by developing credit rationing and efficiency wages models—both based on imperfect information and particularly the mechanism of adverse selection—as two clear examples of how markets may misfire.[75] A comprehensive synthesis of Stiglitz's credit rationing model is captured in the quote below from a commentary on the subject:

> [Stiglitz's] credit rationing model starts with the claim that the probability of borrower default is related to the rate of interest charged on the loan. He argues, for instance, that at high rates of interest, the borrowing pool will be composed of an especially high percentage of deadbeats. ...[Underlying this model is the central asymmetric information assumption that] borrowers have a better idea of their likelihood of default than do lenders. High rates of interest therefore scare off the good borrowers, who expect to repay the loan. In contrast, high rates of interest do not scare off the deadbeats, who know their chance of having to repay the money is slight in any case. This principle then imposes a constraint on how high a rate of interest a lender will charge. Many lenders will keep interest rates artificially low, to maintain a higher quality pool of borrowers and to increase their chance of being paid back.
>
> In this setting, the interest rate will not necessarily clear the market for borrowing and lending. Banks keep interest rates down, but at those low rates demand exceeds supply. Lending must then be rationed. Banks will use non-price criteria, such as their estimation of borrower quality, or perhaps simple favouritism, to determine who can borrow how much money.[76]

Similarly, Stiglitz's efficiency wage model concerns how asymmetric information influences equilibrium in the labour market. According to the model, higher wages cause individuals to work harder.[77] However, since asymmetric information is rife in the labour market—the boss does not always know how hard the employees are working—employers must pay workers a certain premium if they expect to get good effort from them.[78] "When every employer pays a premium, however, some unemployment will result, due to the higher overall level of wages. ... At the going wage rate, more workers would like to have jobs than

[73] "Lemons" is a term used in America to refer to bad quality new or used cars. See idem., p. 489.

[74] Cowen and Crampton (2003a) p. 7.

[75] Idem., p. 6.

[76] Idem., pp. 6–7.

[77] Idem., p. 8.

[78] Idem.

can find them. The market price fails to clear the market and to coordinate all buyers and sellers".[79] In terms of adverse selection, "[h]igher wages will attract a higher quality of job applicants in the first place. Offering the market-clearing wage rate may attract only those individuals who do not have jobs, have been fired or cannot command a high premium for their skills, all of which may serve as examples of labour market 'lemons'".[80]

In essence, the effect of adverse selection is that "if all purchasers have imperfect information about quality, then a market for the product may not exist, or if it does function, it may not be efficient".[81] With specific reference to the application of adverse selection in the field of insurance, some notable commentators have observed that:

> [t]he potential for adverse selection crops up in insurance markets as well. When a firm offers insurance, for instance, it might expect that only the worst risks will be interested in purchasing the contract. The contract therefore must be structured to pay for these high risk individuals, which will further discourage low-risk individuals from buying insurance. Adverse selection models imply that low risk individuals have a hard time finding fairly priced insurance in the marketplace.[82]

Credit rationing and efficiency wage theories have had a significant influence on economic policy, particularly in the US. "Market failure remains one of the most influential arguments for government intervention".[83] Economists have often cited the efficiency wage theory when pushing for an increase in the minimum wage—the claim being that, in an efficiency wage model, the higher real wage would not put as many people out of work as otherwise might be expected.[84] "Credit rationing models have been used to justify a number of governmental interventions into credit markets, including usury laws (maximum ceilings on interest rates), fairness in lending regulations, and government investment subsidies. Credit rationing has also been used to argue for a more activist monetary

[79] Idem.

[80] Idem.

[81] Kunreuther and Pauly (1985).

[82] Cowen and Crampton (2003a) p. 7. See also Chiappori and Gollier (2006) pp. 3–4 where the authors note that:

> The adverse selection problem ... originates from the observation that if insurance companies calculate the premium rate on the basis of the average probability distribution in the population, the less risky agents will purchase less insurance than riskier agents. In the extreme case, the low-risk agents will find the premium rate too large with respect to their actual probability of loss. They will prefer not to insure their risk. Insurers will anticipate this reaction, and they will increase the premium rate to break even only on the population of high-risk policyholders. In summary, the presence of high risk agents generates a negative externality to lower risk agents who are unable to find an insurance premium at an acceptable premium rate.

[83] Cowen and Crampton (2003a) p. 3.

[84] Idem., p. 8.

policy, to encourage banks to lend more to customers".[85] In the insurance sector, economists relying on the foregoing theories have suggested that problems of moral hazard and adverse selection have a negative impact on the insurability of certain risks, and since market failures are inevitable if such risks are left to be insured by private markets, governments should intervene in those markets and either provide the required insurance or act as insurer or guarantor of last resort.[86]

4.2.4 How Market Failure Theories Explain the Behavior of Insurance Markets for Catastrophic Risks

Two leading authors on the subject, Dwight Jaffee and Thomas Russell, have specifically examined the reasons why extreme event insurance markets[87] tend to collapse following the occurrence of a major catastrophic event.[88] Prior to advancing explanations of the post-event behaviour of extreme event insurance markets, they analyze the conditions necessary for the formation of an extreme event insurance syndicate. In this regard, they argue that extreme event insurance is not fundamentally different from other lines of casualty insurance (*e.g.*, auto insurance) since, in both cases, "investors will always be willing to participate in an insurance syndicate portfolio as long as either the premium loading (the premium in excess of the expected loss) is sufficiently large and/or the number of investors is sufficiently large (meaning that each investor takes on a sufficiently small share of the portfolio)".[89] They note further that "[t]his conclusion is true, moreover, even when the expected loss or variance of each policy is large and/or when the individual risks are highly (even perfectly) correlated. Of course, when the risks are larger or more highly correlated, then the premium loading or the number of investors will itself have to be larger to induce investors to purchase a share of the portfolio".[90]

While conceding that the parameter values that reasonably apply to extreme event insurance might be significantly different from those that apply to more

[85] Idem.

[86] See e.g., Moss (2002). Compare with Priest (2003).

[87] Extreme event insurance markets consist of those insurers who provide cover for events characterized by low probability and high losses or consequences. They include natural disaster insurance markets (e.g., earthquakes and hurricanes), insurance markets for catastrophic nuclear accidents, and terrorist insurance markets (e.g., the aviation war risk insurance market).

[88] Their joint essay on the subject is published as a part of a collection of essays in honour of Joseph E. Stiglitz. Despite very careful research, this is the only essay that the present author came across that specifically addresses the issue of extreme event insurance market failure following a major event. See Jaffee and Russell (2003).

[89] Idem., p. 38.

[90] Idem.

standard casualty lines,[91] Jaffee and Russell conclude that, in the long run, the implication is still the same: "the premium loading and the number of investors necessary to induce investors to hold an extreme event insurance portfolio is likely to be larger than for more traditional casualty risks, *but this is a question of degree, not of kind*".[92] Thus, in line with the foregoing, "[i]f capital markets are perfect and all investors hold highly diversified market portfolios, then an equity position in an insurance firm should be an efficient structure for holding even large and highly correlated extreme risks".[93] Drawing upon the concept of imperfect information, however, Jaffee and Russell identify three sets of capital market imperfections which could impede this result: (1) asymmetric information within the syndicate;[94] (2) bankruptcy/agency costs;[95] and, (3) a variety of institutional impediments to accumulating capital reserves against future possible losses.[96]

---

[91] With respect to extreme events, they specify the differences between the relevant parameter values as follows:

1. The size of the risks are larger;
2. The correlation coefficients between individual risks may be higher; and,
3. The performance guarantee costs may be higher as a result of (1) and (2).

See idem., p. 38.

[92] Idem., [emphasis added].

[93] Idem., p. 39.

[94] "In forming an insurance syndicate, there is always the possibility that some members will have more information about the risks at issue than others. This problem is distinct from the insured/ insurer adverse selection problem ... [b]ut this source of asymmetric information can also lead to market failure". See idem.

[95] "If the losses created by an extreme event threaten an insurance firm with bankruptcy, then there is a potential for deadweight bankruptcy costs and related agency costs. In particular, it is clear that the probability that an insurance firm would be made bankrupt by a particularly bad extreme loss during 1 year is substantially higher than the probability that the same firm would be made bankrupt by a particularly bad run of, say, auto insurance losses during a year. It could thus be quite sensible for the insurance firm's managers to refuse to take on extreme risks for fear that the big one will cause the loss of their jobs due to the bankruptcy of their firm". See idem., pp. 38–39.

[96] "Extreme losses tend to be large, often exceeding the annual premiums collected for the coverage by a factor of 10 and possibly by as much as 100. In particular, if the event occurs early in the life of a syndicate, the premiums accumulated to that date will fall far short of the loss, leaving the syndicate responsible for the shortfall. Even with the risk spreading associated with reinsurance [and retrocession], any one risk bearing entity, and certainly the industry as a whole must have access to substantial capital if it is to pay these losses... This compares with routine lines such as auto insurance or dental insurance, where one year's premiums will almost always cover one year's losses, thus requiring the insurance firm to place little of its own capital at risk." See idem., p. 40. Three fundamental problems with insurance companies retaining earnings or raising capital in anticipation of possible future losses have been identified by the same authors in a previous publication:

- U.S. accounting rules preclude "ear-marking" retained profits or other capital funds as "reserves" against future losses, if the actual events have not yet occurred. Insurance firms, of course, are always free to retain their earnings, but the accounting rules preclude pre-committing these funds to pay only catastrophic losses.

Turning to the post-event behaviour of extreme event insurance markets, Jaffee and Russell enquire into the reasons why the simple occurrence of a low probability, high consequence event should cause the failure of a previously well-functioning insurance market. They note as follows:

> The occurrence of an event may contain information requiring the reassessment of the means, variances and co-variances of the underlying risks. But, after an appropriate adjustment in premiums, it would appear insurance syndicates should again be viable. Clearly, however, this is not what happens. Typically, following an extreme event, insurance markets are seriously disrupted. ... In fact, following the September 11 event, a previously well functioning market for terrorist insurance became highly ineffective. Similar breakdowns occur regularly following similar catastrophic events such as hurricanes and earthquakes.[97]

Even though it can be argued that the likelihood of future terrorist attacks was higher after September 11, 2001, than before, this only amounted to a change in the perceived probability of occurrence of such attacks; a new development which could simply be addressed with higher premiums.[98] Alternatively, even assuming that the degree of uncertainty surrounding terrorism went up, either increasing the variance of claims or increasing parameter uncertainty, this could also be handled by an appropriate adjustment in the premium charged for covering the risk.[99] However, Jaffee and Russell observe that apart from the fact that premiums rise steeply after an extreme event has occurred, the quantity of insurance available at any price also becomes severely restricted.[100]

Jaffee and Russell therefore conclude that there is more at stake than simply the fact that premiums rise after an extreme event.[101] In their opinion, although moral

---

- U.S. tax rules require full taxation of profits that are retained as reserves against future losses. This makes retained earnings an expensive way to accumulate funds against possible future losses.
- A firm that accumulates liquidity to cover future large losses could become a takeover target due to its large cash assets. Since the liquidity cannot be pre-committed to catastrophic losses, a third party could take over the firm, allow the policies to mature, and then use the liquidity for another purpose.

See generally: Jaffee and Russell (1997).

[97] Jaffee and Russell (2003) p. 41.

[98] Idem., p. 36.

[99] Idem.

[100] The insurance of Chicago airports offers a practical illustration of the foregoing. Prior to September 11, 2001, Chicago carried $750 million of terrorist insurance for an annual premium of $125,000. Post-September 11, their insurers would only offer $150 million of coverage for the new premium of $6.9 million. Not only had premiums been significantly increased; the upper limit of coverage had also been severely reduced. See idem.The incidence of very steep increases in the rates of premium charged coupled with severe rationing or restriction of the quantity of insurance cover previously available provides the basis for economists to conclude that a market failure has occurred in the war risk insurance market.

[101] Idem.

hazard and adverse selection (the standard explanations offered for insurance market failures) are not completely absent in extreme event insurance markets, "they are unlikely to be a major contributor to an explanation of the puzzle of market collapse"[102] following the occurrence of such an event. Building upon several strands of previous research based on imperfect information, they offer two sets of explanations (distinct from the concepts of moral hazard and adverse selection) for this type of market failure. The first set of explanations offered relates to post-event capital market imperfections and it is discussed in detail below. The other set of explanations is associated with behavioural responses to bad draws and is discussed below separately in Sect. 4.3.

4.2.4.1 Post-event Capital Market Imperfections

Jaffee and Russell argue that one of the underlying causes of post-event market failure in extreme event insurance markets is that, for a number of reasons, "new capital does not immediately flow into catastrophe lines following an event, so that private insurers either limit coverage or withdraw from the line completely".[103] In their own words:

> After a major event wipes out most of the [insurance] industry's capital, firms might be expected to use the financial markets to replenish their capital base. With minor exceptions, however, insurance firms have not issued new equity to replenish their capital following an extreme event. This is puzzling since the period following an event is in many ways the perfect time for a syndicate to raise new capital. Rates normally harden following an event and this will be reflected in higher stock prices, reducing the cost of equity. The markets responded in exactly this way following September 11, yet insurance firms have not used the financial markets to replenish their capital in any significant way.[104]

It is argued that "insurers will respond to a sudden loss of surplus by reducing capacity and slowly building capital internally rather than seeking to raise costly external capital immediately. The reduction in capacity will result in severe increases in prices in the insurance product market. The quantity of insurance traded will then fall substantially, reflecting the withdrawal of capacity and its

---

[102] Idem.

[103] Idem., p. 43.

[104] Idem., pp. 41–42. Two major factors that may account for this situation were identified by the same authors in a previous publication. They are:

- The fact that potential investors in the new securities may be concerned that their funds will be used to pay off past losses and not to support new profitable initiatives; and,
- The possibility that asymmetric information may lead potential investors to evaluate future risks at a higher level than does the issuing firm, causing the new investors to require a lower price for the new securities than the firm is willing to accept.

See generally: Jaffee and Russell (1997).

impact on prices".[105] In an effort to facilitate and/or enhance the general flow of capital into insurance markets, a number of innovative insurance derivatives have been created in recent years, including option and futures contracts and catastrophe bonds.[106] "These securities are motivated by the notion that catastrophe events represent, by and large, zero beta risks, so that capital market investors should be willing to take on these risks at a price that reflects only the expected loss, with little or no risk premium above that amount".[107] Jaffee and Russell are of the view that these securities, also, have failed to provide an effective mechanism for transferring catastrophic risks from insurance firms to capital markets. They identify three basic reasons for this state of affairs:

1. Just as with new security issues, the potential for asymmetric information may lead investors to evaluate future risks at a higher level than does the issuing firm;
2. With the future and option instruments, the need to provide adequate performance guarantees has restricted the amount of risk transfer to relatively small amounts; and,
3. Investors may believe that catastrophic events will depress the economy and stock market generally, creating a positive, possibly even very large, expected beta value, and thus raising the cost of the catastrophe insurance security.[108]

Finally, Jaffee and Russell suggest that perhaps the reluctance of the capital markets to issue new capital to replace the capital lost by the insurance industry following major events could also reflect the hope shared by all that governments might come to the rescue.[109]

---

[105] Doherty et al. (2003) p. 186.

[106] "Catastrophe bonds are a class of securities issued by insurance or reinsurance firms. The issuer places the proceeds from the bond sale in Treasury securities. If the cat [catastrophic] event does not occur, the Treasury securities are sold to repay the principal to the bondholders. If the cat event does occur, then the insurance firm receives the proceeds from the Treasury bond sale, and the firm is also relieved of its obligation to repay the principal and any further interest on the bonds". See Jaffee and Russell (2003) p. 42, fn. 4. Catastrophe bonds have been used extensively in the natural disaster insurance markets (earthquakes, hurricanes, etc.), but not in the terrorism insurance market (e.g., the aviation war risk insurance market). The present author therefore highly recommends that the aviation war risk insurance market could explore the feasibility of adapting such derivatives as a means of raising the much needed capital for the industry.

[107] Idem., p. 42.

[108] Idem. Also, see generally: Jaffee and Russell (1997).

[109] Jaffee and Russell (2003). This suggestion rekindles the debate as to who should bear the cost of aerial terrorism (*i.e.*, as between operators: airlines, airports, air navigation service providers, ground handling service providers and their insurers on the one hand; victims on the ground; and, governments on the other hand). This issue will be revisited in subsequent sections of this book.

4.2.5 Criticisms of the New Market Failure Arguments

As convincing as they may sound, the new imperfect information-based market failure arguments have been criticized both on theoretical and empirical grounds.[110] Critics have argued, for instance, that the arguments have been grossly overstated and applied without sufficient discrimination; and that the models are not very general but, rather, rest on very specific assumptions.[111] Others have questioned the empirical relevance of the anti-market mechanisms, noting that "it is one thing to argue that credit rationing and efficiency wages [and the asymmetric information theories upon which they are based] are theoretical possibilities, but it is quite another to argue that they are significant phenomena in the real world".[112] It may be recalled for instance that, in its extreme form, Akerlof's lemons argument predicts that due to adverse selection it is impossible to buy a good used car. This prediction is, however, countermanded by the millions of used cars that are bought and sold worldwide each year, frequently to the satisfaction of both buyer and seller.[113]

Aside from the numerous empirical tests that have been conducted in insurance markets the results of which have failed to support the lemons hypothesis,[114] it has been suggested that it may be cost efficient for insurers to overcome informational asymmetries in the market, and if they do not attempt to do so, then it may be because it is not worthwhile.[115] Indeed, as far back as the 1930s, Economists such as Friedrich A. Hayek, Ludwig von Mises and others had stressed imperfect information and dispersed knowledge in the economy as fundamental arguments for the continued existence of markets and of any liberal order.[116] "[I]n Hayek's view, markets eliminate asymmetry by revealing relevant aspects of information in market prices".[117] Building upon these views, critics of the new market failure theories have strongly argued that the existence of "informational asymmetries (and simple lack of information) [in the economy] create a demand for product assurance that entrepreneurs can profit from by meeting".[118] They argue further that:

[110] For a collection of key articles challenging the claims of the new market failure arguments in the more recent debates on market failure, See generally: Cowen and Crampton (2003b).

[111] Cowen and Crampton (2003a) pp. 5, 8–9.

[112] Idem., p. 9. Critics refer to the fact that Joseph Stiglitz has never presented empirical work on his basic mechanisms as an added basis for skepticism about the relevance of his research.

[113] Idem., p. 10.

[114] See e.g.: Cawley and Philipson (1999), Bond (1982), and Chiappori and Salanie (2000).

[115] Cawley and Philipson (1999) pp. 842–843. See also Cowen and Crampton (2003a) p. 10.

[116] Cowen and Crampton (2003a) p. 4.

[117] Idem.

[118] Idem., p. 12.

> Buyers and sellers are willing to pay to overcome the problems that information asymmetries cause. Buyers seek assurance that purchased products will meet expectations, and sellers know that confidence in product quality generate sales. Several mechanisms have emerged to meet the demand for assurance. At the most basic level, extended dealings and firm reputation, coupled with a low enough discount rate can engender cooperative transactions and trust. Firms go to considerable expense to foster such extended dealings.[119]

In line with the foregoing, institutions have arisen spontaneously in the market system to mitigate problems of information, quality and certification.[120] "Trusted middlemen [have emerged] between buyers and sellers who would otherwise find it too costly to investigate the trustworthiness of each other. ... Consumer reports, Underwriters Laboratories, CARFAX and a multitude of credit bureaus [to name only a few] reduce the information asymmetries between buyers and sellers of products and credit".[121] The typical insurance company has the ability to process actuarial statistics and to hire specialists for advice.[122] Market failure theory predicts massive deadweight losses accruing from the trades that fail to take place because of informational asymmetries. In reality, alert entrepreneurs see deadweight losses as potential profits to be earned by removing the impediment to trade.[123] Once the underlying informational asymmetry goes away, the adverse selection argument does not get off the ground.[124]

One critic takes the argument against adverse selection in insurance markets one step further.[125] According to this critic, if the phenomenon of adverse selection in insurance markets occurs in reality, then, in line with its underlying assumption that individuals are consistent in risk preferences across physical and financial dimensions, propitious selection must ensue (*i.e.*, people with higher levels of risk avoidance are more likely to both buy insurance and exercise care, whereas those with low levels of risk avoidance, or those who are actually risk seeking, will tend to do neither).[126] However, in reality, this is usually not the case.

Where the theory of adverse selection would, for instance, lead motorcyclists to purchase more insurance, the likelihood is that motorcyclists admitted to hospital after accidents are more likely than car drivers similarly admitted to have no insurance at all, and that un-helmeted motorcyclists (the most risk seeking class) are the least likely to carry any insurance.[127] Similarly, automobile associations

---

119 See idem., citing Klein (2002).

120 Cowen and Crampton (2003a) p. 12.

121 Idem.

122 Idem.

123 Idem., pp. 12–13.

124 Idem., p. 10.

125 Hemenway (1990).

126 Idem., pp. 1063–1064.

127 Idem., pp. 1065–1066. The author demonstrates this phenomenon empirically with statistics from the Boston General Hospital and the Brackenridge Hospital in Austin Texas. Although the empirical evidence relied upon by the author is not very rigorous, it is at least suggestive. See Cowen and Crampton (2003a).

which provide insurance in the form of assistance to member drivers in distress should be comprised of young risky drivers with unreliable cars according to the adverse selection theory. But, in fact, they mostly count richer, older drivers as members.[128] Finally, with respect to rental car insurance which is a voluntary purchase, the theory of adverse selection implies that poor drivers would find the insurance a good deal, while the theory of moral hazard suggests that once the insurance is purchased, the operator will tend to drive less carefully. However, the theory of propitious selection provides findings contrary to these two factors: it suggests that people who are risk avoiders will tend to both drive safely and to purchase insurance.[129] While the theory of propitious selection does nothing to eliminate the moral hazard problem of insurance markets, it does render far less likely insurance market failures associated with adverse selection.[130]

Yet another criticism levelled against the market failure theories is found in the implicit contract model of insurance shocks and post-loss rationing devised by Neil Doherty and Lisa Posey in 1997.[131] According to this model, after a loss occurs, prices for new coverage are raised (reflecting the shortage of capital), but insurance coverage is rationed at this new price. Proponents of this model argue, however, that the rationing of coverage that occurs is not evidence of a market failure, but is rather an implicit part of *ex ante* efficient contract design since, without the prospect of being able to ration coverage after catastrophic losses, insurers would be less willing to offer catastrophic coverage in the first place.[132] In other words, "[t]he model argues that insurers will be more willing to offer coverage for first-event catastrophic events if second-event coverage is both expensive and rationed".[133] Thus the combination of price increases and rationing of coverage that occurs after a major loss does not signify a failure of the market, but instead, accomplishes several goals[134] which are consistent with efficient insurance contracting rather than evidence of a market failure.[135]

---

[128] Hemenway (1990) p. 1066.

[129] Idem., pp. 1066–1067.

[130] Cowen and Crampton (2003a)

[131] See Doherty and Posey (1997).

[132] Idem., pp. 58 ff.

[133] See Doherty et al. (2003) p. 181.

[134] These goals are as follows: "First, undiversifiable risk is passed back to the policyholders. Second insurers can cover their additional costs by raising prices, but do not disassemble since this would involve greater rationing at the post-loss prices. Thirdly, and prospectively, insurers are more willing to offer coverage for such severe events because they know they can raise prices for such coverage and by rationing they need not stretch their depleted capital". See Doherty and Posey (1997) p. 189.

[135] Idem., pp. 181–182.

4.3 Behavioural Explanations of the Post-Event Reactions of Extreme Event Insurance Markets

As mentioned above, in their landmark essay on the subject,[136] Jaffee and Russell do not restrict their analysis of the post-event behaviour of extreme event insurance markets to the field of economics. They also draw upon some behavioural and/or psychological explanations of this phenomenon, "including a new explanation based on a behavioural interpretation of attitudes to risk".[137] These behavioural explanations explore both cognitive and non-cognitive theories[138] of choice under risk or uncertainty in an effort to explain the behaviour of insurance entities and the people within them who are primarily charged with decision making functions. The general premise for these behavioural explanations has been succinctly summarized by one commentator as follows:

> [R]isk involves some chance of a negative – or bad – outcome occurring, [and] the extent of risk therefore depends on both the probability of the event occurring and the size of the negative outcome. In dealing with many risks, however, people (*and even insurance companies*) do not have access to data that allows them to assess and calculate risks in a rational manner. They therefore rely on more tacit or intuitive ways of dealing with risk that involve *feelings* or *emotions*; in addition, *imagination* plays an important role. *Tacit or intuitive knowledge*, however, is limited by past experience and imagination may be insufficient or unrealistic. *In addition, both can be affected by the context of immediate experience that may or may not be relevant to the issues at hand.*[139]

Behavioural explanations of the post-event market reactions of extreme event insurance markets are discussed by Jaffee and Russell under three specific heads: ambiguity aversion; fairness; and, irrational abhorrence. The first two heads involve purely cognitive considerations and, as such, are discussed together. The last head involves additional (non-cognitive) psychological considerations and is therefore discussed separately.

---

[136] See Jaffee and Russell (2003).

[137] Idem., p. 43.

[138] Cognitive theories of choice (also referred to as consequentialist theories) posit that risk-related decisions (and choices) made by human beings are always the result of some conscious intellectual or cognitive activity of the human mind. They assume that people assess the desirability and likelihood of possible outcomes of risky choice alternatives, albeit subjectively and possibly with bias or error, and integrate this information through some type of expectation-based calculus to arrive at a decision. Under these theories, feelings triggered by the decision situation and imminent risky choice are seen as epiphenomenal, i.e., not integral to the decision making process. See Loewenstein et al. (2001). Non-cognitive theories of choice, on the other hand, are premised on the fact that additional psychological factors (such as emotional reactions to risky situations) play a role in decision making processes.

[139] Hogarth (2002) (emphasis added).

4.3.1 Ambiguity Aversion and Fairness

In deciding whether or not to accept a risk, an insurer will typically go through the cognitive process of assessing the likelihood of the risk materializing and the consequent loss exposure that he will face if the risk materializes. One reason the insurance industry has been reluctant to cover certain risks is the ambiguity or uncertainty associated with either the probability of specific events occurring or the magnitude of the potential consequences or both.[140] Ambiguity in this sense may be defined as the extent to which the chances of the risk materializing or the magnitude of the associated losses cannot be estimated with a reasonable degree of certainty by an insurer. Indeed, empirical studies[141] conducted over the years strongly suggest that ambiguity related to both probabilities and losses plays a key role in the decisions made by underwriters, actuaries, insurers and reinsurers on what premiums to charge and what coverage to offer, if any.[142]

The principal reason why actuaries, underwriters, insurers and reinsurers want to charge higher premiums or completely avoid providing coverage when there is considerable ambiguity surrounding a risk is because, in their perception, all potential policyholders are affected in the same way by the uncertainty regarding probability or losses.[143] As noted in one commentary "[i]f there is a lack of understanding concerning the mechanism causing a loss, then this uncertainty will affect all the risks. Similarly, if one is uncertain as to what type of liability ruling will be invoked should a claim be made on one policy, then this uncertainty will affect all policies".[144] As a result of these cognitive considerations, the insurance industry has been unwilling to extend coverage very widely for risks in respect of which there is considerable ambiguity on both the probability and outcome dimensions.[145]

---

[140] Kunreuther and Hogarth (1992) p. 308. The authors demonstrate ambiguous probability with the example of political risks: the reluctance of insurers to provide coverage for industrial firms investing in developing countries with unstable political systems stems from the difficulty in estimating the probabilities associated with losses of different magnitudes. With respect to ambiguous losses, the historic reluctance of insurers to provide coverage to manufacturers of the pertussis vaccine against possible brain damage caused by the use of the vaccine is offered as an example. Although the probability of such serious side effects of the vaccine were well known, the size of court awards from product liability suits against the manufacturer made the costs of insurance prohibitive to the manufacturers.

[141] Idem. See also Kunreuther et al. (1993). The findings made by these authors were based on the results of empirical surveys of actuaries, underwriters and reinsurers.

[142] See Kunreuther and Hogarth (1992) p. 308. See also Kunreuther et al. (1995).

[143] Kunreuther and Hogarth (1992) p. 318.

[144] Idem.

[145] Idem. The example offered is the case of insurance coverage for environmental pollution damage which, at some point in time, was avoided by practically all major insurance firms. Not only was the probability of a claim against the insurer uncertain, but should a suit be filed against the insured party, there was no guarantee that the costs to the insurer would be bounded by the

By their very nature, extreme event insurance markets are more vulnerable to ambiguity than many other lines of insurance. The low probabilities associated with the occurrence of extreme events implies that, usually, there is very little or no historical data on the basis of which insurers can estimate the probability of occurrence of future events. The catastrophic nature of the losses that flow from such events also makes the estimation of potential future losses a rather imprecise task. The occurrence of an extreme event will frequently trigger an increase in the level of uncertainty surrounding future events and thereby deepen the level of ambiguity associated with the risk.[146] Naturally, as most insurers are ambiguity averse,[147] they will tend to either charge very high premiums or completely shy away from covering such risks after such an event has occurred.

Aside from ambiguity, notions of fairness have also been used to explain why certain insurance markets may fail during periods when profit-maximizing models predict that they should be increasing the premiums they charge for covering certain risks in order for the market not to fail. In this regard, it has been argued that when events require a sharp increase in price, markets may fail to clear because the seller is reluctant to increase the price and thereby incur the bad will caused by an apparently unfair price increase.[148] The underlying rationale is that cognitive considerations relating to community standards of fairness and the possible negative outcomes of price increases do in fact restrict the actions of profit-seeking insurance firms in raising premiums.[149] By logical extension, if, as a result of such considerations, insurance firms cannot raise premiums following the occurrence of an event, then the only option open to them is to ration or completely withdraw coverage forthwith.

Proponents of this concept assert, however, that unlike ambiguity, it is less obvious that fairness plays a significant role in extreme event insurance markets.[150] In support, they note that unfairness is generally associated with price increases for which there is no obvious cost justification. Losses created by extreme events—earthquakes, hurricanes and terrorist attacks—on the contrary, are all widely reported, and, in their opinion, this blunts any accusations of opportunism that may arise after premiums are raised.[151] The reaction of the aviation war risk insurance market to the events of September 11, 2001, provides some support for the argument that fairness does not play a significant role in extreme event insurance markets.

---

stated limits of coverage. Coverage for aviation war risks and other extreme events fall within this category.

[146] Jaffee and Russell (2003) p. 43.

[147] The various empirical studies referred to above suggest that actuaries and underwriters will add an ambiguity premium in pricing a given risk whenever there is heightened uncertainty regarding either the probability or the magnitude of losses. For a discussion of the various reasons underlying the ambiguity aversion patterns of insurers, see Kunreuther et al. (1995) pp. 346–349.

[148] Jaffee and Russell (2003).

[149] Kahneman et al. (1986) p. 729.

[150] Jaffee and Russell (2003) p. 44.

[151] Idem.

It will be recalled that following that event, not only were prices raised very steeply; the depth of coverage the market was willing to provide going forward was also severely restricted. Obviously, cognitive considerations regarding the bad will to be incurred by insurers following premium rate increases and rationing/withdrawal of coverage did not influence the decisions made by the insurers in any significant manner.

4.3.2 *Irrational Abhorrence*

Some experts who have studied the psychology of human judgement/decision making processes have recognized that, apart from the cognitive factors discussed above, decision making under risk and uncertainty involves additional psychological (*i.e.*, non-cognitive, emotional) considerations.[152] In their seminal essay on the subject, George F. Loewenstein and his collaborators describe this new approach as "risk-as-feelings".[153] This approach proposes a model of choice under risk and uncertainty that highlights the role of *anticipatory emotions*—immediate visceral reactions (*e.g.*, fear anxiety, dread) that arise at the time of decision-making. The model is fundamentally different from the cognitive/consequentialist models of choice which, to the extent that they incorporate emotions at all, tend to incorporate *anticipated emotions*—emotions that are expected to result from the consequences of the decision.[154] By taking into account the role played by anticipatory emotions that are experienced at the moment of decision making, the new approach explains a variety of phenomena that have eluded explanation by theorists relying on purely cognitive theories of risky choice.

The risk-as-feelings hypothesis posits that "people react to the prospect of risk at two levels: they evaluate the risk cognitively, and they react to it emotionally".[155]

---

[152] Idem., pp. 44–45.

[153] Idem. See also Loewenstein et al. (2001) p. 270, where the authors note as follows: "The risk-as-feelings hypothesis . . . postulates that responses to risky situations (including decision making) result in part from direct . . . emotional influences, including feelings such as worry, fear, dread, or anxiety. People are assumed to evaluate risky alternatives at a cognitive level . . . based largely on the probability and desirability of associated consequences. Such cognitive evaluations have affective consequences, and feeling states also exert a reciprocal influence on cognitive evaluations. At the same time, however, feeling states are postulated to respond to factors such as the immediacy of a risk, that do not enter into cognitive evaluations of the risk and also respond to probabilities and outcome values in a fashion that is different from the way in which these variables enter into cognitive evaluations".

[154] Loewenstein et al. (2001) p. 281.

[155] Idem., p. 280. The authors note further that although the two types of reactions are interrelated, they have different determinants. Whereas cognitive evaluations are sensitive to variables such as probabilities and outcome valences, emotional reactions are sensitive to the vividness of associated imagery, proximity in time, and a variety of other variables that play a minimal role in cognitive evaluations. As a result of these differences, people often experience a discrepancy

Although cognitive evaluations of, and emotional reactions to, risky situations typically work in concert to guide human reasoning and decision making, emotional reactions often diverge from cognitive assessments of risks, and when such divergence occurs, emotional reactions often drive behaviour and produce behavioural responses that depart from what individuals view as the best or most rational course of action.[156] Thus, for example, in the face of heightened risks such as in the period following the occurrence of an extreme event, the overwhelming influence of non-cognitive factors in the decision making process may lead to irrational behaviour by insurers (*e.g.*, a withdrawal of supply of insurance).[157]

These non-cognitive emotional factors have been extensively studied by psychologists such as Ellen Peters and Paul Slovic.[158] In their opinion, the psychological dimensions of risk can be distilled into two primary factors: *dread* defined by Loewenstein et al. as "the extent of perceived lack of control, feelings of dread, and *perceived catastrophic potential*";[159] and *the risk of the unknown*, defined as "the extent to which the hazard is judged to be unobservable, unknown, new or delayed in producing harmful effects".[160] According to Loewenstein et al., "the first of these dimensions [dread] clearly suggests an *affective* rather than a *cognitive* evaluation of hazards".[161] That dread could lead to inaction or irrational behaviour and, in the context of terrorist insurance markets, to a withdrawal of supply is consistent with the observation that individuals typically shun investments that have just experienced a major loss.[162]

This observation provides a unifying framework for the analysis of a number of extreme event phenomena. According to Dwight Jaffee and Thomas Russell,

> [s]ince the essence of insurance is risk sharing, it is essential that anyone contemplating joining an insurance syndicate believes that there are enough other potential members of

---

between the fear they experience in connection with a particular risk and their cognitive evaluation of the threat posed by that risk.

156 Idem., pp. 270–271.

157 Jaffee and Russell (2003) p. 45 where the authors note that "noncognitive factors lead to inaction rather than wrong action in the face of some risks". See also Loewenstein et al. (2001) p. 269, where the authors elaborate further with the following examples: "Fear causes us to slam on the brakes instead of steering into the skid, immobilizes us when we have greatest need for strength, causes sexual dysfunction, insomnia, ulcers and gives us dry mouth and jitters at the very moment when there is the greatest premium on clarity and eloquence".

158 Peters and Slovic (1996).

159 Loewenstein et al. (2001) p. 269 [emphasis added].

160 Idem.

161 Idem. [emphasis added].

162 Idem., pp. 272–273. See also Jaffee and Russell (2003) p. 45. This observation is based on the findings of a series of studies conducted by a group of psychologists. In those studies, subjects were told that they could earn hypothetical money by turning over cards from one of four decks. Two of the decks contained high payouts ($100) and two contained low payouts ($50). The high paying decks however also contained a catastrophe card marked with a very high loss. On average, subjects sampled from all four decks until they drew the catastrophe card, at which point they thereafter avoided the catastrophe deck. For a report on the studies, See Bechara et al. (1997).

> the syndicate to make his or her share of the risk small. For example this appears to have been the case pre-September 11. Following the event, however, even if a non-emotional investor believes that the syndicate could be profitable if sufficiently subdivided, the syndicate will not be viable if (1) the event causes a sufficient number of investors to become unavailable, or (2) it causes sufficient investors to have the belief that a sufficient number of investors will be unavailable. In the latter case, the belief that the syndicate was not viable becomes a self fulfilling prophecy.[163]

In other words, although individual actuaries and underwriters evaluating the risk after an extreme event has occurred may arrive at positive actuarial computations, non-cognitive considerations of dread (in the sense of a perceived lack of control and a perceived uncertainty as to the catastrophic potential of future events) and the risk of the unknown (the extent to which the hazard is judged to be unobservable, unknown, new or delayed in producing harmful effects) may play a more prominent role in their decision making processes and thereby cause them to avoid insuring the risk in question. Such abhorrence of the risk is considered irrational since it runs contrary to the decision that an ordinarily prudent actuary or underwriter acting reasonably will be expected to arrive at under the circumstances.

The occurrence of irrational abhorrence may perhaps be explained by resorting to yet another psychological concept heavily relied upon by proponents of behavioral law and economics.[164] This is the theory of *hindsight bias*, also known as the *availability heuristic*. In their seminal publication on the subject, psychologists Amos Tversky and Daniel Kahneman found that people rely on a limited number of heuristic principles which reduce the complex tasks of assessing probabilities and predicting values to simpler judgmental operations in assessing the probability of an uncertain event or the value of an uncertain quantity.[165] One such heuristic principle, according to the authors, is the availability heuristic by virtue of which people attach high probabilities to events simply because they have occurred before.[166] In other words, the fact that decisions made after a negative event has materialized are often biased toward excessively high estimates of the event recurring is attributable simply to the fact that the negative event in question has materialized before and, as such, can easily be brought to mind.[167] In essence, this reflects the operation of the availability heuristic—people seem to have difficulty putting aside events they know to have occurred. The availability heuristic also explains the reactive bias (rather than proactive approach) observed in the conventional insurance market for aviation war and terrorism risks.

Notwithstanding the foregoing, it appears unlikely that all investors will pass on a positive profit project just because it once generated a bad draw. It is known that some individuals are less prone to irrational abhorrence than others. In particular, there appears to be a remarkable difference between the response of individuals and

---

[163] Jaffee and Russell (2003) p. 45.

[164] Jolls (2007) pp. 14–15; 21 (hindsight bias).

[165] Tversky and Kahneman (1974).

[166] Idem., p. 1127.

[167] Jolls (2007) pp. 14–15.

the response within corporations. It would appear that the tendency to avoid projects that have suffered a loss is more pronounced in corporations than it is in entities run by single individuals.[168] For example, Warren Buffet, an executive who exercises strong individual control over his insurance businesses quickly offered to fill the gap when, following September 11, 2001, the large French insurer AXA Group terminated the international federation of football associations' (FIFA) 2002 Soccer World Cup cancellation insurance policy.[169] Again, in April 2002, while the global aviation insurance market was still reluctant to provide any meaningful war risk insurance coverage to the air transport industry, Warren Buffett's Berkshire Hathaway joined with Allianz and ten other insurance companies to offer terrorism insurance to airlines.[170] The scheme insured against losses arising from aviation war risks and covered a single plane for as much as $1 billion or an airline up to $2 billion a year, but the policy was subject to automatic termination immediately after the occurrence of four major events resulting in losses.[171]

As such, reliance upon the concept of irrational abhorrence to explain the reactions of extreme event insurance markets in the post event period is subject to its own limitations.

4.4 The Systemic Nature of Aviation War and Terrorism Risks and Its Impact on Their Insurability

Some authors have argued that apart from the economic (i.e., market failure) and behavioural theories discussed above, the inherently systemic nature of the risks handled by catastrophic event insurance markets (including the aviation war risk insurance market) offers an alternative or complementary explanation for the steep increases in prices and withdrawal of coverage that occurs in such markets in the immediate post-event period. Although a review of the literature reveals the existence of a number of sector-specific descriptions of systemic risk, a precise insurance-specific definition of the concept is elusive.[172]

Within the broader financial sector for instance, systemic risk has been variously described as: "the danger of an event leading to a loss of economic value and/or

[168] Idem. Other commentators have explained this difference in attitudes by noting that insurance company managers who are rewarded with a share of the profits but suffer a large penalty in case the firm suffers insolvency will behave as if they are risk averse. They provide the following example: "suppose an insurance underwriter is concerned with his future employment opportunities should his firm be declared insolvent. He may then limit the amount of coverage for a particular risk or charge higher premiums than otherwise if he perceives the risks in his portfolio to be highly correlated". See Kunreuther et al. (2004).

[169] Bianco (2002).

[170] Idem.

[171] Idem.

[172] Schwarcz (2008) pp. 196–197.

of confidence in the financial system with grave consequences for the real economy";[173] "the probability that cumulative losses will occur from an event that ignites a series of successive losses along a chain of [financial] institutions or markets comprising . . . a system";[174] "the potential for a modest economic shock to induce substantial volatility in asset prices, significant reductions in corporate liquidity, potential bankruptcies and efficiency losses";[175] "[t]he risk that a default by one market participant will have repercussions on other participants due to the interlocking nature of financial markets. For example, Customer A's default in X market may affect Intermediary B's ability to fulfill its obligations in Markets X, Y, and Z";[176] the likelihood and the degree that the activities of a financial institution will negatively affect the larger economy;[177] and finally, as "risk that is both so extreme and so critical in its impact on society *that governments are required to insure them*, even at the cost of their own economic principles".[178] These definitions emphasize the interconnectedness of the global financial system and the potential for a shock to one part of the system to quickly spread to other parts and cause damage. The classical example of systemic risk in the financial sector is the bank run—where the short term inability of just one bank to handle the demands of account holders can create a global panic and pull down the entire financial system.[179]

In a joint paper on the subject, George Kaufman and Kenneth Scott identify and distill three different concepts from the various descriptions of systemic risk frequently appearing in the literature. In their own words:

> The first refers to a "big" shock or macroshock that produces nearly simultaneous, large, adverse effects on most or all of the domestic economy or system. Here, *systemic* "refers to an event having effects on the entire banking, financial, or economic system, rather than just one or a few institutions". . ..
>
> The other two definitions focus more on the microlevel and on the transmission of the shock and potential spillover from one unit to others. For example, according to the second definition, systemic risk is the "probability that cumulative losses will accrue from an event that sets in motion a series of successive losses along a chain of institutions or markets comprising a system. . .. That is, systemic risk is the risk of a chain reaction of falling interconnected dominos" . . ..
>
> A third definition of systemic risk also focuses on spillover from an initial exogenous external shock, but it does not involve direct causation and depends on weaker and more indirect connections. *It emphasizes similarities in third-party risk exposures among the units involved. When one unit experiences adverse effects from a shock – say, the failure of a large financial or nonfinancial firm – that generates severe losses, uncertainty is created about the values of other units potentially also subject to adverse effects from the same*

173 Baur and Enz (2003) p. 7.

174 Schwarcz (2008) p. 196, citing Kaufman (1996) p. 21 fn. 5.

175 Schwarcz (2008). pp. 196–197, citing Kupiec and Nickerson (2004).

176 Schwarcz (2008)

177 Property and Casualty Insurers Association of America (2009).

178 Mundy (2004) p. 30 [emphasis added].

179 Idem., p. 29.

> *shock. To minimize additional losses, market participants will examine other units, such as banks, in which they have economic interests to see whether and to what extent they are at risk. The more similar the risk-exposure profile to that of the initial unit economically, politically, or otherwise, the greater is the probability of loss, and the more likely it is that participants will withdraw funds as soon as possible.* This response may induce liquidity problems and even more fundamental solvency problems. This pattern may be referred to as a "common shock" or "reassessment shock" effect and represents correlation without direct causation (indirect causation).[180]

Although not specifically relevant to present purposes, it deserves mentioning that the presence of systemic risk (as defined in the immediately preceding paragraph) in the global economy accounted in large part for the global credit crisis which started in 2008 and subsequently precipitated a global economic recession second in rank only to the great depression of 1933. The initial shock to the system was the failure of a significantly small part of the global financial sector—the US housing and sub-prime mortgage sector. This caused a global liquidity crisis in the US as financial institutions became concerned about their own survival and refused to lend to each other. This in turn created adverse effects on the real economy such as job losses, bankruptcies, etc. This development falls very much in line with the observation that: "[n]ot all economic downturns involve systemic risk but the occurrence of systemic risk has almost invariably transformed economic downturns into deep recessions and even depressions".[181]

Outside the financial realm, systemic risk has been broadly defined by the Organization for Economic Cooperation and Development (OECD) as encompassing "*those risks that affect the systems on which society depends* – health, transport, environment, telecommunications, etc.".[182] Five categories of risk explicitly identified by the OECD as falling within this definition are: natural disasters; industrial accidents; infectious diseases; terrorism; and, food safety.[183] Although the precise meaning of systemic risk remains ambiguous,[184] a common factor in the various descriptions of the concept is that a trigger event such as an economic shock or institutional failure in a small corner of an economic system causes a chain of bad economic consequences—sometimes referred to as a domino effect—on the entire economic system.[185] The spreading of the bad economic consequences to other parts of the system is facilitated by the existence of a high level of interconnectedness between financial services institutions or a high degree of correlation between the financial risks of such institutions. As illustrated by one author, "[t]hese consequences could include (a chain of) financial institution and/or market failures. Less dramatically, these consequences might include (a chain of) significant losses

---

[180] Kaufman and Scott (2003) pp. 372–373 [emphasis added].

[181] Acharya et al. (2009) p. 283.

[182] OECD (2003) p. 9 [emphasis added].

[183] Idem.

[184] Kaufman and Scott (2003) p. 371.

[185] Schwarcz (2008) p. 198.

to financial institutions or substantial financial-market price volatility. In either case, the consequences impact financial institutions, markets, or both".[186]

It has been argued that the systemic nature of catastrophic risks (including aviation war and terrorism risks) adversely affects their insurability by conventional insurance methods and thereby causes the commercial insurance markets to withdraw or restrict coverage and increase premiums in the period following the occurrence of such events.[187] It may be recalled that the essence of insurance (including reinsurance and retrocession) is the management of risks through pooling.[188] By bringing together similarly situated but widely distributed purchasers, the mechanism of insurance enables the sharing and reduction of risks amongst individual members of the pool *i.e.*, within the system.[189] However, insurance is possible only when the criteria for insurability of risks have been fulfilled.[190] As one author put it: "[t]he economic role of insurance and reinsurance companies as private mechanisms of risk allocation is closely related to the concept of insurability".[191] Accordingly, in circumstances where some or all of the criteria of insurability cannot be fulfilled in relation to a particular category of risks, the mechanism of conventional insurance is unable to completely spread the risk through pooling.

The systemic nature of catastrophic risks makes them vulnerable to the foregoing in at least two important respects. First, since individual loss exposures within the pool of catastrophic risks are typically concentrated and highly correlated,[192] it is usually difficult (if not impossible) to estimate the magnitude of the maximum

---

[186] Idem.

[187] Fitzsimmons (2004).

[188] According to Fitzsimmons, "[c]lassical insurance works on the basis of pooling of money (the premium) so that when someone suffers an insured loss, their loss is indirectly paid by the many (including reinsurers), out of the premiums received from those who have not suffered loss. There is an additional buffer, for bad times, of the insurer's capital, but even taking account of contingent capital available through reinsurance, this is distinctly finite". See idem., p. 73.

[189] Kendall (2002).

[190] These criteria of insurability include: randomness of the loss occurrence; the size of the maximum probable loss; the average expected loss amount upon occurrence; the average frequency of loss occurrences; the insurance premium; and, the absence of moral hazard. See Fitzsimmons (2004) p. 74.

[191] Mahul (2002) p. 2.

[192] There is another important requirement that the risks in an insurer's pool should not be correlated. This typically means that the realization of one risk within the portfolio must not simultaneously cause the realization of other insured risks in the portfolio. By virtue of their inherently systemic nature, most catastrophic risks are correlated. This affects the availability of commercial insurance for such risks by limiting the potential for insurers to pool individual risks. See Faure and Hartlief (2003) pp. 109–110.

possible loss associated with such risks.[193] Secondly, since such risks only occur infrequently, they are "sufficiently sporadic to be treated as rare and random for much of insurance".[194] It is therefore extremely difficult to predict the probability of occurrence or the loss frequency associated with such risks.[195] In consequence, conventional insurers face immense difficulty in using traditional actuarial methods to determine whether they have the requisite financial capacity at their disposal to back coverage of such risks.[196] These limitations on the ability of the conventional insurance industry to provide coverage for catastrophic risks have led to proposals for governmental involvement in the insurance of catastrophic events.[197]

In 2003, the OECD published a study it had previously commissioned on the implications of increasing and expanding systemic risks (including terrorism) for, *inter alia*, the insurability of the liability of enterprises.[198] After reviewing the theoretical conditions that must be fulfilled in order to guarantee the insurability of a risk, the study found that, in the case of systemic risks, the lack of precise information on the predictability of occurrence and the magnitude of losses associated therewith combines to make such risks largely uninsurable by traditional insurance markets.[199]

---

[193] In this regard, Fitzsimmons notes that the most serious factor in the aviation war risk insurance market following September 11, 2001, was "the absence of an identifiable maximum possible loss from the broad causative factor of terrorism". He notes further that "[e]ven now, aggregate loss estimates are in many cases little more than educated guesses at the outturn. ... there is no way which an insurer insuring terrorism in the traditional manner can now quantify his maximum exposure to terrorism risks across his portfolio in general. That alone was sufficient to make terrorism uninsurable in the traditional manner". See Fitzsimmons (2004) p. 74.

[194] Idem.

[195] According to Fitzsimmons: "It is essential to conventional insurance that history is a reasonable guide to the future as regards loss size and frequency, and this is more important the larger the potential loss. The insurer needs to know that it has enough capital to withstand even unlikely losses with a sufficient degree of confidence. 11 September meant that history ceased to be a predictor of the future, and the big picture of terrorism ceased to be random". See idem.

[196] Mahul (2001). Unlike other businesses, a special quality of the conventional insurance industry is that its financial capacity is determined by the amount of reserves and capital at its disposal. "When large firms such as Daimler or Wal-Mart suffer financial losses, they may defer capital expenditures, but their capacity will be little affected. By contrast, if insurers experience large underwriting or investment losses, the industry's capacity will be depleted". In such situations, given the costs of raising new capital quickly and a reluctance to underwrite risks that might weaken their balance sheets, insurers would typically scale back their underwriting activities. See Laster and Schmidt (2005) p. 10.

[197] Mahul (2001) p. 659. Governmental involvement in extreme event insurance markets, in particular, the aviation war risk insurance market, is discussed in Chapter 7 below.

[198] Faure and Hartlief (2003).

[199] The study stresses that precise information on the probability that a certain loss will occur (*i.e.*, its predictability) and the possibility of making a more or less accurate estimate of the potential magnitude of damage (*i.e.*, magnitude) is necessary not only for the purpose of making an accurate calculation of the premium to be charged, but also for purposes of setting aside a reserve in case the accident for which insurance coverage was taken out does occur. With respect to predictability, the study notes that although insurers may, in theory, charge an additional risk

In spite of the foregoing, it is generally said that the conventional insurance industry as a whole presents a "relatively low [level of] systemic risk because [it] generates relatively little counterparty risk and [its] liabilities are generally independent of economic cycles and other potential systemic failures".[200] Proponents of this assertion argue in support that "while some portions of primary risk are passed on to reinsurers [and retrocessionaires], the risks are not further multiplied or leveraged, and the primary insurer almost always remains obliged and retains a portion of the underlying risk".[201] Proponents also state that with respect to assets, "insurers [unlike banks] do not hold other peoples' money, so there is no vulnerability towards a 'run on the bank'".[202] Also, unlike depository institutions, investment funds, or retirement accounts, insurers normally underwrite risks exclusively on the basis of their own assets "with less leveraging statutorily allowed than for other financial companies".[203]

However, the commercial operations of most insurers and reinsurers engaged in the global insurance industry straddle multiple lines of insurance business such as life insurance, property insurance, liability insurance, aviation insurance, etc. The clustering of insurance-specific risks poses a potential danger to the entire industry and, as a consequence, to financial stability.[204] The attacks of September 11, 2001, presented an unprecedented accumulation of a variety of losses across several lines of insurance. Such an accumulation had not been thought possible before. Accumulation of losses across a variety of lines of insurance business, coupled with the very finite supply of capital at the disposal of the industry, demonstrates the extent of interconnectedness that exists within the conventional insurance industry. The belief that insurance and reinsurance portfolios are traditionally managed to achieve a balancing effect between independent lines of business was scattered by the events of September 11, 2001.

A further qualification must be made in the case of insurance markets for extreme or catastrophic events such as hurricanes, earthquakes and terrorist attacks. The sheer magnitude of the individual risks normally covered in such markets means that such risks are not widely diversifiable in the insurance context,[205] and

premium (known as an ambiguity premium) in situations where there is uncertainty as to the predictability of occurrence of a risk, in practice, there are a number of reasons that strongly militate against charging such premiums. Problems associated with uncertainty about the magnitude of potential losses could also be addressed through the use of insurance techniques such as co-insurance, reinsurance and retrocession. Yet systemic risks may still be of such a large magnitude that even with the use of all the aforementioned techniques, capacity may not be sufficient to cover the risk once it materializes. See idem., pp. 82–89.

[200] Property and Casualty Insurers Association of America (2009).

[201] Idem.

[202] Idem.

[203] Idem.

[204] Krenn and Oschischnig (2003).

[205] Mahul (2002) p. 2. Diversification of risks is discussed in detail in the next chapter under securitization of risks.

the similarities in third-party risk exposures of insurers and reinsurers generate a very pervasive level of systemic risk in the market. Although each insurer takes steps to manage the risks it individually assumes, it may not consider its impact on the risk of the system as a whole, having regard to the limited financial capacity of the industry.[206] There is also a high degree of correlation between the individual risks—particularly when the possibility exists for multiple catastrophic events to occur simultaneously. While the risks of an individual firm are properly dealt with in normal times, the system itself remains, or is induced to be, heavily consolidated, fragile and vulnerable to large macroeconomic shocks. In other words, in spite of the mechanisms of reinsurance and retrocession, the risk pooling mechanism of private insurance is not highly efficient in spreading out and reducing catastrophic risks within the industry.[207] This, coupled with the fact that the financial capacity of the industry (indeed any industry) is limited, naturally results in excessive system-wide consolidation of risks in the industry.

As a result of the pervasiveness of systemic risk in catastrophic event insurance markets, all insurers and reinsurers in the market tend to anticipate that the collapse of an individual insurer or reinsurer due to losses occasioned by a single (or multiple) catastrophic event(s) may trigger a domino effect, eventually pulling down the remainder of the market. In reaction to this anticipation, they curtail their appetite for the risk in question in the period immediately following the occurrence of an insured catastrophic event—the financial market equivalent of credit rationing. This explains why following the occurrence of an insured catastrophic event, there is only limited appetite for covering such risks within the conventional insurance industry. It is instructive to note that this phenomenon is not exclusively confined to extreme event insurance markets. On occasion, other lines of insurance[208] have experienced massive price increases and coverage reductions following periods of dramatic increases in insurers' loss payouts or revisions in expectations concerning future payouts.

In spite of the potential impact of catastrophic risks on the conventional insurance industry attributable to their systemic nature, the literature is replete with statements to the effect that that the global insurance industry was able to absorb the losses created by September 11, 2001, without suffering any significant insolvencies, and that the market has also been able to recapitalize itself back at

[206] Acharya et al. (2009) pp. 283 et seq. The authors observe further that, existing financial regulations [including deposit requirements] are usually directed at limiting each individual's risk in isolation; they are not sufficiently focused on systemic risk.

[207] Mahul (2002) p. 2.

[208] According to the literature, the best known examples of such "availability crises" occurred in the mid 1980s when several lines of commercial liability insurance were subject to massive price increases and coverage reductions primarily as a result of increases in the number and cost of tort awards. During the early 1970s, a similar phenomenon occurred in the medical malpractice insurance market and the satellite insurance market witnessed price and availability problems in the early 1980s. See Doherty and Posey (1997) p. 56.

least to pre-September 11, 2001, levels.[209] As emphasized by one commentator, "[i]t is clear that the collapse of a single reinsurer or insurer has not triggered any problem of capacity or coverage that the market has not been able to absorb. There has been no domino effect which is the fear with the banks. It is also clear that in the wake of the insurance industry's biggest ever disaster ... [September 11, 2001], business went on as usual with remarkably little impact on the global economy".[210] However, the reactions of the insurance industry to those events reflect the systemic effect of catastrophic risks on the industry. Serious concerns have been raised about the capacity of the industry to absorb any future losses caused by multiple and/or highly correlated events on the same scale as those of September 11, 2001.

For instance, it has been argued that underneath the fact that the insurance industry was able to absorb the losses from September 11, "there were clear signs of systemic risk. The aviation insurance industry had to reduce substantially the amount of cover available – reduce it below the level at which airlines could continue to operate. Globally, governments had to intervene to provide the limits of liability necessary to satisfy financiers and regulators ... *arguably, the reason why governments had to intervene was because insurance itself has become systemic*".[211] Another commentator succinctly states the resulting state of the insurance industry as follows: "September 11 has ... reinforced the perception that due to the correlation of both insurance and financial risks, a sudden extreme event could set in motion a 'domino-like' collapse of a large segment of the insurance sector. *This risk can be considered the systemic risk of the industry*".[212]

According to economic theorists, most catastrophic risks (including aviation war and terrorism risks) consist of a combination of systemic components (stemming primarily from the similarities in the impact of terrorist events upon insurers and reinsurers for example), and an idiosyncratic component (which depends on the individual characteristics of the risks covered). As the name implies, the systemic component is usually highly correlated among individual insureds, and since it is not amenable to diversification in the ordinary course of insurance,[213] that part of the risk is retained within the insurance system. Because the financial capacity of

[209] De Mey (2003) p. 66.

[210] Mundy (2004) p. 30.

[211] Idem., [emphasis added].

[212] De Mey (2003) p. 68 [emphasis added]. Although there is general consensus regarding the existence of systemic risk in the aviation insurance industry, opinions differ as to what impact increasing globalization, consolidation and integration within the financial services sector has on systemic risk in the insurance sector. According to De Mey, "the integration of the financial services industry will increase its ability to absorb shocks and spread risks ... integration reduces the probability that the first domino falls down, and therefore reduces systemic risk". On the other hand, Chris Mundy is of the view that "the rate of consolidation and globalization in the primary insurance sector, combined with the insidiousness of insurance into every aspect of our lives is bringing primary insurance ever closer to systemic risk". See Mundy (2004) p. 30.

[213] "Systemic risks can be diversified by pooling them with other economic events that are not usually the subject of insurance. This is achieved through the securitization of risk". See Mahul (2001) p. 656. Securitization is discussed in Chap. 5 of this book.

the insurance industry is not infinite or deep enough to back the systemic risks retained within the industry, it becomes very necessary for the industry to divest itself of those risks. One important means of diversifying systemic risks from the insurance industry is to pool them together with other economic events that are not usually the subject of insurance.[214]

This is achieved through the securitization of risk, a process which entails the development of financial instruments to transfer catastrophic risks to financial investors through capital markets. Securitization therefore relies on the huge financial potential of capital markets to resolve the capacity constraints of the traditional insurance industry. As a prerequisite, securitization of risks is only feasible under circumstances where "the design of an optimal risk sharing contract is based on a decomposition of the risk into systemic i.e., non-diversifiable, and idiosyncratic, *i.e.*, diversifiable parts".[215] Risk securitization is discussed in detail in the next chapter of this book.

4.5 Conclusion

The object of this chapter has been to provide some broader theoretical perspectives on the use of conventional insurance as a risk management tool for catastrophic risks by exploring some fundamental economic and behavioural explanations underlying the reactions of conventional insurance markets to catastrophic risks in the post-event period. It has been established that whenever conventional insurance providers are faced with extreme events such as those which occurred in the US on September 11, 2001, heightened uncertainty about the frequency and magnitude of future attacks are brought to the forefront in both their cognitive and non-cognitive risk assessment and decision-making processes, and this, coupled with the systemic nature of those risks and the financial capacity constraints under which insurers operate, causes them to restrict the width and scope of the insurance coverage that they were hitherto willing to provide for such risks.[216]

Although conventional insurance remains a very versatile means for managing risks of all kinds, it has inherent limitations when those risks are catastrophic in nature or fall into the category of low-probability, high-consequence risks. Commenting generally on the impact of September 11, 2001, on the insurance system, one author offers the following as some of the reasons why the conventional insurance industry has limitations vis-à-vis catastrophic risks:

[214] See footnote 213 above and accompanying text.

[215] Mahul (2002) p. 2.

[216] See Rhee (2005) p. 461 where the author notes that "exogenous shocks create short term 'psychological' distortions in the [insurance] industry as perceptions of the risk are changed by new information". In the footnote accompanying this text, Robert Rhee notes further that "[s]hocks actually have been more psychological than financial due to the benefits of diversification".

> September 11th exposed the vulnerability of the insurance system to catastrophic terrorist attacks. While the industry has fully recovered from the financial shock, it cannot withstand multiple blows on the scale of 9/11 under the current industry model. *The problem is one of capacity at economically feasible levels.* . . . As currently configured, the [global] economy has only three primary sources of compensation: insurance proceeds, government subsidies, and tort recoveries. Litigation is the most inefficient mechanism to deliver compensation and therefore should be avoided; and the fallout from 9/11 exposed the weakness in the insurance sector. These limitations would seem to suggest that only the government has sufficient capital to absorb large losses.[217]

Despite the various innovative mechanisms used by conventional insurers to spread risks as widely as possible within the insurance system, it is clear that the financial capacity of the global aviation insurance industry is finite. Accordingly, the industry cannot be relied upon as a primary means of providing the desired levels of insurance coverage to the air transport industry for catastrophic aviation war and terrorism risks. The question therefore arises as to whether there are in existence any viable complementary or alternative mechanisms that can be used to enhance or substitute the role played currently by the conventional insurance industry in connection with the coverage of aviation war and terrorism risks.

The second part of this book attempts to provide some answers to this question by outlining and analyzing a number of complementary and alternative mechanisms that have been implemented and/or proposed to enhance the provision of insurance coverage or other financial equivalent against aviation war and terrorism risks to the air transport industry. Three broad areas form the focus of part II: (1) alternative risk financing and alternative risk transfer mechanisms aimed at enhancing the financial capacity of the conventional insurance industry to cover catastrophic aviation war and terrorism risks; (2) the adoption of an international treaty to specifically address the challenges posed by compensation of third-party victims of acts of unlawful interference involving aircraft and its effect on the insurability of aviation war and terrorism risks of the air transport industry, and; (3) governmental involvement in the provision of aviation war and terrorism insurance coverage at the domestic and international levels, as well as the fundamental question regarding the appropriate role of governments in the provision of insurance or other financial equivalent for extreme catastrophic events.

After outlining the structure and concepts of the various schemes proposed and/or implemented under each of these three broad areas, an effort is then made to determine whether, and to what extent, the theoretical concerns identified in relation to conventional insurance and catastrophic risks in this chapter are addressed by the said scheme.

[217] Idem., p. 440 [emphasis added].

References

Acharya VV, Pedersen L, Philippon T, Richardson M (2009) Regulating systemic risk. In: Acharya VV, Richardson M (eds) Restoring financial stability – how to repair a failed system. Wiley, Hoboken

Akerlof GA (1970) The market for 'Lemons': quality uncertainty and the market mechanism. Q J Econ 84(3):488–500

Arnott RJ (1992) Moral Hazard and competitive insurance markets. In: Dionne G (ed) Contributions to insurance economics. Kluwer Academic, Boston/Dordrecht/London, pp 325–358

Arnott R, Stiglitz JE (1991) Equilibrium in competitive insurance markets with Moral Hazard. NBER, Cambridge

Bator FM (1958) The anatomy of market failure. Q J Econ 72(3):351–379

Baur P, Enz R (2003) Sigma No. 5/2003: reinsurance – a systemic risk? Swiss Reinsurance Company, Economic Research and Consulting, Zurich

Bechara A, Damasio H, Tranel D, Damasio AR (1997) Deciding advantageously before knowing the advantageous strategy. Sci Magazine 275(5304):1293–1295

Bianco A (2002) Buffett jumps in where others fear to tread – Berkshire Hathaway starts underwriting terrorism policies – and investors approve. Business Week

Bond EW (1982) A direct test of the "Lemons" model: the market for used pickup trucks. Am Econ Rev 72(4):836–840

Booth P (2008) Market failure: a failed paradigm. IEA, London

Cawley J, Philipson T (1999) An empirical examination of information barriers to trade in insurance. Am Econ Rev 89(4):827–846

Chiappori P-A, Gollier C (2006) Introduction. In: Chiappori P-A, Gollier C (eds) Competitive failures in insurance markets – theory and policy implications. MIT Press, Cambridge

Chiappori P-A, Salanie B (2000) Testing for asymmetric information in insurance markets. J Pol Econ 108(1):56–78

Cowen T (1988) Public goods and externalities: old and new perspectives. In: Cowen T (ed) The theory of market failure – a critical examination. George Mason University Press, Fairfax, pp 1–28

Cowen T, Crampton E (2003a) Introduction. In: Cowen T, Crampton E (eds) Market failure or success: the new debate. Edward Elgar, Cheltenham

Cowen T, Crampton E (eds) (2003b) Market failure or success – the new debate. Edward Elgar, Cheltenham

De Mey J (2003) The aftermath of September 11: the impact on and systemic risk to the insurance industry. Geneva Papers (Issues & Practice) 28(1):65–70

Doherty NA, Posey LL (1997) Availability crises in insurance markets: optimal contracts with asymmetric information and capacity constraints. J Risk Uncertainty 15:55–80

Doherty NA, Lamm-Tennant J, Starks LT (2003) Insuring September 11th: market recovery and transparency. J Risk Uncertainty 26(2):179–199

Faure MG, Hartlief T (2003) Policy issues in insurance no, 5: insurance and expanding systemic risks. Organisation for Economic Cooperation and Development (OECD), Paris

Fitzsimmons A (2004) Terrorism – maximizing the insurability of a catastrophe risk. Ann Air Space Law XXIX:67

Hemenway D (1990) Propitious selection. Q J Econ 105(4):1063–1069

Hogarth RM (2002) Insurance and safety after September 11: has the world become a "Riskier" Place? [unpublished]

Jaffee DM, Russell T (1997) Catastrophe insurance, capital markets and uninsurable risks. J Risk Insur 64(2):205–230

Jaffee D, Russell T (2003) Markets under stress: the case of extreme event insurance. In: Arnott R, Greenwald B, Kanbur R, Nalebuff B (eds) Economics for an imperfect world – essays in Honour of Joseph E. Stiglitz. MIT Press, Cambridge

Jolls C (2007) Behavioural law and economics. NBER, Cambridge
Jolls C, Sunstein CR, Thaler R (1998) A behavioral approach to law and economics. Stanford Law Rev 50(5):1471–1550
Kahneman D, Knetsch JL, Thaler R (1986) Fairness as a constraint on profit seeking: entitlements in the market. Am Econ Rev 76(4):728–741
Kaufman GG (1996) Bank failures, systemic risk, and bank regulation. Cato J 16(1):17–45
Kaufman GG, Scott KE (2003) What is systemic risk? and do bank regulators retard or contribute to it. Independent Rev VII(3):371–391
Kendall J (2002) The incalculable risk: how the World Trade Center disaster accelerated the evolution of insurance terrorism exclusions. Univ Rich Law Rev 36:569
Klein DB (2002) The demand for and supply of assurance. In: Cowen T, Crampton E (eds) Market failure or success: the new debate. Edward Elgar, Cheltenham, pp 172–192
Krenn G, Oschischnig U (2003) Systemic risk factors in the insurance industry and methods for risk assessment. OENB Financ Stability Rep 6:62–74
Kunreuther H, Hogarth RM (1992) How does ambiguity affect insurance decisions? In: Dionne G (ed) Contributions to insurance economics. Kluwer Academic, Boston/Dordrecht/London, pp 307–324
Kunreuther H, Pauly M (1985) Market equilibrium with private knowledge: an insurance example. J Public Econ 26(3):269–288
Kunreuther H, Hogarth R, Meszaros J (1993) Insurer ambiguity and market failure. J Risk Uncertainty 7:71–87
Kunreuther H, Meszaros J, Hogarth RM, Spranca M (1995) Ambiguity and underwriter decision processes. J Econ Behav Org 26(3):337–352
Kunreuther H, Pauly MV, Russell T (2004) Demand and supply side anomalies in catastrophe insurance markets: the role of the public and private sectors [unpublished]
Kupiec P, Nickerson D (2004) Assessing systemic risk exposure from banks and GSEs under alternative approaches to capital regulation. J Real Estate Finance Econ 48:123
Laster DS, Schmidt C (2005) Sigma No. 4/2005: innovating to insure the uninsurable. Swiss Reinsurance Company, Economic Research and Consulting, Zurich
Loewenstein GF, Weber EU, Hsee CK, Welch N (2001) Risk as feelings. Psychol Bull 127(2):267–286
Mahul O (2001) Managing catastrophic risk through insurance and securitization. Am J Agric Econ 83(3):656–661
Mahul O (2002) Coping with catastrophic risks: the role of (non)-participating contracts [unpublished]
Mitchell G (2002–2003) Why law and economics' perfect rationality should not be traded for behavioural law and economics' equal incompetence. Geo Law J 91:67–167
Moss DA (2002) When all else fails: government as the ultimate risk manager. Harvard University Press, Cambridge/London
Mundy C (2004) The nature of risk: the nature of systemic risk – trying to achieve a definition. Balance Sheet 12(5):29–31
OECD (2003) Emerging systemic risks in the 21st century – an agenda for action. OECD, Paris
Outreville JF (1998) Theory and practice of insurance. Kluwer Academic, Boston/Dordrecht/London
Peters E, Slovic P (1996) The role of affect and worldviews as orienting dispositions in the perception and acceptance of nuclear power. J Appl Soc Psychol 26(16):1427–1453
Polinsky AM (2003) An introduction to law and economics, 3rd edn. Aspen Publishers, New York
Posner RA (1987) The law and economics movement. Am Econ Rev 77(2):1–13
Priest GL (2003) Government insurance versus market insurance. Geneva Papers (Issues & Practice) 28(1):71–80
Property and Casualty Insurers Association of America (2009) Systemic risk defined [unpublished]

Rhee RJ (2005) Terrorism risk in a post-9/11 economy: the convergence of capital markets, insurance, and government action. Ariz State Law J 37:435

Rothschild M, Stiglitz J (1976) Equilibrium in competitive insurance markets: an essay on the economics of imperfect information. Q J Econ 90(4):629–649

Samuelson P (1954) The pure theory of public expenditure. Rev Econ Stat 36(4):387–389

Schwarcz SL (2008) Systemic risk. Geo Law J 97:193–249

Shavell S (1992) On Moral Hazard and insurance. In: Dionne G, Harrington SE (eds) Foundations of insurance economics: readings in economics and finance. Kluwer Academic, Boston/Dordrecht/London, pp 280–301

Smith A (1977) An inquiry into the causes of the wealth of nations. University of Chicago Press, Chicago, first published in 1776

Stiglitz JE (2003) Information and the change in the paradigm in economics. In: Arnott R, Greenwald B, Kanbur R, Nalebuff B (eds) Economics for an imperfect world – essays in Honour of Joseph E. Stiglitz. MIT Press, Cambridge

Tversky A, Kahneman D (1974) Judgment under uncertainty: heuristics and biases. Science 185(4157):1124–1131

Wilson C (1977) A model of insurance markets with incomplete information. J Econ Theory 16(2):167–207

Winston C (2006) Market failure versus government failure. AEI-Brookings Joint Center for Regulatory Studies, Washington

Winter RA (1992) Moral Hazard and insurance contracts. In: Dionne G (ed) Contributions to insurance economics. Kluwer Academic, Boston/Dordrecht/London, pp 61–96

Wolf C Jr (1979) A theory of nonmarket failure: framework for implementation analysis. J Law Econ 22(1):107–139

Chapter 5
Enhancing the Insurance of Aviation War and Terrorism Risks Through the Use of Alternative Risk Transfer and Risk Financing Mechanisms

5.1 Introduction

This chapter discusses alternative/complementary mechanisms for enhancing the ability of conventional insurance markets to provide sustainable coverage for aviation war and terrorism risks.[1] At the outset, it is important to recall that one of the fundamental reasons why conventional insurance markets withdraw coverage and sharply raise premiums charged for insuring aviation war and terrorism risks following the occurrence of a catastrophic event such as September 11, 2001, is the immense difficulty they experience in raising capital during those periods.[2] As such, the need to find innovative, non-conventional ways of raising capital to back insurance coverage of catastrophic risks has been a subject of much deliberation in the conventional insurance industry over the years, and a number of steps have been taken in that direction. Alternative Risk Transfer (ART) mechanisms are one of the major areas that have been explored.

As the name implies, ART is an umbrella term that encompasses various mechanisms of transferring or financing risks other than through conventional insurance or reinsurance.[3] Conventional insurance and reinsurance usually involve

---

[1] Rhee (2005) p. 461 According to the author, risk management techniques may be categorized into *avoidance*, *reduction*, *control*, *transfer* and *retention*. Conventional insurance falls within the transfer category since it encompasses the process of disaggregating, reconstituting and transferring various forms of risk from individuals and enterprises to the insurance system. The remaining risk management techniques may therefore be used to enhance the ability of conventional insurance to address the risks that are transferred to it.

[2] See idem., p. 453. Conventional insurance companies typically fund the risks they underwrite with capital raised from three primary sources: (1) equity; (2) accumulated reserves from premiums collected and any returns gained from investing same; and, (3) debt. Once a catastrophic event occurs and depletes the reserves of such companies, it becomes impossible to raise from these traditional sources the large amounts of capital needed to recapitalize such companies for them to continue their normal operations.

[3] Godbole (2004) p. 39.

Y.O.M. Nyampong, *Insuring the Air Transport Industry Against Aviation War and Terrorism Risks and Allied Perils*, DOI 10.1007/978-3-642-32433-8_5,

a complete transfer of pure insurable risks under annual contracts of indemnity. On the contrary, some ART mechanisms often do not involve a full or complete transfer of risks, but are simply a means of providing funding for risks.[4] As noted by one commentator, "ART is a true enterprise risk management approach that focuses on protection of value creation processes and not on indemnification of much narrowly defined loss as in the case of traditional insurance".[5] "ART aims at increasing the efficiency of the risk transfer [process], broadening the spectrum of insurable risks and tapping the capital markets for additional capacity".[6] Where limited capital poses a constraint in traditional risk management, ART routes may provide viable solutions.[7]

By their very nature, ART solutions are capable of raising much more capital than the traditional insurance markets can, and are therefore perceived as having the potential to cover those large catastrophic risks not considered suitable for coverage under traditional insurance, including aviation war and terrorism risks. The ART market has two broad segments depending on whether or not there is transfer of risk and, if there is, the manner in which the risk transfer is carried out. The first segment involves coverage of risk through *alternative carriers* and it covers mechanisms such as self-insurance, captives, mutual schemes, risk retention groups and pools. The second segment involves some element of risk transfer (usually to the capital markets) through *alternative products* such as catastrophe bonds, derivatives, finite risk and multiline products.[8]

Following the aforementioned broad categorizations of ART solutions, the next two parts of this chapter investigate the viability and suitability of a number of ART initiatives/proposals that have been proffered at various levels as alternatives/complements to conventional insurance coverage for aviation war and terrorism risks.

5.2 Funding of Aviation War and Terrorism Risks Through Industry Captives, Risk Retention Groups (RRGs) and Other Mutualization Schemes

According to one writer, the classic response of many industries every time insurance becomes unavailable or too pricey is to start their own insurance company for their industry.[9] "Whether they're called risk retention groups (RRG's), captives, or mutual insurance companies, their purpose is the same – spread the risk

[4] Idem.
[5] Idem., p. 40.
[6] Idem., p. 39.
[7] Idem.
[8] Idem., p. 41.
[9] Boyle (2002a).

over the entire industry, charge adequate, but not excessive, premiums and lower the cost of insurance while increasing its availability".[10] As such, a captive can be compared to a cooperative of industry members and it has been described as:

> an insurance or reinsurance entity created and owned, directly or indirectly, by one or more industrial, commercial or financial entities, the purpose of which is to provide insurance or reinsurance cover for risks of the entity or entities to which it belongs, or for entities connected to those entities and only a small part if any of its risk exposure is related to providing insurance or reinsurance to other parties.[11]

In a study report on captive insurance companies published in October 2006, the International Association of Insurance Supervisors (IAIS) comprehensively outlined the historical origins and evolution of the concept of risk retention and funding within an industry as follows:

> The concept of forming an insurance company to insure the risks of its owners can be traced back to the infancy of insurance. There are instances as early as 1782 of mutual insurance companies being formed by members of a particular industry to provide insurance coverage. In 1860, in response to increased insurance rates, a group of London merchants formed their own insurance company called Commercial Union. Similar situations were beginning to occur in North America as well. In the 20th century corporations became more and more involved in forming mutuals or their own insurance companies. In the 1920's and 1930's several major companies, including ICI, BP, Pilkingtons and Unilever in the UK and Lufthansa in Germany, had formed their own insurance companies.

In connection with the development of the modern concept of captive insurance companies, risk retention groups and mutualization schemes, the report continues as follows:

> The modern concept of captive insurance companies did not develop into a real growth industry until the 1950's, when Fred Reiss, the widely acknowledged 'father' of captives took a special interest and initiated the development of the current industry profile. Mr. Reiss was a US fire protection engineer assessing buildings for the Ohio Inspection Bureau. He consistently heard complaints from clients on how difficult it was to obtain coverages from the insurance industry. Owing to losses on failed research and marketing, the confiscation or nationalisation of assets and new health and safety requirements in respect of, for instance, oil plants and new buildings, large corporations were, at that time, faced with enormous premiums in the traditional insurance markets. Reiss was quick to realise that this was an opportunity with a unique and simple solution. What corporations sought, but were unable to find, was a method of financing the covering of their own exposures in a way that could, ultimately, bring down the net cost of insurance to the corporations. Initially, Reiss based his concept on the simple principle of setting up subsidiary companies to insure the risks of the parent companies in Kentucky and Ohio. Reiss began to call such subsidiaries a 'captive', a term believed to originate from his first client, a manufacturer who owned its own mines to produce the company's raw materials that they called 'captive mines'. In 1958 he incorporated American Risk Management and began to assist corporations in setting up captives. Each captive company would insure only the parent's risk and needed only a low level of capital set aside against future losses.[12]

---

[10] Idem.

[11] International Association of Insurance Supervisors (2006) p. 4.

[12] Idem., p. 5 [footnotes omitted].

The insurance market is cyclical and fluctuating costs have an undesirable impact on budgeting and profit forecasting by captive owners. However, there is a view that retaining and developing insurance risk capacity in captives can reduce the impact of insurance market cycles on risk pricing which can enhance the stability of the market both generally and to captives specifically.[13] Although most industries establish captives, mutuals or risk retention groups for microeconomic reasons such as cost reduction or risk control, these mechanisms can also provide other economic as well as non-economic benefits.[14] For instance, "[a] captive can operate at reduced expense compared with traditional commercial insurers because it will probably not have marketing expenses. It will benefit from lower personnel costs, lower underwriting expenses, lower overhead expenses and be willing to accept a minimal underwriting profit. Consequently a captive can accept risk at a higher loss ratio than the traditional market is willing to accept".[15]

The concept of retaining catastrophic risks and funding them internally has been explored in the air transport industry. Following the events of September 11, 2001, several proposals based on this concept were made at various levels. The following sections describe the most prominent of such proposals.

5.2.1 Equitime

In the US, the Air Transport Association (ATA), a domestic trade association of leading US airlines acting in conjunction with Marsh Inc., a global insurance company worked to quickly create a risk retention group/captive insurance scheme following September 11, 2001.[16] The scheme, known as Equitime,[17] called for the establishment of a company under the laws of the State of Vermont to be owned exclusively by ATA member airlines (who together, supply 95 % of all passenger and air cargo transport in the US) as well as airport maintenance and service provider companies.[18] Under its initial plans, the scheme was to issue to its owners insurance policies covering a first layer of up to US$ 300 million in third-party and war risk liability, with no requirement for the insured member to obtain a similar policy from the conventional insurance market.[19] In addition, the scheme envisaged

[13] Idem., p. 12.

[14] Idem., p. 11.

[15] Idem., p. 13. According to this IAIS report, "[t]he portion of commercial premiums paid that are [*sic*] attributable to profit, overhead and acquisition costs can be as high as 40 % of the whole amount charged. The establishment of a captive seeks to mitigate these extraneous costs by allowing the company the benefit of retaining profit for its own account and participating in the risk exposure by paying a premium that more accurately reflects the parent loss history".

[16] See Boyle (2002a). See also Airline group files to form vermont risk group (2002).

[17] In civil aviation, the term "Equitime" refers to the point in flight when the risk of going forward is equal to the risk of returning. See Pinkham (2002).

[18] Boyle (2002a).

[19] Idem.

an additional layer of insurance coverage for third-party war and terrorism risks of up to US$ 2 billion, to be funded (or reinsured) during the first 4–5 years by the US federal government, acting through the FAA.[20] Barring the occurrence of any huge losses in that initial period, the expectation was that Equitime would become fully funded at the end of that initial period and could then have at its disposal the required amount of capital reserves necessary to fund the second layer of coverage in place of the US government.[21]

5.2.2 *Eurotime and New Eurotime*

In Europe, the Association of European Airlines (AEA), the European regional airline association, acting in conjunction with global insurance and brokering companies Marsh, Aon and Willis worked out the general formation of Eurotime—a risk retention group projected as a medium-term solution to the aviation war risk insurance problem.[22] The original Eurotime scheme was roughly equivalent to the Equitime proposal. It was to provide coverage of European airlines for third-party war and terrorism risks up to a policy limit of US$ 1 billion per occurrence, increasing to US$ 1.5 billion per occurrence if passenger war liability was included.[23] Unlike Equitime, however, airlines insured under the original Eurotime scheme would have been required to obtain a first layer of at least US$ 50 million in third-party coverage from the conventional insurance market unless they could show that such coverage had been cancelled or was otherwise no longer available from the private markets.[24]

Beyond the US$ 50 million excess point, the amount to be insured under the Eurotime scheme (otherwise referred to as the industry retention) was set at US$ 150 million per occurrence for the first year, US$ 250 million per occurrence for the second year, and US$ 500 million per occurrence for the third year.[25] Under the

[20] Idem.

[21] According to a comparative study conducted by Marsh Inc., the base premium rate per passenger under the Equitime scheme was to be fixed at 64 cents. This projected a maximum total estimated annual premium of US$ 435 million, assuming 100 % participation by all ATA member airlines. Out of this amount, US$ 75 million was to be paid to the US federal government for its excess coverage, leaving US$ 360 million per annum to fund Equitime plus the US$ 50 million initially garnered to set up the company. At the time, the "usual aviation markets" were asking for premium rates of US$ 1.25 per passenger for coverage of third party and war risks up to US$ 50 million. Additionally, the new "excess third party markets" were demanding premium rates of US$ 1.85 per passenger for coverage of third party and war risks beyond the US$ 50 million up to US$ 1 billion.

[22] Boyle (2002a).

[23] Idem.

[24] Idem.

[25] Hoeven (2005) p. 75.

scheme, the difference between the first two layers combined (i.e., the US$ 50 million that was to be covered by conventional insurance plus the excess coverage to be provided by Eurotime) on the one hand and the policy limit of US$ 1 billion (or 1.5 billion if passenger liability was included) on the other was to be covered by the governments of the respective European countries where the carriers were located, acting as reinsurers.[26]

Eurotime's third-party coverage was to be funded by a premium rate of 50 cents per passenger, and this was projected to generate a total of between US$ 325 and 329 million annually, 20 % (about US$ 65–66 million) of which would be paid to governments as reinsurance premium for their excess coverage.[27] The scheme was brought before the EU Commission for approval. After due consideration, the EU Commission indicated in October 2002 that it preferred to support the Globaltime scheme proposed by ICAO which, in essence, sought to replicate the Eurotime concept on a global scale.[28] The Globaltime scheme is discussed in more detail in the next section of this chapter.

Meanwhile, discussions progressed in Europe following the EU Commission's non-approval of the original Eurotime scheme. As noted by one author, "[i]t was recognized during those discussions that there was the need for a mechanism to deal with the market failure that was likely to occur should there be another major terrorist attack involving air (or perhaps sea) transport".[29] European thinking therefore evolved beyond the original Eurotime concept into a "New Eurotime" concept. The New Eurotime concept involved two standing arrangements the features of which are discussed in turn below: (1) an EU Partial Market Failure Guarantee; and, (2) an EU Total Market Failure Guarantee.

Under the first arrangement, the EU Partial Market Failure Guarantee, "European aviators"[30] were to continue procuring the maximum available limits of primary war and terrorism cover from the conventional insurance markets. EU Member States (EUMSs) would then step in to provide excess third-party coverage for the difference between the existing primary liability cover purchased from the conventional markets and twice the full liability policy limit as existed before September 11, 2001.[31] This measure was aimed at leveling the playing field so that European aviators would have access to approximately the same levels of cover as was available to US airlines, though at much greater cost.[32] Further, EUMSs would also provide *primary* hull, passenger and third-party cover for the following specific heads of third-party liability coverage in respect of which, at the time, there already was

---

[26] Boyle (2002a).

[27] Idem. See also Hoeven (2005) p. 75.

[28] Hoeven (2005).

[29] Fitzsimmons (2004) p. 82.

[30] This term was invented under the scheme to cover all operators, airlines, manufacturers, airports, maintenance service providers, security screeners etc. See idem., p. 83, fn. 26.

[31] Idem., p. 83.

[32] Idem.

market failure: Dirty nuclear; Nuclear weapons; Biological weapons; Chemical weapons; and Electromagnetic pulse.[33] Finally, the arrangement envisaged that the EU would provide *excess* hull, passenger, and third-party cover for the above-mentioned specific heads in respect of incidents of war or terror occurring worldwide and involving European aviators.[34]

On the other hand, the EU Total Market Failure Guarantee Scheme, a scheme involving the establishment of a special purpose mutual insurer with support from EUMSs, was intended to kick in automatically if a market failure were to occur, including prohibitive pricing of the then existing commercial insurance products.[35] Under the arrangement, EUMSs would provide *primary* passenger, third-party and hull war/terrorism coverage for twice the full pre-September 11, 2001, liability policy limits, including coverage for those specific heads identified above for which the private markets were previously not providing any cover. Further, EUMSs would provide unlimited *excess* cover of the above for extreme damages occurring worldwide, and the guarantee would be maintained for at least 3 years, subject to periodic review. It was proposed that if the scheme ever came into effect, the cost as well as the cover available under it should be comparable to the US government funded scheme.[36]

5.2.3 Globaltime

In the aftermath of the events of September 11, 2001, the ICAO Assembly adopted a resolution calling upon contracting states to work together to develop a more enduring and coordinated approach in providing assistance in the field of aviation war risk insurance, and also directed the ICAO Council to establish a Special Group.[37] In accordance with the resolution, a Special Group on Aviation War Risk Insurance (SGWI) was established by the ICAO Council and tasked to review the problem of aviation war risk insurance in light of the then prevailing situation and to develop recommendations for coordinated and appropriate assistance mechanisms for airline operators and other affected parties to be operated if and when necessary to the extent that the conventional insurance markets were unable to provide sufficient coverage.[38]

After holding two meetings, the SGWI recommended that in the short- to medium-term, an international mechanism funded by insurance premiums should be established to provide non-cancellable third-party aviation war risk coverage

[33] Idem.
[34] Idem.
[35] Idem.
[36] Idem.
[37] ICAO (2001c).
[38] ICAO (2001e).

through a non-profit special purpose insurance entity, with multilateral government backing during the initial years.[39] Named as the Globaltime Scheme, it is this proposal and its implementation that forms the focus of this section. As a long-term solution, the SGWI recommended that an international convention be developed which would limit the third-party liability of the aviation industry for losses arising from war, hijacking and related perils.[40] In 2009, two international treaties were adopted by ICAO in response to this second recommendation. They are discussed in detail in Chap. 6.

As initially conceived, the Globaltime scheme entailed the establishment of a non-profit entity for the sole purpose of offering non-cancellable *third party war risk liability* cover in excess of US$ 50 million per insured up to US$ 1.5 billion per occurrence.[41] It was expected that each entity that would be covered under the scheme would have taken out from the conventional market, insurance cover for *passenger war risk liability* and at least US$ 50 million *third-party war risk liability*—the maximum limits then available from commercial insurers. However, in the event that the commercial markets were to withdraw such cover, the plan was that the Globaltime scheme would drop-down to cover the primary US$ 50 million third-party war risk liability and, as well, automatically adjust to provide passenger war risk liability cover. In this latter case, the limit of cover per insured would be US$ 2 billion per occurrence.[42]

The insurance cover to be provided under the Globaltime scheme was to be made available to the entire global aviation industry (including scheduled and non-scheduled operators, cargo operators, general aviation including business aviation operators, airports and other service providers), and was to include domestic and international operations as well as equipment lessors, financiers and manufacturers from any State that joined the scheme.[43] Initial capitalization for the scheme was to be provided by aviation industry participants and not by participating states (unless they expressly desired to do so). If the need arose, however, loans for the initial capitalization of the scheme could be backed by guarantees from participating states.[44] Once the scheme had been initially capitalized, claims under policies issued thereunder were to be met from a pool of reserves built up with premiums collected from each insured party.

The expectation was that this pool of reserves would preclude or at least distance participating states from having to make cash contributions to the scheme in the event of a claim. In turn, insured parties were to pass on the cost of premiums to the

[39] See ICAO (2001d). See also ICAO (2002b).

[40] ICAO (2001d, 2002b).

[41] ICAO (2002b), Appendix 1 at para. 1.1.

[42] Idem.

[43] Idem., Appendix 1 para. 1.3.

[44] Idem., Appendix 1 para. 1.4.

users of air transport, i.e. passengers and air cargo shippers.[45] In addition to paying premiums, each policyholder was to be charged an upfront policy fee of US$ 2500. Most significantly, provision was made for premium rates to be adjusted upwards in the event of a major loss and payout, subject only to a 30-day period of notice.[46]

State participation in the scheme was to be voluntary and was to be based upon signing of a Participation Agreement.[47] Participating states were to act as guarantors or "reinsurers" of last resort only, and their respective back-up guarantees were to be pro-rated on the basis of their respective ICAO contribution rates.[48] The scheme was to commence once a sufficient number of Contracting States representing at least 51 % of ICAO contribution rates had signed the participation agreement and thereby agreed to participate.[49] Signing of the participation agreement *per se* would not trigger an obligation on the part of the signing state to pay money upfront on account of its allocated share of the back-up guarantee. However, concerns were expressed by certain states regarding the lack of any correlation whatsoever between their respective ICAO contribution rates and their differing (perhaps perceived) levels of exposure to aviation war and

[45] Idem., paras. 3.1–3.3. By way of projections, the total amount of premiums expected to be collected in the first year was estimated at US$ 850 million (equivalent to a premium of 50 cents per passenger segment based on an estimated total passenger segments of 1.7 billion). If this was achieved, then the premium for subsequent years could be kept at approximately the same level, provided there were no losses. In addition to allocating premiums on a per passenger segment basis, the SGWI also recommended that these other options for premium allocation be considered: (a) flat rate per departure flight; (b) flat rate per aircraft proportional to the maximum take-off weight; (c) flat rate per ton/km performed, including passenger and freight; and, (d) flat rate premium (for airports, service providers and others).

[46] Idem., paras. 3.4–3.5.

[47] See ICAO (2002a).This participation agreement was intended to be a legal agreement between the contracting states that would sign it and the Insuring Entity to be established under the scheme. Its purpose was for the Participating States to guarantee certain obligations of the Insuring Entity; to establish the proration, limits, and payment mechanisms related thereto; and, to provide for the obligations of the Insuring Entity towards the Participating States.

[48] With the participation of all ICAO states, the collective cap for participating States' contributions was estimated at US$ 15 billion maximum (sufficient to meet 10 maximum claims), or a proportion thereof based on percentage of participation. Each State's maximum liability under the scheme was also to be capped. The maximum exposure of each State would be the equivalent of their ICAO contribution percentage of US$ 15 billion on the basis of 100 % participation, and this individual cap was to remain constant.

[49] The ICAO Assembly is convened once every 3 years. One of the major resolutions adopted at each Assembly concerns how the activities of the organization will be funded during the ensuing 3 years. By convention, the estimated expenses of the organization are apportioned among all contracting states using a Scale of Assessment adopted in accordance with certain principles established by the Assembly in 1980 during its 23rd session. According to those principles, the lowest rate of contribution cannot be below 0.06 % and the highest rate may not exceed 25 %. See ICAO (1980a), published in ICAO (1980b). The contribution rates for 2003 upon which the Globaltime guarantee shares were to be based are found in: ICAO (2001b), published in ICAO (2001a).

terrorism risks.[50] These differences among states in relation to perceived exposure to aviation war and terrorism risks appears to be the source of the most difficult complications that have arisen in the effort to apply the concept of risk retention to the aviation industry on a global scale.[51]

After several refinements of the Globaltime scheme and its accompanying participation agreement,[52] the ICAO Council eventually decided that the scheme would be retained exclusively on a contingency basis, subject to effective

[50] Japan's ICAO contribution rate for 2003, for instance, was set at 14.36 % which meant that its guarantee share would be 14.36 % of the total amount of state guarantees if it decided to participate in Globaltime. The Japanese delegation to the SGWI-RG expressed concern that its Globaltime guarantee share was out of proportion to its exposure to aviation war and terrorism risk. The delegation suggested that, in order to more appropriately reflect each participating state's respective exposure to those risks, the guarantee share of each state could, instead, be based on standards such as flight volume (e.g., the number of passengers carried). Another delegation proposed that indicative factors such as cargo volume and the historical background of states with ICAO contribution rates below the 25 % threshold should be taken into consideration in determining the guarantee share of such states. It was also suggested that Japan's (and indeed other states with large contribution rates) guarantee share be capped at 10 %, and the excess redistributed among remaining participating states The SGWI-RG did not accept any of these suggestions. In its view, a state's level of exposure to aviation war and terrorism risks could not be determined as proposed since, in reality, there is no place or region which could be considered as risk-free or permanently at lower risk from being targeted for terrorism or for initiating or carrying out preparatory terrorism actions. The SGWI-RG also noted that the principles which animate the calculation of ICAO contribution rates take into consideration a Contracting State's importance in civil aviation, measured by the capacity in terms of tonne-kilometres available on each State's scheduled air services, which includes both passenger and cargo services. As such, the computation of the ICAO contribution rates already takes into account factors such as flight, passenger and cargo volume. The SGWI-RG therefore recommended to the Council that Globaltime guarantee shares be allocated among states in the same manner as ICAO contribution rates are allocated. See ICAO (2003b), Agenda Item 2—Review of Globaltime pp. 2-1–2-2.

[51] Most countries consider that the level of any state's exposure to terrorism in general and aviation war and terrorism risks in particular is heavily dependent upon factors such as the domestic and/or foreign policy being pursued by that state. As such, a scheme such as Globaltime which purports to allocate the cost of insurance for aviation war and terrorism risks on a global scale among states without reference to these factors is bound to be rejected by the vast majority of states, particularly those who do not consider themselves to be exposed to terrorism.

[52] Following completion of the SGWI's initial deliberations, the Council decided on 4 March 2002 to establish a Council Group on Aviation War Risk Insurance (CGWI) to work with the ICAO Secretariat to review the recommendations presented by the SGWI. Meanwhile, the President of the Council sent state letters to all ICAO contracting states informing them about the Council's approval in principle of the Globaltime scheme and seeking expressions of intent to participate in it from them. Several responses were received from contracting states some expressing an unconditional interest to participate; others indicating a willingness to participate subject to certain conditions; and some indicating no intent at all to participate. Accordingly, the Council entrusted a sub-group ("review group") of the Special Group on Aviation War Risk Insurance (SGWI-RG) with the task of reviewing the Globaltime scheme in the light of the conditions of participation set by certain states in reply to the State letters and making any adjustments thereto and to the revised draft Participation Agreement. Upon recommendation of the SGWI-RG, the Council decided to approve an amended version of the participation agreement and to retain Globaltime exclusively on a contingency basis.

participation by States representing at least 51 % of ICAO contribution rates.[53] This meant that, the scheme would only become activated if, at any point in the future, the ICAO Council determines that there has been another failure of the commercial insurance market. In that event, the Insuring entity would commence its operations possibly at short notice.[54] In combination with the requirement that to be eligible for war risk coverage under Globaltime, an insured entity must have first obtained the maximum extent of coverage available from the commercial markets, this approach was seen as a means of effectively addressing concerns regarding Globaltime's potential interference with the functioning of the conventional insurance market (market distortion) and state aid issues.[55]

At the last count which took place on 15 June 2004 before the 35th session of the Assembly, 67 ICAO contracting states representing 46.36 % of annual contribution rates had indicated their intention to participate in Globaltime.[56] Out of this number, some 22 states representing 34.93 % of annual contribution rates had indicated that they will participate in the scheme only if certain specified conditions are met.[57] 16 States representing 17.07 % had categorically stated that they would not participate in the scheme.[58] At this writing, although some 21 states had indicated that they would advise the ICAO Council later about their position, the 51 % threshold of intentions to participate has not been attained. Given the continued divergence of views on individual state contributions, in the event that the ICAO Council declares a failure of the conventional insurance market for aviation war and terrorism risks, it is doubtful whether Globaltime can be activated at short notice as envisaged.

5.2.4 The Viability of the Risk Retention Concept in Relation to Aviation War and Terrorism Risks

Theoretically, using the concept of risk retention as a means of funding aviation war and terrorism risks can provide several benefits primary among which is the enhanced availability of capital. In this regard, the circumstances of the air transport industry following the events of September 11, 2001, can be likened to the "capacity crisis" observed in a number of other industries in recent years that, in turn, drove up the rate at which captives, RRGs and mutuals were established in

[53] See ICAO (2003c) pp. 2–3, incorporating and adopting the recommendations of the SGWI-RG as set out in ICAO (2003a).

[54] ICAO (2003a).

[55] Idem.

[56] See ICAO (2004) Appendix A.

[57] Idem.

[58] Idem.

those industries.[59] However, the air transport industry is unique and, in terms of raising capital, has peculiar problems beyond those of most other industries. It is a capital intensive industry characterized by very high fixed costs. The industry's primary equipment—aircraft—is dreadfully expensive to acquire, maintain and operate. Banks finance a large portion of aircraft purchases and a sizeable proportion of many fleets are leased under terms requiring regular monthly capital outlays.[60] Often, many airlines operate at a loss, and this only gets worse in the period following a major event, as demand for air transport softens dramatically. A 3 % net profit margin in any year is considered a "good" year. Although aviation accidents happen infrequently, they do nonetheless occur, and are usually disasters of major proportions with losses running into hundreds of millions of dollars. For an industry that is perennially undercapitalized, the suggestion that the most extreme financial risks that its members are exposed to should be internalized and that an industry-owned insuring entity should be established as a means of marshalling large amounts of capital to fund those risks seems incomprehensible.

As the various risk retention/captive proposals have failed to take root at the domestic and/or regional levels, there is no empirical evidence on the basis of which an assessment of the feasibility of risk retention can be made. It therefore remains to be seen whether, in practice, the concept of risk retention in the air transport industry can be used as a solid alternative or complement to conventional insurance. It is also unclear whether risk retention within the air transport industry will address the problem of heightened ambiguity and uncertainty that causes the conventional insurance markets to avoid covering aviation war and terrorism risks in the period following the occurrence of an extreme insured event. A conclusion drawn by the OECD on the feasibility of using captives as alternatives to commercial insurance is instructive. After noting that captives may be used for alternative risk financing where the conventional insurance market is unable to provide sufficiently flexible, stable and attractive conditions of coverage, the OECD concludes that "[i]t should however be underlined that, with regard to terror-related losses, captives do not seem to have the capacity to offer solutions adapted to the current constraints affecting the availability of reinsurance coverage for the highest layers of terrorism risk exposure".[61]

Notwithstanding the foregoing, applying the broader concept of risk retention within the air transport industry could, to a certain extent, provide a solution to the problems caused by adverse selection in conventional insurance. As discussed in the immediately preceding chapter, conventional insurers are more or less locked into accepting both good and bad (or poor) risks primarily as a result of their inability to identify the specific risk types of individual insureds. Because it is impossible or prohibitively expensive for a conventional insurer to overcome this

[59] For a concise description of the capacity crises that various industries experienced in the years before 2002 and how they resorted to ART schemes in order to resolve them, see Boyle (2002b).

[60] Boyle (2002a).

[61] OECD (2005) p. 56.

informational asymmetry and thereby attain the capability to distinguish between high (bad) and low (good) risks, the price charged by conventional insurers for covering the risk is fixed at an average value which does not really reflect the nature and depth of the risk covered.[62] In consequence, insured companies which take measures to control claims and therefore losses frequently end up subsidizing insurance coverage on the private market for those who do not.[63] Indeed, due to its subsidization effects, the phenomenon of adverse selection causes high risk individuals/entities to purchase more insurance than low risk individuals/entities.

"Setting up a captive or becoming part of a RRG that is based on similar loss histories can mean substantial savings"[64] for insured individuals/entities. Because the captive, RRG or mutual scheme internalizes the risk within the industry, the insurer would technically be the same as, or at the very extreme, be a subsidiary of the insured entities. As such, none of the informational problems which are the root causes of adverse selection in conventional insurance would exist when captives/RRGs/mutuals are created to insure certain risks. As a consequence, it would theoretically be possible to better model the risk exposure of each individual member of the group, thereby disposing of the need to build in an extra premium to address adverse selection. Premium rates could then be set at realistic values that reflect the actual risk covered. In addition if losses are substantially reduced, the profits on any invested surplus will go to the group's members rather than to the equity stakeholders of a private insurance company.[65]

5.3 Capital Market Solutions for Funding and/or Transferring Aviation War and Terrorism Risks Beyond the Insurance System

Unlike the concept of risk retention which underlies the formation of captives, risk retention groups and mutualization schemes to provide alternative means of self-insuring risks in any particular industry, capital market solutions focus on how commercial insurance companies can tap into the deeper capital resources of the capital markets in order to enhance their underwriting capacity. Thus, the role of capital markets in financing and/or insuring risks is best explained from the perspective of the dominant "originators" in this market, namely insurance and reinsurance companies.[66] Again, as a background to this discussion, it is useful to recall that when commercial insurance companies underwrite risks, they do so in reliance upon a very finite supply of capital at their disposal. In order to avoid

[62] Outreville (1998) p. 152.

[63] Boyle (2002b).

[64] Idem.

[65] Idem.

[66] See Ali (2008) p. 352.

over-concentration of risk which may adversely affect the solvency of any insurance company, commercial underwriters traditionally transfer or cede portions of the risks they have underwritten to reinsurers and retrocessionaires in order to spread risks among a wide network of risk bearing entities within the insurance industry. Since reinsurers and retrocessionaires are equally exposed to the same capacity (capital) constraints that primary insurance companies are exposed to, they too must deal with the problem of over-concentration of risk in order to avoid erosion of capital or even insolvency. The possibility of over-concentration of risk in any one primary insurance company, reinsurer or retrocessionaire is heightened when the risk concerned is of catastrophic proportions.

In order to overcome the foregoing limits of the conventional insurance and reinsurance markets, suggestions have been made to turn to domestic and international capital markets with the view to developing new and innovative risk financing and risk transfer solutions.[67] Capital markets offer different types of alternative risk management solutions which can be grouped into two main categories: *alternative risk financing* and *alternative risk transfer* instruments.[68] The main difference between the two categories is that while the former does not involve any transfer of risk and is aimed at securing the availability of funding for recovery on predetermined conditions in case of a catastrophic loss, the latter entails the shifting of all or part of the financial burden associated with the risk from one party to another.[69] In this perspective, only the latter is considered a functional alternative to conventional insurance and reinsurance contracts—the former encompasses means of raising funds and does not involve transfer of risk. Notwithstanding the foregoing, risk transfer and risk financing tools may be used jointly within the framework of an integrated risk management strategy.[70] What follows is a closer look at the viability of the two aforementioned categories of capital market solutions *vis-á-vis* aviation war and terrorism risks.

5.3.1 Capital Market Alternative Risk Financing Instruments

It has been argued in a leading article on the theory of catastrophe risk financing that, the best way to protect the value embedded in a firm is to prearrange equity to be put at favourable rates, when a financially impairing event occurs.[71] Accordingly, "[t]he

---

[67] The driving force behind such suggestions is that, taking their size into consideration, capital markets have a remarkable risk spreading potential and might be willing to take on new risks if they consider them imperfectly correlated with those they routinely accept. In theory, through the diversification of institutional investors' investment portfolios, capital markets may manage to absorb high risk exposures, thereby optimizing investor's risk-return ratios. See OECD (2005) p. 55.

[68] Idem.

[69] Idem.

[70] Idem., p. 56.

[71] Mutenga and Staikouras (2007) p. 238.

purpose of alternative risk financing is not to transfer a risk of loss, but to secure access to future financing opportunities under prearranged conditions".[72] Alternative risk financing arrangements provide capital replenishment opportunities by establishing contingencies in the financial markets that make funding available in case there is the need to recuperate after economic losses have been inflicted.[73] By resorting to alternative risk financing instruments, an insurance company for instance is assured that, after a catastrophic event has occurred thereby reducing its surplus and credit standing, it will still be able to procure capital up to certain agreed limits to help refinance its business.[74] These instruments are therefore purchased with the sole purpose of alleviating the strain on capital and/or enhancing its role when depleted after a catastrophic event.[75] In summary, capital market alternative risk financing instruments offer insurers: partial hedging of risk; credit enhancement; post-loss liquidity; low cost of capital; and as well, mitigate underinvestment and asset substitution problems.[76]

As adeptly portrayed by the OECD in a publication released in 2005,

> [d]ifferent forms of risk financing solutions have been explored within international financial markets, the most important of which are *committed funding arrangements* with commercial banking sector participants, such as committed revolving term facilities and *contingent capital instruments* offered by investment banks and securities firms.[77]

5.3.1.1 Committed Credit Facilities

Committed credit facilities may be drawn down by an insurance company at any time on predetermined conditions in case the need arises, (e.g., after a major disaster has occurred or any other adverse situation that gives rise to incremental liquidity need).[78] In their simplest form, committed funding arrangements may take the form of committed revolving term facilities that provide funding by rolling over short-term credits at a fixed spread over a variable rate indicator like Libor.[79] "More advanced forms of committed funding arrangements may constitute

---

[72] OECD (2005) p. 56.

[73] Andersen (2005) p. 167.

[74] Mutenga and Staikouras (2007) p. 238. According to these authors, this sort of financing redresses the balance between equity and debt, and the potential embedded in the firm's structure could be realized. The catastrophe hits the equity, which in turn triggers the exercise of the hedging device that restores the stock's value. This circularity, known as the feedback effect, is also referred to by other authors as the "apparent paradox".

[75] Idem., p. 227.

[76] Idem., p. 240.

[77] OECD (2005) p. 56, [emphasis added]. Contingent capital instruments may take the form of put option contracts or contingent surplus notes, the aim of which is to guarantee the issuance of medium-term securities on fixed terms if a certain event occurs.

[78] Andersen (2005) p. 167.

[79] Idem.

syndicated credit facilities shared among banks in larger consortia".[80] They may also take hybrid forms somewhere between pure bank lines of credit and capital market instruments. For example, the arrangement could be set up as "short-term commercial paper or medium-term note issuance facilities where debt instruments are placed directly in the market or are offered to a prearranged panel of financial institutions".[81]

Normally, such credit facilities would be further supported by committed back-stop facilities provided by commercial banks for purposes of ensuring future availability of funding in the unlikely event that the capital market dries up or offers funding at uncompetitive rates.[82] Committed funding facilities typically require payment by the insurance company beneficiary of an up-front commitment fee to compensate the provider for the implied liquidity, interest rate and credit risks.[83]

5.3.1.2 Contingent Capital Instruments

In its simplest form, a contingent capital instrument is a put option contract that gives the holder the right to place funding instruments on the market for purposes of raising funds subject to predetermined conditions.[84] "The issuer of contingent capital instruments provides the holder (e.g., an insurance company) with a guarantee that securities can be issued and placed with investors if certain adverse events occur".[85] Thus, should the pre-specified event occur, the holder of the instrument will have the right to sell its own securities or issue debt instruments for a fixed period of time.[86] Contingent capital may also come in the form of a reverse convertible debt instrument (RCDI), where existing debt is converted into equity when the qualifying event occurs.[87] "Capital raised through equity puts or RCDI is treated as equity, which means that it adds directly to [the buying firm's] surplus, providing a stronger balance sheet and protection at a cost that is lower than a traditional secondary equity offering".[88] Contingent capital may also take the form of debt or hybrid security financing.[89]

Typically, the process of raising contingent capital is a multi-year deal in which the buyer of the put option (the insurance company) pays a commitment fee or option premium in exchange for the equity or debt put option that enables it to retain

[80] Idem.

[81] Idem.

[82] Idem.

[83] Idem.

[84] Mutenga and Staikouras (2007) p. 238; see also Andersen (2005) p. 168.

[85] Andersen (2005).

[86] Mutenga and Staikouras (2007) p. 238.

[87] Idem.

[88] Idem.

[89] Idem., p. 240.

access to future financing opportunities on predetermined conditions.[90] One of those conditions is usually a trigger—an event or scenario that activates the holder's right to exercise the option. "When the option is triggered by the performance of the insurance company's actual portfolio of business, the resulting instruments are called *indemnity-based or company specific* instruments. On the other hand, when the option is triggered by the performance of a broad, industry-based index, the resulting instruments are referred to as *index-based or non-indemnity based* instruments".[91]

For the option to be exercised in a typical catastrophe equity put (CatEPut) transaction for example, two contingencies must be satisfied: (a) the specified catastrophic event must occur and, (b) the stock price must fall below the strike price.[92] This is the point in time when the buyer becomes entitled to exercise the right to recapitalize its balance sheet by issuing new shares (or debt instruments) at a pre-determined price.[93] From this time, the capital provider (option writer) starts receiving the dividends (or interest depending on the type of capital raised) on the equity or debt supplied. The next step is for the buyer to redeem the shares (or debt) and repay the capital.[94]

As an alternative to traditional reinsurance, the alternative risk financing instruments discussed above have been used by the insurance industry to finance various types of catastrophic risks. However, it has been reported that, as of 2005, no contingent capital instrument had been issued using natural disasters or terrorist attacks as triggering events.[95] The choice between alternative risk financing instruments and traditional reinsurance is a function of their respective availabilities across markets for different risk financing instruments and the general pricing and affordability of available covers.[96] It is also influenced by the characteristics of the instruments and the implications they have for moral hazard, adverse selection, basis risk and credit risk exposures. In any event, unlike reinsurance, the proceeds of alternative risk financing instruments must be repaid by the buyer according to the terms and conditions agreed upon in advance.[97]

Indemnity-based or company-specific alternative risk financing instruments appeal to insurance companies because they tend to reduce or eliminate basis risk. Basis risk has been defined as "the risk that there may be a difference between the performance of the hedge and the losses sustained from the hedged exposure".[98] Stated differently, "it is the risk that the value of the underlying index used

[90] Andersen (2005) p. 167.

[91] Bouriaux and Scott (2002).

[92] Mutenga and Staikouras (2007) p. 239.

[93] Idem.

[94] Idem.

[95] OECD (2005) p. 56. See also Andersen (2005) p. 168.

[96] Andersen (2005).

[97] OECD (2005). See also Andersen (2005) p. 167.

[98] See American Academy of Actuaries (2001) p. 17.

and/or structure of the settlement (in cash) of the derivative may not provide the desired offset to the insurer's loss".[99] "Instruments that use standardized indexes [as triggers] will often have high basis risk, because it is difficult to apply a general index to an individualized risk exposure".[100] By way of example, in using an index-based ARF instrument, if the specified index value that underpins or triggers the instrument differs significantly from the value of the risk exposure it is intended to cover, the hedge will be exposed to a high basis risk.[101] The existence of high basis risk therefore means that there is no guarantee that those risks intended to be financed by the instruments are perfectly hedged. The implication of the mismatch between the index value and the holder's actual losses is that, although the holder might have suffered substantial losses, it will not be able to exercise the financing options granted by the instrument because the index-based triggering scenario has not materialized.

Capital market investors prefer index-based or non-indemnity alternative risk financing instruments since they tend to minimize moral hazard and adverse selection. In this context, moral hazard relates to the fact that an insurance company that has prearranged financing for its risks on favorable terms from the capital markets will no longer have an incentive to limit its losses.[102] Adverse selection, on the other hand, refers to the tendency of an insurer to hedge the most unattractive parts of its risk portfolio, while keeping the most profitable parts to itself.[103] Index-based ARF instruments are able to minimize moral hazard and adverse selection because the trigger for the instrument is largely outside the control of the holder.[104] For example, if the trigger is a loss index of many insurers, then the only control the holder has over the index is scaled to its share of the index. If it is not in the index, the holder has no influence on the index and there is no moral hazard.[105] Thus, in connection with ARF instruments, there is a trade-off between basis risk and moral hazard.[106]

Using ARF instruments as a means of hedging capital availability to back the insurance of aviation war and terrorism risks entails a number of issues. The moral hazard and adverse selection concerns explained above will cause providers of ARF instruments to charge higher up-front commitment fees if the trigger is associated with the underlying loss exposure. Where index-based triggers are used instead, the concern is that the existence of high basis risk will result in little or no correlation between the actual losses suffered by the holder of the instrument and the

[99] Bouriaux (2001) p. 102.

[100] Andersen (2005) p. 169. Under traditional reinsurance, the payout obligation is usually a function of the reinsured's own losses and so there is little or no basis risk.

[101] Idem.

[102] Bouriaux and Scott (2002) p. 17.

[103] Idem.

[104] Doherty and Richter (2002) p. 11.

[105] Idem.

[106] Idem.

index-based trigger. As a result, the insurance company will exhaust its capital paying claims based on covered events, but will not be able to exercise the financing options granted under the ARF instruments to recapitalize its business.

Further, an insurance company that chooses to hedge its aviation war and terrorism risks on the capital markets using ARF instruments stands to lose the premium or commitment fee it pays to the provider if the specified trigger event or scenario does not occur within the option period.[107] In a sense, this is no different from reinsurance, as premiums paid to reinsurers are usually not refundable. However, considering the fact that reinsurance provides non-refundable indemnity payouts to the reinsured (whereas payouts made under ARF instruments must be repaid by the holder), and also that up-front commitment fees for ARF instruments may be more expensive than reinsurance premiums, a lot remains to be said about the viability of ARF instruments as a substitute for reinsurance in relation to aviation war and terrorism risks.

5.3.2 Capital Market Alternative Risk Transfer Instruments

Unlike alternative risk financing, the concept of alternative risk transfer (ART) involves the actual transfer of risks of all kinds to the capital markets. Typical ART instruments include over-the-counter and exchange-traded financial derivatives such as options contracts, futures contracts, catastrophe risk swap agreements, as well as different types of risk-linked (or insurance-linked) securities. They are all products of securitization, a financial technique that involves the repackaging of income yielding assets into a tradable form via the issuance of financial instruments that are secured against those underlying assets.[108] It is reported that the technique of securitization was first developed in the early 1970s when the US federal government issued mortgage-backed "pass through" securities.[109] Since then, financial institutions and businesses of all kinds have used the technique to reduce their capital requirements and to immediately realize the value of cash producing assets by creating securities separate from their existing debt and equity securities.[110] It is reported, for instance,

[107] Mutenga and Staikouras (2007) p. 239. On the other hand, the severity of the event that triggers the instrument could be substantial, resulting in the insolvency of the holder and leaving the provider with no capital repayment. In the literature, this phenomenon is referred to as credit risk.

[108] Godbole (2004) p. 41. In theory, any stream of receivables can be securitized. However, assets that are commonly securitized are receivables generated from the sale of mortgages (both residential and commercial), credit cards, auto loans, student loans and home equity loans. See Rhee (2005) p. 497.

[109] Rhee (2005).

[110] Helfenstein and Holzheu (2006) p. 3.

that securitization is one of the major factors that has contributed to the recent transformation of the banking industry.[111]

"The [two] forms of securitization that are most commonly encountered in the global financial markets are 'true sale' or 'cash' securitizations (which are primarily a fund-raising tool for banks and corporations) and 'synthetic' securitizations (which are used primarily by banks to manage their risk capital)".[112] In a typical synthetic securitization, an originator[113] transfers the credit risk[114] of a pool of nominated debt instruments (while retaining the other risks associated with the instruments, including liquidity risk[115] and market risk[116]) to a special purpose securitization vehicle[117] by means of a credit derivative. The special purpose securitization vehicle in turn issues securities to investors in the capital markets and uses the funds raised therefrom to support the performance of its obligation to make payments under the credit derivative to the originator should there be a material deterioration in the credit quality of the instruments.

In this way, the credit risk associated with the pool of debt instruments is segregated from the other associated risks and transferred from the originator to the securitization vehicle, and then by the latter on to the capital market investors.[118] The success of synthetic securitization is attributable to the ease

[111] See Wemmer (2008) p. 2. In support, the author reports that, over the 25 year period ending in 2008, commercial banks developed various forms of asset-backed securities (ABS) and sold them to a broad spectrum of market participants. As a result, not only did the return on equity in the banking sector rise from single to double digits; there was also a sizeable reduction in the earnings volatility of commercial banks.

[112] Ali (2008) p. 349. The essential feature of a true sale securitization is that the transaction revolves around the sale (assignment) of the underlying assets from the originator to the SPV. Therefore, the originator sheds all risks (not just credit risk) associated with the assets. In a synthetic securitization, it is only the credit risk of the underlying assets that is transferred from the originator to the SPV. The originator retains all the other risks associated with the assets. See Vries Robbé et al. (2008) p. 6.

[113] Usually a bank that has originated mortgage loans or corporate loans.

[114] Credit risk generally refers to the risk of default. In other words, it is the risk that counterparties to a transaction will not meet their obligations thereunder. See Bouriaux (2001) p. 105. It is the risk of loss of principal or loss of financial reward stemming from a borrower's failure to repay a loan or otherwise meet a contractual obligation. Even if a counterparty to a transaction does manage to ultimately meet its obligations, the value of the underlying debt instrument may decline if its rating is downgraded. See Krenn and Oschischnig (2003) p. 66.

[115] "Closely related to market risk, liquidity risk is the risk of not being able to meet payment liabilities when due. The liquidity of an investment is defined by how quickly and to what extent it can be converted into cash". See Krenn and Oschischnig (2003) p. 67.

[116] Market risk is defined as "potential losses owing to detrimental changes in market prices and/or other financial variables influenced by prices. This includes share prices, interest rates, asset prices or exchange rates. In other words, market risk makes up a key share of investment risks". See idem., p. 65.

[117] The special purpose securitization vehicle is usually a corporate entity specifically established for the purpose of the securitization transaction. They are usually incorporated in countries or jurisdictions with the most favourable tax regimes.

[118] Ali (2008) pp. 349–350.

with which the credit risk as well as the ownership of loans and other debt instruments can be disaggregated from the other risks associated with those instruments. This facilitates hedging of the credit risk by banks and enables them to release the risk capital that would otherwise have to be held to cover the credit risk of those debt instruments.[119]

An adaptation of the technique of synthetic securitization is used in order to transfer insurance and reinsurance risks to the capital markets, so that investors are substituted in place of traditional risk bearers such as reinsurers.[120] The concept of risk disaggregation that is central to synthetic securitizations provides the basis for insurance securitization.[121] In securitizing insurance risks, the originator (generally an insurance or reinsurance company) transfers underwriting risks[122] (while retaining other risks) to the capital markets by transforming insurance receivables—underwriting cash flows—into tradable financial securities. The cash flows resulting from the securities issued are used to fund the securitization vehicle's assumption of risk from the originator which is made contingent upon the occurrence of a specified insurance event or risk.[123] This means that "[i]f the event to which the transferred risk relates does occur, the securitization vehicle will use the proceeds obtained from the investors to make a pre-determined payment to the originator, meaning that the securitization vehicle will then have fewer or even, depending on the severity of the event in question, no or negligible assets with which to meet the investors' claims for the payment of principal and interest on their securities".[124] In this way, the risk of the event occurring (i.e., the underwriting risk)—that would have been borne by the originator—is passed on by the securitization vehicle to the investors, and the originator is thereby relieved from the obligation of carrying capital reserves to back those risks.

Thus, whereas securitization in the banking sector aims at transferring the credit risks linked to certain assets to the capital markets, the risks transferred in insurance securitization are typically linked to liabilities.[125] According to one commentator, the rationale for securitizing a pool of assets (receivables)

---

[119] Idem. Indeed, through securitization, the originator is able to de-link the value of the instruments issued to investors from its own creditworthiness (or the lack of it).

[120] Godbole (2004) p. 41.

[121] Ali (2008) p. 350. See also Doherty and Schlesinger (2002) p. 48 where the authors argue that "[t]he securitization of insurance risk is at issue when risk can be decomposed into an idiosyncratic component and a systemic element that can be indexed".

[122] Underwriting risks are the risks which an insurance contract is supposed to cover. To a large extent, these risks stem from the fundamental business of the insurance industry, namely selling insurance policies. Underwriting risks emanate from the dangers to which the object of the insurance contract is exposed. See Krenn and Oschischnig (2003) p. 63.

[123] De Mey (2007) p. 37. Depending on the terms of the securities, the principal and/or interest owed thereon to investors will be paid instead to the originator once the specified trigger conditions are satisfied. This may take one of two forms. On an indemnity-based deal, the parties agree on a trigger based on the actual loss experience of the originator or on the occurrence of an insured event of a specified magnitude. On a non-indemnity securitization, investor liability on the securities is triggered by an agreed index rather than the actual loss experience of the originator.

[124] Ali (2008) p. 354.

[125] De Mey (2007).

> lies in a cost of capital differential. If the cost of funds needed to generate the assets (i.e., the originator's cost of capital) is more than the cost to securitize the assets (i.e., the interest payments on the bonds), securitization benefits all concerned. By securitizing the receivables, the originator secures funding for the receivables at a cheaper rate than its own cost of capital. The originator can then use the "freed up" capital to originate more assets or return it to its shareholders.[126]

As frequently repeated in this book, conventional insurance and reinsurance markets are highly cyclical. "Following large losses, premia tend to rise due to several factors including the need of the (re)insurance industry to gradually rebuild financial capacity after the loss reserves have been drained; the increased level of generalised uncertainty and ambiguity that translates into higher safety and fluctuation loadings; and the growth in demand for coverage".[127] Historically, these rather significant insurance market disruptions or failures have been the main driving force behind efforts to transfer risks—catastrophic risks in particular—from the insurance markets into the capital markets. It is reported for instance that, in the mid-1990s, the occurrence of two major natural catastrophes in the US—Hurricane Andrew (1992) and the Northridge Earthquake (1994)—sparked several innovations in the capital market, one significant result of which was the introduction of natural catastrophe futures contracts and options in 1995 (also known as Cat spreads) and catastrophe risk-linked bonds (Cat-bonds) in 1997 at the Chicago Board of Trade.[128] These innovative financial instruments were in response to the traditional insurance and reinsurance markets' inability to deal with those catastrophic risks. Thus, as one author succinctly put it, "[i]nsurance securitization has largely evolved as a financial markets response to natural disasters".[129] For present purposes, the balance of this

[126] Rhee (2005) p. 497.

[127] OECD (2005) p. 55 (footnotes omitted).

[128] See Rhee (2005) p. 500. It is reported that the first attempt to access the capital markets as a source for risk transfer capacity was made in 1993 by Dr. Richard Sandor and Morton Lane through the development of the concept of insurance derivatives. The main driver behind this innovation was the occurrence of hurricane Andrew in 1992. Insured losses from this hurricane amounted to approximately US$ 20 billion and this seemed to generate a capacity crisis in the insurance market for natural catastrophes. Richard Sandor and Morton Lane created reinsurance derivatives at the Chicago Board of Trade, based on US nationwide and individual region insurance market loss ratios for natural catastrophe property business. They were so confident about the derivatives that they announced that in 3 years' time, there will no longer be any traditional reinsurance. Unfortunately, however, due to the injection of substantial amounts of fresh capital through existing and freshly established reinsurance companies, the capacity crisis did not materialize. Consequently, the reinsurance derivatives did not generate sufficient trading volume. See Materne (2007).

[129] Ali (2008) p. 350. Simulations conducted by modeling firms in the 1990s suggested that damages caused by a major hurricane in Florida could be at least US$ 75 billion, and those due to an earthquake in California could exceed US$ 100 billion. With prospective event losses exceeding US$ 50 billion, the capitalization of the insurance and reinsurance industry was at issue. Estimates of the total capital and surplus of U.S. insurers and international reinsurers were about US$ 300 billion and US$ 100 billion, respectively. Although such catastrophic losses were large enough to put the insurance industry under severe stress, they were estimated to be lower than one standard deviation of the daily value traded (about US$ 130 billion on average) in the US capital markets. As such, the simulations found that the pool of financial capacity provided by the financial markets is capable of bearing the most pessimistic estimated losses caused by a natural catastrophe. See Mahul (2001).

section focuses on Cat-bonds as an alternative to conventional reinsurance of aviation war and terrorism risks.[130] It should be noted, however, that there are in existence other capital market ART instruments which are of equal significance.

Through the issuance of Cat-bonds, the originator, typically an insurance or reinsurance company can obtain cover for specified exposures in case of predefined catastrophe events, (e.g., storms, hurricanes or earthquakes). Cat-bond issues are typically structured around a special purpose reinsurance vehicle (SPRV), established in a tax favourable jurisdiction such as Grand Caymans or Bahamas.[131] Unlike other securitizations where the securitization vehicle merely makes payments to the originator once the specified trigger event has occurred, the SPRV in a Cat-bond usually enters into a reinsurance contract with the originator.[132]

This reinsurance contract will normally provide the originator with insurance coverage for the securitized catastrophic risks on an excess-of-loss (EOL) basis, corresponding to usual practice in the conventional catastrophe reinsurance market.[133] Hence, "the ceded risk exposure may cover losses associated with particular insurance layers between specified attachment and exhaustion points", and the originator (as the reinsured or ceding party) is obliged to pay an insurance premium to the SPRV for the entire insurance period on a pro-rata basis.[134] The SPRV then transfers the risks it has assumed under the reinsurance contract to the capital markets by issuing the Cat-bonds and selling them to capital market investors. The SPRV receives up-front payments from those investors buying the securities and in turn, is obliged to pay interest on the bonds.[135]

---

[130] To date, Cat-bonds constitute the commonest form of insurance securitizations. It is reported that between 1997 and 2006, a total of 97 Cat-bond securitizations were executed. The range of risks that have been securitized via Cat-bonds has also expanded from natural catastrophes to man-made disasters, and suggestions have been made following the events of September 11, 2001 that Cat-bonds (or a slight variation thereof) can potentially be used to transfer aviation war and terrorism risks to the capital markets. See Ali (2008) p. 351. Aside from Cat-bonds, other forms of insurance securitization include financial derivatives such as exchange traded and over-the-counter options contracts, futures contracts, and catastrophe risk swap agreements.

[131] Andersen (2005) p. 162.

[132] Idem. This is why the securitization vehicle in Cat-bonds is usually referred to as a special purpose reinsurance vehicle (SPRV) and not just a special purpose vehicle (SPV).

[133] Idem.

[134] Technically, this means that the originator of the premium (i.e., the insurer) cedes all or a portion of the premium to the SPRV in return for the reinsurance cover provided. Payment of the premium by the originator is usually synchronized with payment by the SPRV of interest on the Cat-bonds to the investors—typically on a quarterly basis. Thus, nonpayment of premiums by the originator on a matching basis would result in a cancellation of the reinsurance policy, a default of the bond terms, and a termination of the risk to the bondholders. See Rhee (2005) p. 502.

[135] The SPRV uses the up-front proceeds from the bond issue, less the expenses accrued in connection with the placement, to buy a portfolio of liquid securities with high credit quality and low interest rate sensitivity. The securities portfolio is placed in a trust account as collateral for the interest payments due on the Cat-bonds. The SPRV often enters into a fixed-floating interest rate swap agreement that converts the interest returns from the invested securities portfolio into monthly Libor-based floating payments. The investors receive a relatively high spread above the Libor rate to compensate for their exposure to the underlying catastrophe risk. See Andersen (2005) pp. 162–163. Concerning the interest rate swap agreement, see also Rhee (2005) p. 501.

Risks transferred to the capital markets through Cat-bonds "can be dissected and packaged in a number of ways".[136] For instance, the capital invested by bondholders may be treated in different ways. "In a principal-protected bond, only a portion of the principal is [placed] at risk and the remaining portion is paid back to the investors after a period of years, typically a term of five or ten years. In a principal-at-risk bond, the investor puts at risk the entire principal of the bonds, typically for a term of three to five years".[137] Cat-bonds may also use different bases to trigger payment of compensation by the SPRV to the originator under the reinsurance contract.[138] Payment of compensation can be triggered as an indemnity of actual insurance losses incurred by the originator.[139] In the event of a catastrophe materializing, since there would be no mismatch between the actual losses suffered by the originator and the payout received from the SPRV, this type of arrangement would involve little or no basis risk even when the bond is linked to an index-based trigger. As aptly noted by Rhee in his leading article on the subject, the foregoing arrangement "mimics traditional reinsurance which is typically indemnity-based because [reinsurance] treaties are between well developed, symbiotic business relationships".[140]

Insurers who securitize all or parts of the catastrophic risks they have assumed usually prefer such indemnity-based Cat-bonds for obvious reasons.[141] However, "the inability of the investor to oversee or control the [originator's] underwriting and claims processes creates a moral hazard".[142] Accordingly, Cat-bond investors usually prefer a non-indemnity structure where liability is not determined exclusively by the actual losses suffered by the originator, but is triggered on the basis of: (1) a defined, industry-wide loss index, or built on indicators measuring the magnitude of the specified catastrophic event in any number of different ways (e.g., wind speed, magnitude of earthquake, intensity of rainfall, etc.);[143] (2) parametric formulas—a hybrid methodology where the triggers adopted may be closely associated with the originator's actual exposure to loss but at the same time are well defined, objectively measurable and analyzable parameters.[144] Another

---

136 Rhee (2005) p. 502.

137 Idem., pp. 502–503.

138 Andersen (2005) p. 163.

139 Idem.

140 Rhee, *supra* note 2 at 503.

141 These reasons are similar to those discussed above in connection with insurers' preference for indemnity-based ARF instruments over non-indemnity based ARF instruments. See section 5.3.1 above.

142 Rhee (2005) p. 503.

143 Andersen (2005) p. 163.

144 Idem.

important feature of Cat-bonds is that, at the time of their maturity, the investors may only receive from the SPRV payment of principal and/or accrued interest (as the case may be) if no catastrophe losses have materialized in the meantime.[145] As such, "the major risk consideration for Cat-bond investors is the inherent catastrophic risk exposure".[146]

In the conventional insurance industry, reinsurance companies are able to diversify their risk from underwriting risky lines of business (such as hurricanes) by insuring other risky but non-correlated exposures (e.g., earthquakes) at the same time.[147] This spreads the risk, ensuring that an adverse outcome in any one line will not bring down the whole company.[148] As compared to reinsurance, however, insurance securitization enjoys significant advantages over conventional reinsurance.[149] "The principal advantage is the enormous capacity of the global capital markets to absorb the magnitude of losses likely to result from a natural or man-made disaster relative to the global insurance and reinsurance markets".[150] Additionally, "the greater capacity of the global capital markets to absorb losses flowing from catastrophic risks has pricing advantages. The pricing for covering such losses vià securitization is cheaper and less volatile than the pricing of similar coverage in the insurance and reinsurance markets".[151]

From the capital market perspective, there appears to be a steady demand for Cat-bonds, particularly from institutional investors, and this demand is largely driven by—even attributable to—the immense portfolio diversification potential associated with Cat-bonds.[152] According to Paul Ali, "[m]odern portfolio theory—which not only informs institutional investment but also has been incorporated into the legal duty of prudence with which institutional investors must comply when deciding to buy, hold or sell securities—is concerned with maximizing the benefits

---

[145] Idem.

[146] Idem. Investors assume a much greater risk with Cat-bonds as compared to regular corporate bonds. This is because, although rating agencies routinely provide credit ratings for Cat-bonds, information on natural catastrophes is not as voluminous or transparent as information on commoditized receivables. It is therefore difficult to model catastrophic risks. In consequence, Cat-bond investors receive a relatively high rate of return above the LIBOR rate to compensate for the exposure to catastrophic risk. See also Rhee (2005) pp. 500–501.

[147] Bouriaux and Scott (2002) p. 8.

[148] Idem.

[149] p. 354.

[150] Ali (2008) p. 353.

[151] Idem., pp. 353–354. The author notes further that, through securitization, it is possible to obtain multi-year coverage of catastrophic risks at a fixed price in the global capital markets, whereas multi-year coverage in conventional insurance and reinsurance markets is rare or nonexistent. See also OECD (2005) p. 57.

[152] Ali (2008), p. 354.

from portfolio diversification".[153] Since the returns on Cat-bonds are not, or are only weakly, correlated to the returns on conventional investment assets such as shares and corporate bonds,[154] investing in Cat-bonds offers professional asset managers the opportunity to construct investment portfolios that engage different forms of risk exposure so that the risk of the entire portfolio is lower than the risk associated with any of its individual constituents taken separately.[155] Securitization of risks through the issuance of Cat-bonds offers capital market investors the unique opportunity of combining insurance risks with financial risks in the same portfolio in order to create and/or enhance diversification benefits.

Historically, insurance securitization (particularly Cat-bonds) has primarily been used by the insurance industry to hedge against natural disaster type catastrophic risks (e.g., the risk of an earthquake or a hurricane causing very large financial losses). However, in recent years, the range of risks that have been securitized has continued to expand.[156] For instance, securitization has been used to hedge weather risk[157] and the risks associated with man-made

---

[153] Idem., p. 355. In expounding the modern portfolio theory, the author writes at 355–356:

> This theory posits that the extent to which an investor can maximize the riskiness of a portfolio for a given level of risk or minimize the riskiness of the portfolio for a given level of returns depends upon the level of portfolio diversification, as measured by the extent to which the different portfolio constituents are correlated to one another. Thus the inclusion in a portfolio of securities such as those issued in an insurance securitization, whose returns are negatively or weakly correlated or not correlated to the returns of other portfolio constituents should increase portfolio returns (without increasing the riskiness of the portfolio) or reduce the riskiness of the portfolio (without reducing portfolio returns). Where securities bear the same interest rate and credit risk as other securities but, unlike the latter, are not or are only weakly correlated to the constituents of the investor's portfolio (which is the relationship that the returns on cat-bonds bears to the returns on conventional debt securities), modern portfolio theory as well as the legal duty of prudence would favour the selection of the former securities.

[154] All conventional asset classes typically available for investment on the capital markets (e.g., stocks, commodities, real estate, etc.) share economic interdependencies and are therefore highly correlated with the overarching economic framework. To illustrate, a collapse of the Dow Jones Stock Index will certainly affect commodity prices and vice versa. Securitized natural catastrophe risks, on the other hand, provide a "non-correlating asset class". This is because the underlying risk exposure is not affected by what happens within the economic framework. Still using the above example, a collapse of the Dow Jones Stock Index will not generate a natural catastrophe such as an earthquake or a hurricane (although the reverse may be the case—the occurrence of an earthquake or hurricane may affect the performance of the stock index). See Materne (2007) pp. 5–6.

[155] Bouriaux and Scott (2002) p. 8.

[156] Ali (2008) p. 354.

[157] "Weather derivatives are, uniquely, hedges against volumetric risk. They offer protection not against changes in the prices of commodities, financial instruments or indices, but against changes in the volume of demand for, or supply of, commodities or services due to changes in weather conditions. The demand for electricity, for example, rises in hot weather (due to increased use of air conditioners) but tapers off in cooler weather. The demand for gas and heating oil, on the other hand declines during warmer weather but rises in cold weather (due to increased demand for hot water and heating). Electricity utilities, and gas and heating oil suppliers can, by using temperature

disasters.[158] The idea of securitizing terrorism risks (including aviation war and terrorism risks) emerged after the September 11, 2001 attacks. "The shrinkage of capacity [on the insurance and reinsurance markets] following those attacks was seen as an opportunity to develop new financial market instruments that may be used by (re)insurers to enable them to increase their underwriting capacity".[159] Further, these instruments were perceived as being capable of providing other corporate (i.e., non-insurance) entities with "an alternative to limited and possibly expensive conventional terrorism (re)insurance products".[160] So far, there has only been two publicly reported cases of alternative risk transfer of terrorism risk exposures to the capital market, namely: "FIFA's [Fédération Internationale de Football Association] economic cover for cancellation of the 2006 World Cup tournament in Germany and the Swiss Re sponsored Vita Capital cover for excess mortality risk".[161] Although both transactions did not involve the securitization of aviation war and terrorism risks, they are nevertheless considered in detail below for purposes of determining whether they provide a model for future securitization of aviation war and terrorism risks.

FIFA obtained cover through the issuance of risk-linked securities by Golden Goal Finance Ltd., (a special purpose vehicle, SPV, created to securitize FIFA's expected revenues from the World Cup tournament).[162] The US$ 262.5 million transaction was structured on behalf of FIFA by the investment bank Credit Suisse First Boston (CSFB) and closed in late 2003. It was designed to provide cover for lost revenues to FIFA in the event of non-completion of the World Cup. The need for the cover was prompted, among other things,[163] by FIFA's marketing partners to secure repayment of prepaid amounts in case of cancellation, abandonment, or curtailment of the scheduled World Cup tournament. The structure of the transaction followed a conventional risk-linked security. According to the terms of the transaction, the note holders were scheduled to receive 25 % of their initial principal at the scheduled interest payment date in December 2005 and, consequently, only 75 % the principal amount was exposed to the World Cup cancellation risk.[164]

---

swaps, protect their earnings from cooler than usual summers and warmer than usual winters respectively". See idem., pp. 361–362.

[158] Whether or not the diversification potential of insurance securitization exists in the case of terrorism risks (i.e., man-made disasters) is not clear and remains to be seen. For instance, the stock markets fell as a result of the September 11, 2001 terrorist attacks in the US. However, bond markets spiked as the US Federal Reserve liquefied financial markets in view of the attacks. See Bouriaux and Scott (2002) p. 9.

[159] OECD (2005) p. 58.

[160] Idem.

[161] Andersen (2005) p. 178.

[162] Idem.

[163] It is reported that FIFA "opted for this capital market arrangement after having carefully evaluated the traditional insurance alternative, which reportedly no longer met FIFA's objectives. Among the main concerns was the fact that, after September 11, [2001] the insurance market shifted from multi-year to annual renewable cover". See OECD (2005) p. 58.

[164] Idem. See also Andersen (2005) p. 178.

The securities were issued in four tranches, structured as classes A1, A2, A3, and B, and denominated in three currencies.[165] The trigger was defined in an objective and highly verifiable manner.[166] A striking feature of the transaction was that cancellation of the World Cup could be triggered by natural hazards such as windstorms, earthquakes, and floods, as well as different types of terrorist events. However, it would have required extraordinary circumstances for the final tournament to be cancelled, abandoned or truncated since FIFA had the flexibility, under the transaction, to reschedule matches and also to choose different locations.[167] This transaction is said to be the first of its kind to transfer event risk (i.e., the risk of a sporting event being cancelled) and the risks of terrorism, man-made catastrophe, as well as natural catastrophe to the capital markets.[168]

Not only was the Golden Goal transaction the first transaction explicitly covering terrorism risks; it was also oversubscribed, demonstrating that investors were ready to cover such terrorism exposures under certain conditions. Given the unique characteristics of the FIFA bond issuance, however, it may not have broad applications to the overall securitization of terrorism risk, and in particular, the securitization of aviation war and terrorism risks in the near future. For instance, the sponsor was not "an insurance or a reinsurance company, but the world's football governing body, acting in its capacity as event organizer. In this case [therefore], the structured finance transaction replaced primary insurance coverage, not excess of loss reinsurance".[169] Also, the transaction was primarily aimed at covering revenue losses from cancellation of the event and not property damage, business interruption or other third-party liability losses caused by terrorist attacks.[170] Indeed, as noted above, the coverage was requested by FIFA's marketing partners "in order to secure reimbursement of prepaid sums".[171] In such an arrangement, the impact of basis risk is greatly reduced.

---

[165] USD, EUR and CHF.

[166] Class A note holders assumed the financial risk of cancellation of the World Cup "if no official result has been determined or declared in respect of the final match of the 2006 FIFA World Cup . . . and no final match will be held on or before 31st August 2007". Class B note holders, on the other hand, assumed the financial risk if no official result has been announced by FIFA by August 2007 for scheduled matches other than the final match. See Andersen (2005) p. 178.

[167] OECD (2005) p. 59. See also Andersen (2005).

[168] Contrary to this assertion, it is reported that, in 1992, Hanover Reinsurance Company (Hanover Re) launched the world's first portfolio-linked swap using ISDA standard documentation. Known as K2, this transaction is reported to have broadened the scope of risks transferred to the capital markets by including aviation catastrophic risk in addition to property perils for defined peril regions. See Zeller (2008) p. 8.

[169] OECD (2005) p. 59. It has been argued by Neil Doherty and Harris Schlesinger that efficient securitization requires that any systemic risk first be pooled through insurance. See Doherty and Schlesinger (2002) p. 47. Thus, in a transaction such as the FIFA bond issue where the risks concerned were not pooled through insurance before being securitized, the resulting securitization was not considered to be optimal.

[170] OECD (2005).

[171] Idem.

In sum, the special features and circumstances of the FIFA transaction contributed to rendering it somehow special. "[W]hile it could certainly be used as a model for the management of the various risks – including terrorism – affecting similar events in the future, it does not provide clear indications as to the potential for risk-linked securities to become a viable complement to, or substitute for, conventional insurance and reinsurance in the coverage of terrorism risk exposures",[172] including aviation war and terrorism risks.

After the FIFA transaction, another securitization transaction involving certain aspects of terrorism risk was sponsored by Swiss Re Capital Markets Corporation.[173] In December 2003, Swiss Re entered into a financial arrangement with Vita Capital Limited, a specially created insurance-linked security intermediary, to provide payments of up to US$ 400 million to Swiss Re in certain extreme mortality risk scenarios.[174] To fund potential payments under this arrangement, Swiss Re acted as sponsor on Vita Capital's issuance of US$ 400 million principal at-risk variable rate mortality-indexed notes. The notes were linked to a rise in mortality from any source including epidemics, natural disasters, war or terrorist attacks.[175] The transaction constitutes a recent example of the securitization of terrorism risk exposures primarily because it did not explicitly or implicitly exclude increases in the combined mortality index attributable to terrorist attacks.[176] Through it, Swiss Re was able to transfer to the capital markets excess mortality risk caused *inter alia* by terrorist attacks in place of obtaining conventional retrocession agreements to cover those risks.

It is clear from the foregoing that, in theory, there is no reason why aviation war and terrorism risks cannot be transferred by the insurance industry to the capital markets through the technique of securitization. Unlike conventional reinsurance (and retrocession), the prospect of securitization holds immense potential for the coverage of aviation war and terrorism risks in terms of the availability of deeper capital reserves and multi-year coverage at competitive prices. However, the exact reason(s) why this has not happened as yet remains to be seen. Obviously, there are a number of inherent obstacles foreseeable in any effort to securitize aviation war

---

172 Idem., pp. 58–59.

173 Idem.

174 The coverage was based on a combined mortality index similar to other index-based insurance-linked securities. The mortality index measured annual general population mortality in five selected countries (US, UK, France, Switzerland and Italy) by applying predetermined weights to publicly reported mortality data from each country (70 % US; 15 % UK; 7.5 % France; 5 % Switzerland; and, 2.5 % Italy). The risk was also segmented according to age and gender. Payments to Swiss Re under the Vita Capital transaction were to be triggered if, during any single calendar year before final maturity of the notes in January 2007, the combined mortality index as described above fell between 130 % and 150 % of the 2002 baseline level. In terms of an absolute number of extra deaths, this was in the range of approximately 750,000. See idem., p. 60. See also Andersen (2005) p. 178.

175 OECD (2005).

176 Andersen (2005) p. 178.

and terrorism risks, and the following paragraphs only conjecture at some of these likely obstacles. First is the issue of *recharacterization risk*, adeptly portrayed by Paul Ali as follows:

> [t]he major legal risk faced by participants in an insurance securitization is that a regulator or court may characterize the securitization vehicle, in terms of its obligations under the risk transfer instrument, as carrying on an insurance business without the requisite authority. Such a finding carries with it a number of adverse consequences for the transaction participants. Criminal penalties may be imposed upon the securitization vehicle and its officers. In addition, the risk transfer instrument may be rendered unenforceable.[177]

"The carrying on of an insurance business involves the undertaking of liability by way of insurance or reinsurance in respect of losses".[178] As demonstrated in part I of this book, conventional insurance and reinsurance involve the agreement of one party, in exchange for the payment to it of a premium or other valuable consideration by another party, to pay money to, or perform some other obligation for, the latter on the occurrence of a stipulated event. There must be uncertainty as to whether or when that stipulated event will occur. In addition, that payment must be by way of compensation or indemnification for the losses incurred by the insured as a result of the occurrence of the stipulated uncertain event.[179] This latter requirement incorporates the common law concept of insurable interest which requires that the insured under a contract of insurance must stand in a legally recognized relationship with the subject matter of the insurance otherwise the contract may be declared void and unenforceable for being contrary to public policy.[180] Thus, in essence, there are two major features that differentiate an insurance contract from other commercial contracts: (1) an agreement to pay money or perform some other obligation on the occurrence of a stipulated uncertain event; and, (2) the payment of money or performance of the obligation must be by way of compensation or indemnification for the loss or damage of a subject matter in which the recipient of the payment has an insurable interest.[181]

To a large extent, existing ART instruments for securitizing insurance risks satisfy the first requirement. In a Cat-bond transaction for instance, if the stipulated trigger event occurs before the maturity date of the bonds issued to capital market investors, the SPRV will be obligated to make a payment to the originator calculated on the basis of the trigger, and there is uncertainty as to whether or when the stipulated trigger event will happen.[182] However, the fulfillment of this requirement alone is not sufficient to constitute a Cat-bond or any other ART instrument for securitizing insurance risks into an insurance contract. The requirement of an

177 Ali (2008) p. 364.

178 Idem.

179 Idem.

180 Salah El Din (1971) p. 27.

181 Ali (2008) p. 365.

182 Idem.

insurable interest on the part of the originator in relation to the subject matter of the securitization must also be met.[183]

"In certain common law jurisdictions (including New York and Australia, but not the United Kingdom), the requirement that the recipient of a payment under a putative insurance contract must have an insurable interest in the subject matter of the contract will be satisfied by that party having a pecuniary or economic interest in the subject matter".[184] However, in an insurance securitization, the originator's pecuniary interest in the Cat-bond or other risk transfer instrument (i.e., its interest in receiving payment from the SPV or SPRV on the occurrence of the stipulated event) is not sufficient for purposes of meeting the common law insurable interest requirement.[185] This is because the insurable interest requirement mandates the possession of "a risk that subsists in respect of the subject matter of the insurance contract, not a risk that has been created by the contract itself".[186] Thus, apart from the risk of non-payment under the Cat-bond or other ART instrument, "the originator must be subject to a corresponding risk that, should the stipulated event occur, that event will result in a loss or damage to the subject matter of the ... risk transfer instrument".[187]

In view of the foregoing, a Cat-bond or other ART instrument securitizing aviation war and terrorism risks will likely be characterized as an insurance contract if the payment to be made to the originator by the SPV or SPRV will be by way of compensation or indemnification to the originator for losses incurred in respect of the underlying subject matter.[188] Stated differently, an SPV or SPRV that issues Cat-bonds or other ART instruments in respect of aviation war and terrorism risks

---

[183] It is this requirement that actually differentiates insurance and reinsurance contracts from other agreements to make payment conditional upon an uncertain event (i.e., gaming and wagering contracts which are generally illegal and unenforceable under common law). See idem.

[184] In those jurisdictions, the possession of a pecuniary or economic interest equates to the payee suffering a loss through damage to, or a diminution in the value of, the subject matter of the contract as a result of the occurrence of the stipulated event. See idem., p. 366.

[185] Idem., p. 366.

[186] Idem.

[187] In other words, the originator must have a pecuniary interest beyond the amount that may or may not be paid to it under the Cat-bond or other ART instrument which presently exists in the subject matter of that agreement. If the originator has no interest other than the amount to be paid on the occurrence of the stipulated event, the Cat-bond or other ART instrument cannot constitute an insurance contract, as the originator's only risk is the risk created by the agreement. See idem.

[188] Idem., pp. 366–367. It will be recalled from the discussion above that although originators prefer such indemnity-triggered bonds because they ensure full coverage of actual losses through the elimination of basis risk, they are usually the exception as capital market investors tend to prefer non-indemnity triggered instruments. As a result, a critical feature of most ART instruments usually encountered in insurance securitizations is that the SPV or SPRV's obligation to make payment to the originator is not conditional upon the actual suffering of a loss by the originator in relation to the subject matter. It is possible that the payment may have the effect of putting the originator back into the financial position in which it was before the occurrence of the loss, but this would only be coincidental. This is because the obligation to make payment is de-linked from the originator's actual losses.

and whose payment obligations under the risk transfer instruments backing those bonds are subject to an indemnity trigger is exposed to the risk that its conduct could be characterized as the carrying on of an (unauthorized) insurance business.[189] This is one of the principal reasons why most SPRVs used in insurance securitizations are incorporated in places like Jersey, Bermuda, Cayman Islands or Guernsey—aside from the favourable tax treatment these countries/places offer to such entities, they also offer regulatory exemptions and concessions that enhance or facilitate the execution of such deals.[190]

The upshot of this discussion is that, an important consideration in the securitization of aviation war and terrorism risks is to ensure that all necessary measures are taken to avoid a recharacterization of the securitization vehicle (i.e., the SPV or SPRV) as an entity carrying on an insurance business in a jurisdiction where it is not authorized to do so. This concern becomes particularly important in scenarios where the Cat-bond model described above is used—an SPRV is established as the securitization vehicle, and the underlying risk is transferred from the originator to it via a reinsurance contract prior to the issuance of any securities.

Another major foreseeable obstacle inherent in the securitization of aviation war and terrorism risks arises from the non-existence or limited availability of actuarial models for accurately analyzing, estimating and predicting such risks. The ability to analyze, predict and estimate risk is a prerequisite not only for insurance, but also for securitization of risks.[191] As such, current challenges in predicting the frequency and severity of terrorist acts with some degree of reliability appear to be among the main obstacles to the securitization of aviation war and terrorism risks,

---

[189] Idem., pp. 367–369. Although this conclusion suggests that non-indemnity triggered ART instruments used in insurance securitizations are wholly free from the risk of an adverse judicial or regulatory recharacterization, in reality, this is not the case. Paul Ali points out that in late 2003, the Property and Casualty Insurance Committee of the US National Association of Insurance Commissioners (NAIC) voiced the opinion that weather derivatives were, in substance, insurance contracts. This caused a lot of unrest in the industry, and following intense lobbying by various industry associations, the NAIC white paper was withdrawn from publication. According to Paul Ali, this event well illustrates the persistent risk of an adverse judicial or regulatory recharacterization, notwithstanding that transaction participants may believe they have solid legal reasons for a contrary characterization. This event serves to highlight the fragile legal foundations of insurance securitization. If there is no statutory safe harbor from insurance laws for weather derivatives (and the securitizations that make use of them) in the jurisdiction whose laws are the proper law of the weather derivatives, they will be subject to the risk that a regulator or court may recharacterize them as insurance contracts. That concern also applies to the risk transfer instruments employed in other insurance securitizations.

[190] Rhee (2005) p. 501. For instance, in Bermuda, there is a statutory exemption for catastrophe bonds by virtue of which the transaction participants are deemed not to be carrying on an insurance business. See Bermuda Insurance Act, 1978 s. 57A(4). In the US also, a majority of states have passed statutes exempting catastrophe bond issuers from the insurance laws. See generally, Ali (2008) p. 369.

[191] OECD (2005) p. 60.

in the same manner as they are obstacles to (re)insuring those risks in the conventional insurance markets.[192] Over the years, specialized firms have been developing new risk evaluation models, but, in comparison to assessing the risk of natural disasters, estimating the probabilities associated with man-made catastrophes (particularly terrorist acts) remains intrinsically far more subjective. As compared to conventional (re)insurance markets, capital market investors tend to demand an even higher degree of precision in the modeling of the underlying risk: being more transaction based, they place a premium on tradability.[193] "Yet, risk uncertainty and the perception that terrorism risk modeling is too new and subjective to be fully relied upon may, in particular, be limiting investors' appetite for terrorism bonds".[194]

According to the OECD, "[f]inancial market tools suitable to cover catastrophic terrorism risks have not yet been developed, and no sustainable risk-linked securities market covering losses associated with terrorism acts has emerged so far, owing mainly to the extremely high level of uncertainty and ambiguity that affects modern-day terrorism risk".[195] As a result of the uncertainty associated with the measurement of the underlying risk and the fact that such transactions are relatively new, insurance securitizations tend to be complex, long to put in place, and expensive as compared with traditional reinsurance, if it is available.[196] The Bond Market Association has also been emphatic on this issue. In a paper published in 2005, its opinion was expressed as follows: "the current unavailability of affordable terrorism insurance is not due to a lack of capacity as much as to a mismatch in the perception of risk between protection buyers and sellers. Until there is a way to accurately measure and price terrorism risk, it is not likely that derivatives and other capital markets instruments will provide a viable solution".[197]

Finally, any contemporary discussion of the viability of capital market risk transfer solutions as alternatives and/or complements to conventional insurance coverage of aviation war and terrorism risks will not be complete if nothing is said about the impact of the global credit crisis of 2007–2009 on those capital market solutions going forward. As will be recalled, the said credit crisis was precipitated by a meltdown of the US sub-prime mortgage market (and as a consequence the housing market)—a segment of the domestic US banking industry—which had been heavily securitized, thereby creating serious interdependencies among financial institutions within the global financial system with attendant systemic risk problems. It is these matters then that we turn our attention to in the next section of this chapter.

---

[192] Idem.

[193] Idem.

[194] Idem.

[195] Idem., p. 61.

[196] Idem., p. 60.

[197] David (2005) p. 168.

5.3.3 The Viability of Capital Market ART Solutions Following the Global Credit Crisis of 2007–2009

In order to put the discussion in its proper perspective, a brief primer on the global financial crisis of 2007–2009 is necessary here.[198] "In essence, the financial crisis resulted from an unprecedented period of excessive borrowing, excessive lending and excessive investment incentivized by a series of significant economic and regulatory factors. Excessive borrowing and lending most directly arose in the context of the market for subprime residential mortgages in the United States".[199] During the early part of the 2000–2010 decade, US federal government policies encouraged the Federal National Mortgage Association (Fannie Mae) and the Federal Home Loan Mortgage Corporation (Freddie Mac)—both government-sponsored enterprises—to expand rapidly, in significant part to support lending to low income home buyers.[200] Also, the Community Reinvestment Act[201] and pressure from the Department of Housing and Urban Development similarly encouraged commercial banks in the US to expand mortgage lending in low income, minority neighbourhoods.

As a result of these policies, consumer lending and borrowing in the United States reached new levels of excess during the decade. As succinctly noted by one commentator,

> [t]he period of greatest excess was 2005–2006. During this period, borrowers, lenders, arrangers of transactions, credit support providers such as insurance companies, investors and advisors such as rating agencies all combined in an environment of low interest rates, freely available capital and regulatory distraction to produce the greatest financial crisis since the [great depression of the] 1930's. ... Arrangers and advisors such as rating agencies became caught up in the fee generating orgy. At the same time, regulators, thinking originate and distribute on balance beneficial for financial stability and economic growth, focused on other areas such as Basel II, hedge funds and sovereign wealth funds.[202]

In particular, subprime mortgage lending—"loans backed by residential mortgages to borrowers which for a variety of reasons (such as credit history or type of residence), did not comply with ordinary standards for mortgage underwriting",[203] and also characterized by low initial interest rates and little

[198] For a comprehensive account of the background causes and consequences of the credit crisis, see Arner (2009).

[199] Idem., p. 1.

[200] Harrington (2009) p. 786.

[201] Pub. L. 95-128, Title VII (1977).

[202] Arner (2009) p. 21.

[203] Vries Robbé et al. (2008) p. 7. The most extreme example of subprime borrowers of lesser credit quality is the now infamous "NINJA" borrowers—borrowers with No Income, No Job, and No Assets). See Arner (2009) p. 21.

required down payment—accelerated throughout the middle part of the decade.[204] This stimulated demand for housing by individuals deemed traditionally uncreditworthy, and by speculators.

At the same time, the state of the global capital markets was such that investors were finding it hard to find products yielding a favourable return. Investors therefore pursued yield with little consideration for risk, fuelling stronger demand for higher yielding (i.e., riskier) investments. One such market generating higher yields was the US subprime mortgage market.[205] The application of the concept of securitization enabled originators[206] to repackage the subprime mortgages they had originated and to transfer them to capital market investors in the form of debt securities of various kinds.[207] Since most of these transactions were carried out through the establishment of off-balance sheet entities (i.e., special purpose vehicles), the originators were able to effectively shed the credit risk associated with house price declines and defaults on the subprime mortgages they had originated, thereby evading regulatory capital requirements.[208] Coupled with the fact that the funds obtained from issuing mortgage-backed securities were simply used to originate new subprime mortgages, this enabled the originators to aggressively expand

[204] Harrington (2009) pp. 787–788. Because many subprime borrowers acquired property with little or no money down, they faced relatively little loss if housing prices fell and they defaulted on their mortgages. Many people took low-cost mortgages on investment property to speculate on housing price increases. Others took low-cost second mortgages to fund consumption.

[205] Vries Robbé et al. (2008) p. 7.

[206] According to one author, "loans came to be made not by banks with an ongoing interest in their repayment but instead by specialists – mortgage brokers for real estate ... – intent on profiting from charging to arrange loans and with no intention of maintaining an interest in the ability of the borrower to repay in the future". See Arner (2009) p. 3.

[207] This was driven in large part by the "originate and distribute" model of universal banking, initially adopted by the majority of international banks and investment banks in the early 1990s. Under the model, financial institutions would on a continual basis either create or purchase underlying assets from the originators. The assets would be pooled together into structured pools of risks designed to appeal to various classes of investors and held. Such pooling would take place either on-balance sheet or off-balance sheet through separate (though often not truly independent) entities such as conduits and Structured Investment Vehicles (SIVs). Pools where necessary would be supplemented by synthetic credit risk through credit default swaps (CDSs) to meet the requirements of complex quantitative models designed on the basis of portfolio theory to reduce risk and enhance return, including those of rating agencies. Pools then would be used to back a structure of securities rated by external credit rating agencies. Resulting securities would be sold or held (warehoused) depending on prevailing market conditions, with purchasers including banks and investment banks, insurance companies and pension and investment funds, including hedge funds. Funds resulting from the sales of securities (which might in turn be repackaged into collateralized debt obligations (CDOs) and eventually CDO^2s etc.) would be used to collect new assets, thus continuing the process, so long as investors continued to be willing to purchase the resulting securities. See idem., pp. 21–22.

[208] Harrington (2009) p. 787.

mortgage lending in competition with investment banks and other financial institutions.[209]

Following their initial transfer to the capital markets by the originators, the subprime mortgages were re-securitized over and over again through various kinds of derivative mechanisms[210] altogether known as Collateralized Debt Obligation (CDO)[211] and Asset-Backed Securities Collateralized Debt Obligation (ABS CDO)[212] transactions. Driven by strong investor demand, CDO arrangers and portfolio managers steadily increased the percentage of these subprime mortgage loans and financial derivatives based on them in the portfolio of ABS CDOs to over 50 %, making these structures particularly vulnerable to adverse events in the subprime market.[213] Securitization thus became the central linkage between

---

[209] Idem. See also Arner (2009) pp. 18–19 where the author notes: "From the standpoint of financial institutions . . . [the 'originate and distribute'] model had two benefits. First, it increased profitability by increasing velocity of transactions which in a low interest rate environment relied more on fees charged for the origination than on spread based income produced over the life of the asset. Second, it reduced the risks of any potential defaults because the originators did not own the assets originated; instead the resulting securities were widely distributed in the markets. From the standpoint of regulators, this model likewise had two benefits. First, banks were less risky because they were holding fewer loans and hence were exposed less to default risk in any future economic downturn. Second, by repackaging and distributing credit risks widely into the market, this brought down the charges which lenders had to charge borrowers, increasing home ownership and economic activity".

[210] In this context, the technology of securitization was expanded to encompass a range of ever more complex techniques and structures. Simple securitization techniques (such as pooling of risks, off-balance sheet structure, and capital markets funding) were combined with over-the-counter (OTC) derivative techniques, especially credit derivatives such as credit default swaps. See Arner (2009) p. 4.

[211] "CDO securities are backed by – and thus their payment derives principally or entirely from – a mixed pool of mortgage loans and/or other receivables owned by an SPV". See Schwarcz (2008) p. 376.

[212] "ABS CDO securities, on the other hand, are backed by a mixed pool of ABS and/or MBS securities owned by the SPV, and thus their payment derives principally or entirely from the underlying mortgage loans and/or other receivables ultimately backing those ABS and/or MBS securities". See idem., p. 376. In fact, ABS CDOs are CDOs referencing other securitizations and this is why those transactions are sometimes referred to as "re-securitization". On this, see Vries Robbé et al. (2008) p. 8.

[213] Vries Robbé et al. (2008). ABS CDO securities are typically issued in tranches, ranked by seniority of payment priority. The highest priority class is called senior securities, whereas lower priority classes are usually known as mezzanine securities, with the lowest priority class, which has a residual claim against the SPV, called the equity. "The senior classes of securities are more highly rated than the quality of the underlying receivables. For example, senior securities issued in a CDO transaction are usually rated AAA even if the underlying receivables consist of subprime mortgages, and senior securities issued in an ABS CDO transaction are usually rated AAA even if none of the MBS and ABS securities supporting the transaction are rated that highly. This is accomplished by allocating cash collections from the receivables first to pay the senior classes, and thereafter to pay more junior classes (the so-called waterfall of payment). In this way the senior classes are highly overcollateralized to take into account the possibility, indeed likelihood, of delays and losses on collection". See Schwarcz (2008) pp. 377–378 [footnotes omitted].

excessive investment in credit securities and excessive borrowing and lending.[214] In theory, risk spreading by aggregating properties, coupled with an assumption that the historical trend toward higher housing prices would continue unabated led to exuberant investment in the security portfolios, which, in turn, created more investment capital for low-interest, no down-payment mortgages and wild speculation in housing, until the bubble burst.

At the apex of these complex securitization and re-securitization transactions involving subprime mortgages, capital market investors holding those securities entered into Credit Default Swap (CDS) agreements with financial entities to hedge part or all of the credit risk they had assumed. "A CDS is a bilateral derivative transaction which may be seen as a type of protection against default or as a synthetic loan".[215] "In a basic credit default swap, the protection seller agrees to protect the protection buyer against credit risk events associated with specified underlying securities. If a specified credit event occurs, the protection seller is obligated to make either a cash payment to the buyer or pay the notional amount of the underlying securities in exchange for the underlying securities".[216] Investment bank Lehman brothers, AIG Financial Products[217] and several other entities became major writers of CDS instruments which offered domestic and foreign financial institutions relatively low-cost protection against reductions in values of mostly subprime mortgage-related securities.[218]

The securitization of subprime mortgages and the explosion of CDS and more complex derivatives linked to residential mortgages caused the risk of housing price declines and mortgage defaults to be spread widely among global financial institutions in a complex and opaque set of transactions, which created substantial

[214] Arner (2009) p. 3.

[215] "In essence, the seller of a CDS agrees to pay the buyer if a credit event occurs, typically some sort of default by an unrelated borrower. The buyer of the CDS agrees to pay the seller a stream of payments roughly equivalent to the payments that would be made by the identified but unrelated borrower. As such, the seller of the CDS receives a stream of payments which mimic a loan – thus for one party, the CDS is a form of synthetic loan: a mechanism to acquire credit risk of an unrelated party. If the notional creditor defaults, the seller must pay the value of the defaulted obligation or deliver the underlying obligation to the buyer. The buyer in turn purchases a form of protection against the default of the underlying borrower/obligation, thereby hedging an actual credit to the notional borrower or speculating on notional credit risk". See idem., p. 5.

[216] Harrington (2009) p. 790. Although CDSs have economic characteristics similar to insurance (i.e., they transfer risk from the protection buyer to the protection seller, and involve some degree of risk spreading by the protection buyer), they are not legally considered to be insurance since the protection buyer does not need to have an insurable interest in the underlying securities or exposure. In the US for instance, insurance regulation prohibits insurance companies from writing CDS.

[217] It is reported that at the end of 2007, AIG had US$ 533 billion (net notional amount) of CDS outstanding, out of which some US$ 61 billion represented its exposure to subprime mortgages. See idem., pp. 790–791.

[218] Idem., p. 787.

uncertainty about the financial exposure of different institutions.[219] This set the stage for the global financial crisis:

> by the end of 2006, real estate prices in the United States and a range of other Western countries had reached unsustainable levels. As central banks around the world began to raise interest rates to address potential inflationary concerns resulting from rapid global economic growth, weaker residential mortgage borrowers in the United States began to have difficulties meeting their obligations and defaults on loans began to increase. At the same time, as new purchasers stopped entering the markets, real estate prices began to decrease rapidly.[220]

"With home prices unexpectedly plummeting and adjustable rate mortgage (ARM) interest rates skyrocketing, many more borrowers defaulted than anticipated, causing collections on subprime mortgages to plummet below the original estimates".[221] As equity and mezzanine classes of securities based on the subprime mortgages were impaired, if not completely wiped out, and in many cases even senior classes were impaired, investors in these securities lost billions, creating a loss of confidence in the financial markets.[222] In reaction, the markets ceased to deal in instruments the values of which were now uncertain. Additionally, "throughout the first half of 2007, investor preferences changed from high-yield credit products to simpler investments such as emerging market equities and commodities".[223] As a result, financial institutions holding large amounts of impaired and now unmarketable securities based on subprime mortgages found themselves unable to raise capital to fund their continuing operations, leading to their eventual demise. The most notorious example was Bear Stearns which, in the face of severe liquidity problems, had no option but to file for bankruptcy protection or put itself up for acquisition by another firm.[224]

As a result of the widespread credit defaults on the underlying subprime mortgages, the major CDS writers in turn had to post increasing amounts of collateral with their multi-sector CDO swap portfolio counterparties. Unfortunately, the CDSs sold by AIGFP and other financial entities were not backed by the large amounts of capital that would be held to back the sale of insurance with catastrophe exposure. Clearly, these CDS contracts were not backed by anything close to the amount of capital that would have been needed to respond to reductions in the value of the underlying securities and collateral calls by counterparties. As a result, the credit protection offered by major CDS writers such as AIGFP was severely underfunded. If AIGFP's credit protection was underfunded, its

[219] Idem.

[220] Arner (2009) p. 6.

[221] Schwarcz (2008) pp. 378–379.

[222] Idem.

[223] Arner (2009).

[224] Idem. Bear Stearns was eventually bought by J.P. Morgan in May 2008.

counterparties either were unaware or did not care, perhaps in part because they believed that AIG either could not or would not be allowed to default.[225] Governmental infusion of massive amounts of capital in what has come to be known in popular parlance as the bailout was therefore required to prevent AIGFP and other major CDS writers from failing.[226]

In the aftermath of the global financial crisis, Steven L. Schwarcz, an eminent scholar in the field of structured global financing, has conducted a detailed (albeit post-mortem) analysis of the subprime crisis using various hypotheses. One of his major findings is that:

> there is little structurally wrong about how structured financing worked in the mortgage context. Although the originate-and-distribute model of structured finance may have created a degree of moral hazard, the model is critical to underlying funding liquidity. Moreover the moral hazard cost can be mitigated if as likely will occur in the future, investors learn from the subprime crisis and require mortgage originators to retain a direct risk of loss beyond the sometimes illusory risk borne through representations and warranties.[227]

What implications therefore does the global credit crisis have for the securitization of aviation war and terrorism risks? What lessons can be learnt from the crisis going forward? How best can the technique of securitization be adapted to enable the global capital markets provide a sustainable alternative/complement to the coverage of aviation war and terrorism risks by the conventional insurance markets?

First and foremost, in accordance with the view expressed by Schwarcz, it is significant to note that the securitizations at the centre of the subprime crisis were not backed by anything close to the amount of capital that would have been needed to respond to reductions in the value of the underlying securities and collateral calls by counterparties. Secondly, the then existing regulatory framework enabled widespread reliance on the concept of originate-and-distribute[228] within the subprime lending market.[229] This allowed the issuance and re-securitization of mortgage-backed securities in such a way that the originators neither had ownership of the underlying loans or portions thereof nor any interest in their future repayment. Indeed, it is reported that the emergence of specialist mortgage brokers,

---

[225] It was generally thought that the extent of AIGs interconnectedness within the global financial system made it "too big to fail". See Harrington (2009) p. 791. See also Saporito (2009).

[226] Initially, an amount of US$ 85 billion was put up by the federal government. This was subsequently modified on several occasions bringing the total federal government commitment in bailout assistance to AIG to US$ 182.5 billion. Most of this assistance money was paid by AIG to bank and investment bank counterparties in CDS transactions. See Harrington (2009) p. 789.

[227] Schwarcz (2008) p. 393.

[228] This concept enabled mortgage lenders to sell off loans as they were made.

[229] Pub. L. No. 96-221 (1980) and Pub. L. No. 106-102 (1999) had significantly reduced regulatory control over financial institutions and effectively allowed unprecedented leverage relative to reserves.

"intent [only] on profiting from charging fees to arrange loans and with no intention of maintaining an interest in the ability of the borrower to repay in the future"[230] as major loan arrangers and providers in the subprime lending market was heavily facilitated by the originate-and-distribute concept. This created moral hazard to the extent that mortgage lenders did not have to live with the credit consequences of their loans.[231] It also brought about a classic case of adverse selection: as a result of the re-packaging and re-repackaging of the subprime loans into CDOs and other complex financial derivatives, no one knew who really owned the underlying loans and stood the greatest risk of being primarily impacted by the residential real estate price decreases and the increasing defaults. In reaction to this uncertainty, the markets ceased to deal in such instruments at the outbreak of the crisis.[232]

To avoid such pitfalls it is important to ensure that any effort to securitize aviation war and terrorism risks is carried out in a manner that guarantees that capital reserves would be available when needed to pay collateral calls, and that originating insurance companies do not use capital market securitization mechanisms simply as a means of evading their regulatory, economic and accounting capital requirements.[233] One way of dealing with the moral hazard problem would be to securitize aviation war and terrorism risks exclusively on an excess-of-loss basis.[234] This would help mitigate the moral hazard inherent in risk securitization by compelling originators (insurance or reinsurance companies) to retain a specified portion of the catastrophic risks they underwrite and by permitting securitization of the upper portions of those risks only, between specified attachment and exhaustion points. In this manner, insurers will have to place their own capital at risk whenever they securitize portions of the aviation war and terrorism risks they have underwritten and thereby transfer them to the capital markets. As alternative means of spreading risks, insurance securitization carried out in this manner would essentially not be any different from reinsurance and retrocession except that with securitization, the risks will no longer be concentrated within the insurance industry but will be more widely dispersed and held in the capital markets.

[230] Arner (2009) p. 3.

[231] Schwarcz (2008) p. 383.

[232] Arner (2009) p. 7.

[233] In most countries, insurance laws and regulations require underwriters to maintain substantial contingency reserves, including a general requirement that half of all premiums written each year be held as a contingency reserve for 10 years. See. Harrington (2009) pp. 788–789.

[234] When insurance is contracted for on an excess-of-loss basis, the insured retains a portion of the risk and this is known as the deductible. This means that upon the occurrence of an insured event, the insured will be responsible for all losses that fall within the deductible limit, and the insurer will only cover losses that fall over and above the limit, if any.

For purposes of addressing the problem of adequate capital reserves[235] in connection with the securitization of aviation war and terrorism risks, it is instructive to consider how similar concerns were addressed in the international banking sector with the advent of the era of globalization. Starting from the 1970s, hitherto domestic banks in several countries increasingly sought for new business opportunities overseas. As these financial institutions expanded their international lending and commercial activities, they also increased their exposure to various types of lending and credit risks.[236] According to one commentator,

> [t]his gave rise to concerns about the profitability, financial soundness [and solvency] of internationally active banks. An international regulatory organization, the Bank for International Settlements, responded to these concerns by developing a new regulatory framework designed to strengthen the financial integrity of banks and increase public confidence in the stability of national financial systems. This new framework, the Basel Capital Accord, established a set of formulas and rules to bolster the capital adequacy of internationally active depositary institutions and offset the risk exposure associated with volatile international lending markets.[237]

The Bank for International Settlements is an international organization of central banks. It was established in 1930 and is headquartered in Basel, Switzerland.[238] In 1974, in response to the rapid expansion of international lending activities by national financial systems, "the Bank formed the Committee on Banking Regulations and Supervisory Practices (otherwise known as the Basel Committee)

---

[235] "Adequate capital reserves are essential to the sound management of financial institutions. Good capitalization requires that ... [financial institutions] have sufficient financial resources at their disposal to provide adequate protection against financial losses and declines in the value of assets. A ... [financial institution's] capital serves to cushion the effect of temporary operating losses. Capital reserves absorb these losses until profitability is restored, allowing the ... [financial institution] to remain solvent and thus providing a measure of protection to depositors and creditors. Profitability and solvency are linked to the composition of a ... [financial institution's] portfolio of loans and deposits; therefore, the proper management of capital reserves is essential to both of these objectives. However, determining the "right" amount of capital reserves requires finding the right balance between a ... [financial institution's] profitability and solvency. Diverting too many funds into capital reserves can drain a ... [financial institution] of its liquidity and thus put it at a competitive disadvantage. On the other hand, if the level of capital reserves is too low, the ... [financial institution] will be at greater risk of insolvency. Public confidence in the soundness of a financial institution depends on the perception that it holds satisfactory amounts of capital over assets (the capital ratio). If depositors believe their ... [financial institution] is financially unsound, and that their deposits are at risk, there is an increased chance of an unexpected and substantial withdrawal of funds by depositors (i.e., a run on the bank). Even in cases where the liquidation of assets is considered unnecessary, a loss of public confidence can increase a ... [financial institution's] cost of raising funds. If the cost increase is significant, profitability will be impaired, once again putting pressure on an already thinly capitalized institution. Thus, by keeping adequate capital reserves, a ... [financial institution] can help preserve public confidence in its financial integrity, reduce the risk of bank runs and thus lower its costs of doing business". See Dupuis (2006) pp. 1–2.

[236] Idem., p. 2.

[237] Idem., p. 3.

[238] Idem.

to promote the monetary and financial stability of national economies".[239] The Basel Committee "does not possess any formal supranational supervisory authority, and its conclusions do not, and were never intended to, have legal force. However, it formulates broad supervisory standards and guidelines and recommends statements of best practice in the expectation that individual state authorities will take steps to implement them through detailed arrangements – statutory or otherwise – which are best suited to their own national systems".[240]

In 1988, the work of the Basel Committee culminated in the introduction of a capital measurement system for internationally active banks commonly referred to as the Basel Capital Accord.[241] Among many other things, this system recommended that internationally active banks must maintain minimum capital reserves equal to at least 8 % of their risk-adjusted assets by the end of 1992.[242] Since its introduction in 1988, "this framework has been progressively implemented not only in member countries [of the Bank for International Settlements] but also in virtually all other countries with internationally active banks".[243]

In June 1999, following the Asian financial crisis, the Basel Committee issued a proposal for a new capital adequacy framework to replace the 1988 Accord. The revised framework (Basel II Accord),[244] which was eventually adopted on 26 June 2004 after extensive consultations, consists of three pillars: (1) minimum capital requirements, which seek to refine the standardized rules set forth in the 1988 Accord; (2) supervisory review of an institution's internal assessment process and capital adequacy; and, (3) effective use of disclosure as a lever to strengthen market discipline and to encourage safe and sound banking practices.[245] The text of the Basel II Accord has since served as a basis for national rule-making. It was subsequently updated in November 2005, and a comprehensive version incorporating unchanged elements of the 1988 Accord and all subsequent amendments[246] was issued on 4 July 2006.[247]

---

[239] Idem.

[240] Basel Committee on Banking Supervision (2009) p. 1.

[241] Basel Committee on Banking Supervision (1988).

[242] The weights assigned to each class of assets were adjusted according to the credit risk associated therewith and they ranged from 0 % (for assets thought to be very safe, such as government debt in developed countries) to 100 % (for unsecured loans to consumers and companies). See Dupuis (2006) p. 4.

[243] See Basel Committee on Banking Supervision (2009) p. 2. In September 1993, a statement was issued confirming that all the banks in the G10 countries with material international banking business were meeting the minimum requirements laid down in the 1988 Accord.

[244] Basel Committee on Banking Supervision (2004).

[245] Basel Committee on Banking Supervision (2009) p. 3.

[246] Most significantly, these amendments include a consensus document governing the treatment of banks' trading books under the new Framework published in July 2005 in close cooperation with the International Organization of Securities Commissions (IOSCO), the international body of securities regulators who monitor the activities of securities firms and investment houses. See idem., p. 3.

[247] Basel Committee on Banking Supervision (2006).

The Basel capital framework was not intended to be static but to evolve over time.[248] Accordingly, in July 2009, the Basel Committee issued a package of documents to strengthen the framework, with regard notably to the treatment of certain complex securitization positions, off-balance sheet vehicles and trading book exposures.[249] "These enhancements are part of a broader effort the Committee has undertaken to strengthen the regulation and supervision of internationally active banks, in light of weaknesses revealed by the financial market crisis which started in 2007".[250] Further, on 12 September 2010, the Group of Governors and Heads of Supervision (the oversight body of the Basel Committee) announced a substantial strengthening of the Basel II capital requirements in what is expected to eventually become Basel III.[251] These capital reforms, together with the introduction of a global liquidity standard, deliver on the core of the global financial reform agenda and were presented to the Seoul G20 Leaders summit in November 2010.[252]

In spite of the increased cooperation between the Basel Committee and other relevant international financial regulatory bodies,[253] the minimum capital requirements described above have remained exclusively applicable to internationally active banks, and even so, at the discretion of national supervisory authorities. As demonstrated by the subprime mortgage crisis, non-bank entities that are heavily involved in complex securitization transactions on international capital markets are typically not subject to any such minimum capital requirements. If adequate capital reserves are to be retained by such entities for purposes of backing the securitized insurance instruments they purchase or sell on international capital markets, then it is imperative as a starting point to have in place some sort of national or international framework concerning minimum capital reserves. The international banking sector's Basel Capital Accords provide a model worthy of emulation in this regard.

[248] Basel Committee on Banking Supervision (2009) p. 2.

[249] Idem., p. 4.

[250] Idem.

[251] See Basel Committee on Banking Supervision No. 35/2010 (2010). The Committee's package of reforms will seek to increase the minimum common equity requirement from 2 % to 4.5 %. In addition, banks will be required to hold a capital conservation buffer of 2.5 % to withstand future periods of stress, bringing the total common equity requirements to 7 %. This reinforces the higher capital requirements for trading, derivative and securitization activities to be introduced at the end of 2011.

[252] See idem.

[253] The Basel Committee has been working closely with securities and insurance supervisors to study the challenges presented by the development of diversified financial conglomerates. Initially this cooperation was through an informal tripartite group of supervisors from each of the three sectors. This group was succeeded in 1996 by the Joint Forum on Financial Conglomerates, constituted under the aegis of the Basel Committee, IOSCO and the International Association of Insurance Supervisors (IAIS). In addition, the Committee, together with IOSCO, has issued ten joint reports since 1995 dealing with the management, reporting and disclosure of the derivatives activities of banks and securities firms. See Basel Committee on Banking Supervision (2009) p. 4.

5.4 Conclusion

This chapter has considered various alternative and/or complementary means securing the required capital for conventional insurance coverage of aviation war and terrorism risks and completely transferring such risks from the conventional insurance markets into capital markets. Underlying the alternatives explored are the concepts of: risk retention within the air transport industry at the domestic, regional and international levels; provision by the capital markets of funding for conventional insurance coverage of aviation war and terrorism risks; and, complete transfer of aviation war and terrorism risks from the conventional insurance markets to the capital markets through the techniques of securitization. It was found that the application of the concept of risk retention for the coverage of aviation war and terrorism risks within the air transport industry poses unique challenges at each of the various levels. At the domestic and regional levels, the question of availability of capital remains unresolved whereas at the international level, the problem seems to lie in the unequal perception of exposure to risk among different countries.

In connection with the use of capital market alternative risk funding (ARF) mechanisms as alternatives to conventional reinsurance and retrocession of aviation war and terrorism risks, it was found that indemnity triggered ARF instruments hold the best promise. However, considering the fact that reinsurance and retrocession provides indemnity payouts to the reinsured (whereas ARF instrument payouts must be repaid by the holder), and also that up-front commitment fees for ARF instruments may be more expensive than reinsurance premiums, a lot remains to be said about the viability of ARF instruments as a substitute for reinsurance in relation to aviation war and terrorism risks.

Finally, it was found that the complete transfer of aviation war and terrorism risks from the realm of conventional insurance into the capital markets via the techniques of insurance securitization could provide a meaningful way of truly spreading those catastrophic risks within the deeper capital pools of the international capital markets. In order to do so successfully, however, the lessons learned from the global financial crisis of 2007–2009 ought to be taken into serious consideration. In the next chapter, we turn our attention to recent developments in international law that have taken place under the aegis of ICAO and assess whether they provide a workable solution to the problems of insuring the air transport industry aviation war and terrorism risks.

References

Airline group files to form Vermont risk group (2002). Insurance Times, 11 June 2002

Ali PU (2008) Insurance securitization. In: de Vries Robbé JJ (ed) Securitization law and practice in the face of the credit crunch. Kluwer Law International, Alphen aan den Rijn

American Academy of Actuaries (2001) Catastrophe exposures and insurance industry catastrophe management practices. [unpublished]

Andersen TJ (2005) International financing solutions to terrorism risk exposures. In: Policy issues in insurance no. 9 – terrorism risk insurance in OECD countries. Organisation for Economic Cooperation and Development (OECD), Paris, pp 149–188

Arner DW (2009) The global credit crisis of 2008: causes and consequences. [unpublished]

Basel Committee on Banking Supervision (1988) International convergence of capital measurement and capital standards (updated to April 1998). Bank for International Settlements, Basel

Basel Committee on Banking Supervision (2004) International convergence of capital measurement and capital standards: a revised framework. Bank for International Settlements, Basel

Basel Committee on Banking Supervision (2006) International convergence of capital measurement and capital standards: a revised framework – comprehensive version. Bank for International Settlements, Basel

Basel Committee on Banking Supervision (2009) History of the Basel Committee and its Membership. [unpublished]

Basel Committee on Banking Supervision (2010) Group of Governors and Heads of Supervision announces higher global minimum capital standards. No. 35/2010, September 12, 2010. Available via http://www.bis.org/press/p100912.htm

Bouriaux S (2001) Basis risk, credit risk and collateralization issues for insurance-linked derivatives and securities. J Insur Regul 20(1):94

Bouriaux S, Scott WL (2002) Alternative solutions to terrorism risk coverage. [unpublished]

Boyle CE (2002a) Airlines look to provide their own war and terrorist coverage. Insur J (November 11, 2002)

Boyle CE (2002b) Risk retention: the growing role of the alternative market. Insur J (August 5, 2002)

David M (2005) The potential for new derivatives instruments to cover terrorism risks. In: Policy issues in insurance no. 8 – catastrophic risks and insurance. Organisation for Economic Cooperation and Development (OECD), Paris, pp 163–170

De Mey J (2007) Insurance and the capital markets. Geneva Papers (Issues & Practice) 32(1):35–41

Doherty NA, Richter A (2002) Moral hazard, basis risk and gap insurance. J Risk Insur 69(1):9–24

Doherty NA, Schlesinger H (2002) Insurance contracts and securitization. J Risk Insur 69(1):45–62

Dupuis J (2006) The Basel capital accords. Library of Parliament, Government of Canada, Ottawa

Fitzsimmons A (2004) Terrorism – maximizing the insurability of a catastrophe risk. Ann Air Space Law XXIX:67

Godbole D (2004) Alternative risk transfer. BimaQuest IV(2):37–45

Harrington SE (2009) The financial crisis, systemic risk, and the future of insurance regulation. J Risk Insur 76(4):785–819

Helfenstein R, Holzheu T (2006) Sigma no. 7/2006: securitization: new opportunities for insurers and investors. Swiss Reinsurance Company, Economic Research and Consulting, Zurich

Hoeven E (2005) Current state of the coverage for war and terrorism risks in the aviation sector. In: Policy issues in insurance no. 8 – catastrophic risks and insurance. Organisation for Economic Cooperation and Development (OECD), Paris, pp 73–79

ICAO (1980a) Apportionment of the expenses of ICAO among contracting states (principles to be applied in the determination of scales of assessment). ICAO Assembly Resolution A23–24 (1980)

ICAO (1980b) Assembly resolutions in force as of 7 October 1980 ICAO Doc. 9349

ICAO (2001a) Assembly resolutions in force as of 5 October 2001 ICAO Doc. 9790

ICAO (2001b) Assessments to the general fund for 2002, 2003 and 2004. ICAO Assembly Resolution A33–26 (2001)

ICAO (2001c) Coordinated approach in providing assistance in the field of aviation war risk insurance. ICAO Assembly Resolution A33–20 (2001)

ICAO (2001d) Report of the First Meeting of the special working group on aviation war risk insurance, 6–7 December 2001. ICAO Doc. SGWI/1

ICAO (2001e) Summary of decisions: assistance in the field of aviation war risk insurance (Subject No. 24.3). ICAO Council Decision No. C-DEC 164/1

ICAO (2002a) Draft participation agreement for the global scheme regarding the provision of aviation war risk insurance. ICAO Council Working Paper No. C-WP/11794

ICAO (2002b) Report of the Second Meeting of the special group on aviation war risk insurance, 28–30 January 2002. ICAO Doc. SGWI/2

ICAO (2003a) Assistance in the field of aviation war risk insurance. ICAO Council Working Paper No. C-WP/12003

ICAO (2003b) Report of the meeting of the review group of the special group on aviation war risk insurance, 30 April–1 May 2003. ICAO Doc. SGWI-RG/1

ICAO (2003c) Summary of decisions: assistance in the field of aviation war risk insurance (Subject No. 24.3). ICAO Council Decision No. C-DEC 169/11

ICAO (2004) Assistance in the field of aviation war risk insurance. ICAO Doc. A35-WP/17 LE/2

International Association of Insurance Supervisors (2006) Issues Paper on the regulation and supervision of captive insurance companies. [unpublished]

Krenn G, Oschischnig U (2003) Systemic risk factors in the insurance industry and methods for risk assessment. OENB Financ Stability Rep 6:62–74

Mahul O (2001) Managing catastrophic risk through insurance and securitization. Am J Agric Econ 83(3):656–661

Materne S (2007) Transfer of risk insurance – will risk securitization replace traditional reinsurance as the preferred means? [unpublished]

Mutenga S, Staikouras SK (2007) The theory of catastrophe risk financing: a look at the instruments that might transform the insurance industry. Geneva Papers (Issues & Practice) 32(2):222–245

OECD (2005) Financial market solutions for terrorism risk. In: Policy issues in insurance no. 9 – terrorism risk insurance in OECD countries. OECD, Paris, pp 55–65

Outreville JF (1998) Theory and practice of insurance. Kluwer Academic, Boston/Dordrecht/London

Pinkham R (2002) At odds. Airline Bus 18(5):72–74

Pub. L. 95-128, Title VII 91 Stat. 1147 12 USC 2901 (1977) Community Reinvestment Act. (US)

Pub. L. No. 106-102 113 STAT. 1338 (1999) Gramm-Leach-Bliley Act (Financial Services Modernization Act of 1999). (US)

Pub. L. No. 96-221 94 STAT. 145 12 U.S.C. 226 note (1980) Depository Institutions Deregulation and Monetary Control Act of 1980. (US)

Rhee RJ (2005) Terrorism risk in a post-9/11 economy: the convergence of capital markets, insurance, and government action. Ariz State Law J 37:435

Salah El Din A (1971) Aviation insurance practice, law and reinsurance. Clowes, London

Saporito B (2009) How AIG became too big to fail. Time Magazine 173(12):24–30

Schwarcz SL (2008) Protecting financial markets: lessons from the subprime mortgage meltdown. Minn Law Rev 93(2):373–406

Vries Robbé JJd, Ali PAU, Coyne T (2008) Securitization law and practice: in the face of the credit crunch. Kluwer Law International, Alphen aan den Rijn

Wemmer D (2008) The securitization of insurance liabilities: the view from Zurich. Geneva Papers (Issues & Practice) 33:1–6

Zeller W (2008) Securitization and insurance – characteristics of Hannover Re's Approach. Geneva Papers (Issues & Practice) 33:7–11

Chapter 6
The Insurability of Aviation War and Terrorism Risks Under ICAO's Unlawful Interference Convention of 2009

6.1 Introduction

In the aftermath of the events of September 11, 2001, the Council of the International Civil Aviation Organization (ICAO) established a Special Group on Aviation War Risk Insurance (SGWI). The Special Group was tasked to review the problem of aviation war risk insurance in light of the then prevailing situation, and to "develop recommendations for coordinated and appropriate assistance mechanisms for airline operators and other affected parties to be operated if and when necessary to the extent that the conventional insurance markets were unable to provide sufficient war risk coverage".[1] As a short term solution, the SGWI recommended the establishment of a captive insurance organization that would provide aviation war risk coverage to operators in the global air transport industry, with multilateral government support. ICAO's attempt to implement this recommendation resulted in the rather unsuccessful Globaltime scheme discussed in the immediately preceding chapter.

By way of a long-term solution, the SGWI recommended the expedited preparation of a new international treaty to limit or exclude the aviation industry's exposure to third-party liability for losses arising from war, hijacking, terrorism and related perils in order to make those risks insurable on the conventional markets.[2] After due consideration, the ICAO Council decided,[3] on 4th March 2002, that this latter recommendation should be addressed by the ICAO Legal Committee as part of its

[1] ICAO (2001a). See also ICAO (2001c).

[2] See ICAO (2001b). See also ICAO (2002a).

[3] See ICAO (2002b). See also Jennison (2005) p. 790.

Y.O.M. Nyampong, *Insuring the Air Transport Industry Against Aviation War and Terrorism Risks and Allied Perils*, DOI 10.1007/978-3-642-32433-8_6,

ongoing[4] work program concerning the modernization of the 1952 convention on damage caused by foreign aircraft to third parties on the surface (Rome Convention of 1952).[5] Following a number of preparatory activities, the entire 32nd Session of the Legal Committee held in March 2004 was devoted to the subject, and a draft new convention previously prepared by an ICAO secretariat study group as a replacement for the Rome Convention of 1952 was discussed and modified with several refinements. The ICAO Council considered the draft convention and decided that it was not yet mature for submission to a Diplomatic Conference, but required further study. Accordingly, the Council established a Special Group on the Modernization of the Rome Convention (SGMR) in 2004 to further develop and refine the text, both on substantive legal issues and with respect to drafting and editorial concerns.[6]

The work of the SGMR eventually culminated in the development of two draft Conventions which were considered and approved by the Legal Committee at its 33rd session in 2008, and subsequently adopted and opened for signature at a Diplomatic Conference held under the auspices of ICAO in Montreal from 20 April to 2 May 2009. The two new treaties are titled: convention on compensation for damage caused by aircraft to third parties[7] (referred to informally as the General Risks Convention); and, convention on compensation for damage caused to third parties, resulting from acts of unlawful interference involving aircraft[8] (referred to as the Unlawful Interference Compensation Convention). As their titles indicate, they spell out new regimes for allocating liability and compensating third-parties for damage caused by civil aircraft as a result of the general risks inherent in the conduct of air transport, and for damage caused as a result of acts of unlawful interference involving aircraft respectively. One of the fundamental objectives that the drafters of these new

---

[4] It is important to note that, prior to these developments efforts had already been initiated by the Legal Committee to revise the Rome Convention of 1952. Indeed, the adoption of the new passenger liability regime—the Montreal Convention of 1999 provided the initial impetus for the modernization of the 1952 Rome Convention. It is reported that, during the 31st session of the ICAO Legal Committee held in August–September 2000, the Swedish delegate proposed that modernization of the 1952 Rome Convention should be included in the work program of the Legal Committee. This proposal was favorably received and preparatory work was already being carried out on it by the ICAO Legal Bureau before the terrorist events of September 11, 2001 occurred.

[5] 310 UNTS 181 ICAO Doc. 7364 (1952). This Convention applied to damage caused on the surface of the territory of one Contracting State by an aircraft in flight registered in another Contracting State. It imposed strict liability on the operator of the aircraft without regard to fault. Only limited defenses were available. Liability for death or personal injury was limited with the values expressed in gold francs and varying according the weight of the aircraft. See Jennison (2005) p. 787. The biggest concern with this regime of third-party liability stemmed from the unrealistically low liability limits prescribed therein. In spite of the adoption in 1978 of an Amending Protocol that revised the liability limits upwards and expressed them in Special Drawing Rights, the Convention failed to attract the desired support from States.

[6] In 2006, the title of the project was amended from "Consideration of the Modernization of the Rome Convention of 1952" to read: "Compensation for damage caused by aircraft to third parties arising from acts of unlawful interference or from general risks". See ICAO (2008a) p. 1.

[7] ICAO Doc. 9919 (2009).

[8] ICAO Doc. 9920 (2009).

conventions sought to achieve with the new liability regimes they propounded therein was to make the air transport industry's exposure to aviation war and terrorism risks insurable. Accordingly, the object of this chapter is to analyze relevant aspects of these new treaties to determine whether the offer a viable solution to the problem of insuring the global air transport industry against aviation war and terrorism risks.

6.2 The General Risks Convention of 2009

The General Risks Convention (GRC) is intended to govern the allocation of liability and payment of compensation to third-parties for damage caused by civil aircraft in flight as a result of all risks except those involving acts of unlawful interference.[9] It imposes strict liability on the operator[10] for such third-party damage. Unlike the Rome Convention of 1952 which the GRC seeks to replace, the liability of the operator under the GRC is generally unlimited. However, in line with a concept derived from the passenger liability provisions of the Montreal Convention of 1999,[11] the liability of an operator may be limited to a specified maximum per-event sum, calibrated according to the Maximum certificated Take-Off Mass (MTOM)[12] of the aircraft involved if the

[9] ICAO Doc. 9919 (2009) art. 2(1).

[10] Under the GRC, "operator" means the person who makes use of the aircraft, provided that if control of the navigation of the aircraft is retained by the person from whom the right to make use of the aircraft is derived, whether directly or indirectly, that person shall be considered the operator. A person shall be considered to be making use of an aircraft when he or she is using it personally or when his or her servants or agents are using the aircraft in the course of their employment, whether or not within the scope of their authority. The operator shall not lose its status as operator by virtue of the fact that another person commits an act of unlawful interference. See idem., art. 1(f).

[11] See Caplan (2008) p. 186.

[12] For this purpose, the GRC replicates the minimum insurance requirements prescribed for air carriers operating within, to and from European territory under EC Regulation 785/2004 OJ L 1 (2004b). The operator's liability is thus limited according to the weight of the aircraft as follows:

Category	MTOM (kg)	Limit of operator's liability (SDRs)
1	Less than 500	750,000
2	More than 500 but not exceeding 1,000	1,500,000
3	More than 1,000 but not exceeding 2,700	3,000,000
4	More than 2,700 but not exceeding 6,000	7,000,000
5	More than 6,000 but not exceeding 12,000	18,000,000
6	More than 12,000 but not exceeding 25,000	80,000,000
7	More than 25,000 but not exceeding 50,000	150,000,000
8	More than 50,000 but not exceeding 200,000	300,000,000
9	More than 200,000 but not exceeding 500,000	500,000,000
10	More than 500,000	700,000,000

See ICAO Doc. 9919 (2009), art. 4(1).

operator is able to prove either that the damage was not due to its negligence or other wrongful act or omission or that of its servants and agents; or that the damage was solely due to the negligence or other wrongful act or omission of another person.[13]

The effect of this concept is that, once a third-party establishes that it has suffered damage as a result of an aircraft accident not involving an act of unlawful interference, a legal presumption to the effect that the said damage was caused by the negligence, wrongful act or omission of the operator and/or its servants and agents is automatically raised, thereby exposing the operator to unlimited liability. The limits on the operator's liability prescribed by article 3 of the GRC only become applicable if the operator is able to rebut this onerous presumption by proving the absence of negligence, wrongful act or omission on its part.[14] Although the operator's liability for third-party damages is strict, the convention prescribes two limited circumstances under which the operator may exonerate itself from liability. Thus, the operator is not liable if the damage is the direct consequence of armed conflict or civil disturbance.[15]

The GRC has been heavily criticized as being unnecessary[16] and as well, driven by misguided and misdirected motives and driving forces.[17] In any event, the commercial availability of conventional insurance coverage for the third-party liability exposure of

[13] See ICAO Doc. 9919 (2009), art. 4(3).

[14] This is considered to be an onerous burden because it is more difficult to establish the absence of fault than to positively offer proof of fault.

[15] ICAO Doc. 9919 (2009), art. 3(8).

[16] See Tompkins (2008) p. 82 where the author persistently points out that the GRC is unnecessary because the Rome Convention of 1952 which it seeks to replace has not played any part in compensating victims of any major accident over the last 50 years owing primarily to the fact that each state has existing laws governing liability to pay compensation for accidents, and adequate insurance has always been available.

[17] The efforts that eventually culminated in the adoption of the GRC were heavily influenced by the victim oriented features of the new passenger liability regime established under the Montreal Convention of 1999. That treaty represented a formal recognition by states of industry initiatives signifying a fundamental shift from the previous era in which the air transport industry needed protection from potentially debilitating passenger and cargo liability damages awards to one in which the need to compensate passengers and cargo shippers who suffered death, injury or damage to property during the course of transportation by air was of eminent concern. Owing to its broad acceptance among the majority of states, the victim oriented Montreal Convention of 1999 has been largely hailed as a success. As clearly pointed out by several commentators, however, there is no relationship between the passenger liability rules of the Montreal Convention of 1999 and the liability for damage to persons and property on the ground. Whereas passengers on a commercial aircraft are a confined and known group who are familiar with the liability limits and can take "self protective" measures through personal accident insurance, the same cannot be said about persons on the ground. According to one commentator, the latter is an "undefined group of random persons in relation to any aircraft accident and should be entitled to the same liability rules including damages as any other person who happens to be a victim of an accident involving a bus, car, taxi, railroad, objects falling from buildings, etc.". As such the rules derived from the passenger liability provisions of the Montreal Convention of 1999 are wholly inappropriate for compensating third party victims on the ground. Much of the difficulty with the GRC, therefore, stems from the drafters insistence on implementing a liability regime for third-party compensation that closely mirrors the novel passenger liability regime laid out in the Montreal Convention of 1999. See Tompkins (2008) pp. 82–83; Caplan (2008) p. 188; Britton (2005) pp. 272 et seq.

air transport operators attributable to those general risks envisaged under the GRC has never been a problem. As such, beyond setting out its main characteristics, this chapter will not pay any further attention to the provisions of the GRC. Thus, the remainder of this chapter analyzes those aspects of the unlawful interference compensation convention relevant to the insurance of aviation war and terrorism risks. However, since some of the major features of the GRC closely mirror those of the UIC, they will be discussed in parallel as a matter of necessity and convenience. Where necessary, any striking differences between the relevant features of the two regimes will also be pointed out.

6.3 The Insurability of Aviation War and Terrorism Risks Under the Regime of Third-Party Liability and Compensation Established by the Unlawful Interference Compensation Convention of 2009

The Unlawful Interference Compensation Convention (UIC Convention) is intended to govern the allocation of liability and payment of compensation when damage is caused by an aircraft in flight to third-parties as a result of an act of unlawful interference involving aircraft. The convention defines an "act of unlawful interference" by reference to certain acts which are classified as offences in some existing aviation security instruments[18] and, from an insurance perspective, the

[18] Article 1 of ICAO Doc. 9920 (2009) defines an "act of unlawful interference" as: "an act which is defined as an offence in the *Convention for the Suppression of Unlawful Seizure of Aircraft*, Signed at The Hague on 16 December 1970, or the *Convention for the Suppression of Unlawful Acts Against the Safety of Civil Aviation*, Signed at Montréal on 23 September 1971, and any amendment in force at the time of the event." Under the Hague Convention of 1970, "[a]ny person who on board an aircraft in flight (a) unlawfully, by force or threat thereof, or by any other form of intimidation, seizes, or exercises control of that aircraft, or attempts to perform any such act, or (b) is an accomplice of a person who performs or attempts to perform any such act commits an offence…". The definition contained in the Montreal Convention of 1971 is even more extensive:

Any person commits an offence if he unlawfully and intentionally:

(a). performs an act of violence against a person on board an aircraft in flight if that act is likely to endanger the safety of that aircraft; or
(b). destroys an aircraft in service or causes damage to such an aircraft which renders it incapable of flight or which is likely to endanger its safety in flight; or
(c). places or causes to be placed on an aircraft in service, by any means whatsoever, a device or substance which is likely to destroy that aircraft, or to cause damage to it which renders it incapable of flight, or to cause damage to it which is likely to endanger its safety in flight; or
(d). destroys or damages air navigation facilities or interferes with their operation if any such act is likely to endanger the safety of aircraft in flight; or
(e). communicates information which he knows to be false thereby endangering the safety of aircraft in flight.

majority of those offences invariably fall within the purview of the aviation war and terrorism risks with which this book is primarily concerned.[19]

At the outset, it must be pointed out that the stated objective of the UIC is to achieve a balance between the seemingly incompatible goals of: (1) protecting the interests of third-party victims and the need for equitable compensation on the one hand; and, (2) protecting the aviation industry from the financial consequences of damage caused by unlawful interference with aircraft on the other hand.[20] Although protecting and equitably compensating third-party victims of acts of unlawful interference involving aircraft is not an undesirable objective *per se*, it is obvious that the UIC Convention was heavily influenced by the victim protection concerns which animated the new international passenger liability regime established under the Montreal Convention of 1999. However, since passengers and third-party victims differ in many respects, the criticisms leveled against the GRC on account of the inappropriateness of its victim protection leanings equally apply to the UIC Convention.[21]

On the other hand, it has been established in earlier chapters of this book that aviation war and terrorism risks pose the greatest danger of financial ruin on operators in the air transport industry owing to the catastrophic proportions of the losses associated therewith. Conventional insurance markets are usually unwilling to provide the desired depth and width of insurance coverage for these risks because they are typically not amenable to the law of large numbers. As such, in those limited instances where the conventional markets do provide some coverage, it is heavily circumscribed by conditions and exclusions, and premium rates are very expensive. When considered against this backdrop of inadequate and/or expensive conventional insurance coverage, the UIC convention's desire to protect the air transport industry from the consequences of large scale damages caused by aircraft as a result of acts of unlawful interference falls into its proper perspective.

The question that remains unanswered, however, is whether the UIC convention strikes an acceptable (and insurable) balance between these two competing goals. In other words, will the application of the UIC convention facilitate the availability of conventional insurance (or other financial) coverage for aviation war and terrorism risks on a global scale so as to make it possible for third-party victims of acts of

---

[19] In Chap. 4 above, these were identified as the risk of:

(a). War, Invasion, Civil War, Warlike Operations, Hostilities, Insurrection, Rebellion, Revolution, Military or Usurped Power;
(b). Hostile Detonation or use of any Nuclear Weapon of War, Radioactive Force or Matter, Chemical, Biochemical or Biological Materials;
(c). Strikes, Riots, Civil Commotions or Labour Disturbances;
(d). Acts for Terrorist or Political Purposes;
(e). Malicious Acts and Acts of Sabotage;
(f). Confiscation, Nationalization, Seizure, Restraint, Detention, Appropriation, and Requisition for Title or Use; and,
(g). Hijacking or any Unlawful Seizure or Wrongful Control of the Aircraft or Crew.

[20] See ICAO Doc. 9920 (2009), preamble.

[21] For these criticisms, see sources cited in footnote 16 above.

unlawful interference involving aircraft to be adequately compensated for their losses? Developments that have occurred since the adoption of the UIC convention suggest that this is indeed not the case. For instance, despite the length of time and effort that went into its preparation, the final version of the treaty that was opened for signature on May 2, 2010, has failed to attract the support of states, many of whom consider the regime as being neither fair nor insurable.[22] At this writing, only six states had signed the convention and none had ratified it. As such, the perception that the UIC convention will never enter into force is widely held. The sections following will attempt to describe and analyze the relevant features of the UIC convention in an effort to provide some answers to this question.

The UIC convention places very heavy reliance on the concept of risk disaggregation, the rationale being that, by slicing the catastrophic losses associated with aviation war and terrorism risks into manageable proportions, their insurability on conventional insurance markets (at least in the lower tiers) will be significantly enhanced. The convention therefore creates three stratified layers of compensation along the spectrum of what it considers to be a typical air transport operator's maximum financial exposure to one catastrophic event, and it allocates liability for paying compensation within each of those tiers to a different entity.[23] It also prescribes the specific conditions that must be fulfilled in order for compensation to be paid. The UIC convention's three tiers of compensation are set out on the basis of per-event monetary limits of compensation. They are as follows: (1) third-party claims amounting to a total not exceeding 700 million Special Drawing Rights (SDRs); (2) third-party claims amounting to a total that exceeds 700 million SDRs but does not exceed 3 billion SDRs; and (3) third-party claims beyond the 3.7 billion SDRs combined threshold of the first two tiers.[24]

6.3.1 *The First Tier of Compensation: Liability of the Operator*

Within this tier, liability for third-party damages is limited to an absolute maximum of 700 million SDRs per event,[25] and this is calibrated in steps according to the maximum

[22] Article 40 of ICAO Doc. 9920 (2009) provides that the Convention shall enter into force 180 days after the deposit of the 35th instrument of ratification on condition that the total number of passengers departing in the previous year from airports in the states that have ratified the convention is at least 750 million.

[23] This is referred to as the three layer approach. See Kjellin (2008) p. 67.

[24] See ICAO Doc. 9920 (2009), arts. 4, 18 and 23.

[25] Under the UIC convention, an "event" occurs when damage results from an act of unlawful interference involving an aircraft in flight. See idem., art. 1. This is a system-wide limit applicable to the totality of claims from all third-party victims deriving from any one event. It is not a limit on the amount of compensation that each third-party victim can claim against the operator.

certificated take-off mass (MTOM) of the aircraft involved.[26] All claims for compensation within this tier are channeled exclusively through the operator.[27] This means that, in all cases, third-party claims for compensation must be brought against the operator who is by law designated as the sole entity liable to pay compensation for the third-party damage that has occurred.[28] Thus, even in a situation where the person responsible for the act of unlawful interference that caused the damage can be identified and legally proceeded against, the claim for compensation in this tier must still be brought by the third-party against the operator.[29] Further, the operator's liability to pay compensation for damage to third-parties in this first tier is strict.[30] This means that third party claimants are not required to prove any fault on the part of the operator in order to succeed on their claims for compensation within this tier. All that is required in order to succeed is proof of the fact that a third-party has suffered some form damage deemed compensable[31] under the convention, and that the damage is "a direct consequence of the event giving rise thereto".[32] It has been said that, as a *quid-pro-quo* for being relieved of the onus of proving the operator's fault, the totality of all third-party claims deriving from any one event cannot exceed the absolute limit of 700 million SDRs.[33]

---

[26] This first tier of compensation of the UIC is similar in many respects to the GRC the only exception being that the liability of the operator under the UIC is absolutely limited to 700 million SDRs. See idem., art. 4(1). Compare with ICAO Doc. 9919 (2009), art. 3.

[27] The definition of the term "operator" in article 1 of the UIC convention is the same as that contained in the GRC. See footnote 10 above.

[28] Article 29 of the Convention reinforces the concept of channelling by providing that: "... any action for compensation for damage to a third party due to an act of unlawful interference, however founded, whether under this Convention or in tort or in contract or otherwise, can only be brought against the operator ... and shall be subject to the conditions and limits of liability set out in this Convention. No claims by a third party shall lie against any other person for compensation for such damage." See ICAO Doc. 9920 (2009), art. 29.

[29] The operator is granted a right of recourse against: (a) any person who has committed, organized or financed the act of unlawful interference; and, (b) any person. See idem., art. 24.

[30] See idem., art. 3(1) which provides that: "the operator shall be liable to compensate for damage within the scope of this Convention upon condition *only* that the damage was caused by an aircraft in flight." [emphasis added].

[31] Compensable damage includes: damages due to death, bodily injury and mental injury; damage to property; and, environmental damage. Damage due to mental injury is compensable only if it is caused by a recognizable psychiatric illness resulting either from bodily injury or from direct exposure to the likelihood of imminent death or bodily injury. Damage caused by a nuclear incident as defined in 956 UNTS 263 (1960) or for nuclear damage as defined in 1063 UNTS 265 (1963) and any amendment or supplements to these Conventions in force at the time of the event, as well as punitive, exemplary or any other non-compensatory damages are not compensable under the convention. See ICAO Doc. 9920 (2009), art. 3.

[32] ICAO Doc. 9920 (2009), art. 3(2).

[33] See Kjellin (2008) p. 68 where he notes: "In a fair exchange for taking on the liability up to a high level and securing it by insurance, the operators would get a hard cap on their liability. In practice this means that the liability in the first layer is strict but limited." The question as to whether this is a fair tradeoff particularly when considered from the point of view of operators was heavily debated during the diplomatic conference.

More importantly, each State party to the convention undertakes that it shall require its operators to maintain adequate insurance or guarantee covering their liability under the convention.[34] As a means of enforcing this undertaking, an operator may be required by a State party in or into which it operates to furnish evidence that it maintains adequate insurance or guarantee to cover its liability under this tier.[35] Although the convention is silent about what measures may be taken against an operator in the event of default, it is foreseeable that a state may revoke a foreign operator's right to operate in its territory on account of non-compliance with these insurance requirements. In brief, the first tier of compensation established by the UIC Convention is characterized by: channelling of liability through the operator; a system-wide per-event liability limit of 700 million SDRs; strict liability of the operator; and, mandatory procurement of insurance or guarantee by each operator to cover its liability. These features are analyzed in detail below to determine whether they enhance the insurability of the operator's liability.

6.3.1.1 Channelling of Liability Through the Operator and Limitation of the Operator's Liability

The incorporation of the concept of channelling into the framework of the UIC convention draws heavily upon experiences gained from an analogous international regime governing civil liability for nuclear damage.[36] The development of mankind's facility to utilize the power of the atom and the subsequent emergence of the civil nuclear energy program in the 1950s presented the insurance industry with two separate but inter-related problems:[37] first, "how best to provide insurance cover for the emerging nuclear industry in general";[38] and, secondly, "how to provide protection for the general public without exposing insurers' solvency margins to the potentially catastrophic losses that could arise from widespread radioactive contamination".[39] According to Anthony Fitzsimmons, "[a] special regime was considered essential for the development of civil nuclear energy as the devastation that could be caused by a major nuclear accident was so large that no manufacturer or operator would otherwise be prepared to be involved in the nuclear energy field".[40]

---

[34] ICAO Doc. 9920 (2009), art. 7(1).

[35] Idem., art. 7(2).

[36] This regime comprises 956 UNTS 263 (1960) and 1063 UNTS 265 (1963) adopted (as amended to date) under the auspices of the OECD and the IAEA respectively.

[37] As can be seen, these problems bear striking resemblance to the dual objectives expressed in ICAO Doc. 9920 (2009).

[38] Comprising nuclear power stations, nuclear fuel enrichment and manufacture, nuclear waste treatment and disposal, and also, in certain cases, radioisotopes. See Nuclear Risk Insurers Ltd. (2008).

[39] Idem.

[40] Fitzsimmons (2004) pp. 87–88.

With the adoption of the Paris and Vienna Conventions in 1960 and 1963, respectively, and their subsequent amendment, what eventually emerged was a two-tiered liability regime aimed at ensuring that in the case of a nuclear accident, meaningful levels of compensation are available with a minimal level of litigation and difficulty. Civil liability for nuclear damage within the first tier is limited in amount[41] and is legally channeled to the operator (or licensee) of the nuclear installation from which the damage ensues to the exclusion of any other party potentially liable under general tort law in substitution of or in conjunction with that operator.[42] For nuclear damage that exceeds the monetary limits of the first tier, liability is passed on from the individual operator either to the state or a mutual collective of nuclear operators, or indeed both.[43] "In essence this limitation recognizes the benefits of nuclear power and the tacit acceptance of the risks a State takes by permitting power plant construction and operation, as with other major infrastructure".[44]

In spite of the fact that "nuclear liability risks are generally considered too dangerous for most insurers to contemplate because of the potential scale of destruction",[45] the introduction of the concepts of channelling and liability limitation as fundamental elements of the first tier of the nuclear damage regime has "enabled insurers to contemplate underwriting Paris/Vienna Convention liability since it ... [has become] easy to arrange their affairs so that they ... [have] no doubt about the amount of their aggregate exposure to any particular event".[46] In light of the foregoing, commercial insurance coverage for nuclear damage suffered by third parties can be easily obtained.

On account of the fundamental role played by the concepts of channelling and liability limitation in making third party nuclear damage insurable (at least in the first tier of compensation), the architects of the UIC convention reasoned that similar results could be achieved in connection with the insurance of air transport operators against third-party damage caused by aircraft as a result of acts of unlawful interference. Unfortunately, they failed to appreciate the fine but nonetheless important distinction(s) between the risks envisaged under the third-party nuclear damage regime and those envisaged under the UIC convention.[47] Channelling and liability limitation under the Paris/Vienna conventions are

---

[41] Under 1063 UNTS 265 (1963), the upper ceiling for operator liability within the first tier is not fixed but is left within the legislative discretion of each member state. The lower limit may not be less than US$ 5 million. Under the 1960 Paris convention, liability is limited to not more than 15 million and not less than 5 million SDRs.

[42] IAEA (2007) p. 10.

[43] See World Nuclear Association (WNA) (2012).

[44] Idem.

[45] Fitzsimmons (2004) p. 88.

[46] Idem.

[47] The drafters of the UIC convention also failed to take into account the relative profitability of the nuclear energy industry as compared to the air transport industry. The nuclear energy industry can afford the cost of channelling and high liability limits because it is a very profitable endeavour.

effective tools only because the risks contemplated by those treaties are necessarily internal or central to the operation of the nuclear facility and, as such, are largely within the control of, and can be influenced by the behavior of, the operator. It is precisely for this reason that the Paris and Vienna conventions completely absolve the operator from liability for damage caused by a nuclear incident that is directly attributable to an act of armed conflict, hostilities, civil war, insurrection, grave natural disasters or exceptional circumstances—risks which are completely outside the control of the operator of a nuclear facility.[48]

The same cannot be said about "acts of unlawful interference involving aircraft"—the risks contemplated by the regime of third-party liability established under the UIC convention. Being purely external or incidental to the normal conduct of air transport operations, such acts are by their very nature, outside the control of any air transport operator, and if exceptional situations are excluded, the probability that any of these acts will be carried out has very little correlation to the behavior of the operator. The economic and risk management rationale underlying the concept of channelling is that it is designed and intended to address some of the problems of moral hazard by influencing the behavior of the entity through whom the risk is channeled.[49] As such, application of the concept is only effective in situations where the entity through whom the risk is channeled has some level of control or influence over the risk. Thus, a simple transposition of the concepts of channelling and liability limitation from the regime of civil liability for third-party nuclear damage (where they have no doubt been successful) to the regime of third-party liability for damage resulting from acts of unlawful interference involving aircraft cannot be expected to achieve the same results in both regimes.

6.3.1.2 Strict Liability of the Operator

As noted earlier, the liability of the operator within the UIC convention's first tier of compensation is strict. This means that third-party victims are not required to prove intent, negligence or fault on the part of the operator in order to succeed on their claims against the operator in this tier.[50] The choice of liability rule in any regime is determined by the goals sought to be achieved by the regime. This notwithstanding, the incorporation of a strict liability rule in any legal regime carries with it several legal and economic connotations. For instance, under the compensation scenarios envisaged by the UIC convention, it is expected that acts of unlawful interference will often cause losses to many third-party victims.

[48] See 956 UNTS 263 (1960), art. 9. See also 1063 UNTS 265 (1963), art. IV(3)(a) and (b).

[49] The fact that the operator of a nuclear facility for instance is singled out and designated as the only liable party in the event of an accident causes the operator to avoid this liability by taking the appropriate amount of care to ensure that accidents do not happen.

[50] See ICAO Doc. 9920 (2009), art. 3(1), which provides that "[t]he operator shall be liable ... upon condition only that the damage was caused by an aircraft in flight".

In such situations, a strict liability rule typically leads to the accumulation of risk upon one party (the injurer) whereas a negligence rule would have spread the risks among all the parties (the injurer and the victims).[51]

It will be recalled that one of the primary goals of the UIC convention is to achieve a balance between the need to protect the interests of third-party victims (including the need for equitable compensation) and the need to protect the aviation industry from the consequences of damage caused by unlawful interference with aircraft. The architects of the UIC convention claim that their choice of a strict liability rule within the first tier of liability was not driven by concepts of fault-finding, apportionment of blame and punishment, but rather by ideas of burden sharing and solidarity.[52] It would appear, however, that the choice of the strict liability rule as the preferred liability rule within the first tier of the UIC convention was driven primarily by its distributional advantage of always providing compensation to third-party victims.[53] In this section, we resort to some fundamental principles underlying the economic analysis of law in order to provide some useful insights concerning the appropriateness of the UIC's choice of strict liability as the applicable liability rule in the first tier of compensation.

In the law and economics literature dealing with the selection of an appropriate liability rule in a legal regime that governs highly risky activities, much support is generally given to a strict liability rule as against a fault-based (or negligence) rule if a market relationship does not exist between the parties (i.e., the injurer and the victim).[54] The underlying premise for this preference is that the risk of an accident occurring is influenced not only by the *level of care* taken but also by the number of times the parties are involved in the risky activity—that is the *activity level*.[55] Hence, not only should an optimal liability rule give the parties in a potential accident setting incentives to take an efficient level of care[56] in order to escape liability; it should also

[51] See Nell and Richter (2003) p. 32.

[52] It is reported that, during the meetings of the SGMR, the suggestion was made that the air transport sector ought to be liable for damage caused by acts of unlawful interference because it profited and reaped the main economic gains from the activity that provided the opportunity for terrorists to commit their acts. A majority of the group, however, refuted these claims, embracing instead the idea of burden sharing and solidarity. Thus, in moving away from the concepts of fault, blame and punishment, the group expressed a preference for strict liability of the operator, subject to liability limits in the first tier, as a means of ensuring that the financial viability of operators is not sacrificed in the process of adequately compensating victims. See Kjellin (2008) p. 70.

[53] This is because strict liability helps the victim in obtaining compensation since he is released from the heavy burden of proving fault under the negligence rule. See Faure (1995) p. 23.

[54] Typical liability scenarios in which a market relationship exists between the parties include product liability. In such cases, liability arises from a defective product that the injurer places on the market. In contrast, third-party liability as well as liability for environmental damage does not envisage any form of market relationship between the injurer and the victims. See Nell and Richter (2003) p. 32. See also Faure (1995).

[55] Faure (1995) p. 23.

[56] Efficient care can be found where the marginal costs of care are equal to the marginal benefits of accident reduction, assuming risk neutrality. See idem., p. 22.

encourage them to adopt an optimal activity level. According to the literature, both negligence and strict liability "are equivalent with regard to loss prevention incentives, but strict liability seems to be a better solution in terms of controlling highly risky activities"[57] in a non-market relationship setting. This is because, whereas both negligence and strict liability induce the injurer to take efficient care, it is only strict liability that provides him with further incentives to engage in an efficient or optimal level of the risky activity itself.[58] One commentary succinctly sums it up by noting that "only strict liability creates incentives to research and develop new security technologies".[59]

However, in order for these findings and their underlying analyses to be valid, certain exclusive conditions must exist. The statement that strict liability is superior to negligence as a liability rule if a market relationship does not exist between the parties is correct only if the parties are risk neutral.[60] Also, the setting must be a unilateral one in which the behavior of the injurer bears a heavy influence or a direct correlation to the accident risk.[61] Indeed, in the realms of civil liability for nuclear damage and for oil pollution damage, this latter condition does exist. The setting is truly unilateral in the sense that whether or not a nuclear accident or oil tanker spill occurs depends to a very large extent on the level of care taken and the general activity level engaged in by the operator. As a result, the introduction of a strict liability rule in the third party liability and compensation regimes governing these activities naturally achieves the desired effect of inducing operators of nuclear facilities and oil tanker vessels to maintain efficient levels of care and also optimal activity levels during their respective operations.

Unfortunately, however, the same cannot be said about the nature of the risks giving rise to strict liability under the UIC convention's regime of operator liability for third-party damage resulting from acts of unlawful interference. The setting is not a unilateral one in which the risk is influenced largely or exclusively by the behavior of the operator. In terms of the activity level, it is a fact that the number of

---

57 Nell and Richter (2003) p. 32.

58 According to the literature, a negligence rule will not give incentives to the injurer to adopt an optimal activity level since the activity level is not incorporated in the due care standard that the court applies. Thus, when the negligence rule is applied, a defendant is not held liable if she exercises a level of care that equals or exceeds what amounts to due care under the legal system. As such, the defendant will not take the remaining risk into account and will therefore exceed the welfare maximizing activity level. In contrast, strict liability would lead to optimal care *and* control activity in an efficient way, since a defendant would in any case internalize the entire liability risk. This is because, under a strict liability rule, adopting an efficient activity level is also a way to minimize the total expected accident costs that the injurer has to bear. See Faure (1995) p. 23. See also Nell and Richter (2003) p. 32.

59 See Nell and Richter (2003).

60 The standard assumption of risk neutrality is especially crucial in this context considering that areas subject to strict liability usually bear extreme risks. If the parties are risk averse in reality, the results from an analysis based on risk neutrality might lead to substantial misjudgments and therefore incorrect policy recommendations. See idem., pp. 32–33.

61 Faure (1995) p. 23.

times an operator conducts commercial flights does not, in and of itself, expose the operator to a higher risk of acts of unlawful interference—there is no evidence that those who carry out such acts typically target air transport operators with extensive networks and/or massive daily operations. On the contrary, since the setting under the UIC convention is one in which a market relationship does not exist between the operator (the injurer by operation of law) and the third-party victims, the economic effect of the imposition of strict liability upon the operator in this tier is that it will probably lead to an activity level which is too low as compared to the welfare maximizing level.[62] It has been argued that with the introduction of a per-event system-wide limit on the operator's liability in this tier, the operator's actual share of the risk will decrease as the number of victims increases.[63] It however remains unclear whether this will improve the efficiency of the regime by causing operators to become neutral to their liability risk exposure in the first tier.

With regard to the level of care, although there is a likelihood that maintaining an efficient level of care in the conduct of air transport operations (by, for example, implementing enhanced security procedures) could reduce the chances of an act of unlawful interference occurring, the fact remains that those enhanced security measures can be, and are usually, defeated by determined terrorists bent on carrying out acts of unlawful interference against civil aviation. Thus, the choice of strict liability as the preferred liability rule in the first tier of the UIC convention does not appear to make any difference. A negligence rule would equally give operators incentives to take an efficient level of care for the purpose of preventing acts of unlawful interference while also achieving a better allocation of the risk between the operator and the victims. In sum, since the risk of acts of unlawful interference in air transport operations is not entirely within the unilateral control of the operator, the choice of strict liability does not really achieve its intended economic effect of reducing the chances that an act of unlawful interference will occur.

Moreover, it has been said that the incorporation of the strict liability rule in the UIC convention's first tier of liability was intended to facilitate the insurability of the underlying risks on the conventional insurance market.[64] The validity of this argument is, however, questionable since the insurability of any risk is not solely dependent on the level of certainty associated with the probability of occurrence of the risk or the extent of losses associated with it but on a multiplicity of

[62] See Nell and Richter (2003) p. 33.

[63] Idem., p. 45.

[64] The rationale underlying this argument is that, by capping the exposure of the operator to liability for third-party damages resulting from acts of unlawful interference at 700 million SDRs per event and making the operator strictly liable, it is envisaged that the extent of losses associated with the risks will thereby become amenable to actuarial assessment, and this in turn would have the effect of enhancing the insurability of the risks in the conventional insurance markets. In the words of Henrik Kjellin, one of the principal architects of the UIC, "[t]he first layer builds on a modern approach to liability issues where the risk is attributed to a person who is in a good position to insure it, but who is also in need of protection from the potential financial consequences of the risk". See Kjellin (2008) p. 68.

considerations none of which is singularly determinative.[65] Also, strict liability of the operator means that those commercial insurers who underwrite these risks will be faced with the prospect of having to make automatic payouts whenever an act of unlawful interference occurs. This aspect of the matter will definitely play a significant role in their decisions as to whether or not to accept the risk and at what price. Given that unlike the negligence rule, strict liability does not admit of any defences or justifications that could be used by the operator to avoid or abate the extent of liability, the most likely rating outcomes will be that conventional insurers will either refuse to cover these risks or charge very high premiums to cover them if they decide to accept them at all.

6.3.2 *The Second Tier of Compensation: The International Civil Aviation Compensation Fund*

The second tier of compensation under UIC Convention involves the establishment of an International Civil Aviation Compensation Fund (the International Fund)[66] to pay additional compensation not exceeding a maximum of 3 billion SDRs per event to third-parties who suffer damage in the territory of a state party as a result of acts of unlawful interference involving aircraft.[67] Within this tier, additional compensation shall be paid by the International Fund "under the same conditions as are applicable to the liability of the operator",[68] and to the extent that the total amount of damages arising from any one event exceeds the limit of the operator's liability in the first tier (i.e., 700 million SDRs in the worst case scenario). Thus, whenever there is third-party damage as a result of acts of unlawful interference,

---

[65] For a summary of considerations commonly taken into account by the conventional insurance market in determining the insurability of any risk, see Table 2.1 and accompanying discussion in Chap. 2 above.

[66] The International Civil Aviation Compensation Fund established by the UIC Convention is an organization with international legal personality separate from, but having its seat at the same place as, the International Civil Aviation Organization. It is made up of a Conference of Parties, consisting of the States Parties to the UIC Convention, and a Secretariat headed by a Director. Within the territory of States Parties, the International Fund enjoys tax exempt status and immunity from legal process except in respect of actions relating to credits obtained in accordance with article 17 or to compensation payable in accordance with article 18 of the Convention. See ICAO Doc. 9920 (2009), art. 8.

[67] Idem., art. 18. The International Fund is only liable to pay additional compensation if the damage is caused by an act of unlawful interference involving an aircraft engaged in an international flight. Third-party damage caused by an aircraft engaged in a domestic flight will fall within the scope of the UIC Convention only if the State Party concerned has made a declaration to that effect under article 2(2) of the Convention.

[68] Idem., art. 18(1). In effect, this means that the liability of the International Fund to pay additional compensation within this layer is strict. Also, third-party claims for additional compensation not exceeding the 3 billion SDR per event limit may only be brought against the International Fund.

the operator will be strictly liable to pay compensation up to the level of its cap, determined on the basis of the weight of the aircraft involved, and if need be, the International Fund will pay additional compensation above and beyond the level of the operator's cap up to a maximum of 3 billion SDRs.

Under what has come to be known as the "drop-down mechanism", the International Fund may, at its discretion, step in the shoes of operators and pay the first tier compensation for which the operators are strictly liable (thereby completely discharging the operators from liability) if and when a determination is made by the Conference of Parties that insurance for such liability of the operator is wholly or partially unavailable or is only available at a cost incompatible with the continued operation of air transport generally.[69] Further, the Conference of Parties may also decide on a case-by-case basis that the International Fund shall provide financial support to operators from States Parties when, as a result of acts of unlawful interference, their aircraft causes third-party damage in the territories of States that are not party to the UIC Convention.[70]

In order to enable the International Fund perform these functions, the UIC Convention makes provision for it to be funded primarily from contributions to be collected from the users of air transport.[71] Accordingly, under and by virtue of article 12 of the UIC convention, the contributions to the International Fund shall be:

(a) the mandatory amounts collected in respect of each passenger and each tonne of cargo departing on an international commercial flight from an airport in a State Party. Where a State Party has made a declaration to bring its domestic flights within the scope of coverage of the UIC Convention, such amounts shall also be collected in respect of each passenger and each tonne of cargo departing on a commercial flight between two airports in that State Party; and,
(b) such amounts as the Conference of Parties may specify in respect of general aviation or any sector thereof.[72]

Operators are required to collect these contributions from passengers and consignors/consignees of goods and to remit them to the International Fund.[73] Contributions which are in arrears shall bear interest.[74]

For their part, States Parties to the UIC Convention are required to take appropriate measures, including sanctions, to ensure that operators fulfill their obligations to collect contributions from passengers, cargo shippers and general aviation operators

[69] Idem., art. 18(3). If such a determination is made, the Conference of Parties shall also decide on a fee to be paid by the operators during the period to be covered, and payment of the fee shall be a condition for the performance of this action by the International Fund.

[70] Idem., arts. 9(k) and 28.

[71] "Where the International Fund is unable to meet valid compensation claims because insufficient contributions have been collected, it may obtain credits from financial institutions for the payment of compensation and may grant security for such credits". See idem., arts. 9(n) and 17(4).

[72] Idem., art. 12(1).

[73] Idem., art. 12(1).

[74] Idem., art. 15(1).

and remit them to the International Fund.[75] States Parties must also provide to the International Fund information concerning: the number of passengers and quantity of cargo departing on international commercial flights from their airports; such information on general aviation as the Conference of Parties may decide; and, the identity of the operators performing such flights.[76] Where a State Party does not fulfill its reporting obligations and this failure results in a shortfall in contributions for the International Fund, the State Party shall be liable for such shortfall.[77]

The UIC Convention itself does not fix the rate of the contributions and the period during which they are to be collected. Instead, it sets out a number of principles to guide the Conference of Parties in the performance of the rate-setting function. With regard to the basis for fixing contributions, the following principles must be taken into account by the Conference of Parties: the efficient achievement of the objectives of the International Fund; the non-distortion of competition within the air transport sector; the maintenance of the competitive edge of the air transport sector in relation to other modes of transport; and, in connection with general aviation, ensuring that the costs of collecting contributions are not excessive when compared to the amount of such contributions.[78] Contributions are also to be fixed in a manner that does not discriminate between States, operators, passengers and consignors or consignees of cargo.

The UIC convention provides that the period and rate of contributions shall be equal for all States Parties[79] and shall be fixed so that within four years, the funds available amount to 100 % of the prescribed limit of compensation in the second tier (i.e., 3 billion SDRs).[80] "If the funds available are deemed sufficient in relation to the likely compensation or financial assistance to be provided in the foreseeable future and amount to 100 per cent of that limit, the Conference of Parties may decide that no further contributions shall be made until the next meeting of the

[75] Idem., art. 16(1).

[76] Idem., art. 16(2) and (3). Where a State Party has by declaration included domestic flights within the scope of the UIC Convention, it is required to provide information on such domestic flights to the International Fund. In each case, such statistics shall be deemed to be *prima facie* evidence of the facts stated therein.

[77] Idem., art. 16(3).

[78] Idem., art. 13(1). Based on a budget to be drawn up by the Director of the International Fund, contributions are to be fixed having regard to:

(a). The upper limit of compensation set out in article 18(2)—3 billion SDRs
(b). The need for reserves where article 18(3) is applied
(c). Claims for compensation, measures to minimize or mitigate damages and financial assistance under the Convention
(d). The costs and expenses of administration, including the costs and expenses incurred by meetings of the Conference of Parties
(e). The income of the International Fund; and
(f). The availability of additional funds for compensation pursuant to article 17(4).

See idem., art. 13(3).

[79] Idem., art. 14(1).

[80] Idem., art. 14(2).

Conference of Parties".[81] In any event, the total amount of contributions collected by the International Fund within any period of two consecutive calendar years shall not exceed three times the maximum amount of compensation the International Fund is liable to pay in respect of one event (i.e., 9 billion SDRs).[82]

Proponents of the UIC convention claim that the International Fund is intended to be a modern and cost effective scheme to provide victim compensation in case of large scale damage caused by acts of unlawful interference involving aircraft.[83] However, the UIC Convention's choice of the International Fund mechanism as the second tier of compensation has been heavily criticized. According to Harold Caplan, one of the most vocal critics of the scheme, the International Fund

> has a superficial resemblance to a system of insurance as it will, in effect, collect premiums from a worldwide community, and use this resource to pay claims. However, it is intended to be far more versatile than any insurer on earth – it may become a substitute for insurance of the First Layer if the Conference of Parties deems it necessary; and on a case-by-case basis, it may also give protection to operators who crash in non-participating States.[84]

Caplan then goes on to point out that, by the standards of the insurance world and its regulators, the International Fund "would be a most imprudent insurer".[85] In support, he argues that the International Fund would have "no capital base or reinsurance, and could be liable not merely to pay claims up to the maximum limit on its first day of operation [*plus* possible support for operators who crash in non-participating states] but also to supply some or all of the insurance which the parties deem necessary for countless operators".[86] In the event that the International Fund does not have sufficient reserves to pay claims, it must borrow from financial institutions and may grant security for such credits.[87]

Proponents of the UIC Convention concede that to a very large extent, the International Fund is "built upon the International Oil Pollution Compensation Fund, but [it is] adapted to the specific circumstances of air transport".[88] Caplan's

[81] Idem., art. 14(2). However, the period and rate of contributions shall be applied in respect of passengers and cargo departing from a State in respect of which the Convention subsequently enters into force.

[82] Idem., art. 14(3).

[83] See e.g., Kjellin (2008) p. 69.

[84] Caplan (2008) p. 201.

[85] Idem.

[86] Idem.

[87] Although, the International Fund has power to obtain lines of credit from financial institutions to pay compensation in the event that contributions collected are insufficient to meet claims, there is no guarantee that this option will be feasible in practice. In the absence of State guarantees, the only security that the International Fund can provide is revenue streams expected from future contributions. Financial institutions may not be impressed by such security because it is the very source from which the International Fund has been unable to build sufficient reserves thus bringing about the need to borrow in the first place. See idem., p. 202.

[88] See Kjellin (2008) p. 69.

view of the matter is, however, to the contrary. He points out that the similarities between the IOPC Fund scheme and the International Fund are few and far between whilst the differences are truly striking, not merely in scale.[89] He argues that, probably, the most important single difference between the two schemes is that:

> today's oil pollution scheme was not set up to deal with terrorism. It is the result of nearly 40 years of dialogue, experience and compromise between the main stakeholders – shipowners and oil importers – who, between them, finance the complete scheme. This became necessary and possible because it was recognized from the beginning that both groups of stakeholders were essential contributors to the oil pollution problem usually caused by errors of human judgement – not by criminal intent. There are no similar arguments, which can be used to support the financing of terrorism victims by air transport users. Eventually the aviation debate will require active participation and consent by those representing air transport users (passengers and cargo shippers). Their voice has not yet been heard. It is not likely that they will see themselves as the equivalent of big corporations whose business it is to import a minimum of 150,000 tons each year of the commodity involved in pollution accidents.[90]

It is instructive to note in this regard also that, under the international regime of civil liability for nuclear damage (from which the UIC convention's concepts of channelling and strict liability were obviously borrowed), the risk of radioactive contamination which is essentially third-party in nature has always been excluded from coverage by national nuclear pools and their international reinsurers on account of its potentially catastrophic proportions and the fact that it is considered simply uninsurable by conventional actuarial methods.[91]

In view of the foregoing, the fundamental question that remains unanswered following the adoption of the UIC convention is whether there is any justification in turning to the aviation industry (i.e., the first tier) or the users thereof (i.e., the second tier) to compensate for the third-party damage caused to persons and property

---

[89] See generally Caplan (2008) p. 202. In terms of similarities, both schemes have a primary layer financed by operators and higher layers financed by users. Beyond these, there are significant differences between the two schemes. For instance, under the IOPC scheme, shipowners are not required to be liable for the criminal acts of other parties and can defend themselves in the event that pollution is caused by terrorists. In fact, shipowners may defend themselves not only in the event of terrorist attacks, but also in the event of major onslaughts outside their control such as war hostilities, insurrection or a natural phenomenon of an exceptional, inevitable and irresistible character. See 973 UNTS 3 (1969) art. III as amended by 1956 UNTS 255 (1992) art. 4(2). Under the UIC Convention, aircraft operators will not be able to avoid such liability within the first tier. Also, under the UIC Convention, the International Fund alone will have to provide compensation many times greater than all three layers of the IOPC scheme. On this, see Franklin (2006) p. 96 where the author notes: "While the IOPC may have been successful in practice, the amounts it has dealt with have been peanuts compared to the liabilities that can arise after a major aviation surface damage loss of 9/11 proportions".

[90] Caplan (2008) p. 203.

[91] "The Governments of the countries in Western Europe have provided, and are in some cases still providing compensation to the affected population in their territories for contamination arising from Chernobyl, and these amounts alone in total have exceeded by several times the capacity of the nuclear insurance industry, thus reinforcing the view that such compensation can be considered solely for the account of Governments and not for the private insurance industry". See Nuclear Risk Insurers Ltd. (2008).

on the ground as a result of acts of unlawful interference simply because the perpetrators of the acts chose to use aircraft or other aviation installations as their preferred instrument(s) of destruction.[92] In this regard, George N. Tompkins Jr., another vocal critic of the UIC convention, questions whether "rail service providers and their passengers, bus service providers and their passengers, taxi service providers and their passengers, restaurants and their patrons, night clubs and their patrons" are expected to "compensate the victims of terrorism carried out by bombing surface and underground trains, buses, cars, taxis, restaurants and night clubs" in the same manner as air transport operators and users are obliged to compensate third-party victims of acts of unlawful interference involving aircraft under the UIC convention.[93]

Quite apart from the foregoing, it has also been argued that the legality of the mandatory departure charges imposed by the UIC convention upon passengers and shippers of cargo for purposes of funding the International Fund is doubtful as the scheme potentially contravenes the provisions of article 15 of the 1944 Convention on International Civil Aviation.[94] For our present purposes, the relevant portion of article 15 provides that "[n]o fees, dues or other charges shall be imposed by any contracting State in respect solely of the right of transit over or entry into or exit from its territory of any aircraft of a contracting State or persons or property thereon".[95] In effect, article 15 permits states to levy charges on airlines for airport services and air navigation facilities on a non-discriminatory basis, but strictly prohibits states from imposing fees, levies or other charges solely for the grant of rights of transit, entry or exit of aircraft over, into or from their territories respectively. According to one commentator, this prohibition cannot be evaded merely by ascribing the fees, levies or charges to some purpose other than the mere grant of rights of transit, entry or exit.[96] Since the

[92] See Tompkins (2008) p. 83. Purely and simply stated, acts of unlawful interference are crimes. Where aircraft or other aviation installations are used to carry out such acts, the operator involved is very much a victim of the crime as are persons and property on the ground.

[93] Idem.

[94] 15 UNTS 295 ICAO Doc. 7300/8 (1944). "Article 15 requires contracting States to make available all public airports and air navigation services on the same terms and conditions to all civil aircraft. There must be no discrimination as between national and foreign aircraft. The charges for such services must be publicized and notified to ICAO". See Caplan (2008) p. 207.

[95] 15 UNTS 295 ICAO Doc. 7300/8 (1944), art. 15.

[96] See, Caplan (2008) p. 207. By way of illustration, the author notes that "a charge levied on all arriving passengers and said to be payment for (say) promotion of the Olympic Games would be precluded" under article 15. In support, he cites two recent examples of the principle in practice, namely: (a) Carl Burleson's (FAA Director of Environment and Energy) heavy reliance on article 15 in strong opposition to the EU's proposed aviation emissions trading scheme; and (b) the UK's Federation of Tour Operators claim that the introduction of an Air Passenger Duty by the British government was in breach of article 15.

mandatory departure charges envisaged under the UIC Convention do not relate to airport services or air navigation facilities, there appears to be a clear conflict between the UIC Convention and the provisions of article 15 of the Chicago Convention.[97]

6.3.3 *The Third Tier of Compensation: Unlimited Liability of the Operator Based on Proof of Fault*

Throughout the numerous deliberations that preceded the April–May 2009 diplomatic conference at which the UIC convention was eventually adopted, (including deliberations of the SGMR and the 33rd Session of the ICAO Legal Committee), the third tier was proffered as an invisible, unspecified and non-binding layer of compensation to be "provided by the government or governments concerned in accordance with their laws and policies and perhaps other governments in a spirit of solidarity".[98] At several stages of the development of the convention, the drafters were at pains to point out that the third tier of compensation was not intended to appear in the written text of the resulting treaty in any manner whatsoever. Instead, their intention was that it would stay invisible—the only reference to it was to be found in the preamble to the convention or in the final act of the diplomatic conference in the form of an exhortation.[99] At the end of the diplomatic conference, however, that which was initially conceived as an invisible layer of compensation had been fundamentally transformed into a very visible layer in which the operator is subject to unlimited liability on the basis of proof of fault.[100]

Thus, in the UIC convention's third tier of compensation, third-party claimants may claim additional compensation from the operator where the total amount of damages resulting from an event involving an act of unlawful interference exceeds the aggregate amount of compensation payable under the first two tiers (i.e., 3.7 billion SDRs in the worst case scenario).[101] The basis of the operator's liability for additional compensation in this tier is not strict liability but proof of fault—"the operator shall be liable … to the extent the person claiming compensation proves that the operator or its employees have contributed to the event by an act or omission done with intent to cause damage or recklessly and with knowledge that damage would probably result".[102] The liability of the operator in this tier is unlimited as

[97] It has been suggested that, in practice, ICAO does not treat article 15 as an absolute prohibition on all charges unrelated to the use of airports or air navigation facilities. Copious reference is made to several resolutions of the ICAO Council contained in ICAO (2000, 2009). However, it is important to note that these Council resolutions are, at best, unilateral interpretations of article 15 and they do not amend the express provisions of the Chicago Convention by any means whatsoever.

[98] ICAO (2008b) para. 2.3.1.

[99] Kjellin (2008) p. 70. See also ICAO (2008b) para. 2.3.1.

[100] See generally ICAO Doc. 9920 (2009), art. 23.

[101] Idem., art. 23(1).

[102] Idem., art. 23(2).

there are no provisions in the convention prescribing an upper limit for this tier. However, the operator may exonerate itself from, or reduce its exposure to, liability in this tier by resorting to two defences specifically provided for in the Convention.

First, where an employee has contributed to the third-party damage, the operator shall not be liable for additional compensation beyond what is available within the first two tiers if it proves that it has established and implemented an appropriate system for the selection and monitoring of its employees.[103] Secondly, the UIC convention raises a presumption of non-recklessness in favour of an operator or its senior management (if it is a legal person) if the operator proves that it has established a system that is in compliance with the security requirements specified pursuant to Annex 17 to the 1944 Chicago Convention[104] "in accordance with the law of the State Party in which the operator has its principal place of business, or if it has no such place of business, its permanent residence".[105] Due to the extensive scope and comprehensive nature of the Standards and Recommended Practices contained in Annex 17, this presumption can be easily rebutted upon submission of proof by third-party claimants that the security system established by the operator falls short of just one requirement specified in the Annex. It therefore does not offer much protection to the operator.

Although the UIC convention is completely silent as to governmental involvement in the third tier, ardent supporters still maintain that, in the long run, the payment of compensation in the third tier will inevitably invoke governmental support. They start by admitting that, having regard to the amounts of compensation envisaged at this level, the likelihood is that the assets of any one operator (irrespective of how well funded or well insured it is) will not be sufficient to enable it pay additional compensation in this tier. Caplan has signified his agreement with this admission by noting that "[b]ecause this extraordinary situation can only arise if claims arising from any one event exceed the first two layers, the total potential liability of the operator would be several multiples of all available insurances and must therefore [necessarily] result in the bankruptcy of the operator".[106] Proponents of the UIC, however, argue further that, in recognition of factors such as the indispensable role played by the air transport sector in driving and/or facilitating economic growth and development in the majority of countries, governments will not sit idle and watch while their air transport operators are made bankrupt by such claims.[107]

---

[103] Idem., art. 23(3).

[104] ICAO (2006).

[105] ICAO Doc. 9920 (2009), art. 23(4).

[106] Caplan (2008) pp. 205–206.

[107] This argument probably underscores the claim that the third tier of the UIC Convention is indeed invisible. The operator is by law, made primarily liable to pay additional compensation in this tier. However, since the operator's assets (including any insurance it may have taken out) will not be sufficient to pay such additional compensation, it is expected that governments would step in one way or the other to make good those claims. Governmental involvement then (as opposed to operator liability) is the invisible part of the third tier since there is no express reference to it in the substantive text or even the preamble of the UIC Convention.

The expectation that governments will somehow inevitably get themselves involved in the settlement of claims in the third tier derives from the so-called concept of "solidarity within a society and between States",[108] first identified by the SGMR. In an effort to explain the origin and basis of application of this concept, Henrik Kjellin, chairman of the SGMR wrote in a June 2008 article explaining the work of the SGMR (albeit in his personal capacity) that:

> [t]he experience of 9/11 and similar events clearly shows that there is a readiness on behalf of States to intervene to assist victims. If a similar event would [*sic*] take place in the European Union for instance, most probably the Solidarity Fund would be used to ease the economic consequences. And the tsunami 2004 also clearly shows the solidarity of States and individuals towards victims of a catastrophic nature.[109]

According to Kjellin, the SGMR considered the payment of compensation in the third tier of the UIC Convention as one of those obligations properly falling within the general responsibilities of States which are "*normally not put on paper*".[110] He goes on to say that, it was the understanding of the SGMR that, when claims reach the notional third layer, they would be "reasonably administered by the State where the damage occurred",[111] and "any action for additional compensation would most likely be made by that State on the basis of subrogation".[112] Accordingly, the UIC Convention does not contain any provisions requiring operators to maintain any form of insurance or guarantee whatsoever covering their exposure to liability beyond the first tier.[113]

It is difficult to rationalize the reasoning process employed by the drafters of the UIC convention to arrive at the third tier of compensation and its underlying aspect of invisible governmental support. Admittedly, governmental provision of financial

---

[108] Kjellin (2008) p. 70.

[109] Idem.

[110] Idem., [emphasis added].

[111] Idem., p. 75.

[112] Idem. Harold Caplan raises the question as to whom these rights of subrogation will be exercised against and hazards a guess that perhaps it would be exercised against terrorists and their supporters.

[113] ICAO Doc. 9920 (2009), art. 7(1) provides as follows:

> *Having regard to Article 4*, States shall require their operators to maintain adequate insurance or guarantee covering their liability under this Convention. If such insurance or guarantee is not available to an operator on a per event basis, the operator may satisfy this obligation by insuring on an aggregate basis. State Parties shall not require their operators to maintain such insurance or guarantee to the extent that they are covered by a decision made pursuant to Article 11, paragraph 1(e) or Article 18, paragraph 3. [Emphasis added].

Since article 4 spells out the liability of the operator in the first tier only (i.e., up to 700 million SDRs in the worst case scenario), this provision as a whole can only be construed reasonably as limiting the scope of mandatory insurance exclusively to the operator's liability exposure in the first tier. Even then, the operator is free of this obligation at any time when the drop-down mechanism is in effect.

support and/or compensation to victims of catastrophes is nothing new,[114] and so the expectation that governments will continue to provide some form of financial support or compensation to victims of future catastrophes is, indeed, a legitimate one. However, it is submitted with due respect that, to make air transport operators primarily liable to pay unlimited compensation to third-parties in the silent and uncertain hope that governments will come to their aid (as the UIC Convention does in its third tier of compensation) amounts to an unjustifiable stretching of a legitimate expectation far beyond its scope of legitimacy.

A much more acceptable balance would have been achieved at this stage if, in place of the silent reliance on the uncertain hope of governmental intervention, express provisions were included in the UIC Convention committing each ratifying State to assume primary responsibility for providing financial assistance or compensation to third-party victims whenever claims from any one event exceed the amounts of compensation available in the first two tiers.[115] If the assumption underlying the UIC convention's third tier—that governments will ultimately provide compensation and/or financial support to victims of acts of unlawful interference involving aircraft—is a valid one, then, technically, there is no reason why governments would not have expressly committed themselves to do so in an international treaty.

In fact, the primary reason advanced by the drafters of the UIC convention that such general responsibilities of society are normally not put on paper is not supported by the evidence. In the European Union, member states have, since 1983, been under a mandatory obligation to ensure that victims of violent crime are adequately compensated.[116] Also, as far back as 1985, the United Nations General Assembly passed a resolution adopting a *Declaration of Basic Principles of Justice for Victims of Crime and Abuse of Power*.[117] With respect to compensation of victims of crime, the Declaration provides in material part as follows:

---

[114] See e.g., Dauber (2003–2004) p. 290, where the author notes that "the federal government [of the US] has been involved in compensating the victims of calamities of various kinds, including victims of what we now call terrorism since the earliest days of the Republic." In this article, the author compares the compensation schemes set up by Congress after the war with England in 1812 and the events of September 11, 2001 and points out striking similarities between the popular and political aftermath of each scheme.

[115] See Tompkins (2008) p. 83. This suggestion falls very much in line with the widely accepted principle that when violence is directed towards a State, it is the State (and not the industrial sector involved) that must assume ultimate responsibility for prevention (i.e., security) and for making reparations (i.e., paying compensation to innocent victims). It is also underscored by the doctrine that when compensation is not fully available from other sources, the State must contribute to compensate those who have suffered death, injury or property damage as a result of a violent crime, and that such State compensation must be paid even when the offender cannot be prosecuted or punished.

[116] See ETS No. 116 (1983). See also Council Directive 2004/80/EC OJ L 15 (2004a).

[117] UN General Assembly (1985). See also Caplan (2008) pp. 194–195, where the author notes that, although the Declaration does not create enforceable rights for victims, it has been supplemented by a Handbook on Justice for Victims and a Guide for Policymakers.

12. When compensation is not fully available from the offender or other sources, States should endeavour to provide financial compensation to:

    (a) Victims who have sustained significant bodily injury or impairment of physical or mental health as a result of serious crimes;
    (b) The family, in particular dependants of persons who have died or become physically or mentally incapacitated . . .

13. The establishment, strengthening and expansion of national funds for compensation to victims should be encouraged. Where appropriate, other funds may also be established for this purpose, including in those cases where the State of which the victim is a national is not in a position to compensate the victim for the harm.[118]

The practical reality is that, where States are expected to provide compensation to victims of crime, express mention is made of it, and in the majority of cases, States do comply with these express obligations.[119] Thus, it is clear that in the absence of an express or binding legal obligation, there is no guarantee that governments will automatically assist air transport operators facing bankruptcy as a result of the financial consequences of an act of unlawful interference.

The drafters of the UIC convention also claim that the failure of the Globaltime scheme to garner the required level of State participation in order to come into effect provided further reason not to incorporate express State commitments to provide additional compensation in the UIC Convention's third tier. The Globaltime situation can, however, be distinguished from the proposal being made here. The State guarantees envisaged under the Globaltime scheme called for States to make financial contributions into an international fund that would be used to pay claims in the event that the scheme's reserves were deemed insufficient to pay claims following another catastrophic aviation event. The rate of contributions was to be fixed according to each contracting State's established ICAO contribution rate. As noted above, the Globaltime scheme failed to attract State interest because there were numerous unresolved issues associated with it, principal among which was the lack of any correlation whatsoever between the basis of determining State contribution rates to the fund and the self-perceived non-exposure of certain major aviation nations to acts of unlawful interference.[120]

On the contrary, the proposal that the UIC Convention should have included express State commitments to provide additional compensation in the third tier does not require States to make any kind of monetary contributions to an international fund as envisaged under Globaltime. Instead, the proposal would require each contracting State to undertake expressly, on an individual basis but within a multilateral setting, to provide additional compensation to third-party victims with respect to

[118] See Annex to UN General Assembly (1985), Sections 12 & 13.

[119] The US government has, since 2004, compiled and updated a Directory of International Crime Victims Compensation Programs which provides details of such schemes in 36 countries. The Directory is publicly available online at http://www.ojp.usdoj.gov/ovc/publications/infores/intdir2005/welcome.html.

[120] See discussion of industry mutualization schemes in Chap. 5 above.

acts of unlawful interference involving aircraft which occur within its territory or involve its operators. Each contracting State would have absolute discretion as to the most suitable means of performing of this commitment. Thus, for instance, the government of a State could decide that it would be characterized either as the sole entity against whom all claims in this tier may be brought or as the insurer or guarantor of last resort if some other entity is made liable.[121] Since this proposal would only commit States to do that which they already do anyway, its broad acceptance would have been much more likely.

In the final analysis, it is obvious that States and their governments have an important role to play in compensating third-party victims for damages suffered as a result of acts of unlawful interference involving aircraft. States also have a moral obligation to ensure that air transport operators are not driven into bankruptcy as a result of paying unlimited compensation to third-party victims of acts of unlawful interference. Though these obligations are not legally binding, they are underscored by the fact that, in the majority of cases, acts of unlawful interference involving aircraft are directed primarily at the State, its people, values and institutions.[122] Therefore, it is perhaps an understatement to say that the drafters of the UIC convention missed the best opportunity to transform these moral State obligations into internationally binding legal obligations. The next chapter of this book takes a closer look at various modes of state involvement in the provision of insurance coverage or other financial equivalent against aviation war and terrorism risks to the air transport industry, as well as the repercussions thereof. Prior to delving into this matter, however, it is essential that mention be made here of a handful of alternative proposals that were put forward during the period that the UIC convention was being developed.

6.4 Alternative Proposals for an International Liability Regime for Third-Party Damages Caused by Acts of Unlawful Interference Involving Aircraft

During the eight year interval between the events of September 11, 2001 and the adoption of the UIC convention in May 2009, there was no shortage of alternative ideas on how to allocate liability for purposes of ensuring that third-party victims of acts of unlawful interference involving aircraft are properly compensated

[121] A detailed discussion of the modalities for governmental involvement in the provision of insurance or guarantees for aviation war and terrorism risks is contained in the next chapter.

[122] See Tompkins (2008) p. 83, where the author states that "acts of terrorism are directed against governments and the political and religious beliefs and ideals of governments that are not acceptable to the political and religious beliefs and ideals of those who commit the acts of terrorism". See also Fitzsimmons (2004) p. 87 where the author states that "[a]rguably, it is States (and of course terrorists) that ultimately cause and should therefore provide compensation for terrorism, since terrorism is the ultimate consequence of the failure of domestic policy or diplomacy at the highest levels".

without compromising the financial sustainability of the air transport industry. Although each suggestion was unique in its content and effect, they all shared a distinct common feature in calling upon States and their governments to assume liability and/or provide compensation beyond a certain level to third-party victims. For instance, as reported by one author, "at the first meeting of the ICAO Special Group on War Risk Insurance [SGWI] held in December 2001, the International Coordinating Council of Aerospace Industries Association proposed a draft convention that [would]... impose[...] primary liability on states with security responsibilities to pay for Third Party losses caused by unlawful seizure [of aircraft], terrorism or war".[123]

In an article published in 2004, Anthony Fitzsimmons suggested to ICAO that, in searching for a sustainable global solution to the problem, ICAO should consider the concept of channelling as used in the Paris and Vienna conventions on third party liability in the Nuclear Energy industry.[124] There is no doubt that this suggestion played an immense role in determining the ultimate form of the UIC convention. Needless to say, however, it appears that little or no attention was paid to the full ramifications of the suggestion, particularly the overall scheme within which the concept of channelling operates in the nuclear energy industry. Beyond channelling the first layer of limited liability to the operator of the nuclear plant (to be covered by insurance or other financial security), both the Paris and Vienna Conventions and their subsequent amending protocols explicitly provide for a second layer of liability to be covered by the installation State.[125] Indeed, there is also a third layer of liability in which states parties to the Brussels Supplementary Convention have explicitly agreed to be jointly liable (up to a certain grand total amount) according to a prescribed formula.[126]

Fitzsimmons' suggestion to ICAO was therefore premised on the assumption that, at some point, governments would have to explicitly assume liability for third-party losses resulting from acts of unlawful interference involving aircraft. This was amply exemplified in his suggestion as follows:

> Governments could decide that specified aviation operators should be the exclusive channel for no-fault liability for terrorist acts in aviation, and to provide that the channelling is accompanied by a financial limit of liability for such acts set at a level that is likely to remain insurable in the long term... *Whatever the scheme, governments would have to decide whether to assume liability for losses above that level whether on a national or international (i.e., treaty) basis.*[127]

Also, writing in his personal capacity in 2007,[128] Christopher M. Petras (then a senior officer of the US Air Force) proposed the adoption of a new treaty modeled

[123] Caplan (2008)198, citing Abeyratne (2004) p. 271.

[124] See Fitzsimmons (2004).

[125] i.e., the state in which the nuclear plant is situated.

[126] 1041 UNTS 358 (1963) art. 3.

[127] Fitzsimmons (2004) p. 88, [emphasis added].

[128] Petras (2007).

along the lines of the system for the imposition of international liability and compensation for damage on the surface of the earth and to aircraft in flight caused by space objects as prescribed in the 1972 convention on international liability for damages caused by space objects.[129] Under that regime, a state that is deemed to be a launching state of a space object is held absolutely liable for any damage caused by the space object on the surface of the earth or to aircraft in flight.[130]

Under Petras' proposal, absolute and unlimited liability for third-party damage resulting from acts of unlawful interference would be cast upon the "state of embarkation"[131] on two bases. First, the state of embarkation would be subject to liability for third-party damage if the persons committing and/or the devices used in the commission of the act of unlawful interference were on board the aircraft when it departed from that state's territory or facility.[132] Secondly, in the case of an act of unlawful interference carried out from the ground, liability would only attach to the state of embarkation if the devices or substances used in the commission of the offence were launched, employed or remotely controlled from within its territory.[133]

After voicing his deeply incisive criticism of the penultimate draft of the UIC Convention, Harold Caplan proposed in an article published in 2008 that ICAO could most appropriately sponsor a new convention to promote international cooperation in the financing and provision of compensation for victims of terrorism for consideration by the United Nations.[134] Provisionally named the Terrorism Solidarity Agreement (TSA), the new convention would not be restricted to aviation but would cover compensation for all forms of terrorism everywhere.[135] As basic elements of this new convention, Caplan proposed that the TSA should include among other things: (1) a declaration that it is a pact of mutual assistance between contracting states to share the economic burdens of terrorist attacks; (2) a declaration of sharing principles based on each state's contributions to the cost of the United Nations and that *sharing between states is to operate only in excess of a first loss to be borne by each contracting state*; (3) a long-term commitment to develop principles for a universal form of partnership between

[129] 961 UNTS 187 TIAS 7762; 24 UST 2389 (1972). However, the proposal is restricted to the no-fault regime of the Convention applicable to damage caused on the surface of the earth and to aircraft in flight.

[130] The 1972 Liability Convention also establishes a fault-based regime for allocation of liability and payment of compensation with respect to damage caused by space objects to other space objects in space.

[131] This is used as an equivalent of the launching state concept that appears in the 1972 Liability Convention. Although it is oversimplified in the proposal, the state of embarkation probably refers to the state from which the flight in question last originated. However, the proposal envisages situations in which there will be multiple states of embarkation and provides that in such cases, the states concerned will be jointly and severally liable.

[132] Petras (2007) p. 335.

[133] Idem.

[134] Caplan (2008) p. 211.

[135] Idem.

contracting states and their respective insurance/reinsurance communities governing all branches of commercial insurance to provide cover for terrorist risks . . . .[136]

Given the limited scope of this research and the fact that these proposals were put forward only in a conceptual manner, it is impossible to subject each one of them to a detailed analysis in order to determine their practical viability. However, the drafters of the UIC convention were fully aware of the existence of these and other similar proposals, but decided that the final version of the UIC convention would not include an explicit governmental obligation to insure the air transport industry or provide compensation to third-party victims for damages resulting from acts of unlawful interference involving aircraft. The wisdom of their choice will be determined by the acceptance or otherwise of the UIC convention by the broad majority of states.

6.5 Conclusion

ICAO's second attempt at enhancing the insurability of aviation war and terrorism risks following the events of September 11, 2001, resulted in the adoption of the UIC Convention in May 2009. One of the fundamental objectives of the convention is to strike a balance between (1) protecting the interests of third-party victims and the need for equitable compensation on the one hand; and, (2) protecting the aviation industry from the financial consequences of damage caused by unlawful interference with aircraft on the other hand. The convention attempts to achieve this objective by segregating the entire spectrum of third-party liability resulting from acts of unlawful interference involving aircraft into three tranches and establishing mechanisms to provide compensation in each tranche.

In the first tranche, the operator is strictly liable to pay compensation and, owing to the fact that liability exposure within this tranche is capped on the basis of the weight of the aircraft involved and in any case to a maximum of 700 million SDRs, it is envisaged that the operator can (and indeed must) take out sufficient insurance or other financial security to protect itself. Nevertheless, operators will have to pay insurance premiums for such coverage and these will invariably translate into higher ticket prices for passengers and cargo charges for consignors/consignees. Thus, ultimately, the first tier of compensation under the UIC convention will be financed by the operators and users of air transport.

In the second tier of compensation, the UIC convention establishes an International Civil Aviation Compensation Fund to pay compensation to third-party victims when their claims exceed the limits of the first tier. The International Fund may additionally pay compensation to third-party victims in the first tier if a determination is made that operators cannot obtain commercial insurance to cover their exposure to liability in this tier. The International Fund will be financed by mandatory departure charges to be levied against each departing passenger and each tonne of cargo

[136] Idem., pp. 212–213, Appendix [emphasis added].

departing on an international flight. Again, the burden of paying third-party compensation within this tranche ultimately falls upon the shoulders of operators and users of air transport. Although the International Fund may borrow money from financial institutions for the performance of its intended obligations when contributions are deemed insufficient, there is neither likelihood nor requirement that the International Fund will procure reinsurance or other financial security to cover its potential liability.

In the third tranche, the operator is again made liable to pay unlimited compensation to third-parties upon proof of fault. Although the operator may avoid or abate liability in this tier by resorting to certain specified defences, the fact remains that a prudent operator will take steps to secure some form of insurance or financial protection against its exposure to unlimited liability. This is because, the expectation of governmental support upon which this tier is based will not only remain invisible but also unachievable indefinitely[137] in the absence of express commitments on the part of contracting States to provide such support. Thus, even assuming that conventional insurance or guarantees are available for such exposure, they will require payment of very high premiums which in turn will have negative repercussions on the pricing of, and demand for, air transport services. However, this is not the case since conventional insurance at that level is simply not available.

Viewed in its entirety, one cannot help but conclude that the UIC convention is heavily skewed against the interests of air transport operators and users. It does not offer a viable solution to the insurance problems brought to the limelight in the aftermath of the terrorist events of September 11, 2001. In view of the foregoing, there is widespread doubt as to whether the convention will ever enter into force. This uncertainty is further exacerbated by article 40 of the convention which not only requires ratification by 35 contracting States for it to enter into force but also imposes a condition to the effect that, in the year preceding entry into force, the total number of passengers departing from airports in the States that have ratified, accepted, approved or acceded to the convention should amount to at least 750 million.[138]

References

1041 UNTS 358, (1963) Convention supplementary to the convention on third party liability in the field of nuclear energy (as amended by the Additional Protocol of 28th January 1964 and by the Protocol of 16th November 1982)

1063 UNTS 265, (1963) Convention on civil liability for nuclear damage

15 UNTS 295, ICAO Doc. 7300/8 (1944) Convention on International Civil Aviation

1956 UNTS 255, (1992) Protocol to the international convention on civil liability for oil pollution damage of 29 November 1969

2242 UNTS 350, ICAO Doc. 9740 (1999) Convention for the unification of certain rules for international carriage by air

[137] Idem., p. 205.

[138] ICAO Doc. 9920 (2009), art. 40(1).

310 UNTS 181, ICAO Doc. 7364 (1952) Convention on damage caused by foreign aircraft to third parties on the surface
956 UNTS 263, (1960) Convention on third party liability in the field of nuclear energy
961 UNTS 187, TIAS 7762; 24 UST 2389 (1972) Convention on international liability for damage caused by space objects
973 UNTS 3, (1969) International convention on civil liability for oil pollution damage
Abeyratne RIR (2004) Aviation in crisis. Ashgate, Aldershot, Burlington
Britton J (2005) Roads from Montreal do not lead to Rome: criticism and alternatives to the draft convention on third party liability. Air Space Law XXX(4–5):269–301
Caplan H (2008) Liability for third party damage on the ground – some fundamental issues for consideration by the council of ICAO prior to a diplomatic conference. Air Space Law XXXIII (3):183–213
Council Directive 2004/80/EC (2004a) Council Directive 2004/80/EC of 29 April 2004 relating to compensation of crime victims. OJ, L 261/15
Dauber ML (2003–2004) The War of 1812, September 11th and the politics of compensation. DePaul Law Rev 53:289–354
EC Regulation 785/2004 (2004b) Parliament and Council Regulation (EC) 785/2004 of 21 April 2004 on insurance requirements for air carriers and aircraft operators. OJ, L 138/1
ETS No. 116 (1983) European convention on the compensation of victims of violent crime
Faure MG (1995) Economic models of compensation for damage caused by nuclear accidents: some lessons for the revision of the Paris and Vienna conventions. Eur J Law Econ 2(1):21–43
Fitzsimmons A (2004) Terrorism – maximizing the insurability of a catastrophe risk. Ann Air Space Law XXIX:67
Franklin M (2006) Is a successful new convention on airline liability for surface damage achievable? Air Space Law 31(2):87–97
UN General Assembly (1985) Declaration of basic principles of justice for victims of crime and abuse of power, UNGA Resolution 40/34 (1985)
IAEA (2007) The 1997 Vienna convention on civil liability for nuclear damage and the 1997 Convention on supplementary compensation for nuclear damage – explanatory texts. IAEA International Law Series No. 3.
ICAO (2000) ICAO's policies on taxation in the field of International Air Transport, ICAO Doc. 8632/3 3rd edn, (2000)
ICAO (2001a) Coordinated approach in providing assistance in the field of aviation war risk insurance. ICAO Assembly Resolution A33-20
ICAO (2001b) Report of the First Meeting of the special working group on aviation war risk insurance, 6–7 December 2001. ICAO Doc. SGWI/1
ICAO (2001c) Summary of decisions: assistance in the field of aviation war risk insurance (Subject No. 24.3). ICAO Council Decision C-DEC 164/1
ICAO (2002a) Report of the second meeting of the special group on aviation war risk insurance, 28–30 January 2002. ICAO Doc. SGWI/2
ICAO (2002b) Summary of decisions – assistance in the field of aviation war risk insurance (Subject No. 24.3). ICAO Council Decision No. C-DEC 165/6
ICAO (2006) International standards and recommended practices: security – safeguarding International Civil Aviation against Acts of Unlawful Interference, Annex 17 to the Convention on International Civil Aviation, 15 UNTS 295 8th edn
ICAO (2008a) Introductory note presented by the Secretariat – agenda Item 3: compensation for damage caused by aircraft to third parties arising from acts of unlawful interference or from general risks. ICAO Doc. LC/33-WP/3-1
ICAO (2008b) Report of the Rapporteur on agenda Item 3: draft convention on compensation for damage caused by aircraft to third parties, in case on unlawful interference ICAO Doc. LC/33-WP/3-3
ICAO (2009) ICAO's Policies on charges for airports and air navigation services ICAO Doc. 9082/8, 8th edn, 2009

ICAO Doc. 9919 (2009) Convention on compensation for damage caused by aircraft to third parties

ICAO Doc. 9920 (2009) Convention on compensation for damage caused to third parties, resulting from acts of unlawful interference involving aircraft

Jennison M (2005) Rescuing the Rome convention of 1952: six decades of effort to make a workable regime for damage caused by foreign aircraft to third parties. Unif Law Rev 10(4):785–824

Kjellin H (2008) The new international regime for third party liability. Air Space Law XXXIII (2):63–80

Nell M, Richter A (2003) The design of liability rules for highly risky activities – is strict liability superior when risk allocation matters? Int Rev Law Econ 23(1):31–47

Nuclear Risk Insurers Ltd. (2008) The insurance of nuclear installations and associated risks. Nuclear Pools website http://www.nuclearpools.com/aboutUs.asp

Petras CM (2007) An alternative proposal to modernize the liability regime for surface damage caused by aircraft to address damage resulting from hijackings or other unlawful interference. Gonz J Int Law 10(3):315–347

Tompkins GN (2008) Some thoughts to ponder when considering whether to adopt the new aviation general risks and unlawful interference conventions proposed by ICAO. Air Space Law XXXIII(2):81–84

World Nuclear Association (WNA) (2012) Liability for nuclear damage. WNA website http://www.world-nuclear.org/info/default.aspx?id=504&terms=liability

Chapter 7
Governmental Involvement in the Insurance of Aviation War and Terrorism Risks

7.1 Introduction

At various points throughout this book, the case has been strongly made that States and their governments quite clearly have, at the very minimum, a moral obligation to provide insurance coverage or other suitable financial equivalent to the air transport industry against aviation war and terrorism risks (at least in the upper echelons where these risks are largely considered to be uninsurable by conventional means). Although these State obligations may not be legally binding and/or enforceable, they are nonetheless underscored by the fact that, in the overwhelming majority of cases, the acts of unlawful interference involving aircraft that underlie aviation war and terrorism risks are directed primarily at States, their peoples, values, governments and other institutions.[1] As such, it seems highly inappropriate to even characterize such risks as forming part of the core risks which the air transport operators must necessarily address in the course of their routine operations. Air transport operators are victims of such catastrophic risks in much the same way as third-party victims.

It is instructive to note that, aside from the air transport industry there are many other sectors of any country's economy which are equally exposed to large catastrophic risks in respect of which conventional insurance markets behave the same way they do as regards aviation war and terrorism risk. For instance, conventional insurance markets dealing with catastrophic property and casualty risks such as floods, earthquakes and terrorism, and the civil nuclear energy insurance market, to name a few, behave in exactly the same manner as the aviation war and terrorism risks

[1] See Tompkins (2008) p. 83, where the author notes that "acts of terrorism are directed against governments and the political and religious beliefs and ideals of governments that are not acceptable to the political and religious beliefs and ideals of those who commit the acts of terrorism". See also Fitzsimmons (2004) p. 87, where the author notes in support that "[a]rguably, it is States (and of course terrorists) that ultimately cause and should therefore provide compensation for terrorism, since terrorism is the ultimate consequence of the failure of domestic policy or diplomacy at the highest levels".

Y.O.M. Nyampong, *Insuring the Air Transport Industry Against Aviation War and Terrorism Risks and Allied Perils*, DOI 10.1007/978-3-642-32433-8_7,

insurance market does when the large catastrophic risks they cover materialize—be they natural or man-made.[2] In most of these other economic sectors, however, governments consider such unilateral, supply-side interruptions in the provision of insurance coverage for large catastrophic risks to be a matter of serious concern for the economy as a whole since "[t]he economic and social development of a country or of a region depends on uninterrupted access to essential needs",[3] including insurance. Accordingly, governments in many countries have designed, established and operated various schemes to directly provide insurance coverage, or indirectly facilitate the provision of insurance coverage, to operators in the industry concerned for those large catastrophic risks which the conventional insurance market is either reluctant or unable to fully underwrite.[4]

In view of the foregoing, the question that remains unresolved is that, given that States and their governments must, as a matter of necessity, be involved in the provision of insurance coverage or other suitable financial equivalent to the air transport industry for aviation war and terrorism risks, what are States and governments expected to do in the proper discharge of this role? This chapter attempts to provide some answers to this question by surveying and analyzing the manner in which a handful of States and their governments have gone about performing this role over the years, particularly in the aftermath of September 11, 2001. Before addressing this matter, however, it must be pointed out that governmental involvement in the provision of catastrophic risk insurance or other financial security to any sector of a country's economy may, at the discretion of the government, be implemented on a domestic or international scale. Thus, in an effort to provide a comparative basis for determining how governments should go about performing this role in connection with the air transport industry, the next two sections of this chapter provide a bird's eye view of a handful of governmental schemes implemented in different sectors of the economy at the domestic and international levels, respectively.

7.2 Governmental Involvement in the Provision of Domestic Insurance Coverage for Large Catastrophic Risks in Property and Casualty Lines of Insurance

Terrorist acts, floods and earthquakes are usually characterized as large catastrophic events within property and casualty lines of insurance in most countries since the probability of their occurrence is low, and yet when they do occur, losses are typically immense and widespread. Many countries have faced situations in which following

[2] Empowered by short-notice cancellation clauses, insurers in these markets usually withdraw coverage soon after the occurrence of a large catastrophic event, and if it is subsequently restored, only partial coverage is made available, usually accompanied by dramatic price increases.

[3] Michel-Kerjan (2005) pp. 11–12.

[4] Cluff and Jonkman (2002) p. 214.

terrorist attacks, their local property and casualty insurers have sought to exclude coverage for terrorism risks from their insurance policies, frequently citing lack of reinsurance support as the basis for their actions.[5] In recognition of the adverse financial and economic consequences of not having widely available and affordable commercial insurance coverage for terrorism as part of general property and casualty insurance contracts, a variety of programs have been established in a number of countries, all with the common objective of facilitating the availability of domestic insurance coverage for damage caused by terrorism.

As noted by one writer, "[s]uch arrangements have usually been created in response to difficulties that were specific to the country in question, and naturally, the provisions that have been put in place reflect both the nature of those local problems and the nature of local insurance markets".[6] As such, these programs vary widely, both in structure and detail, and they usually involve a multiplicity of stakeholders.

The commonest examples of national schemes established to enhance the provision of terrorism insurance coverage under property and casualty insurance policies include:[7] the Pool Reinsurance (Pool Re) scheme established by the UK government in 1992–1993 after UK commercial property insurers had threatened to exclude from their policies damage caused by terrorist acts that resulted in fire or explosion;[8] the *Gestion de l'Assurance et de la Réassurance des Risques*

[5] In the majority of countries where the law does not require mandatory provision of terrorism insurance coverage under routine property and casualty insurance policies, the first line of action of insurers is to threaten withdrawal of terrorism coverage soon after a terrorist activity occurs and causes damage. These direct insurers typically reinsure their exposure to the risks they underwrite, including terrorism risk. However, as reinsurance markets are global in scope and neither the prices nor the conditions of coverage are subject to direct regulation, reinsurers have little difficulty excluding terrorism from coverage following the occurrence of a major event. Since the direct insurers basically rely on reinsurance capacity to underwrite terrorism as part of their property and casualty policies, they have no option but to withdraw coverage when there is no reinsurance capacity. See idem.

[6] Atkins (2007).

[7] For a comprehensive overview of the above-mentioned terrorism risk insurance/reinsurance programs, See idem., pp. 132–145.

[8] The Pool Reinsurance scheme was developed in the UK in the early 1990s following a wave of terrorist (mostly IRA) attacks that caused commercial property insurers and reinsurers in the UK to announce that they would exclude damage caused by terrorist acts that resulted in fire or explosion from their policies and reinsurance treaties with effect from the start of 1993. Given the level of terrorist activity at that time, the prospect of terrorism exclusions in insurance contracts was of great concern and the lack of cover was considered likely to have adverse economic and financial consequences. The evidence of these potential economic and financial consequences convinced the UK government that it should be willing to play a specific role as a partner with others in supporting a resolution to the problem. Pool Re was thus established as a collaborative arrangement between the insurance industry and the UK government. Its object was to provide reinsurance capacity to enable commercial insurers to reinstate the terrorism insurance cover that they had found it necessary to exclude for lack of commercial reinsurance support. As such, Pool Re has a mutual structure: its members are those primary insurers who reinsure the terrorism risks they have underwritten into the pool. Pool Re was set up as a self-funding reinsurance mechanism—to pay claims from the reinsurance premiums received from its reinsured members. However, it was

Attentats et Actes de Terrorisme (GAREAT) scheme established by the French government in 2002;[9] the Australian Reinsurance Pool Corporation (ARPC) scheme established by the government of Australia through the Terrorism Insurance Act of 2003;[10] the *Extremus Versicherungs AG* scheme of the German

recognized that the nature of terrorism risk and the lack of predictability of losses was such that for Pool Re to operate on the scale intended, it needed retrocessional cover sufficient to secure any potential liabilities. This retrocessional role was, and continues to be, supplied by the UK government. The Retrocession Agreement is a contractual agreement under which the retrocessionaire (i.e., the UK government) guarantees to provide funding to Pool Re in the event that Pool Re's accumulated assets are exhausted by claims made on it by its members. Pool Re pays a premium to the government for this retrocessionary cover and any amounts paid by the government under the retrocession agreement stand to be repaid by Pool Re from future operating surpluses. Because the indemnity from the government is unlimited, Pool Re is able to accept all cessions passed to it by its members. The insurer members can therefore provide terrorism cover to their insureds for full values. The reinsurance cover provided by Pool Re to its members provides indemnity for claims they pay in respect of damage and consequential business interruption to commercial property caused by an act of terrorism. An act of terrorism is defined in the enabling legislation as: acts of persons acting on behalf of, or in connection with any organization which carries out activities directed towards the overthrow or influencing, by force or violence, of Her Majesty's government in the United Kingdom or any other government de jure or de facto. Terrorism cover has to be attached to an underlying general policy so the reinsurance provided by Pool Re applies to some of the losses covered by the underlying policy. See idem., pp. 137–139. In response to September 11 2001, the British government expanded the range of perils covered by Pool Re from damage caused by fire and explosion to include damage caused by biological contamination, impact by aircraft, and flood damage related to terrorism. Starting from January 1 2003, Pool Re has also provided reinsurance coverage for nuclear contamination resulting from terrorism. See Cluff and Jonkman (2002) p. 219.

[9] The French GAREAT Pool is a reinsurer of direct insurers that cover commercial and industrial risks located in France and its overseas territories. The arrangements cover direct property damage and related business interruption losses caused by terrorism. Insurance against terrorism is compulsory in France and direct insurers who underwrite terrorism risk may transfer their terrorist exposure to the pool which thereby acts like a reinsurer. GAREAT is a co-reinsurance pool structured as a four-layer risk sharing system. The first layer of 400 million Euros is covered by the insurers in proportion to the risk assigned to the pool. A second layer is covered by reinsurers and other large insurers up to 1.25 billion Euros, with an annual stop loss set at 400 million Euros. A third layer provides additional coverage of up to 350 million Euros and is taken up by several major international reinsurers. Thus, in total, the insurance and reinsurance industry cover terrorist risks in France up to a total limit of 2 billion Euros. Beyond that, the French government covers all insurance compensation required as a result of terrorist attacks through the *Caisse Centrale de Réassurance* (CCR). The government guarantee is unlimited. Premiums collected by participating insurers for covering terrorism risks are transferred to GAREAT and are shared in the following manner: the pool retains 30 %; participants in the second layer keep 50 %; reinsurers in the third layer keep 10 %; and the government also receives 10 % of premiums in exchange for the unlimited guarantee which it provides. See Atkins (2007) pp. 140–141. See also Michel-Kerjan (2005) pp. 40–41.

[10] Australia's ARPC was established by the Terrorism Insurance Act of 2003. The Act overrides terrorism exclusions in the relevant direct policies and consequent exposure can then be reinsured by the insurer with ARPC. The scheme provides reinsurance cover for insurance that covers commercial property and consequential business interruption losses. It also covers insurance provided for liability arising from ownership or occupation of property falling within the provisions of the Act. The cover provided under the scheme follows the underlying cover provided

government which began operations in 2002;[11] The Terrorism Risk Insurance Act (TRIA) scheme of the US government;[12] and, the *Consorcio de Compensacion de Seguros* scheme established by the Spanish government as far back as 1928.[13]

---

by the property policy which has been issued. Thus if the underlying property policy covers fire only, then fire losses that result from an act of terrorism would be covered under the scheme. The extent of indemnity available from the government is capped and there is provision for claims payments to be reduced on a pro rata basis in the event that total losses exceed the resources of the scheme. See Atkins (2007) pp. 141–143.

[11] In contrast to the schemes described above, the German *Extremus Versicherungs AG* scheme is a primary insurer rather than a reinsurer. It is a private company with a diversified shareholding that includes a range of German insurers and reinsurers, and it covers terrorism risks exclusively. Policies are distributed by insurers that operate in the German market and insurance brokers, and there are arrangements for market insurers to participate in claims settlement. The scheme provides cover for property and business interruption losses caused by an act of terrorism and due to fire, explosion, and certain other perils. The scheme covers policyholders up to a maximum loss limit that may be less than the sum insured. Capacity for the scheme is limited to 10 billion Euros comprising successive layers. Extremus itself is engaged in the first tier for damages of up to 1.5 billion Euros. Beyond that, a second tier of 500 million Euros is covered by several insurers and reinsurers drawn from both the German and international reinsurance markets. The German government finally provides an excess layer of up to 8 billion Euros. Since Extremus is liable for all insured losses caused by terrorist activity on German soil and its capacity is limited to 10 billion Euros, it follows that any damages exceeding 10 billion Euros will force it into bankruptcy.

[12] Following September 11, 2001, most property and casualty insurers in the US began excluding terrorism from the policies they issued to their policyholders. In response, Congress passed the Terrorism Risk Insurance Act in 2002. The Act made exclusions in respect of terrorist losses ineffective and required insurers to make cover available in all property and casualty insurance policies. Policyholders were given the option to decline terrorism cover. A financial backstop was provided by the US federal government to affected insurers, beyond a certain level of retention. No premium was payable by the insurers. Following passage of the Act, insurers had a period of time within which to negotiate the price at which terrorism coverage would be provided or to receive confirmation from policyholders that cover was not required. Participation in the program is mandatory for insurers and insurer loss retentions are computed based on the relevant premium income of the insurer. Indemnity from the federal government is subject to an aggregate limit of US$ 100 billion for the whole program, and there are provisions allowing the government to recoup certain amounts in the event that it is required to make payment. Initially, TRIA was intended as a temporary program and it was scheduled to expire on December 31st 2005. However, it was renewed for another 2 years in 2005 with the enactment of Pub. L. No. 109-144 (2005); and, for a further 7 years afterwards with the enactment of Pub L 110-160, 121 Stat. 1839-1843 (2007).

[13] Spain's *Consorcio de Compensacion de Seguros* is a state owned company that deals with a range of special risks that go far beyond just terrorism. It handles many forms of natural catastrophe as well as political risks. The scheme provides cover within a range of property, motor and personal accident risks. The cover is mandatory and automatic with a series of rates applied to sums insured. Insurers may deduct a 5 % charge and the indemnity provided follows the underlying monetary limits and policy conditions. The scheme is backed by an unlimited state guarantee which is activated in the event that losses sustained are beyond the financial resources of the Consorcio.

7.3 International Cooperation Between States in the Provision of Insurance Coverage for Large Catastrophic Risks

There are certain industries which are perennially exposed to large catastrophic risks whose potential damage impact transcends national boundaries. On the strength of this realization, governments in a number of countries have cooperated to put in place mechanisms to facilitate the provision of insurance coverage (or some other financial security) for the large catastrophic risks that such industries are exposed to. Notable among these are the civil nuclear energy sector where it is widely acknowledged that although there is a very low likelihood of occurrence, a single catastrophic event involving a nuclear power plant or the radioactive material used therein may lead to damages that exceed the capacity of any country's national insurance industry, let alone that of a single insurer.

Accordingly, 14 mostly Western European states negotiated and signed the 1960 Paris Convention on Third Party Liability in the field of Nuclear Energy[14] and thereby established an international regime under which liability for damage to, or loss of, life and property (with a few exceptions) caused by a nuclear accident was channelled exclusively to the operator of the nuclear plant in question. The basis of the operator's liability was strict liability and it was subject to an upper limit of US$ 22 million.[15] The operator's liability exposure was to be covered by conventional insurance or other appropriate financial security.[16]

In 1963, a Convention Supplementary[17] to the 1960 Paris Convention was adopted in Brussels and it was signed by a large majority of the states party to the 1960 Paris Convention. Under the Brussels Supplementary Convention, States parties agreed that third-party compensation for nuclear accidents would be provided in three layers. The first layer comprises the liability of the operator as specified under the 1960 Paris Convention. The second layer involves payment of additional compensation by the

[14] 956 UNTS 263 (1960) as subsequently amended by Additional Protocols of January 28, 1964, and November 16, 1982. The Paris convention includes all Western European countries except Ireland, Austria, Luxembourg and Switzerland.

[15] This amount could be increased or decreased by each one of the States bound by the convention, but could never be fixed below US$ 7 million under any circumstances. In fixing the amount, the possibility of obtaining commercial insurance coverage or other financial security was to be taken into consideration.

[16] Such insurance for nuclear energy operators in a good number of countries is organized through the mechanism of nuclear insurance pools. According to the International Association of Nuclear Pools, "[a] Pool is essentially a mechanism whereby a number of insurers agree to appoint a common agent to underwrite jointly a particular risk or class of business. It is a mechanism commonly employed where the risks in question are few in number, or require a capacity beyond the individual means of the members even if arranged on a traditional co-insurance basis, or which presents [*sic*] some particularly hazardous aspect which would render acceptance by conventional methods difficult if not impossible". See Nuclear Risk Insurers Ltd. (2008).

[17] 1041 UNTS 358 (1963).

installation state up to a maximum of 70 units of account[18] (inclusive of the amount provided in the first layer), in the event that the compensation available in the first layer is insufficient.[19] In the third layer, *all states* party to the Brussels Supplementary Convention agreed to be jointly liable, according to a prescribed formula, for third-party damages not exceeding 120 million units of account in the event that the compensation available from the first two layers is insufficient.[20]

Instead of simply joining the 1960 Paris Convention, a bloc of mostly Eastern European states negotiated and adopted their own Convention on Civil Liability for Nuclear Damage in Vienna in 1963.[21] In essence, the basic principles of the 1963 Vienna Convention and the 1960 Paris Convention (as subsequently amended) are identical in all material respects except one.[22] In any event, the two regimes have been linked together by a Joint Protocol[23] since 1988. Thus, under and by virtue of the Joint Protocol, the applicability of each convention is extended to states bound by the other convention. Steps were also taken in 1997 to significantly improve the total amount of compensation available under the unified international liability regime for nuclear damage.[24] The total amount of compensation for nuclear damage was thus increased to 600 million SDRs, comprising 300 million SDRs from the three layers described above plus a further 300 million SDRs of supplementary compensation to be provided by an international fund, financed by contributions from the *public funds* of contracting states.[25]

The mechanism used for providing compensation to victims who suffer as a result of oil pollution damage caused by spills of persistent oil from tankers also provides a good international example of how state cooperation may be used to achieve certain goals when private commercial insurance is not forthcoming.

---

[18] For the purposes of the Brussels Supplementary Convention, "unit of account" meant the unit of account of the European Monetary Agreement as defined at the date of the Paris Convention. See idem., art. 3(g).

[19] Idem., art. 3(b)(ii). The "installation state" is the state within whose territory the nuclear facility is situated.

[20] Idem., arts. 3(b)(iii) & 12.

[21] 1063 UNTS 265 (1963).

[22] The only notable exception between the two regimes is that the 1963 Vienna Convention enables states to lower the liability limit of the operator within the first layer to US$ 5 million, whereas the 1960 Paris Convention allows US$ 7 million.

[23] EC Regulation 285/2010 OJ L 19 (2010).

[24] These steps comprised the adoption of 2241 UNTS 270 (1997) as well as Appendix to IAEA INFCIRC/567 (1997).

[25] According to 2241 UNTS 270 (1997), the liability of the operator in the first layer may be limited by the installation state to an amount not less than 300 million SDRs or 150 million SDRs provided that, in the latter case, public funds will be made available by the installation state to compensate for nuclear damage suffered by third parties in excess of 150 million SDRs and up to at least 300 million SDRs. The Appendix to IAEA INFCIRC/567 (1997), on the other hand, provided for the payment of supplementary compensation of up to 300 million SDRs by an international fund to be financed by contributions from public funds of contracting states.

A succession of international treaties dating back from 1969 has culminated in the establishment of a three-tiered international compensation regime for victims.[26] The first tier involves payment of compensation by the ship owner. The 1992 Civil Liability Convention lays down the principle of strict liability of ship owners[27] and creates a system of compulsory liability insurance.[28]

The registered owner of the tanker concerned (or his insurer as the case may be) is the only person against whom claims for pollution damage arising under the convention may be brought. Although liability under the convention is channelled through the ship owner, "[t]his does not preclude victims from claiming compensation arising outside the convention from persons other than the ship owner".[29] In exchange for being strictly liable, the ship owner is normally entitled to limit his liability to an amount which is linked to the gross tonnage of his ship.[30]

In the second tier, the 1992 Fund Convention establishes a regime for compensating victims in situations where: the ship owner is exempt from liability under the 1992 Civil Liability Convention; or the compensation available under the first tier (usually from insurance proceeds) is inadequate; or, the damage exceeds the ship owner's liability under the 1992 Civil Liability Convention.[31] In such situations, compensation is paid by the International Oil Pollution Compensation Fund, 1992 (IOPC Fund 1992), a worldwide intergovernmental organization established for

---

[26] Compensation for pollution damage caused by spills from oil tankers is governed by an international regime elaborated under the auspices of the International Maritime Organization (IMO). The framework for the regime was originally established in 973 UNTS 3 (1969) and 1110 UNTS 57 (1971). This old regime was successively amended by Protocols adopted in 1976 and 1984. It was amended again in 1992 by yet another two Protocols: 1956 UNTS 255 (1992) and 1956 UNTS 330 (1992). As a result of the amendments introduced by the 1992 Protocols, the new regime now comprises two Conventions which entered into force on 30 May 1996 and are known as the 1992 Civil Liability Convention and the 1992 Fund Convention, respectively. In May 2003, a third tier of compensation was established by means of IMO Doc. No. LEG/CONF.14/20 (2003). This Protocol which entered into force on 3 March 2005 created a Supplementary Fund to provide additional compensation over and above that available under the first two tiers. It is optional and participation in it is open to those States which are party to the 1992 Fund Convention. See International Oil Pollution Compensation Funds (2009).

[27] 1956 UNTS 255 (1992), art. III. The ship owner is however exempt from liability if he proves that: (a) the damage resulted from an act of war or a grave natural disaster; or (b) the damage was wholly caused by sabotage by a third party; or, (c) the damage was wholly caused by the negligence of public authorities in maintaining lights or other navigational aids.

[28] Idem., art. VII.

[29] International Oil Pollution Compensation Funds (2009) p. 3.

[30] These limits, last revised on 1 November 2003, are specified on a graduated scale based on the gross tonnage of the ship concerned. At the upper end of the graduated scale, the liability limit for a ship of 140,000 units of gross tonnage or more is set at 89,770,000 SDRs (US$ 144 million as of 2 December 2009). See idem., p. 2.

[31] 1956 UNTS 330 (1992), art. 4(1).

the purpose of administering the regime created by the 1992 Fund Convention.[32] The Fund is financed by contributions levied on any person who, in one calendar year, has received more than 150,000 tonnes of crude oil or heavy oil (contributing oil) in a State party to the 1992 Fund Convention.[33] The Fund does not pay compensation if the pollution damage resulted from an act of war or was caused by a spill from a warship, or the claimant cannot prove that the damage resulted from an incident involving one or more ships falling within the ambit of the convention.[34]

In May 2003, a third tier of compensation was established by means of yet another Protocol to the 1992 Fund Convention which created a Supplementary Fund to provide additional compensation over and above that available under the first two tiers.[35] The 2003 Supplementary Fund Protocol is optional and participation in it is open only to those states which are party to the 1992 Fund Convention. The 2003 Supplementary Fund is also financed by contributions levied on persons receiving at least 150,000 tonnes of oil in any one calendar year in a Member State. However, for the purpose of paying contributions, it is deemed that each Contracting State has received a minimum of 1 million tonnes of oil each year,[36] and in situations where the aggregate quantity of oil actually received in a Member State is less than 1 million tonnes, the Contracting State concerned must pay the contributions due on behalf of the contributors in its territory insofar as no liable person exists for the aggregated

[32] The maximum amount payable by the 1992 Fund in respect of any incident is 203 million SDRs (US$ 326 million as of 2 December 2009), and this includes the sum actually paid by the ship owner or his insurer in the first tier. See International Oil Pollution Compensation Funds (2009) p. 3.

[33] "The levy of contributions is based on reports of oil receipts in respect of individual contributors. Member States are required to communicate every year to the 1992 Fund the name and address of any person in that State who is liable to contribute, as well as the quantity of contributing oil received by any such person. This applies whether the receiver of the oil is a Government authority, a State-owned company or a private company. ... Oil is counted for contribution purposes any time it is received at a port or terminal installation in a Member State after carriage by sea. The term Received refers to receipt into tankage or storage immediately after carriage by sea. The place of loading is irrelevant in this context; the oil may be imported from abroad, carried from another port in the same State or transported by ship from an off-shore production rig. Also oil received for transhipment to another port or received for further transhipment by pipeline is considered received for contribution purposes. ... The contributions are payable by the individual contributors directly to the 1992 Fund. A State is not responsible for the payment of contributions levied on contributors in that State, unless it has voluntarily accepted such responsibility". See idem., pp. 4–5.

[34] See idem., p. 3. See also 1956 UNTS 330 (1992), art. 4(2).

[35] IMO Doc. No. LEG/CONF.14/20 (2003). The 2003 Supplementary Fund is intended to pay compensation to any person suffering pollution damage if such person has been unable to obtain full and adequate compensation for an established claim for such damage under the terms of the 1992 Fund Convention, because the total damage exceeds, or there is a risk that it will exceed, the applicable limit of compensation laid down in the 1992 Fund Convention in respect of any one incident. See idem., art 4(1).

[36] Idem., art. 14(1).

quantity of oil received.[37] The total amount available for compensation for each incident in the States which become Members of the Supplementary Fund is 750 million SDRs, and this includes the amounts payable under the first tier (the Civil Liability Convention) and the second tier (the 1992 Fund Convention).

The schemes described above were all created in response to specific market problems and public policy goals, but what is common to all of them is the fact that they directly involve contracting states and their respective governments in the provision of compensation to victims of catastrophic events in each of these industries. Thus, a strong case can be made for governmental involvement in the provision of some form of support to the air transport industry in connection with aviation war and terrorism risks. It is also important to note that various stakeholders were involved in the design and implementation of these schemes, each with different and sometimes conflicting objectives. Commenting on this aspect of the process, Steve Atkins notes:

> [t]he main interest of the ultimate insured is the ability to buy cover of a breadth and size to deal with anticipated losses, at reasonable cost. Insurers have an interest in ensuring that while providing cover to their customers, they do so in a way that does not inappropriately expose their balance sheets or lead to unreasonable operational concerns. *Governments have an interest to ensure that economic development is not hampered by lack of insurance protection and in helping to promote financial resilience generally.*[38]

Governments are also interested in ensuring that their citizens who suffer damage as a result of catastrophic events receive full and adequate compensation for their losses. As such, most of the schemes involving government participation usually have protection and compensation of victims as their top priorities. In order for such schemes to be successful, they must take all these interests into account, both at the design and implementation stage. They need to be structured in such a way that encourages the positive involvement of all major stakeholders, and they "must reflect the intended balance of interests between insureds, insurers, government and others who may share the risk, or have clear interest in the arrangements, such as those involved in distribution".[39]

Before discussing the rationale underlying the call for governmental involvement in the provision of support to the air transport industry in connection with aviation war and terrorism risks and, as well, assessing its limits and drawbacks, the next section of this chapter describes a number of air transport sector-specific programs that were implemented by governments in a few selected countries/ regions of significant importance in air transportation both before and in the immediate aftermath of the events of September 11, 2001.

---

[37] Idem., art. 14(2).

[38] See Atkins (2007) p. 135 (emphasis added). This commentator identifies several other considerations which are relevant to our present purposes. He notes at 136 that: "Insureds will wish to know that there will be a reasonable level of continuity in the availability of cover. There is little merit in arrangements that can be bought when risk levels are considered low but cease to be available whenever perception of risk increases. . . . Also, they have a legitimate interest in price stability".

[39] Idem., p. 135.

7.4 Existing Types of, and Modalities for, Governmental Involvement in the Provision of Insurance Coverage (or Other Support) for Aviation War and Terrorism Risks

Governments can and do involve themselves in the provision of insurance coverage or financial guarantees for aviation war and terrorism risks in any number of ways. A variety of governmental schemes designed to facilitate, complement, and in certain countries, even to substitute or replace the insurance coverage for war and terrorism risks provided to air transport operators by the conventional markets have been established in a number of countries across the world. As the governments of the most prominent aviation nations of the world have been reactive rather than proactive in this regard, most of these governmental schemes were established immediately following periods when air transport operators had faced severe difficulty in obtaining the desired or required levels of war and terrorism risk insurance coverage from the conventional markets. One author has described the process of governmental involvement as follows:

> [t]he initial decision to intervene will generally be made in the aftermath of a major terrorist attack, with private insurers and reinsurers withdrawing from the market, and with rising concerns for major macroeconomic losses if the government does not intervene. In this context, initial government intervention is likely to be both necessary and warranted.[40]

Despite the apparent necessity of governmental intervention under such circumstances, the underlying issue of fundamental concern which needs to be addressed both from a theoretical and practical perspective is whether or not (and why) governments should involve themselves in the provision of war and terrorism risk insurance coverage and/or guarantees to the aviation sector in the period before or after the occurrence of an extreme event. There are strong arguments for and against governmental involvement. For instance, it is argued on the one hand, that governmental involvement in the provision of insurance coverage for aviation war and terrorism risks stifles the development of the private insurance markets through a phenomenon known as "crowding out". On the other hand, it is argued that the very nature of aviation war and terrorism risks; the large amounts of capital required to insure them; and, the fact that their occurrence may be attributable to specific aspects of foreign policy adopted exclusively by governments all lead to the inevitable conclusion that governments must play a role in the provision of insurance coverage for such risks.

As will be seen below, the majority of such governmental schemes were established in the wake of an extreme event. Again, it is useful to recall that, following the occurrence of an extreme event, the two major factors that causes disruptions in the conventional insurance markets forcing them to restrict coverage and increase prices are: (a) the limited availability of financial capacity; and, (b) the heightened

[40] Jaffee (2004).

level of general uncertainty and risk ambiguity.[41] Governmental involvement typically aims at addressing these factors. In order to address the financial capacity problems that arise in the wake of an extreme event, governmental intervention may take the form of *indirect or implicit* policy measures aimed at providing specific incentives to restart the private (insurance and non-insurance) markets.[42]

In this respect, the object of the governmental action would be to attempt to revitalize the conventional markets and not to set up a substitute for, or a complement to, purely private solutions.[43] Examples of this type of governmental intervention could be fiscal, accounting and regulatory measures aimed at facilitating the raising and reserving of capital by insurance firms involved in aviation war and terrorism risk insurance. Another example would be targeted regulatory measures aimed at fostering the development of alternative risk transfer tools that would serve the purpose of spreading the risk on capital markets.[44] The legal framework could also be used as a means of facilitating private capacity building and larger mutuality. This could be achieved by, for instance, providing incentives and favourable regulatory environments such as granting tax-free conduit status to private sector risk mutualization schemes.[45]

While these indirect/implicit governmental initiatives may provide at least partial solutions to the shortage of financial capacity following an extreme event, they do not address the crucial issue of risk ambiguity and generalized uncertainty. As such, *direct or explicit* forms of government intervention, aimed at addressing both the financial capacity and uncertainty issues outlined above, are contemplated as means of increasing the availability and affordability of insurance coverage for aviation war and terrorism risks. Such types of governmental intervention may take a wide range of different forms.[46] The most far-reaching form of explicit intervention has the government acting as the *primary insurer*, taking on all insurance functions, including defining the coverage, setting the prices and bearing the risk.[47] Other forms of direct intervention have the government serving as the *reinsurer of last resort*, within a layered approach to terrorism risk coverage.[48] According to one author,

> [t]his integrated risk management strategy involves the private and public sector, the government stepping in to provide reinsurance at the highest risk levels, while private insurers and possibly reinsurers retain some or all of the lower tiers of risk. . . . This solution

---

[41] OECD (2005) p. 69.

[42] Idem.

[43] Idem.

[44] Idem.

[45] Idem. See also discussion of ART and ARF mechanisms in Chap. 5 above.

[46] Idem.

[47] Idem. See also Jaffee (2004) p. 206. According to this latter author, the provision of full government insurance would seem appropriate when the losses incurred are the result of a common national policy such as a war. By logical extension, full governmental provision of war and terrorism risk insurance coverage to the aviation sector would seem appropriate if the losses are somehow attributable to the foreign policy adopted by the government.

[48] OECD (2005).

allows accessing the exclusive capacity of the government to provide coverage for the larger risks as it enjoys much wider diversification capabilities – it may spread the loss over the entire population as well as across time to future generations of taxpayers, while insurers operate under far shorter time constraints.[49]

Finally, the government may act as *lender of last resort*.[50] Private insurance firms refuse to offer aviation war and terrorism coverage due in part to the costs of financial distress that arise if the firms do not have access to the resources to pay future claims. By acting as lender of last resort, the government basically provides cash flow payments to insurance companies when extreme events occur causing catastrophic losses, but only receives premium repayment in future years.[51] This requires that a designated government agency will be ready to make loans to insurance firms who are in need of liquidity after a terrorist event. Thus, by acting as lender of last resort, the government may serve to activate the private markets for aviation war and terrorism insurance at a comparatively low cost to itself.[52]

The two major forms of governmental involvement (i.e., direct/explicit and indirect/implicit measures) are not mutually exclusive: both may be combined depending on the underlying rationale and the policy goals sought to be achieved. For instance, in respect of aviation war and terrorism risks, governments may act as primary insurer and guarantee fund. "More commonly, governments may combine the functions of reinsurer and lender of last resort".[53]

7.4.1 The U.S. Federal Government's Aviation War Risk Insurance Program

By far, the most elaborate governmental scheme in existence providing insurance coverage for aviation war and terrorism risks is that implemented by the federal government in the United States. Prior to the events of September 11, 2001, the availability of aviation war risk insurance coverage on the commercial markets in the United States was very limited. American insurance companies avoided this segment of the market and solidified their position with the use of war risk exclusions such as the Common North American War Exclusion Clause (CWEC).[54] Although American insurance companies wrote back some of the war risks excluded by the CWEC into their all-risks policies upon payment of an additional premium, this was done on a very limited scale, and there was practically no commercial market in existence in the United States for providing full insurance coverage for the war and terrorism risks

[49] Idem.

[50] Idem., p. 70.

[51] Jaffee (2004) p. 218.

[52] Idem.

[53] OECD (2005) p. 70.

[54] See discussion in Chap. 3 above for a comprehensive overview of the Common North American War Exclusion Clause (CWEC). See also Libby (1995) p. 645.

associated with civil aviation.[55] As such, U.S. airlines and aviation operators had no option but to turn to the London market for full war risk coverage.

As far back as 1951, Congress passed legislation thereby establishing the scheme which has evolved into what is now known as the Federal Aviation Administration (FAA) Aviation Insurance Program.[56] The scheme was initially established in response to the limited availability of war risk insurance coverage on the conventional insurance markets in the U.S. for those commercial carriers that were providing essential airlift services to the U.S. government.[57] The program (as amended to date) has three elements. Under the first two, the Secretary of Transportation is given discretion: (1) to directly provide insurance and reinsurance;[58] or (2) to reimburse[59] insurance costs to U.S. aircraft manufacturers or airlines in respect of damage or loss arising out of any risk from the operation of aircraft registered either in the United States or in a foreign country.

The third element of the program was introduced following the events of September 11, 2001. It consists of a limitation of the third-party liability of American flag carriers arising from any future terrorist attacks to US$ 100 million in the aggregate, with the federal government assuming responsibility for any liability above the US$ 100 million aggregate limit.[60] Thus, under the enabling

[55] Margo (2000) p. 333.

[56] The FAA Aviation Insurance Program was originally established in 1951 by the insertion of Title XIII into the Civil Aeronautics Act of 1938. In 1958, the Civil Aeronautics Act of 1938 was repealed by the Federal Aviation Administration Act of 1958. However, the Aviation Insurance Program was continued under the 1958 FAA Act. See Government Accountability Office (1994) p. 2.

[57] When the program was originally established, its objective was to provide *war risk* insurance for commercial aircraft that supplied essential airlift services to the U.S. government when such insurance was not available commercially or was available only on unreasonable terms and conditions. On 9th November 1977, Congress enacted Pub. L. 95-163, 91 Stat. 1286 thereby amending the FAA Act of 1958 to expand the FAA's authority to provide *all risk* insurance under the program. See idem., p. 2. Again, on 12th December 2003, Congress enacted Pub. L. No. 108-176 (2003b) § 106(a)(1) of which amended the 1958 FAA Act by adding American Aircraft Manufacturers to the list of entities eligible to be insured under the program.

[58] 49 USC §44302(a). Initially, the mandate of the Secretary of Transportation under the program was limited to the issuance of insurance coverage for international operations. Following September 11, 2001, however, the mandate was extended thereby enabling the program to provide insurance cover for both domestic and international operations.

[59] 49 U.S.C. § 44302(b).

[60] Pub. L. No. 107-42, 115 STAT. 230 (2001a), § 201(b), codified at 49 U.S.C. § 44303(b). For acts of terrorism committed on or to an air carrier, the Secretary may certify that the air carrier was a victim of an act of terrorism and in the Secretary's judgment, based on the Secretary's analysis and conclusions regarding the facts and circumstances of each case, shall not be responsible for losses suffered by third parties that exceed $100,000,000, in the aggregate, for all claims by such parties arising out of such act. If the Secretary so certifies, the air carrier shall not be liable for an amount that exceeds $100,000,000, in the aggregate, for all claims by such parties arising out of such act, and the Government shall be responsible for any liability above such amount. No punitive damages may be awarded against an air carrier (or the Government taking responsibility for an air carrier under this subsection) under a cause of action arising out of such act. The Secretary may extend the provisions of this subsection to an aircraft manufacturer of the aircraft of the air carrier involved.

legislation, the scope of the program is very broad and it technically allows the U.S. government to provide all kinds of insurance coverage for a broad range of aviation-related risks.

In spite of the broad mandate entrusted to the Secretary of Transportation, however, the program has so far been restricted exclusively to the issuance of war risk policies to airlines and other eligible entities. The effective ending date of the entire program has been extended on numerous occasions since 1958. Most recently, the effective ending date of the program was extended till March 30, 2008,[61] and subsequently, till December 31, 2013.[62]

The FAA (the agency within the Department of Transportation which has been delegated direct responsibility for the implementation of the program by the Secretary of Transportation),[63] issues two forms of aviation war-risk insurance policies covering both liability and hull war risks. The first type of coverage is known as Non-Premium Insurance and it is provided to eligible airlines at no cost aside from a one-time registration fee.[64] The second type of war risk coverage provided by the FAA under the program is known as Premium Insurance and it requires the insured airlines to pay premiums for the coverage provided. Premiums charged by the FAA for this type of coverage are computed on the basis of, and are supposed to be commensurate with, the risks involved.[65]

Provision of premium war risk insurance by the FAA is subject to a number of conditions. The Secretary of Transportation may only issue premium aviation insurance policies to air carriers, aircraft manufacturers and other eligible entities when the following conditions exist:

(a) The President of the United States has determined that the continuation of specified air services, whether conducted by American or foreign flag carriers, is necessary in the

[61] Pub. L. No. 108-176, 117 STAT. 2490 (2003a) § 106(d).

[62] Pub. L. No. 110-181 (2008) § 378.

[63] See Government Accountability Office (1994) p. 3.

[64] FAA registers aircraft for non-premium insurance when the carriers perform contract services for federal agencies that have indemnification agreements with the Department of Transportation (DOT), usually under the Civil Reserve Air Fleet (CRAF) program. Under the indemnification agreements, these federal agencies reimburse FAA for the insurance claims it pays to the airlines. Prior to 1994, a large part of the non-premium insurance written by the FAA concerned flights sponsored by the Department of Defense. Such flights moved troops, cargo and relief supplies (such as food and medical supplies) to foreign locations subject to civil or military unrest. See idem., p. 3.

[65] 49 U.S.C. § 44306(a). See also Margo (2000) p. 334; Government Accountability Office (1994) p. 3.

interest of air commerce or national security or to carry out the foreign policy of the United States Government;[66]

(b) The operation of the aircraft is in foreign air commerce or between two or more points all of which are outside the United States; and,

(c) The Secretary has found that insurance for the particular operation cannot be obtained on reasonable terms from the commercial insurance market.[67]

The FAA began issuing premium war risk insurance policies to commercial airlines on September 24, 2001 following announcement of Presidential Determination number 01-29 dated September 23, 2001.[68] At the same time, the U.S. Congress enacted the Air Transport Safety and System Stabilization Act[69] and thereby limited the third-party liability of American flag carriers arising from any future terrorist attacks to US$ 100 million in the aggregate, with the federal government assuming responsibility for any liability above the US$ 100 million aggregate limit.[70]

To the extent that the Secretary is authorized to provide insurance under the program, the Secretary may also reinsure any part of the insurance provided by a direct insurer. For this purpose, the Secretary is allowed to reinsure with, transfer to, or transfer back to, the direct insurer any insurance or reinsurance provided by the Secretary under the program.[71] With the approval of the Secretary, a person having an insurable interest in an aircraft may insure the aircraft with other underwriters in an amount over and above that insured under the program.[72] In such situations, the Statute does not allow the Secretary to benefit from the additional insurance procured by the insured, although it preserves the right of the Secretary to make contracts of

[66] 49 U.S.C. § 44302(c). Over the years, several Presidential Determinations have been made under this provision, extending the mandate of the FAA to continue provision of aviation war risk insurance to eligible entities. At the time of this writing, the most recent of such Presidential Determinations was made by President Barack Obama on August 31st 2009. It contains (1) a determination that the continuation of U.S. flag commercial air service is necessary in the interest of air commerce, national security, and the foreign policy of the United States; and, (2) an approval of provision by the Secretary of Transportation of insurance or reinsurance to U.S. flag air carriers against any loss or damage arising out of any risk from the operation of an aircraft in the manner and to the extent provided for in Chap. 443 of 49 U.S.C., until August 31st 2010 when he (the Secretary of Transportation) determines that such insurance or reinsurance cannot be obtained on reasonable terms and conditions from any company authorized to conduct an insurance business in a State of the United States. See 74 Fed. Reg. 43617 (2009) (to be codified at 14 C.F.R § 198).

[67] 49 U.S.C. § 44302(a) & (c). See also Margo (2000) p. 333.

[68] 66 Fed. Reg. 49075 (2001) (to be codified at 14 C.F.R § 198). A template of the war risk insurance policy issued by the FAA to eligible entities between January 1, 2011 and September 30, 2011 is reproduced in the Appendix of this book.

[69] Pub. L. No. 107-42 (2001b).

[70] Idem., § 201(b).

[71] 49 U.S.C. § 44304.

[72] 49 U.S.C. § 44302(e).

co-insurance.[73] The Aviation Insurance Program is self-financed through the Aviation Insurance Revolving Fund (the Fund). Moneys deposited into the Fund to pay claims are generated from insurance premiums, the one-time $200-per-aircraft registration fee charged for non-premium insurance, and interest on investments in U.S. Treasury securities.

According to the FAA, the fundamental premise underlying the aviation insurance program is that "the government should not provide insurance on a regular or routine basis; rather, the government should be the insurer of last resort".[74] As such, the first aviation war risk policies issued by the FAA in 2001 were valid initially for 60 days and were renewable upon expiry for further periods of 60 days. In the Homeland Security Act of 2002,[75] the US Congress decided that the short-term administrative extensions of the FAA-issued policies were unsatisfactory and therefore instructed the FAA to provide war risk coverage through August 31, 2003, with the discretion to extend through December 31, 2003.[76] Congress extended each of those dates by 1 year in the Emergency Wartime Supplemental Appropriations Act, 2003.[77] It also extended the $100 million act-of-terrorism liability cap. Since then, Congress has extended war-risk insurance policies issued by the FAA and the liability cap yearly, via Appropriations Acts and Resolutions.[78]

In December 2006, the U.S. Congress in its Continuing Appropriations Resolution, 2007, extended the war-risk insurance and liability cap programs through February 15, 2007, which is the date that the Continuing Appropriations Resolution ended. After that extension, the Secretary of Transportation, using general authority to issue aviation insurance, extended war-risk insurance policies through August 31, 2007. The Secretary, however, had no authority to extend the liability cap which was due to expire on February 15, 2007 unless Congress acted. Congress responded by first enacting the Revised Continuing Appropriations Resolution, 2007,[79] authorizing the Secretary of Transportation to extend policies issued by the FAA and the liability cap until September 30, 2007, and subsequently, the Consolidated Appropriations Act, 2008,[80] pushing the date forward to December 31, 2008. From then onwards, the authority of the Secretary to extend insurance policies issued by

[73] This essentially means that, unless the Secretary expressly states that the contract being made is one of co-insurance, the doctrine of contribution will not apply whenever the insured suffers a loss covered simultaneously under both the FAA policy and the additional insurance policy.

[74] Government Accountability Office (1997) p. 2.

[75] Pub. L. No. 107-296 (2002).

[76] Air Transport Association (U.S.) (2007).

[77] Pub. L. No. 108-11 (2003) § 4001.

[78] See e.g., Pub. L. No. 108-447 (2004) § 106; Pub. L. No. 109-115 (2005) § 108.

[79] Pub. L. No. 110-5 (2007), §§ 106, 21002 (a) & (b).

[80] Pub. L. No. 110-161 (2004), Division K, Title I, § 114.

the FAA and also the liability cap has been extended on numerous occasions for short periods ranging from 2 to 6 months at a time.[81]

At this writing, the US Senate was considering a bill passed by the House of Representatives which, if enacted, will authorize the Secretary of Transportation to extend FAA-issued policies until December 31, 2019,[82] and the liability cap until December 31, 2012.[83] The bill envisages this as the final extension. As such, it makes provision for the establishment of a successor program when the authority of the Secretary to extend policies runs out after December 31, 2019. Under the provisions of the bill, "[c]overage for the risks specified in a policy that has been extended ... [by the Secretary] shall be provided in an airline sponsored risk retention or other risk-sharing arrangement approved by the Secretary".[84]

Initial funding for the airline sponsored risk retention or other risk-sharing arrangement that will replace the FAA Aviation Insurance Program will be provided from premiums collected by the Secretary from the airline industry for policies issued between September 22, 2001 and December 31, 2019, and any interest earned thereon, less any claims paid out during the period; claims pending as of December 31, 2019; and, the cost of administering the provision of insurance coverage by the FAA from September 22, 2001 to December 31, 2019 as determined by the Secretary.[85] It is widely expected that the bill will be enacted into law especially since the Senate has concluded consideration of President Obama's Health Care proposal which overshadowed all other legislative projects in the latter half of 2009.

The direct provision of war risk insurance coverage to the aviation industry by the US government for close to a decade (close to two decades if the impending FAA Reauthorization Bill is passed) has provided grounds for criticism by many commentators. It has been argued for instance that a commercial insurance market for aviation war and terrorism risks in the US has not been able to develop simply because of the cheap availability of government-provided coverage.[86] At a much more fundamental level, questions have been raised concerning the appropriate role to be played by the U.S. government in the war risk insurance arena when commercial markets

---

[81] See e.g., Pub. L. No. 110-253 (2008) § 3(c)(7)—extending FAA insurance policies till March 31 2009; Pub. L. No. 110-330 (2008) §§ 5(c) & (d)—extending FAA insurance policies and the $100 million third partly liability limit for air carriers till May 31 2009; Pub. L. No. 111-12 (2009) §§ 5(b) & (c)—extending FAA insurance policies and the $100 million third partly liability limit for air carriers till December 31 2009. See also Pub. L. No. 111-69 (2009) §§ 5(c) & (d); Pub. L. No. 111-116 (2009) §§ 5(b) & (c); and, Pub. L. No. 111-117 (2009) §§ 114(a) & (b).

[82] 915 RFS (2009) § 701(a).

[83] Idem., § 702.

[84] Idem., § 701(b).

[85] Idem.

[86] Kjelgaard (2002). This commentator reports that Maurice Greenberg, then chief executive of AIG, had lambasted the Department of Transportation on several occasions for its continuing agreement to extend war risk cover to US airlines. Although AIG was unlikely to suffer serious financial difficulty from as a result of the government's support of US airlines' insurance arrangements, Greenberg argued that the DOT's intervention was preventing commercial insurers from restoring competitiveness.

encounter crises such as that which ensued after September 11, 2001. These and other recurring issues which bear striking semblance to the moral hazard problems encountered in conventional insurance are considered in greater detail below in this chapter.

7.4.2 The Federal Government of Canada's Aviation War Risk Indemnity Program

Until the late 1980s, the federal government of Canada owned and managed Trans-Canada Airlines (now Air Canada), airports and the air navigation system in Canada, and it provided their insurance as part of their day-to-day management.[87] However, beginning in the early 1990s the federal government has pursued a policy of commercialization and/or privatization that has resulted in the divestiture from government ownership and management of the bulk of Canadian air transport infrastructure. Today, Air Canada is no longer a Crown corporation; almost all of the major Canadian airports have been privatized under the National Airports Policy; and, NAV CANADA, the nation's air traffic control operator, is a commercialized entity.[88] As part of the divestiture program, the federal government of Canada also gave up the provision of insurance for the airline(s), airports and the air navigation system.

On September 22, 2001, in reaction to the insurance aftermath of the events of September 11, 2001, the federal government adopted an Order in Council authorizing the Minister of Transportation to provide an indemnity to anyone involved in the air transportation industry for war risk liability insurance coverage, for a period of 90 days.[89] Acting on this mandate, the Minister issued an undertaking agreeing to indemnify "any person covered under an insurance policy held by an airline, an airport operator, NAV CANADA, or any supplier of goods or services to an airport operator, an airline in Canada or NAV CANADA who is insured against general liability under an insurance policy"[90] in accordance with the terms and conditions set out in the Undertaking and the Schedule attached thereto. Once the Undertaking was issued by the Minister, acceptance thereof on the part of any person covered was presumed without any formal communication by that person being necessary.[91]

Under the terms and conditions of the first Undertaking and the Schedule, the indemnity thereby issued applied to those entities[92] that already carried war risk

---

[87] Jack (2001).

[88] Dempsey et al. (2005) pp. 23 et seq.

[89] Government of Canada (2001b) (P.C. 2001-1675).

[90] See definition of "Persons covered" in the Schedule to Transport Canada (2009b). The most recent version of the entire undertaking, schedule and declaration at this writing is reproduced in the Appendix to this book.

[91] Idem.

[92] These included: airlines, defined to encompass traditional airlines within the meaning of the Canadian Transportation Act as well as any person operating a commercial air service; airports, referring to operators of airports in Canada; NAV CANADA—the sole air navigation services provider in Canada; and other essential service providers at airports such as ground handlers and refuellers. See idem.

coverage as part of their insurance policies prior to September 11, 2001, and only up to the limits of their existing policies.[93] The indemnity applied specifically to those portions of their existing war risk coverage[94] which had become commercially unavailable as a result of the events of September 11, 2001. According to the Undertaking, "commercially available" aviation war risk liability coverage refers "to aviation war risk liability coverage that is available in the insurance market, but does not include coverage that the Minister of Transport, Infrastructure and Communities may, from time to time, in his sole discretion, declare in writing to be not commercially available on reasonable terms during any period specified in the declaration".[95] Thus, under the Undertaking and the Schedule, the Minister had the discretion at any time to declare the level of aviation war risk liability coverage that, in his opinion, was commercially available, and the indemnity applied to the difference between this declared level of commercially available coverage and the previous limits of war risk coverage that each entity held under its own commercial insurance policy.[96] Subsequently, the indemnity was extended to new entrants on

---

[93] This meant for instance that, for entities such as Air Canada or Toronto's Lester B. Pearson Airport, the limits applicable to the indemnity were the same as that for which they had taken out commercial insurance coverage for war and terrorism risks prior to September 11, 2001; (i.e., up to $1 billion and $1.5 billion, respectively). See Stewart (2001).

[94] The war risks covered by the indemnity were specifically defined in the schedule as:

> Risks listed in the clause headed "War, Hi-jacking and Other Perils Exclusion Clause" in the standard aviation insurance policy to the extent that such risks have been included in a standard write-back endorsement to a policy and any other such risk that is not included in the standard write-back endorsement that the Minister of Transport, Infrastructure and Communities may, from time to time, in his sole discretion, declare in writing to be subject to this Undertaking to the limit of the amount covered for aviation liability under the insurance policy, less whatever coverage is commercially available during the period referred to below.

See Transport Canada (2009b).

[95] See definition of "commercially available" in idem.

[96] Initial declarations made by the Minister pegged the level of commercially available war risk insurance coverage at $50 million. Subsequent declarations have generally followed market trends and have revised the figure upwards. At the time of writing, the most recent declaration of the Minister was dated April 28th 2009. It provided that:

> Any additional coverage in respect of aviation war risk liability for Third Party Bodily Injury and Property Damage in excess of the first US $150 million covered by insurance underwriters under AVN52E or other standard write-back endorsement in respect of an airline or in excess of US $50 million covered by insurance underwriters under AVN52G or other standard write-back endorsement in respect of all other persons covered or where a person covered by the Undertaking has purchased insurance covering war risk liability for Third Party Bodily Injury and Property Damage of more than US $150 million in respect of AVN52E or US $50 million in respect of AVN52G, any additional coverage in excess of the amount purchased are deemed not to be commercially available on reasonable terms during the period while this declaration remains in effect (i.e., May 1, 2009 until seven days after it has been rescinded or varied and notice of its rescission or variation has been posted on the Transport Canada web site). See Transport Canada (2009a).

terms equivalent to those applicable to existing essential air service operators in Canada.[97]

In essence, by issuing the undertaking, the government of Canada promised to place in the same financial position as before, any eligible Canadian air transport entity which pays compensation for damages sustained as a result of the occurrence of a covered aviation war or terrorism risk for which insurance coverage had been withdrawn by the conventional markets following September 11, 2001. While not an insurance policy in the strict sense of the term, the indemnity covers the difference between the amount of war risk insurance coverage that Canadian airlines, airports NAV CANADA and other essential air service providers can freely obtain from the conventional markets (as determined from time to time by the Minister), and the previous levels of war risk coverage that were withdrawn by international insurers following September 11, 2001.

Initially, the indemnity was intended as a temporary measure, aimed at preventing the collapse of the Canadian air transport industry as a result of lack of insurance coverage during the time that air transport operators negotiated with London-based, commercial war risk insurers to restore the coverage that had been hitherto withdrawn. However, the Canadian government has continually and progressively renewed the authority of the Minister of Transportation to continue to provide the indemnity each time it expires.[98] Accordingly, it is reasonable to conclude that the indemnity has become a permanent program although the government insists that it is still a temporary indemnification.[99]

In spite of the numerous occasions on which the indemnity has been renewed, and in spite of the grave financial consequences that it exposes the federal government of Canada (and ultimately Canadian taxpayers) to in the event that a covered risk should materialize in Canada, the government has chosen not to seek legislative endorsement of its aviation war risk indemnity. To date, the Minister's authorization to issue the indemnity has always proceeded from an executive decision of the Cabinet—an Order of Her Majesty the Queen in Council—which, when issued, is not even published as subsidiary legislation in the Canada Gazette under the Statutory Orders and Regulations (SOR) series or the Statutory Instruments (SI) series.

---

[97] A new entrant is an air service operator that has started since September 11, 2001, or intends to start in the near future, the operation of an airline, the operation of an airport, the supplying of goods or services to an airport operator, or the provision of goods or services to the Canadian Air Transport Security Authority or NAV CANADA. See Transport Canada No. H057/02 (2002c).

[98] See e.g., Government of Canada (2001a) (P.C. 2001-1827), Transport Canada No. H151/01 (2001), Government of Canada (2002b) (P.C. 2002-0369), Transport Canada No. H009/02 (2002b), Transport Canada No. H026/02 (2002d), Transport Canada No. H079/02 (2002a), Government of Canada (2002a) (P.C. 2002-2228), Government of Canada (2003) (P.C. 2003-1833), Government of Canada (2004) (P.C. 2004-1538), Government of Canada (2005) (P.C. 2005-2248), Government of Canada (2007) (P.C. 2007-1867), Government of Canada (2008) (P.C. 2008-1849), and Government of Canada (2009) (P.C. 2009-1648).

[99] Indeed, at the very inception of the program in 2001, David Collenette, then Minister of Transportation is reported to have hinted that the Canadian government was considering making the program a permanent one. See Jack (2001) p. FP2.

Again, the sustained provision of this indemnity by the Canadian government raises both theoretical and practical questions about the appropriate role of national governments in the insurance arena. Before addressing those issues, however, the next section considers some initiatives that were implemented by individual European countries in the aftermath of September 11, 2001, and the reactions of the European Commission to those initiatives.

7.4.3 The Legality of European Governmental Schemes Providing Insurance Coverage/Guarantees to Air Transport Operators for Aviation War and Terrorism Risks Under EU State Aid Regulations

Prior to September 11, 2001, there were no specific governmental schemes in existence in Europe to substitute or supplement the aviation war and terrorism insurance coverage available on the conventional insurance markets. A number of European countries which had previous terrorism experiences had established general schemes to address the insurance implications of those incidents, but none of those schemes specifically addressed aviation war and terrorism insurance coverage.[100] Following the issuance of 7-day cancellation notices by insurers worldwide set to expire on September 24, 2001, however, at least 15 Member States of the European Union announced their intention to establish temporary mechanisms to either offer additional insurance guarantees to their air transport operators or to assume the risks directly themselves.

In the United Kingdom for instance, a captive insurance company called Troika was jointly established by three insurance brokering firms: Aon, Marsh and Willis, fully reinsured by Her Majesty's Treasury, and administered by Global Aerospace.[101] Troika provided additional insurance coverage to British airlines and air transport operators for third party war and terrorism risks beyond the $50 million limit that was then available from the conventional insurance markets. Most other countries issued governmental guarantees promising to indemnify their air carriers

[100] The United Kingdom and Spain are the two European countries which had the most extensive terrorist experiences prior to September 11, 2001. The UK government established the Pool Re scheme in 1992–1993 after commercial insurers had threatened to withdraw terrorism coverage following the IRA bombings in central London. Spain established the *Consorcio de Compensacion de Seguros* scheme as far back as 1928 in order to address the insurance implications of terrorist campaigns conducted by the ETA and other Basque separatist or nationalist movements.

[101] Under the Troika scheme, airlines were initially required to obtain third party war risk insurance coverage for up to $50 million from the commercial market, and the scheme provided coverage for limits beyond $50 million up to $1 billion for a premium ranging between 20 and 50 cents per passenger carried. See Margo (2002) p. 393.

and other air transport operators against any compensation or premium increases they may be required to pay as a result of the events of September 11, 2001. Appendix C provides a snapshot of the various temporary mechanisms that were announced by the EU Member States as of September 17, 2001.

European law generally prohibits member state governments from offering State aid. "State aid" is defined as: "any aid granted by a Member State or through State resources in any form whatsoever, which distorts or threatens to distort competition by favouring certain undertakings or the production of certain goods . . .",[102] and, in so far as it affects trade between the Member States, it is incompatible with the European common market. This notwithstanding, there are certain categories of State aid that are explicitly exempted from this general prohibition.[103] Although the EU Commission is the entity entrusted with responsibility and power to ensure that the State aid rules are enforced against Member States so as to ensure the proper functioning of the common market,[104] actual law-making power resides in the Council and the Parliament of Europe. Up until the early 1990s, the Commission faced considerable resistance from the Council in its push for the extension of competition and State aid rules to the air transport sector. It was only after the achievement of full liberalization of the European air transport sector in 1992 that the Council finally agreed to the recommendation of the Commission to bring the air transport sector under the scope of application of the European competition and State aid rules.[105]

The government-backed and/or operated insurance schemes that were announced by Member States following September 11, 2001 were categorized as State aid to the air transport industry since: they involved a direct or indirect transfer of state resources; they conferred an advantage on air carriers and service providers since, in their absence, the carriers and service providers would not have had sufficient insurance to operate; and, they were selective in nature as they favoured the aviation sector only.[106] In addition most of the schemes—especially the State guarantees—did

[102] EC Treaty OJ C 22 (2002) (subsequently amended in 2007 by Treaty of Lisbon), art. 87(1).

[103] Idem., art. 87(2) lists three types of State aid which *shall* be compatible with the common market and art. 87(3) list those which *may* be compatible with the common market. Most notably, "aid to make good the damage caused by natural disasters or exceptional occurrences" shall be compatible with the common market under art. 87(2)(b).

[104] Idem., art. 88. The Commission has power to investigate instances of State aid.

[105] The application of the EU State aid rules as prescribed in articles 87 and 88 of the EC Treaty to the aviation sector has had a rather chequered history. Initially, the governing bodies of the EC/EU were reluctant to extend the application of the State aid rules to the air transport sector, despite having the authority to do so under the EC Treaty. It was not until the passage of the Third Package of liberalization in 1992 that the Commission finally decided to take up the subject of State aid on the grounds that State aid was more of a danger to the market now that it had been fully liberalized. State aid guidelines were thus laid down by the Commission in 1994 and they have since applied to direct and indirect subsidization of air carriers as well as any operations that are accessory to air transport, such as flight schools, duty free shops, airport facilities, etc. The Guidelines are contained in EC 94/C 350/07 (1994). For a comprehensive discussion of EU State aid regulations and their application to the air transport sector, see Dempsey (2004) pp. 126–138. See also: Bovis (2004–2005).

[106] See EC COM(2001) 574 final (2001) p. 8.

not require payment of any premium for the complementary insurance cover provided to the aviation sector. The Commission therefore reacted immediately to the announcement of the temporary insurance schemes by Member States.

From the outset, the Commission took the position that it was desirable to limit distortions of competition caused by State aid to airlines.[107] Loyola de Palacio, then EU Transport Commissioner met with and reminded the Chairmen's Committee of the Association of European Airlines of the Commission's position on State aid. "[W]hile recognizing the exceptional situation facing the airlines, [she] ruled out any possibility that the Commission might accept measures which would create distortion between States and between airlines".[108]

In order to have a coordinated response to the specific issue of emergency State assistance in connection with insurance, the Commission referred the temporary schemes to the Ministers of Financial Affairs for consideration during their meeting of September 21–22, 2001. During their deliberations, the Ministers sought to strike a balance between the urgency of the situation and the risks which such governmental intervention could pose for the operation of the European internal market. Thus, they recommended criteria against which emergency State aid in connection with insurance could be permitted.[109] They agreed that Member States could exceptionally provide cover for aviation war and terrorism risks or assume the cost of the increase in premiums on condition that such aid was strictly regulated[110] and duly notified to the Commission.[111] The Ministers also recommended that the various governmental schemes be operated for a period of one month only, while work continued on finding a lasting solution and to encourage the commercial insurance industry to return to the market as soon as possible.[112]

On October 10, 2001, the EU Commission issued a communication to the Parliament and Council on the repercussions of the terrorist attacks on the air transport industry.[113] In this communication, the Commission endorsed the recommendations of the Ministers of Financial Affairs and stated that it would tolerate emergency State aid granted to make good the damage caused by natural disasters and exceptional occurrences in accordance with article 87(2)(b) of the EC Treaty.[114] In essence, this meant that State assistance in connection with insurance would only be allowed

[107] Balfour (2002).

[108] Idem., p. 399.

[109] European Commission IP/01/1306 (2001).

[110] The measures adopted by Member States were to be restricted to the immediate situation of higher premiums and were also to be proportionate to the risks incurred—governments were to charge a reasonable premium which, as far as practicable, reflected the risks covered by the schemes introduced, although this condition could be waived in the short term. The measures were also to be limited to addressing a failure in the commercial insurance market in order to ensure that third party cover for war and terrorism risks remained available. See EC COM (2001) 574 final (2001) p. 8.

[111] Idem., p. 9.

[112] Idem., p. 8.

[113] Idem.

[114] EC Treaty OJ C 22 (2002).

provided: it applied uniformly without restriction to all companies in a Member State;[115] it was exclusively intended to compensate for the extra cost of insurance and, did not place airlines in a more favourable situation than before 11 September.[116] The Commission asked the governments which had taken such measures to notify it of them and it examined each of those measures in the light of the State aid rules in order to find ways of coordinating them and avoiding distortion of competition.[117]

Almost all the temporary measures announced by Member States were valid for a period of 30 days initially. In the Commission's opinion, however, "[d]evelopments in the insurance market at the time suggest[ed] that it was unlikely that the temporary measures ... [could] be terminated after one month".[118] Accordingly, the communication stated that if the situation should continue beyond the initial 30 day period, the Member State concerned could decide either to continue providing supplementary guarantee to the insurance companies or to underwrite the risk itself.[119] The Commission decided that it will examine any government aid or renewal/extension thereof notified to it by virtue of Article 87(2)(b) of the EC Treaty in line with the criteria discussed above. Furthermore, the Commission requested Member States to terminate the costs of providing supplementary cover by 31 December 2001 at the latest and to pass them on to airlines "in order to restore equal conditions of competition between Community carriers".[120]

As was expected, the Member States extended or renewed the various temporary governmental schemes following their expiration at the end of the initial 30-day period. The extensions/renewals were duly notified to the Commission which examined and approved them in due course.[121] In yet another communication to the Council and Parliament issued by the Commission on July 2, 2002,[122] the Commission surveyed the state of the commercial insurance market for aviation war and terrorism risks and determined that the conditions which justified the application of Article 87(2)(b) of the EC Treaty to authorize national aid schemes were still present. The Commission therefore decided that, on condition that the conditions prescribed in its previous communication[123] were fulfilled, it would

[115] EC COM (2001) 574 final (2001) p. 9.

[116] Idem.

[117] European Commission IP/01/1306 (2001) p. 2.

[118] EC COM (2001) 574 final (2001) p. 9.

[119] Idem.

[120] Idem.

[121] See: EC State Aid No. NN 52/2002 OJ C 5 (2003e), EC State Aid No. NN 171/2001 OJ C 21 (2003l), EC State Aid No. NN 125/2002 OJ C 4 (2003i), EC State Aid No. NN 169/2001 OJ C 20 (2003k), EC State Aid No. NN 19/2002 OJ C 19 (2003a), EC State Aid No. NN 32/2002 OJ C 19 (2003b), EC State Aid No. NN 47/2003 OJ C 17 (2003d), EC State Aid No. NN 124/2002 OJ C 4 (2003h), EC State Aid No. NN 173/2001 OJ C 4 (2003m), EC State Aid No. NN 55/2003 OJ C 17 (2003f), EC State Aid No. NN 168/2001 OJ C 20 (2003j), EC State Aid No. NN 43/2002 OJ C 32 (2003c), and EC State Aid No. NN 123/2002 OJ C 19 (2003g).

[122] EC COM (2002) 320 final (2002).

[123] i.e., EC COM (2001) 574 final (2001).

authorize any prolongation of the temporary governmental schemes until October 31, 2002 subject to review should circumstances change significantly.[124]

The EU finally banned State subsidization or provision of war and terrorism insurance coverage to the air transport sector by Member States as from October 31, 2002 despite complaints from European airlines that the U.S. government was subsidizing its airlines through provision of cheap war and terrorism insurance and other forms of financing.[125] The decision of the EU to ban State subsidization or provision of aviation war and terrorism risk insurance coverage as from October 31, 2002 was primarily driven by the fact that, at the time, there were strong signs that the commercial markets were beginning to emerge from the market failure that occurred following the events of September 11, 2001. Indeed, three major privately capitalized schemes had been established and were offering varying levels of insurance coverage for aviation war and terrorism risks.[126] Two of those schemes emerged from financial groups that included both aircraft lessors and financiers and insurance operations.[127]

[124] EC COM (2002) 320 final (2002) p. 11.

[125] See Fitzsimmons (2004) p. 80. The EU responded to those pleas by setting up the means to deal with unfair aviation competition particularly by US carriers, using the more direct mechanism of anti-dumping tariffs on US airlines to neutralize the effects of aid received by them. See EC Regulation 868/2004 OJ L 1 (2004).

[126] The three private schemes were: (1) the *Berkshire Hathaway/Axis/AIG/GE Frankona Scheme* which offered up to US$ 1 billion war/terrorism of "third party" liability cover per aircraft excess of the "third party" cover purchased from conventional underwriters, up to US$ 2 billion in the aggregate on any one airline. The scheme also provided war and terrorism "passenger" liability cover and primary "third party" cover if the conventional aviation insurance market were to cancel their war and terrorism cover—but not hull war/terrorism cover. The cover, made available exclusively to selected airlines was for a period of 12 months and was non cancellable; (2) the *AIG-Led Scheme* which offered up to US$ 1 billion war/terrorism of "third party" liability cover per aircraft excess of the "third party" cover purchased from conventional underwriters, in the aggregate any one insured. It did not provide war and terrorism passenger liability cover or primary "third party" cover in the event that the conventional aviation insurance market was to cancel its primary war/terrorism cover. Neither did it provide hull war coverage. The cover, made available to airlines, manufacturers and service providers including security screeners, was for 12 months but was cancellable on 30 days notice by underwriters; and, (3) the *Allianz Scheme* which offered up to US$ 1 billion war/terrorism of "third party" liability cover per aircraft excess of the "third party" cover purchased from conventional underwriters, but limited to US$ 2 billion in the aggregate any one insured. There was also an overall aggregate limit of US$ 4 billion or four "Master Events" across all insureds covered under the scheme. The scheme did not provide war and terrorism passenger liability cover or primary third party cover if the conventional aviation insurance market was to cancel its primary war/terrorism cover. Neither did it provide hull war coverage in the event that that too was cancelled by the conventional insurance market. The cover, made available to airlines, manufacturers and service providers but not to security screeners, was for 12 months but cancelled automatically if four "Master Events" were to occur. For a comprehensive account of these schemes, see Fitzsimmons (2004) pp. 84–85.

[127] Idem., p. 80.

7.5 Rationale for Governmental Involvement in the Provision of Insurance Coverage for Aviation War and Terrorism Risks

So far, this chapter has outlined a variety of governmental initiatives designed and implemented in certain countries for the purpose of restoring sanity into the aviation war and terrorism risk insurance market and also mitigating the disruptive effects of insurance market failures/disruptions on the air transport industry. Although these governmental initiatives are typically designed and initially implemented as short-term measures, they invariably evolve into medium- to long-term measures, as they are repeatedly renewed by the governments upon expiry. For our present purposes, a question of paramount importance is whether governmental involvement in the provision of aviation war risk insurance and guarantees through the variety of schemes described above is a sustainable alternative to conventional insurance.

To answer this question, this and the next section of this chapter provide an analysis as to whether the various forms of governmental involvement address the economic and behavioural phenomena responsible for the disruptions that occur in the commercial aviation war and terrorism risk insurance markets following an extreme event. They also analyze the arguments made on both sides of the debate as to whether or not it is prudent (particularly in the US and Canada) to continually extend or renew those governmental initiatives following their initial expiration.

It has been argued that governmental involvement in the provision of insurance and financial guarantees against war and terrorism risks to the aviation sector (or in the compensation of terrorism related losses) may be supported on political grounds.[128] Proponents claim that each country's foreign policy choices have a decisive impact on transnational terrorism[129] and since paying compensation for terrorism losses is a matter of national security, they argue that governments should participate in national insurance programs covering economic losses due to terrorist attacks as part of their broader national security policies.[130] One author succinctly sums this argument up as follows: "[a]rguably, it is States (and of course terrorists) that ultimately cause and should therefore provide compensation for terrorism, since terrorism is the ultimate consequence of the failure of domestic policy or diplomacy at the highest levels".[131]

From an economic perspective,

> the discussion about the proper role that governments may be called upon to play in the field of [aviation war and] terrorism insurance stems from the recognition of certain failures that may negatively affect the functioning of the private insurance markets. Consequent market incapacity to provide sufficient insurance cover at affordable rates may have negative

---

[128] OECD (2005) p. 68.

[129] See for example Pillar (2001).

[130] Levmore and Logue (2003). These authors argue that governments should cover losses from terrorism because doing so would cause them to carefully consider the costs and benefits of their foreign policies.

[131] Fitzsimmons (2004) p. 87.

spill-over effects on the broader economy, result in a contraction of economic activity, and threaten both recovery and growth in the aftermath of an attack.[132]

Accordingly, it has been argued that there are at least three fundamental reasons why government intervention in the terrorism insurance market will be beneficial to any country: (1) imperfect information; (2) the private sector's underproduction or failure to produce public goods; and, (3) externalities that may not be taken into account.[133]

With respect to the first reason, those in favour of government intervention rely on some of the market failure arguments identified in Chap. 3, noting that the problem of imperfect information is often the central challenge facing insurance sellers and buyers.[134] In elaboration, they argue that:

> Insurance contracts promise future delivery and rely on *price inversion* i.e., the price is set before the costs of production (claims and expenses) are known. Insurers and their insureds both face uncertainty with respect to these costs. When this uncertainty is especially pronounced due, for example, to changes in the legal, judicial or social landscape [or the risk environment], markets become suboptimal. Insurers will not provide every type of coverage for which demand exists. In particular, they avoid risks characterized by heightened adverse selection, basic ambiguity or a lack of diversification opportunities.[135]

Due to these imperfect information problems, proponents of governmental involvement conclude that aviation war and terrorism risks carry such a high level of ambiguity that makes them prone to market failure. As a remedial measure, they propose that "[t]he provision of a government backstop would inject some much needed certainty into the market, making it economically viable for the [private] insurance industry to provide adequate coverage at affordable prices".[136]

The second economic reason advanced by proponents of governmental involvement in the terrorism insurance market is the public goods theory. A public good is one that "all enjoy in common in the sense that each individual's consumption of such a good leads to no subtractions from any other individual's consumption of the good".[137] Proponents argue that the ability of free riders to enjoy public goods without paying for them makes it less profitable for businesses to produce them.[138] The tendency of businesses to underproduce public goods sometimes makes it beneficial for governments to produce these goods and services at an efficient level.

---

[132] OECD (2005) pp. 68–69.

[133] Karl and Laster (2007) p. 9.

[134] Idem.

[135] Idem.

[136] Idem.

[137] Samuelson (1954).

[138] Even when society's collective willingness to pay for these goods exceeds their cost of production, individuals may be unwilling to pay a price high enough to warrant the production. Businesses will therefore tend to produce fewer of these goods than is socially optimal, or none at all. See Karl and Laster (2007) p. 10.

Proponents argue that whereas government counter-terrorism and crisis management policies following an attack mitigate the risks associated with global terrorism, they are also natural extensions of the government's role in national defence and law enforcement—traditional public goods.[139] In like manner, the presence of a terrorism insurance market with enough capacity to meet the needs of the economy is a public good which reduces the level of uncertainty both before and after a terrorist event.[140] The upshot of this argument then is that, if governments are willing to continue provision of other public goods, then they must equally play a role in the provision of aviation war and terrorism insurance since "[s]ecurity, stability, respect for property rights and the absence of violence and coercion are among the cornerstones of any society".[141]

A third economic reason advanced by proponents of governmental involvement in the provision of terrorism insurance takes its roots from the concept of externalities. "Externalities arise when the actions of one party make another worse or better off, yet the first party neither bears the costs nor receives the benefits of his effect on others".[142] A major terrorist attack might easily result in externalities with cascading losses, even for those who are insured against the risk. After an attack, insurers' forced sale of securities in order to raise capital could adversely affect the bond and stock markets. The corporate bond market will be especially hurt since in the US, insurers hold about 25 % of all corporate bonds, many of which are thinly traded.[143] Bankruptcies of insurers and other companies would impose further deadweight losses on the economy. In the aviation sector, the unavailability of adequate and affordable aviation war and terrorism risk insurance coverage following September 11, 2001, caused airlines to threaten to severely cut back their operations, with disruptive implications for the global economy as a whole. According to proponents, a government backstop can help prevent these losses in the event of a major attack by: helping insurers remain solvent, assuring that insured victims of terrorist attacks receive policy benefits promptly; and, by preventing a run on insurers and the forced sale of securities.[144]

7.6 Limits and Drawbacks of Governmental Involvement in the Provision of Insurance Coverage for Aviation War and Terrorism Risks

According to one author, "[t]hree primary theories of public policy are involved in evaluating the role of government in addressing market failures in the insurance industry: laissez faire, public interest and market

[139] Idem.

[140] Idem.

[141] Idem.

[142] Idem.

[143] Idem.

[144] Idem., pp. 10–11.

enhancement".[145] At one end of the spectrum, "[l]aissez faire theory maintains that any market-based equilibrium, however imperfect, provides a more efficient allocation of resources within the economy than an equilibrium involving government intervention".[146] The theory therefore claims that government insurance programs create several types of inefficiencies in the market. By way of examples, proponents of the theory point out that provision of subsidized insurance by the government is likely to displace private market activity that would have taken place, thereby "crowding out" private attempts to enter the market and permanently locking in an inefficient solution to financing catastrophe losses.[147] This "crowding out" effect is particularly characteristic of prolonged governmental involvement and it would seem to explain why a private market for aviation war and terrorism risk insurance has failed to develop in the U.S. over the years, despite the high demand for that kind of insurance.

According to proponents of the laissez faire theory, government programs also tend to develop constituencies that engage in intensive lobbying to maintain government support, strengthening concerns about rent-seeking by special interest groups.[148] In support, they argue that government intervention in markets occurs primarily as a result of the rent-seeking behaviour of special interest groups. Thus, industry calls for government protection against catastrophic risks are viewed as opportunistic attempts by these special interest groups to secure an *ex ante* transfer of wealth from taxpayers.[149]

Further, the laissez faire theory maintains that government subsidized insurance tends to create moral hazard problems whereby policyholders underinvest in loss prevention. The availability of insurance at subsidized rates tends to reduce risk mitigation efforts on the part of the insureds since they will receive indemnification for their losses irrespective of their mitigation efforts. *Ex post* indemnification of losses, as in the case of most government provided emergency guarantee programs, similarly decrease the incentive to mitigate the amount of expected losses. Such drawbacks have been cumulatively described as the mitigation incentive effects of governmental intervention in the provision of terrorism insurance.[150] Actuarial (i.e., risk-based) pricing of government provided insurance can alleviate some of these problems. However, because the design of government-provided war risk insurance programs is determined by politics rather than the operation of markets, even unsubsidized insurance programs are not likely to represent the most effective alternative.[151]

---

[145] Cummins (2006) pp. 370–371.

[146] Idem., p. 371.

[147] Jaffee (2004) p. 213.

[148] Cummins (2006) p. 371.

[149] Jaffee (2004) p. 214. See also Stigler (1971).

[150] Jaffee (2004).

[151] Cummins (2006) p. 371.

At the other end of the spectrum, the public interest theory of regulation contests the laissez faire view. This theory suggests that market failures can lead to suboptimal allocation of resources and that government intervention targeted at addressing the market failures can improve welfare.[152] Although laissez faire policy suggests that private sector coordination is the *sine qua non* for optimal allocation of resources, public interest theory suggests that, in specific instances, the government can improve upon the market equilibrium by substituting for private sector coordination. Proponents of public interest theory therefore maintain that the information asymmetries and bankruptcy costs associated with the private market for terrorism insurance may necessitate the role of the government in "completing" the market for terrorism insurance.[153] However, as discussed in Chap. 4 such theories are premised upon assumptions that governmental intervention in the market will effectively overcome the problems posed by the conditions of imperfect competition (i.e., imperfect information, existence of externalities and transaction costs).

The third view of public policy intervention—the market-enhancing view—lies somewhere between the two extremes. This theory recognizes that market failures can create suboptimal allocations of wealth (as argued by the laissez faire theory), and that private sector coordination is not always effective (as maintained by the public interest theory). From a "best of both worlds" perspective, the market-enhancing view recognizes that government intervention can help facilitate the creation or enhancement of private institutions for solving market failures and holds that "public policy should facilitate the development of the private market but should not create new governmental institutions to substitute for private institutions".[154]

7.7 Conclusion

This chapter has explored the issue of governmental involvement in the provision of insurance coverage or other suitable equivalent to the air transport industry in connection with aviation war and terrorism risks. A strong case has been made for such governmental involvement in the air transport industry based, at the very minimum, on what pertains in other areas of economic endeavour prone to large catastrophic risks. Clearly, sustained governmental involvement in the provision of

[152] Idem.

[153] Idem.

[154] Idem. See also Lewis and Murdock (1999) p. 53, where the authors suggest that one way of financing catastrophic risks is for the government to provide initial liquidity for the creation of new financial instruments (e.g., an industry excess-of-loss contract), a facility that would enable the insurance industry inter-temporally diversify extreme risks. The authors argue that if the market is provided with sufficient mechanisms for the private sector to crowd out the public sector, such governmental intervention will allow insurance companies to make the necessary investments in business systems to support the new market. The governmental intervention will then be seen as facilitating the revival of, instead of replacing, the private insurance market.

insurance ultimately stifles the recovery and growth of the conventional markets as probably demonstrated in the US. Thus, any government plan should provide a clear path or at least a strategy for a path to termination.[155] As regards the most appropriate manner in which governments may go about performing this role, it appears that, the market-enhancing viewpoint offers the most appealing alternative. This has been appositely summed up by one writer who notes that, the market enhancing viewpoint presupposes that[,] in the event of an insurance market failure, governmental intervention in the provision of insurance should be conceived as a temporary means of facilitating the restoration of the private markets and not as a permanent solution to the market failure. Governments may have deeper pockets but governmental resources are not infinite. Consequently, for governmental involvement to be meaningful and sustainable, it should give priority to actions that reactivate the private markets.[156]

References

1041 UNTS 358, (1963) Convention supplementary to the convention on third party liability in the field of nuclear energy (as amended by the additional protocol of 28th January 1964 and by the protocol of 16th November 1982)

1063 UNTS 265, (1963) Convention on civil liability for nuclear damage

1110 UNTS 57, (1971) International Convention on the Establishment of an International Fund for Compensation for Oil Pollution Damage

1956 UNTS 255, (1992) Protocol to the International Convention on Civil Liability for Oil Pollution Damage of 29 November 1969

1956 UNTS 330, (1992) Protocol of 1992 to amend the International Convention on the Establishment of an International Fund for Compensation for Oil Pollution Damage of 18 December 1971

2241 UNTS 270, (1997) Protocol to Amend the Vienna Convention on Civil Liability for Nuclear Damage

66 Fed. Reg. 49075 (2001) Presidential Determination No. 01-29 of September 23, 2001—Provision of Aviation Insurance Coverage for Commercial Air Carrier Service in Domestic and International Operations. (US)

74 Fed. Reg. 43617 (2009) Presidential Memorandum of August 21 2009 – Provision of Aviation Insurance Coverage for Commercial Air Carrier Service in Domestic and International Operations. (US)

915 RFS (2009) FAA Reauthorization Act of 2009. (U.S.)

956 UNTS 263, (1960) Convention on third party liability in the field of nuclear energy

973 UNTS 3, (1969) International Convention on Civil Liability for Oil Pollution Damage

Air Transport Association (U.S.) (2007) Extension of the Federal Aviation Administration War-Risk Insurance Program. ATA Issue Brief

Appendix to IAEA INFCIRC/567 (1997) Convention on supplementary compensation for nuclear damage (not yet in force)

Atkins S (2007) State involvement in provision of terrorism insurance. In: Marangos H (ed) War risks and terrorism. Insurance Institute of London, London, pp 132–145

Balfour J (2002) EC policy on state aid to airlines following 11th September 2001. Air Space Law XXVII(6):398–405

[155] Jaffee (2004).

[156] Idem., p. 217.

Bovis CH (2004–2005) The application of state aid rules to the European Union transport sectors. Colum J Eur Law 11(3):557–604

Cluff LD, Jonkman S (2002) Terrorism insurance post 9/11: principles for designing private/public programs. In: Liedtke PM, Courbage C (eds) Insurance and September 11 – one year after – impact, lessons and unresolved issues. International Association for the Study of Insurance Economics – The Geneva Association, Geneva, pp 211–222

Cummins JD (2006) Should the government provide insurance for catastrophes? Fed Res Bank St Louis Rev 88(4):337–379

Dempsey PS (2004) European aviation law. Kluwer Law International, The Hague

Dempsey PS, Buzdugan M, Nyampong Y (2005) The evolution of Canadian Air Transport Policy. In: The McGill Concordia Report on International Aviation Policy for Canada. Center for Research of Air and Space Law, Montreal, pp 11–36

EC COM (2001) 574 final (2001) Communication from the Commission to the European Parliament and the Council on the repercussions of the terrorist attacks in the United States on the air transport industry

EC COM (2002) 320 final (2002) Communication from the Commission on Insurance in the Air Transport sector following the terrorist attacks of 11 September 2001 in the United States. COM (2002) 320 final/

EC 94/C 350/07 (1994) Application of Articles 92 and 93 of the EC Treaty and Article 61 of the EEA agreement to State aids in the aviation sector

EC Regulation 285/2010 (2010) Commission Regulation (EU) No. 285/2010 of 6 April 2010 amending Regulation (EC) No. 785/2004 of the European Parliament and of the Council on Insurance Requirements for Air Carriers and Aircraft operators. OJ, L 87/19

EC Regulation 868/2004 (2004) Parliament and Council Regulation (EC) 868/2004 of 21 April 2004 concerning protection against subsidisation and unfair pricing practices causing injury to Community air carriers in the supply of air services from countries not members of the European Community. OJ, L 162/1

EC State Aid No. NN 123/2002 (2003g) Authorisation for State aid pursuant to Articles 87 and 88 of the EC Treaty – Cases where the Commission raises no objections: State Aid No. NN 123/2002 – United Kingdom – Extension of guarantee scheme for aviation insurance (1 January 2001–31 October 2002). OJ, C 206/19

EC State Aid No. NN 124/2002 (2003h) Authorisation for State aid pursuant to Articles 87 and 88 of the EC Treaty – Cases where the Commission raises no objections: State Aid No. NN 124/2002 – Austria – Extension of the State-guaranteed scheme for aviation industry (1 January 2002 to 31 October 2002). OJ, C 230/4

EC State Aid No. NN 125/2002 (2003i) Authorisation for State aid pursuant to Articles 87 and 88 of the EC Treaty – Cases where the Commission raises no objections: State Aid No. NN 125/2002 – Germany – Extension of the State-guaranteed scheme for aviation industry (1 January 2002 to 31 October 2002). OJ, C 230/4

EC State Aid No. NN 168/2001 (2003j) Authorisation for State aid pursuant to Articles 87 and 88 of the EC Treaty – Cases where the Commission raises no objections: State Aid No. NN 168/2001 – Sweden – Extension of aviation insurance grarantee (25 October 2001–30 June 2002). OJ, C 206/20

EC State Aid No. NN 169/2001 (2003k) Authorisation for State aid pursuant to Articles 87 and 88 of the EC Treaty – Cases where the Commission raises no objections: State Aid No. NN 169/2001 – Spain – Extension of guarantee scheme for aviation industry (1 January 2002 to 31 October 2002). OJ, C 206/20

EC State Aid No. NN 171/2001 (2003l) Authorisation for State aid pursuant to Articles 87 and 88 of the EC Treaty – Cases where the Commission raises no objections: State Aid No. NN 171/2001 – Denmark – Extension of Guarantee scheme for aviation industry (25 November 2001 to 31 July 2002). OJ, C 206/21

EC State Aid No. NN 173/2001 (2003m) Authorisation for State aid pursuant to Articles 87 and 88 of the EC Treaty – Cases where the Commission raises no objections: State Aid No. NN 173/2001 – Portugal – Extension of the state-guaranteed aviation-risk cover scheme. OJ, C 230/4

EC State Aid No. NN 19/2002 (2003a) Authorisation for State aid pursuant to Articles 87 and 88 of the EC Treaty – Cases where the Commission raises no objections: State Aid No. NN 19/2002 – France – Extension of State-guarantee scheme for aviation industry (1 January 2002 to 31 October 2002). OJ, C 206/19

EC State Aid No. NN 32/2002 (2003b) Authorisation for State aid pursuant to Articles 87 and 88 of the EC Treaty – Cases where the Commission raises no objections: State Aid No. NN 32/2002 – Ireland – Extension of guarantee scheme for aviation industry (1 January 2002 to 31 October 2002). OJ, C 206/19

EC State Aid No. NN 43/2002 (2003c) Authorisation for State aid pursuant to Articles 87 and 88 of the EC Treaty – Cases where the Commission raises no objections: State Aid No. NN 43/2002 – United Kingdom – Extension of airline insurance (23 October–31 December 2001). OJ, C 87/32

EC State Aid No. NN 47/2003 (2003d) Authorisation for State aid pursuant to Articles 87 and 88 of the EC Treaty – Cases where the Commission raises no objections: State Aid No. NN 47/2003 – Netherlands – Extension of guarantee scheme for aviation industry (1 January 2002 to 31 October 2002). OJ, C 206/17

EC State Aid No. NN 52/2002 (2003e) Authorisation for State aid pursuant to Articles 87 and 88 of the EC Treaty – Cases where the Commission raises no objections: State Aid No. NN 52/2002: Belgium – Extension of State guaranteed scheme to cover aviation risks (25 November 2001–31 October 2002). OJ, C 230/5

EC State Aid No. NN 55/2003 (2003f) Authorisation for State aid pursuant to Articles 87 and 88 of the EC Treaty – Cases where the Commission raises no objections: State Aid No. NN 55/2003 – Finland – Extension of State-guarantee scheme to cover aviation risks (26 December 2001 to 31 October 2002). OJ, C 206/17

European Commission (2001) Terrorist attacks and air transport: commission takes a series of urgent measures. IP/01/1306, 24 September 2001. Available via http://europa.eu/rapid/pressReleasesAction.do?reference=IP/01/1306&format=HTML&aged=0&language=EN&guiLanguage=en

Fitzsimmons A (2004) Terrorism – maximizing the insurability of a catastrophe risk. Ann Air Space Law XXIX:67

Government Accountability Office (1994) Aviation insurance: Federal Insurance Program needs improvements to ensure success. GAO/RCED-94-151

Government Accountability Office (1997) Aviation insurance: issues related to the reauthorization of FAA's Aviation Insurance Program. GAO/T-RCED-97-115

Government of Canada, Privy Council (2001a) Amendments to order in Council P.C. 2001–1675 which allow the Minister of Transport to provide an indemnity to any supplier of goods or services to an airport operator or an airline in Canada. Order in Council No. P.C. 2001–1827, October 4 2010

Government of Canada, Privy Council (2001b) Authority to provide an indemnity to anyone involved in the air transportation industry for war risk liability insurance coverage, for a period of ninety days. Order in Council No. P.C. 2001–1675, September 22 2001

Government of Canada, Privy Council (2002a) Authority to continue to provide an indemnity to essential air service operators in Canada for WAR RISK LIABILITY INSURANCE COVERAGE, up until December 31, 2003. Order in Council No. P.C. 2002–2228, December 13 2002

Government of Canada, Privy Council (2002b) Authority to provide an indemnity to essential air service operators in Canada for WAR RISK LIABILITY INSURANCE COVERAGE, effective March 22, 2002. Order in Council No. P.C. 2002–0369, March 15 2002

Government of Canada, Privy Council (2003) Authority to continue to provide an indemnity to essential air service operators in Canada for WAR RISK LIABILITY INSURANCE COVERAGE, up until December 31, 2004. Order in Council No. P.C. 2003–1833, November 19 2003

Government of Canada, Privy Council (2004) Authority to continue to provide an indemnity to essential air service operators in Canada for WAR RISK LIABILITY INSURANCE COVERAGE, up until December 31, 2005. Order in Council No. P.C. 2004–1538, December 14 2004

Government of Canada, Privy Council (2005) Authority to continue to provide an indemnity to essential air service operators in Canada for WAR RISK LIABILITY INSURANCE COVERAGE, up until December 31, 2007. Order in Council No. P.C. 2005–2248, November 28 2005

Government of Canada, Privy Council (2007) Authority to continue to provide an indemnity to essential air service operators in Canada for AVIATION WAR RISK LIABILITY PROGRAM, from January 1, 2008 to December 31, 2008, renewable at 120-day intervals. Order in Council No. P.C. 2007–1867, December 6 2007

Government of Canada, Privy Council (2008) Authority to continue to provide an indemnity to essential air service operators in Canada for WAR RISK LIABILITY INSURANCE COVERAGE over the 120-day period commencing on January 1, 2009 and ending on April 30, 2009. Order in Council No. P.C. 2008–1849, December 4 2008

Government of Canada, Privy Council (2009) Authority to continue to provide an indemnity to essential air service operators in Canada for WAR RISK LIABILITY INSURANCE COVERAGE for the period commencing on May 1, 2009 and ending on December 31, 2010. Order in Council No. P.C. 2009–1648, April 23 2009

IMO Doc. No. LEG/CONF.14/20, (2003) Protocol of 2003 to the International Convention on the Establishment of an International Fund for Compensation for Oil Pollution Damage, 1992

International Oil Pollution Compensation Funds (2009) The international regime for compensation for oil pollution damage [unpublished]

Jack I (2001) Feds consider insuring aviation against terrorists: private firms shy away: air industry prefers reaching deal with insurers. National Post, 5 October 2001

Jaffee DM (2004) The role of government in the coverage of terrorism risks. In: Policy issues in insurance no. 9 – terrorism risk insurance in OECD countries. Organisation for Economic Cooperation and Development (OECD), Paris, pp 189–230

Karl K, Laster D (2007) The economic case for a private-public terrorism insurance partnership. Swiss Re Economic Research and Consulting, Zurich

Kjelgaard C (2002) Risky business. Flight International 42–45

Levmore S, Logue KD (2003) Insuring against terrorism – and crime. Mich Law Rev 102:268

Lewis C, Murdock KC (1999) Alternative means of redistributing catastrophic risk in a national risk-management system. In: Froot KA (ed) The financing of catastrophe risk. University of Chicago Press, Chicago, pp 51–92

Libby JB (1995) War risk aviation exclusions. J Air Law Com 60:605

Margo RD (2000) Aviation insurance: the law and practice of aviation insurance, including hovercraft and spacecraft insurance, 3dth edn. Butterworths, London

Margo RD (2002) 11 September 2001 – an aviation insurance perspective. Air Space Law XXVII (6):386–397

Michel-Kerjan E (2005) Financial protection of critical infrastructure: uncertainty, insurability and terrorism risk. Institut Veolia Environnement, Paris

Nuclear Risk Insurers Ltd. (2008) The insurance of nuclear installations and associated risks. Nuclear Pools website http://www.nuclearpools.com/aboutUs.asp

OECD (2005) Possible role of government in the coverage of terrorism risk. In: Policy issues in insurance no. 9 – terrorism risk insurance in OECD Countries OECD, Paris, pp 67–86

Pillar PR (2001) Terrorism and U.S. foreign policy. Brookings Institution Press, Washington

Pub L 110-160, 121 Stat. 1839-1843 (2007) Terrorism Risk Insurance Program Reauthorization Act of 2007. (US)

Pub. L. No. 107-296 116 STAT 2138 (2002) Homeland Security Act of 2002. (US)

Pub. L. No. 107-42 115 STAT. 230 (2001b) Air Transportation Safety and System Stabilization Act. (USA)

Pub. L. No. 107-42, 115 STAT. 230 (2001a) Air Transportation Safety and System Stabilization Act. (US)

Pub. L. No. 108-11 117 STAT. 559 (2003) Emergency Wartime Supplemental Appropriations Act, 2003. (US)
Pub. L. No. 108-176 117 STAT. 2490 (2003b) Vision 100 – Century of Aviation Reauthorization Act. (US)
Pub. L. No. 108-176, 117 STAT. 2490 (2003a) Vision 100 – Century of Aviation Reauthorization Act
Pub. L. No. 108-447 118 STAT. 2809 (2004) Consolidated Appropriations Act, 2005. (US)
Pub. L. No. 109-115 119 STAT. 2396 (2005) Transportation, Treasury, Housing and Urban Development, the Judiciary, the District of Columbia, and Independent Agencies Appropriations Act, 2006. (US)
Pub. L. No. 109-144 119 STAT. 2660 15 U.S.C. 6701 note (2005) Terrorism Risk Insurance Extension Act of 2005. (US)
Pub. L. No. 110-161 121 STAT. 1844 (2007) Consolidated Appropriations Act, 2008. (US)
Pub. L. No. 110-181 122 STAT. 3 (2008) National Defense Authorization Act for Fiscal Year 2008. (US)
Pub. L. No. 110-253 122 STAT. 2417 (2008) Federal Aviation Administration Extension Act of 2008. (US)
Pub. L. No. 110-330 122 STAT. 3717 (2008) Federal Aviation Administration Extension Act of 2008, Part II. (US)
Pub. L. No. 110-5 121 STAT. 8 (2007) Revised Continuing Appropriations Resolution, 2007. (US)
Pub. L. No. 111-116 123 STAT. 3032 (2009) Fiscal Year 2010 Federal Aviation Administration Extension Act, Part II. (US)
Pub. L. No. 111-117 123 STAT. 3043 (2009) Consolidated Appropriations Act, 2010. (US)
Pub. L. No. 111-12 123 STAT. 1457 (2009) Federal Aviation Administration Extension Act of 2009. (US)
Pub. L. No. 111-69 123 STAT. 2054 (2009) Fiscal Year 2010 Federal Aviation Administration Extension Act. (US)
Samuelson P (1954) The pure theory of public expenditure. Rev Econ Stats 36(4):387–389
Stewart S (2001) Ottawa covers air insurance: 90-day emergency aid: gives airlines, airports coverage against terrorism. National Post, 24 September 2001
Stigler GJ (1971) The theory of economic regulation. Bell J Econ Manag Sci 2(1):3–21
Tompkins GN (2008) Some thoughts to ponder when considering whether to adopt the new aviation general Risks and unlawful interference conventions proposed by ICAO. Air Space Law XXXIII(2):81–84
Transport Canada (2001) Government extends indemnity for air industry insurance. No. H151/01, December 6, 2001. Available via http://www.tc.gc.ca/eng/mediaroom/releases-nat-2001-01_h151e-4337.htm
Transport Canada (2002a) Government extends indemnity for air industry insurance. No. H079/02, July 18, 2002. Available via http://www.tc.gc.ca/eng/mediaroom/releases-nat-2002-02_h079e-4348.htm
Transport Canada (2002b) Government extends indemnity for air industry insurance. No. H009/02, February 1, 2002. Available via http://www.tc.gc.ca/eng/mediaroom/releases-nat-2002-02_h009e-5056.htm
Transport Canada (2002c) Government of canada extends indemnity for air industry insurance to new entrants. No. H057/02, June 5 2002. Available via http://www.tc.gc.ca/eng/mediaroom/releases-nat-2002-02_h057e-4704.htm
Transport Canada (2002d) Government renews indemnity for air industry insurance. No. H026/02, March 15, 2002. Available via http://www.tc.gc.ca/eng/mediaroom/releases-nat-2002-02_h026e-3482.htm
Transport Canada (2009a) Declaration (2009-05-01)
Transport Canada (2009b) Undertaking with respect to Aviation War Risk Liability (2009-05-01)
EC Treaty (2002) Treaty establishing the European Community. OJ, C 325/22

Chapter 8
Findings and Conclusions: Towards Sustainable Insurance of Aviation War and Terrorism Risks

The object of this book has been to explore the central issues underlying the perennial problem of providing the air transport industry with adequate and sustainable insurance coverage for aviation war and terrorism risks. We began by describing the manner in which the conventional insurance industry has been used as the primary risk management tool for addressing the massive economic repercussions of such risks upon the air transport industry. We also made an effort to identify the fundamental reasons why conventional insurance markets covering such large catastrophic risks "fail" in the period immediately following the occurrence of an extreme insured event. We then analyzed various complementary solutions that have been advanced for the purpose of enhancing the ability of the conventional insurance industry to provide coverage for such risks as well as alternative solutions advanced and even implemented as substitutes for conventional insurance coverage. Below, we conclude by setting out some of the major findings and conclusions that were made during this research.

8.1 Can the Conventional Insurance Industry Be Expected to Provide Sustainable and Adequate Insurance Coverage to the Global Air Transport Industry for Aviation War and Terrorism Risks?

To a very large extent, aviation war and terrorism risks are considered to be non-actuarial risks. As a risk management mechanism, conventional insurance involves transfer of risk at a price fixed *ex ante*, and this presupposes that a premium corresponding to the risk transferred can be calculated and charged. This, in turn, requires that two conditions are met. It must be possible to calculate the maximum probable loss associated with the risk (i.e., the probability of insured damage multiplied by the estimated size of the damage). These

Y.O.M. Nyampong, *Insuring the Air Transport Industry Against Aviation War and Terrorism Risks and Allied Perils*, DOI 10.1007/978-3-642-32433-8_8,

probabilities are best obtained from historical data and empirical experience. When no such data and experience is available as is usually the case with aviation war and terrorism risks, insurers must rely on assessments. However, such assessments are deemed to be more or less unreliable resulting in a greater degree of uncertainty. Secondly, the Law of Large Numbers must be applicable to the risk in question. The risks must be similar but not highly correlated—the larger the number of such risks, the closer the real damage cost will approach the underlying probability.

The conventional insurance industry often claims that capacity constraints emerge because one or both of these conditions are not met. If the characteristics of the risk are such that the probable maximum loss cannot be estimated with confidence, a situation of heightened uncertainty arises and the risk is deemed not amenable to estimation by actuarial principles. If the number of similar risks is too low, the Law of Large Numbers is not applicable. Such risks too are considered to be non-actuarial. In each of these cases, the capital that needs to be reserved by insurers to back coverage of the risk cannot be fully determined; hence the risk cannot be priced with confidence. Conventional insurers normally resolve this dilemma by behaving in a risk-averse manner, venturing only a small amount of their capital on the incalculable risk.

Flowing from their very nature and as demonstrated by the events of September 11, 2001, it is difficult (if not impossible) for the conventional insurance industry to estimate the probable maximum loss associated with aviation war and terrorism risks, particularly where third-party liability is involved. Also, application of the Law of Large Numbers does not yield any useful results in the case of aviation war and terrorism risks because, as compared to other lines of insurance, the global pool of aviation operators is relatively small and yet heavily concentrated. In addition, the air transport industry's potential claims exposure from aviation war and terrorism risks is truly enormous both in absolute amounts and in relation to the conventional insurance industry's overall capital base.

It is quite clear from the foregoing that, conventional insurance is not well suited to fully provide the desired depth and scope of coverage to the air transport industry for aviation war and terrorism risks. The insurance industry's standard procedure of building up adequate reserves from current premium income to pay claims in each line of insurance is not practicable for large catastrophic risks such as aviation war and terrorism risks. The industry also faces immense difficulty in raising the level of capital required to provide adequate and sustainable coverage to the air transport industry for such risks, particularly in the post-event period when uncertainty and ambiguity are heightened. Nonetheless, if such non-actuarial risks are to be reasonably covered by the conventional insurance industry, then alternative methods of obtaining risk capital must be considered and pursued as a matter of necessity.

8.2 Is It Possible to Enhance the Capacity of the Conventional Insurance Industry to Cover Aviation War and Terrorism Risks Through the Use of Alternative Risk Financing and Alternative Risk Transfer Mechanisms?

It is the author's firm belief that resorting to a number of Alternative Risk Financing (ARF) and Alternative Risk Transfer (ART) instruments, particularly those that tap into the deeper reserves of the capital markets in innovative ways should be able to bridge the gap between sound asset-to-liability ratios and the solvency threshold of conventional insurance companies which insure aviation war and terrorism risks. Within the insurance system, the reinsurance and retrocessionary markets for catastrophic aviation war and terrorism risks are quite well developed, "but market capacity and price developments are highly influenced by recent loss experiences. Furthermore, the insurance premiums for higher risk layers can become excessively expensive if the uncertainties associated with ... [large catastrophic] events are high. This condition is highly relevant for terrorism risk exposures".[1]

Captives, risk retention groups and other mutual arrangements among air transport operators may be capable of providing some insurance coverage for aviation war and terrorism risks but are likely to suffer from the same capital capacity constraints that affect conventional insurance markets. Several capital market mechanisms may be used as a means of enhancing the capacity of the conventional insurance industry to handle aviation war and terrorism risks. The use of different risk financing channels in sourcing contingent capital, for instance, could reduce volatilities in the cost of capital, and in so doing, could also lower financing expenditures.[2] In the author's opinion, however, the securitization of aviation war and terrorism risks in similar fashion as Cat-bonds presents the best potential. In this regard, it has been observed by one writer that:

> risk-linked securities have evolved into a relatively independent market segment for catastrophe risk-transfer where the dependency on the traditional reinsurance market is reduced. This might help dampen price volatilities in the global reinsurance market and could gradually help expand reinsurance capacity. As a potential sign of this development, the price reaction to the WTC incidence appeared more measured than the reaction observed after Hurricane Andrews in 1992. FIFA's Golden Goal Finance transaction to cover potential loss of revenues and the Swiss Re sponsored Vita Capital transaction in cover of excess mortality risk also show that it is possible to securitize terrorism risk exposures and that the cat-bond market can provide incremental capacity for terrorism risk insurance.[3]

It has been suggested that, in order to achieve an effective and optimal means of enhancing the capacity of the conventional insurance market *vis-à-vis* aviation war and terrorism risks, a variety of risk financing instruments should be used and each

[1] Andersen (2005) p. 179.

[2] Mutenga and Staikouras (2007) p. 228.

[3] Andersen (2005) p. 179.

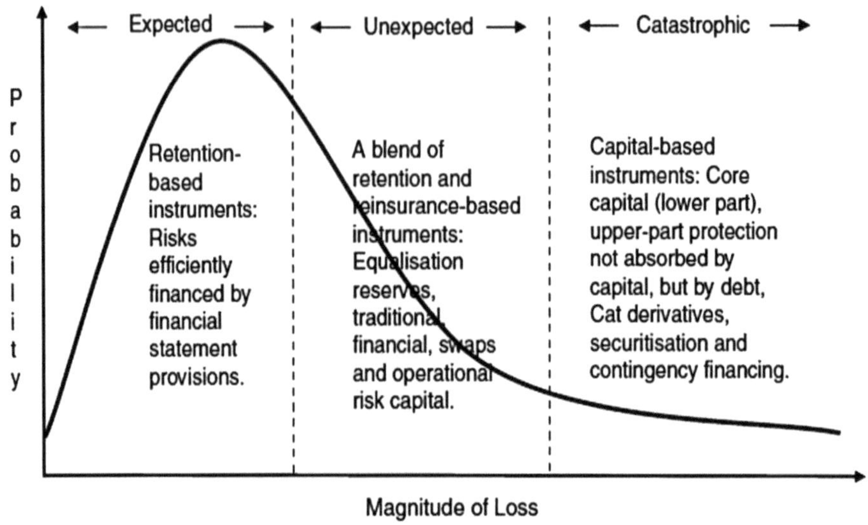

Fig. 8.1 Efficient utilization of insurance equity: a layered risk financing structure. Source: Mutenga and Staikouras (2007), p. 228

should target specific classes of cash flows.[4] According to this suggestion, the entire range of any large catastrophic loss could be segregated into successive loss layers as depicted in Fig. 8.1, and "proper structuring of the risk financing process must entail understanding of the specific characteristics at each loss layer (or risk tier), simply because such structures should recognize the particular underlying cash flow features".[5] On the basis of this understanding, different risk financing channels could then be used to match different sections on the loss distribution.[6]

According to the proponents, this proposed "risk financing structure is designed to reallocate risk to those who have the competitive advantage to bear it. At the same time, it enables those who seek to strengthen their financial position to source leveraged capital at reduced costs. The structure aims to stabilize risk portfolios

[4] Mutenga and Staikouras (2007) p. 228.

[5] Idem.

[6] Idem. According to proponents of this theory, "[r]etention and reinsurance-based techniques do not go far enough in satisfying the risk transfer requirements of cash flows occupying the upper tails of the loss distribution. Losses on the tail of the loss distribution are best financed by capital market-based instruments. These instruments are bought with the sole purpose of alleviating the strain on capital and/or enhancing its role when depleted after a catastrophic event. They are efficient at financing the upper part of the loss distribution because vast amounts of capital are easily accessible, making it cheaper than accumulated reinsurance and retention-based equity. On the other hand, retention and reinsurance-based techniques are efficient in financing risks associated with higher probability of occurrence. Retention-based techniques are efficient at financing risk using the all-purpose equity supplied by shareholders and accumulated from retained earnings. Reinsurance-based instruments are used to provide protection for cash flows occupying the unexpected loss region – up to the tails of the loss distribution".

through the enhancement of the cost of risk trading, lower default probabilities, and make contingent capital available while maintaining target financial structures. The intention is that risk financing should be able to release assets committed to liabilities and should reduce the cost of risk capital in sponsoring all-purpose equity".[7]

8.3 Does the Unlawful Interference Compensation Convention of 2009 Provide a Viable, Sustainable and Insurable Solution?

ICAO's second attempt at enhancing the insurability of aviation war and terrorism risks following the events of September 11, 2001, resulted in the adoption of the UIC convention in May 2009. One of the fundamental objectives of the convention is to strike a balance between (1) protecting the interests of third-party victims and the need for equitable compensation on the one hand; and, (2) protecting the aviation industry from the financial consequences of damage caused by unlawful interference with aircraft on the other hand. The convention attempts to achieve this objective by segregating the full extent of third-party liability resulting from acts of unlawful interference involving aircraft into three tranches and establishing mechanisms to provide compensation in each tranche.

In the first tranche, the operator is strictly liable to pay compensation and, owing to the fact that liability exposure within this tranche is limited on the basis of the weight of the aircraft involved and, in any case, to a maximum of 700 million SDRs per-event, it is envisaged that the operator can (and indeed must) take out sufficient insurance in the conventional manner or other financial security to protect itself. Nevertheless, operators will have to pay insurance premiums for such coverage and these will invariably translate into higher ticket prices and cargo charges for passengers and consignors/consignees, respectively. Thus, ultimately, the first tier of compensation under the UIC convention will be financed by the operators and users of air transport.

In the second tier of compensation, the UIC convention establishes an International Civil Aviation Compensation Fund to pay compensation to third-party victims when their claims exceed the limits of the first tier. The International Fund will be financed by mandatory departure charges to be levied against each departing passenger and each tonne of cargo departing from a contracting state on an international flight. Again, the burden of paying third-party compensation within this tranche ultimately falls upon the shoulders of operators and users of air transport.

In the third tranche, the operator is again made liable to pay unlimited compensation to third-parties upon proof of fault. Although the operator may avoid or abate liability in this tier, the fact remains that a prudent operator will take steps to secure

[7] Idem., pp. 228–229.

some form of financial protection against its exposure to unlimited liability. This is because, the expectation of governmental support upon which this tier is based will not only remain invisible but also unachievable indefinitely in the absence of express commitments on the part of contracting States to provide support. Thus, even assuming that conventional insurance or guarantees are available for such exposure, they will require payment of very high premiums which in turn will have negative repercussions on the pricing of, and demand for, air transport services. However, this is not the case since conventional insurance at that level is simply not a tenable proposition.

Viewed in its entirety, one cannot help but conclude that the UIC convention is heavily skewed against the interests of air transport operators and users. It does not offer a viable solution to the insurance problems brought to the limelight in the aftermath of the terrorist events of September 11, 2001. In view of the foregoing, there is widespread doubt as to whether the convention will ever enter into force. This uncertainty is further exacerbated by article 40 of the convention which not only requires ratification by 35 contracting States for it to enter into force but also imposes a condition to the effect that, in the year preceding entry into force, the total number of passengers departing from airports in the States that have ratified, accepted, approved or acceded to the convention should amount to at least 750 million.[8]

8.4 Do States and Their Governments Have a Role to Play in the Insurance of Aviation War and Terrorism Risks?

Governments are already involved in the provision of insurance coverage or other financial security for large catastrophic risks in several other industrial sectors considered important drivers of economic development in their countries. The air transport industry is one such sector and therefore deserves to be given the necessary governmental support. States and their respective governments therefore have a role to play in the provision of insurance or other financial guarantee to the air transport industry to cover at least the upper layers of their liability exposure to aviation war and terrorism risks. As regards the appropriate manner in which this role is to be performed, it was found that there are in existence various models of governmental involvement in the provision of insurance. However, the overriding consideration in each case is that governmental involvement should not crowd out or stifle private sector initiatives towards the provision of such insurance. Accordingly, the market enhancing theory of governmental involvement appears to be the most appealing alternative.

[8] ICAO Doc. 9920 (2009), art. 40(1).

References

Andersen TJ (2005) International financing solutions to terrorism risk exposures. In: Policy issues in insurance no. 9 – terrorism risk insurance in OECD countries. Organisation for Economic Cooperation and Development (OECD), Paris, pp 149–188

ICAO Doc. 9920 (2009) Convention on Compensation for Damage Caused to Third Parties, Resulting from Acts of Unlawful Interference involving Aircraft

Mutenga S, Staikouras SK (2007) The theory of catastrophe risk financing: a look at the instruments that might transform the insurance industry. Geneva Papers (Issues & Practice) 32(2):222–245

Appendix A
Specimen FAA War Risk Insurance Policy

UNITED STATES OF AMERICA
DEPARTMENT OF TRANSPORTATION
FEDERAL AVIATION ADMINISTRATION

Policy No. ___________

WAR RISK INSURANCE FOR AIRCRAFT HULL, PASSENGER AND CREW LIABILITY, AND THIRD PARTY LIABILITY ISSUED PURSUANT TO CHAPTER 443 OF TITLE 49 OF THE UNITED STATES CODE DESCRIPTION OF COVERAGE UNDER THIS CONTRACT OF INSURANCE AND THOSE TERMS, CONDITIONS AND DEFINITIONS APPLICABLE TO ALL PARTS OF THIS CONTRACT OF INSURANCE

I. Coverage

The United States of America (hereinafter, the Insurer), represented by the Administrator of the Federal Aviation Administration, acting for the Secretary of Transportation (hereinafter the Administrator or FAA), hereby provides coverage of this War Risk Insurance Policy to ___________ (hereinafter the Insured), in accordance with applicable provisions of law and subject to all limitations thereof, and upon the payment of premiums, pursuant to the provisions of chapter 443 of title 49 of the United States Code (49 U.S.C. Sections 44301 through 44310 et seq.) (hereinafter, chapter 443) consisting of the following three parts:

A. Part I: Hull Insurance, covering physical damage to Equipment (including aircraft, aircraft spare parts and engines);
B. Part II: Comprehensive Liability Insurance, covering Premises, Products/Completed Operations, Hangarkeepers, Cargo and Mail Liabilities and Passenger and Crewmember Personal Injury, Bodily Injury or Death (excluding Third Party War Risk Liability); and
C. Part III: Third Party War Risk Liability.

Y.O.M. Nyampong, *Insuring the Air Transport Industry Against Aviation War and Terrorism Risks and Allied Perils*, DOI 10.1007/978-3-642-32433-8,

II. Terms and Conditions

A. The sections in this part shall apply to Part I (Hull Insurance), Part II (Comprehensive Insurance) and Part III (Third Party Insurance) of this Contract of Insurance.

B. Parts I, II, and III, set forth below, shall be considered to be separate elements of this War Risk Insurance Policy, and the deletion, cancellation, or any other means through which any one Part might be terminated or suspended shall have no effect upon the validity of any remaining Part or Parts.

C. The terms and conditions set forth in each Part shall be independent of any other Part, and shall not be construed to affect any other Part, provided, however, that the aggregate amount of insurance provided under all three Parts of this War Risk Insurance Policy shall not exceed US___________ per occurrence/per aircraft incurred by the Insured for the higher of third party losses or passenger liability limits set forth in Parts II or III of this Policy of Insurance.

D. The premiums for each Part of this War Risk Insurance Policy shall be separately determined, provided, however, that for air carriers who did hold a policy of insurance with the FAA on June 19, 2002, the total premium paid for this War Risk Insurance Policy shall not exceed twice the premium (annual and pro rata) paid by the Insured for Third Party War Risk Liability Insurance issued by the Administrator as of June 19, 2002, and for air carriers who did not hold a policy with the FAA on June 19, 2002, the total premium paid by the Insured for all three Parts of this War Risk Insurance Policy shall not exceed twice the premium for Third Party War Risk Liability Insurance as stipulated in Part III, Article IX, of this contract of insurance. The Insured shall provide any and all records and information requested by the Administrator for the purpose of calculating the premium for each Part of this War Risk Insurance policy. Failure to provide such records and information in a reasonable time as directed by the Administrator, shall void this War Risk Insurance Policy, and be cause for cancellation or non-renewal of this Policy of Insurance at the sole discretion of the Administrator.

E. This Policy of Insurance may be amended by the Administrator or terminated by either Party, and shall be either amended or terminated through the occurrence of any condition under chapter 443 that would affect the operation of this agreement.

F. Coverage of any aircraft listed as insured under this Policy of Insurance shall be held in abeyance if that aircraft is either (1) under charter by an agency of the United States or (2) is under the control of the Department of Defense during activation of the Civil Reserve Air Fleet (CRAF); and in either case, non-premium insurance is available pursuant to 49 U.S.C. Section 44305 of chapter 443. Coverage in full under this Policy of Insurance for such aircraft shall be restored when the aircraft completes said charter operations or is released from CRAF activation and non-premium insurance becomes unavailable under 49 U.S.C. Section 44305.

G. Coverage under this Policy does not apply to the following aircraft operations: (1) those that are intentionally conducted into or within geographic areas prohibited by a FAA Special Federal Aviation Regulations (SFAR); (2) operations that are not authorized by the air carriers operation specifications issued in compliance with Part 119 of Title 14 of the Code of Federal Regulations; or (3) any operations that are excluded by separate endorsement to this policy. If an endorsement to hold coverage afforded by this policy in abeyance is a condition of a waiver, exclusion or part of an FAA special permission, this Policy shall not be effective while the Insured is operating aircraft pursuant to that waiver, exclusion or FAA special permission.
H. The Insured shall notify the Insurer, in writing, of a pending Material Change which will affect the operational control of aircraft. Notification of the actual Material Change shall occur no later than 48 h after implementation. Notification by electronic mail will satisfy the reporting requirement so long as the Insured supplies the Insurer with a paper copy of this notice as soon as practicable thereafter.

III. Reconciliation of Actual and Estimated Premiums

Within 30 days of the expiration or termination of this Policy of Insurance, the insured shall calculate and submit data to reconcile the actual premium owed with the deposit premium estimated.

1. If the premium owed is greater than the deposit premium paid by the Insured, the Insured shall pay the premium difference to the Insurer.
2. If the premium owed is less than the deposit premium paid by the Insured, the Insurer will refund the premium difference.

IV. Activation, Amendment and Termination

A. Insurance coverage shall commence upon activation by the FAA, and this Policy of Insurance shall remain in effect until amended by the Administrator or terminated by either party.
B. This Policy of Insurance shall automatically terminate:

   1. Upon effective expiration of the authority of the Secretary of Transportation, subject to retroactive reauthorization, to provide insurance pursuant to chapter 443 of Title 49 of the United States Code; or
   2. Seven days after notice of termination has been directly communicated to the Insured, in writing, by the Administrator. A confirmation copy of this notice may be sent by facsimile or other additional means of communication or delivery to the Insured.

C. Termination of the entirety of this of Policy of Insurance shall terminate each and every Part of this War Risk Insurance Policy.
D. The Insurer has the right at its sole discretion to terminate this Contract of Insurance as of the date of a Material Change in the status of the Insured, if such Material Change to the Insured's status results in a condition which exceeds the statutory authority of the Insurer to provide insurance.
E. The Administrator may terminate this Policy of Insurance for default if the Insured fails to pay the premium or comply with the terms of the policy. In the event of default, the Insurer will forward a Notice of Default to the Insured. The Insured agrees to:

   1. Calculate the actual premium for all operations conducted by the Insured between acceptance of the Insured's application for insurance and the date and time of termination for default, and submit the calculation for the actual premium to the Insurer within 30 days of the date on the Notice of Default; and
   2. Pay the actual premium for all operations conducted by the Insured between acceptance of the Insured's application and the date and time of termination for default.
   3. Produce a list of all Other Insured Parties in accordance with paragraph VIII. A. of this part of the Policy of Insurance.

F. The Insured shall provide any and all records and information requested by the Administrator, including (but not limited to) copies of its commercial aviation liability and hull insurance policies applicable to the period of insurance and all schedules and attachments thereto, for the purpose of verifying the terms and scope of applicable commercial insurance coverage. The Insurer will maintain such Insured-provided commercial aviation liability and hull insurance information as confidential. Failure to provide such records and information in a reasonable time when requested shall be grounds for termination of this Policy of Insurance.

V. Definitions

A. "Air Transportation Business" means:

   1. The ownership, maintenance, sale or use of aircraft by an air operator, or
   2. Operations necessary or related to the providing of air transportation by the Insured, or
   3. Operations, including maintenance and supply of goods or services provided for, or by others which are necessary or related to the provision of air transportation by the Insured, or others approved by the Insured, or
   4. All non-revenue operations involving the operation of aircraft by the Insured, including company sponsored activities, events, promotions,

award programs and other events or happenings designed to further the Air Transportation Business, image and good will of the Insured.

B. "Air Operator" means the party exercising operational control (authority) over initiating, conducting or terminating a flight operation.
C. "Bodily Injury" means Bodily Injury sustained by any person caused by an Occurrence during the policy period, including sickness, disease, mental anguish, trauma, fright, disability or death at any time resulting therefrom or resulting from the apprehension thereof.
D. "Personal Injury" means:

  1. False arrest or imprisonment, delay, detention, malicious prosecution, discrimination, wrongful entry to or eviction from any Premises or Aircraft or vehicle or other invasion of the right of private occupancy; and
  2. Incidental medical malpractice, error or mistake by any physician, surgeon, nurse, medical technician or other person performing medical services on behalf of the Named Insured in the provision of immediate medical relief occasioned by a War Risk Occurrence.

E. "Policy Territory/Geographical Limits" means anywhere in the world.
F. "Property Damage" means (1) injury to or destruction of tangible property and (2) under Part III Third Party coverage, loss of use of tangible property, which has been physically injured or destroyed, provided such loss of use is caused by a War Risk Occurrence.
G. "War Risk Occurrences" (also "Occurrences" or "Occurrence") are defined as any loss or damage directly or indirectly arising from, or occasioned by, or happening through or in consequence of:

  1. War (whether declared or not, including war between Great Powers), invasion, acts of foreign enemies, warlike hostilities, civil war, rebellion, revolution, insurrection, martial law, exercise of military or usurped power, or any attempt at usurpation of power.
  2. Any hostile detonation of any weapon of war, including any employing atomic or nuclear fission and/or fusion or other like reaction of radioactive force or matter.
  3. Strikes, riots, civil commotions, or labor disturbances.
  4. Any act of one or more persons, whether or not agents of a sovereign power, for political or terrorist purposes and whether the loss or damage resulting therefrom is accidental or intentional, except for ransom or extortion demands. Payments in response to ransom or extortion demands are hereby specifically denied under this policy.
  5. Any malicious act or act of sabotage, vandalism or other act intended to cause loss or damage.
  6. Confiscation, nationalization, seizure, restraint, detention, appropriation, requisition for title or use by or under the order of any foreign government (whether civil or military or de facto) or foreign public or local authority. This policy will not cover any lawful government seizures of aircraft or spare parts that are the result of outstanding legal debts, taxes, fines, or

unlawful acts committed with the knowledge of airline officials or the unlawful operation of such aircraft by the named insured.

7. Hijacking or any unlawful seizure or wrongful exercise of control of the aircraft or crew (including any attempt at such seizure or control) made by any person or persons onboard the aircraft or otherwise, acting without the consent of the Insured.
8. The discharge or detonation of any weapon or explosive device while on an aircraft covered by this Policy of Insurance.

H. "Passenger," when mentioned under any liability provision of this Policy of Insurance, means a person who enters into a contract of transportation or other agreement by which the person is to be transported by the Insured, and who has acted upon that contract or other agreement by checking in for transportation and receiving a boarding pass or other means of identification for that transportation, whose subsequent movements are made in direct response to the places, times and means of transportation that are directly involved with, made as a consequence of, and thus governed by, the air operations conducted by the Insured. A person shall cease to be a passenger when that person's movements are no longer governed by the air operations conducted by the Insured pursuant to the contract of transportation or other agreement with the Insured. A person who is identified, at any time and in any way, as a knowing participant in the commission of a War Risk Occurrence shall not be considered as a passenger for the purposes of this Contract of Insurance.

I. "Additional Insureds" are persons with whom the Insured has entered into contracts of indemnity for coverage pursuant to Paragraphs I. B, Parts II and III of this Contract of Insurance.

J. "Material Change" is any substantial change in corporate ownership, financial or operational structure which affects the normal operation of insured aircraft, the operational control of insured aircraft by the Insured, or a change in the type of flight operation or configuration of aircraft operated by the Insured.

K. "Aircraft Accident" means Property Damage and/or Bodily Injury resulting from an Occurrence which has not been determined to be the consequence of items 1–8 as defined in "G" under the Definition section of this Policy.

VI. Coverage for Aircraft Outside the Control of the Insured

This Policy, subject to the exclusions contained herein, covers claims arising while an aircraft under the operational control of the Insured, is outside the control of the Insured by reason of any of the above perils. The aircraft shall be deemed to have been restored to the control of the Insured on the safe return of the aircraft to the Insured at an airfield which is entirely suitable for the operation of the aircraft. Such safe return shall require that the aircraft be parked with engines shut down with the crew under no duress. The Insurer waives no rights of subrogation or indemnification by virtue of this clause.

VII. Notification to the FAA

In all instances when notification to the FAA by the Insured is required by Article IV of Parts I, II, and III of this policy of insurance, it shall be made to the following:

Director, Aviation Insurance Program Office, AEP-20
Federal Aviation Administration
800 Independence Ave., SW
Room 939
Washington, DC 20591
Phone: 202-267-3331
FAX: 202-267-3278

Insurance Staff, Aviation Insurance Program Office AEP-20
Federal Aviation Administration
800 Independence Ave., SW
Washington, DC 20591
Phone: 202-267-3090, 202-267-9943, 202-267-3315, or 202-267-8947
FAX: 202-267-3324

At any time that notification cannot be made to the above numbers, the Insured shall contact the FAA Washington Operations Center at (202) 267-3333. The caller shall give the name of the Insured, a contact name, title, and telephone number.

VIII. Other Insured Parties

A. Definition and Identification of Other Insured Parties. For purposes of Parts I, II and III of this Policy of Insurance, the term "Insured" shall include Other Insured Parties, which are legal or private persons (1) that are aircraft lessors, lendors, lienholders, or other persons to the extent of their ownership or interest in an aircraft operated by ____________ (hereinafter, Other Insured Parties) and (2) that are listed in the commercial insurance policy of ____________ provided, however, that ____________ shall certify in writing that its agreements with the Other Insured Parties require the inclusion of the Other Insured Parties in the war risk insurance coverage obtained by ____________. Upon request by the Insurer, ____________ shall, within 10 working days, identify in writing all such Other Insured Parties to the Insurer.
B. Warranties Applicable to Other Insured Parties. The following warranties shall apply to Other Insured Parties identified under part A of this Article VIII:

1. Respecting equipment loss coverage under Part I to this Policy of Insurance, the Other Insured Parties shall be named as loss payees as their respective interests may appear;
2. Provisions of this Policy of Insurance, including this Article VIII, shall apply worldwide and have no territorial restrictions or limitations;
3. Respecting the interests of the Other Insured Parties in this Policy of Insurance, the insurance shall not be invalidated or impaired by any act or omission (including misrepresentation and nondisclosure) by the Insured or any other person (including use for illegal purposes of any Insured Equipment), and shall insure the Other Insured Parties regardless of any breach or violation of any representation, warranty, declaration, term, or condition contained in such policies by the Insured or any other Person;
4. If the Insurer terminates this Policy of Insurance for any reason whatsoever, or if it is allowed to lapse for nonpayment of premium, or if any material change is made in the Policy of Insurance which adversely affects the interest of any of the Other Insured Parties, such cancellation, lapse, or change shall not be effective as to the Other Insured Parties for 7 days after receipt by the Other Insured Parties of written notice from the Insured of such cancellation, lapse or change, or publication of notice of cancellation by the Insurer in the Federal Register;
5. The Insurer waives any rights of subrogation or any right of setoff (including for unpaid premiums), recoupment, counterclaim, or other deduction, whether by attachment or otherwise, against each Other Insured Party;
6. Insurance proceeds from this Policy of Insurance shall be primary without right of contribution from any other insurance that may be available to any Other Insured Parties;
7. All of the liability insurance provisions of the Policy of Insurance, except the limits of liability, shall operate in all respects as if a separate policy had been issued covering each Other Insured Party;
8. None of the Other Insured Parties shall be liable for any insurance premium; and
9. The Policy of Insurance authorizes a 50/50 Clause per Lloyd's Aviation Underwriters' Association Standard Policy Form AVS 103, or its equivalent.

IX. Supplemental Coverages

This Policy of Insurance shall pay, within the Limits of Liability stated elsewhere herein, the following expenses incurred by the Insured, provided, however, with respect to paragraphs A–E below, the Insurer's Limit of Liability for A–E combined shall not exceed the greater of \$25,000 per passenger or \$5,000,000 for any one War Risk Occurrence unless approved in advance by the Insurer.

A. Reasonable expenses incurred as a result of a War Risk Occurrence in respect of:

    1. The repatriation of Passengers;
    2. The repatriation of the body of any Passenger for burial and/or cremation;
    3. The funeral of any Passenger;
    4. Any necessary first aid, hospital, dental, mental health services, nursing treatment and medical services;
    5. The search for and/or recovery and/or identification of bodies of Passengers;
    6. Where possible, the reasonable transportation of a relative or friend of a Passenger killed or injured in a War Risk Occurrence to and from a place near the scene of the War Risk Occurrence or to and from a place where the Passenger has been removed or taken including necessary living expenses incurred by the relative or friend including but not limited to food, lodging, local transportation, and incidentals while they are away from home for a period not exceeding 1 year from the date of the War Risk Occurrence; and
    7. Other acts of humanity reasonably incurred.

B. Reasonable search and rescue operations for an aircraft insured under this Policy of Insurance which is determined to be missing and unreported after the computed maximum endurance of the flight has been exceeded.
C. Any attempted or actual removal of wreckage of an Aircraft insured under this Policy of Insurance, including the transportation, security costs, and storage or said wreckage and fees incurred by the Insured or its contractors to accomplish these tasks.
D. The foaming of a runway to prevent or mitigate possible loss or damage.
E. Any public inquiry or inquiry by the Federal Aviation Administration, National Transportation Safety Board or similar domestic or foreign governmental agency having investigative authority into an Occurrence involving an Aircraft insured under this Policy of Insurance that the Insured is called upon to pay.
F. For each War Risk Occurrence, all reasonable expenses, incurred by the Insured and/or the Insured's contractors, not to exceed the greater of $25,000 per passenger or $5,000,000, unless approved by the Insurer in advance, for each Aircraft/War Risk Occurrence incurred by the Insured not otherwise payable under this Policy, which arise out of and are a result of efforts expended by the Insured and/or assessed against the Insured solely by virtue of, (1) the requirements of the Aviation Disaster Family Assistance Act of 1996 (as may be amended from time to time) and any regulations imposed by the appropriate federal governmental agency as a result thereof, and/or (2) the "Principles of Understanding between ATA Carriers and the NTSB Regarding Certain Aviation Expenditures Related to the Recovery and Identification of Aviation Accident Victims."
G. For each war Risk Occurrence, all reasonable expenses not to exceed $5,000,000 unless approved by the Insurer in advance, incurred by the Insured and/or the Insured's contractors for the Occurrence site investigation (not otherwise covered by paragraph IX.E), security, and remediation.

X. Allocation of Costs Between the Insurer and Other Insurers with Whom the Insured Has a Policy of Insurance

A. If in the event of an Aircraft Accident, the information at the time of the response does not clearly identify the event as being a War Risk Occurrence, the Insured shall have the right to use airline service providers including the commercial aviation insurance company that would respond on behalf of the Insured to an Aircraft Accident to provide services, activities, or actions that are usual and customary following an Aircraft Accident. If the Aircraft Accident is subsequently determined to be a War Risk Occurrence, the FAA will reimburse the Insured for expenses the Insured incurred for items that are identified in Supplemental Coverages, Article IX, of this policy, subject to adherence to the limits and preapproval conditions specified therein.

B. If, in addition to this Policy of Insurance which, inter alia, covers the risks excluded by AVN48B/the Common North American Airline War Exclusion Clause, the Insured has another policy of insurance in full force and effect that has a "Hull All Risks" and/or a "Liability All Risks" policy which, inter alia, contains the War Hi-Jacking and Other Perils Exclusion Clause (AVN 48B) and/or the Common North American Airline War Exclusion Clause, the insurer agrees that in the event of an Occurrence involving loss or damage to an aircraft on the schedule of aircraft forming part of this Policy of Insurance and where agreement is reached between the "Hull All Risks" and/or the "Liability All Risks" insurers and the Administrator that the Insured has a valid claim under one or the other policy where nevertheless it cannot be resolved within 21 days from the date of the Occurrence as to which policy is liable, each of the aforementioned groups of insurers agree, without prejudice to their liability, to advance to the insured 50 % of such amount as may be mutually agreed between them until such time as final settlement of the claim is agreed, provided that:

1. The "Hull All Risks" and/or the "Liability All Risks" policies, and this Policy of Insurance are identically endorsed with this provisional claims settlement clause;
2. Within 12 months of the advance being made all insurers specified above in this paragraph agree to refer the matter to arbitration in the United States in accordance with the Statutory provision for arbitration for the time being in force;
3. Once the arbitration decision has been conveyed to the parties concerned, the "All Risks" insurers or the Insurer, as the case may be, shall repay the amount advanced by the other group of insurers together with interest for the period concerned, which is to be calculated using the London Clearing Banks' Base Rate;
4. If the "Hull All Risks" and/or the "Liability All Risks" policies and this Policy of Insurance contain differing amounts payable, the advance will not exceed the lesser of the amounts involved. In the event of Co-insurance or risks involving uninsured portion(s), the appropriate adjustment will be made.

XI. Warranty by Insured

The Insured warrants this Policy of Insurance to be free from any claim for loss, damage, or expense covered under any commercial policy in effect for the benefit of the Insured (except any insurance which may be mandated by the Terrorism Risk Insurance Act of 2002), and to be free from any claim for loss, damage, or expense not covered by any policy of insurance whatsoever.

XII. Final General Provisions

A. Notwithstanding any other provision of this Policy of Insurance, no errors or omissions in furnishing notification or reports required by this Policy of Insurance shall prejudice the protection afforded by this Policy of Insurance, but shall be corrected by the Insured when such errors or omissions in furnishing notification or reports are discovered.
B. The Administrator authorizes the Insured to enter into indemnity agreements (and this Policy of Insurance will insure) for war risk liability awards under Parts II and III of this Policy of Insurance with vendors, agents and subcontractors whose goods and services are necessary to the operation of aircraft by the Insured. Upon request, the Insured will provide copies of any or all such indemnity agreements.

XIII. Effective Date and Authorized Signatures

The entirety of this War Risk Insurance Policy (including Parts I, II and III below), becomes effective as of 00:00 GMT of the ____________, subject to the submission of a Schedule of Aircraft as required by Part I, Article IIA and unless one or more Parts are terminated, shall remain in effect until 23:59 GMT on the ____________, or until amended or terminated in accordance with the terms of this Policy of Insurance. In accordance with the Memorandum of Agreement of ____________ and amendments thereof between the Insured and the United States of American regarding the power to bind a contract of insurance:

For the UNITED STATES OF AMERICA
By:
Eric Nelson
Date:
Title: Acting Director of Aviation Insurance Program Office
Federal Aviation Administration
For the INSURED, ____________
By an Individual Empowered to Bind the Insured

By:
Date:
Title:

UNITED STATES OF AMERICA
DEPARTMENT OF TRANSPORTATION
FEDERAL AVIATION ADMINISTRATION
Policy No. ___________

Part I: Hull Insurance

I. Coverage

The Insurer, represented by the Administrator acting for the Secretary of Transportation, shall provide by this Part I of the Policy of Insurance, in accordance with applicable provisions of law and subject to all limitations thereof, and upon the payment of a premium, pursuant to the provisions of chapter 443, physical damage insurance (hereinafter, Hull Insurance) for aircraft (including aircraft spare parts, engines and appliances, hereinafter collectively referred to as "Equipment") in the amounts shown herein for War Risk Occurrences arising from the Air Transportation Business of ___________ (hereinafter, the Insured), for the aircraft described in the attached "Schedule of Equipment" (hereinafter the Schedule) for the account of the Insured for risks associated with the operation of such Equipment by the Insured (or operated by others but for which the Insured is responsible to another party or parties, by reason of contract or agreement, for insurance against physical loss of or damage to said Equipment.)

II. Sum Insured to Be Determined by the Administrator

A. The Equipment values insured by this Policy of Insurance shall be the same as, for air carriers who held an FAA policy as of November 25, 2002, those set forth in the Schedule from the Insured's commercial hull and/or equipment policies as of November 25, 2002, and operated by the Insured as of the date of issuance of this Policy of Insurance or as amended thereafter, and for those who did not hold an FAA policy on November 25, 2002, those set forth in the Schedule from the Insured's current commercial hull and/or equipment policies for those hulls and/or equipments operated by the Insured as of the date of issuance of this Policy of Insurance or as amended thereafter. The value of each item of Equipment set forth in the Schedule shall represent the amount of war risk physical damage insurance in effect for such Equipment and shall be deemed to be the Sum Insured; provided, however, the Sum Insured for each item of

Equipment shall be determined by the Administrator to be the Agreed Value of the item of Equipment in the exercise of her discretion pursuant to 49 U.S.C. Sections 44302 and 44306. For purposes hereof, "Agreed Value" means: (i) the amount in effect on the commercial policy immediately prior to the effective date of this Policy of Insurance as set forth in the Schedule and/or FAA pre-approved self-insurance, or (ii) the stipulated value required by a bona fide agreement reached at arm's length between the Insured and a third party lender or lessor, or (iii) for items of equipment that are not subject to encumbrance, Agreed Value means, at the discretion of the Administrator, the greater either of, (a) the amount that represents the fair and reasonable value of the aircraft, or (b) the net book value of the aircraft at the time of loss. The Insured shall provide the Administrator with a Schedule of Aircraft (the Schedule) from the Insured's current commercial hull policy, or other reasonable document certified as true by the Insured that reflects the aircraft in operation (or the future date of operation of) during the period of this Contract of Insurance within 10 calendar days of issuance of this War Risk Insurance Policy.

B. The Insured agrees that, if the Sum Insured of Equipment insurance carried against loss or damage from risks other than war risks is voluntarily reduced or increased by the Insured on its commercial policy to an amount other than the Sum Insured under this Policy, the Sum Insured under this Policy shall be considered to have been automatically amended to the new amounts at the time of such change on the commercial policy unless a specific value has been predetermined by the Insurer prior to a loss incident resulting from a War Risk Occurrence. Such variations shall conform to changes incurred on the Insured's commercial policy schedule of Equipment valuations.

C. Insurance coverage of this policy is limited to operations of aircraft listed in the Schedule. It is the Insured's responsibility to verify the accuracy of the Schedule and the Schedule must be revised by the Insured to add or delete Equipment, or to change aircraft registration numbers.

1. Any Equipment acquired by the Insured as Owner (or for which they have agreed to provide coverage) shall be attached hereto as of the precise time delivery occurs or title is vested in the Insured, or risk of loss transfers to the Insured, whichever occurs first. The Sum Insured of such Equipment shall be the purchase price to the Insured (unless another value shall be specifically declared to and agreed by the Insurer subject to the determination of the Administrator, in the exercise of her discretion pursuant to 49 U.S.C. Sections 44302 and 44306).
2. Any Equipment operated by the Insured under lease or other agreement under the terms of which the Insured assumes responsibility therefore or is to provide War Risks physical damage insurance therefore shall be attached hereunder as of the precise time such assumption of responsibility or such Insurance is to attach in accordance with the terms of such lease or other agreement. If no value has been specifically declared in the lease or other agreement and reported to the Insurer, then the Sum Insured shall be,

the equitable and reasonable value agreed to between the Insured and the Administrator in the exercise of her discretion pursuant to 49 U.S.C. Sections 44302 and 44306. It is agreed that the Equipment values stated in the Lease agreements or other agreements are subject to amendment in accordance with the terms thereof.

3. As to any particular item of Equipment, cover hereunder ceases automatically when the Equipment is sold or otherwise disposed of and for which the Insured has no responsibility to provide War Risks physical damage insurance.

D. The Equipment values set forth in the Schedule shall be used to calculate the final reconciled premiums at the end of the policy period. The values on the Schedule will reflect the Insured's commercial insurance policy schedule of Equipment unless the Administrator determines prior to a loss incident that a valuation under Article II. A. (iii) of this Part is appropriate. The Administrator may alter the Agreed Values at her discretion with 10 days notice to the Insured.

III. Conditions

A. Subject to the terms, conditions, and exclusions of this Policy, this insurance covers all physical loss or damage to the Equipment described and set forth in the Schedule, while being operated by the Insured (or others approved by the Insured) and engines, navigational instruments, parts and appliances insured under the Insured's commercial hull loss policy.

B. The Insurer will pay, subject to the terms, conditions, and exclusions of this Policy: (1) in respect to total loss, the Sum Insured; and (2) in respect to partial loss:

1. If repairs are made by other than the Insured, the actual cost, as evidenced by bills rendered to the Insured less any discounts granted to the Insured, excluding the cost of overtime and its related overhead unless previously agreed to by the Insurer, to repair the damaged property with material or parts of like kind and quality, plus the reasonable cost of transporting new and/or damaged parts and/or the damaged Equipment to the place of repair and the return of the repaired Equipment to the control of the Insured, plus the reasonable and necessary costs incurred by the Insured in association with these repairs.
2. If repairs are made by the Insured, the total of the following items:

   (a) Actual cost of material or parts of like kind and quality.
   (b) Actual wages paid for direct labor, excluding extra charges for overtime, unless such overtime is consistent with sound business practices and the Insured's obligation to expeditiously and economically repair the damaged Equipment.

(c) Overhead costs incurred by the Insured which shall be determined by the Administrator as (i) A reasonable percentage of Item 2 in lieu of all overhead, including supervisory services, (ii) actual overhead costs, or (iii) the relevant percentage provided in the Insured's previously effective commercial hull Policy.
(d) The reasonable cost of transporting new and/or the damaged parts and/or the damaged Equipment to the place of repair and return of the repaired Equipment to the place of accident or home airport.
(e) If repairs are not made and the Equipment is subsequently disposed of, then the estimated cost by the Administrator (consistent with the usual business practices of the Insured's commercial insurers) of making such repairs to the damaged Equipment with material of like kind and quality or the difference between the Sum Insured of the Equipment before it was damaged and the value of the Equipment in its damaged state.

C. The amount due under this Policy in respect to a partial loss shall not exceed the Sum Insured should the loss payable be for a total loss. When the amount paid hereunder is equal to the Sum Insured, any salvage value remaining shall inure to the benefit of the Insurer. There shall, however, be no abandonment without the consent of the Insurer.
D. The Sum Insured, remaining after loss or damage from a War Risk Occurrence, shall be reduced by the amount of any loss or damage, whether or not covered by this Policy, until repairs have been completed and the value automatically restored in kind.

IV. Prompt Notice of Loss

A. In the event of any known or suspected War Risk Occurrence which may result in loss, damage, or expense for which the Insurer may become liable, prompt notice thereof, on being known to the Insured, shall be given by the Insured to the Administrator consistent with this section. Failure to give such prompt notice because of uncertainty of the event causation, the occasion of War Risk Occurrences, or intervening regulations shall not necessarily prejudice this insurance.

1. Notification must be immediate at any time there are fatalities or injuries to crew, passengers or third parties, there is property damage, or damage to the hull is likely to be in excess of $10,000.
2. Notification may be given as soon as practicable, or as a written claim submission consistent with Article IV., Paragraph B. of this Part, within 60 days to the FAA only when the aircraft suffers superficial damage; there were no fatalities or injuries to crew or passengers or third parties; there was no property damage, the air carrier has documented the aircraft damage with

digital photography or by video tape and includes the records with the claim; and the amount of the claim is estimated to be under $10,000.

B. For all claims, the Insured shall render to the Administrator a proof of loss claim signed and sworn to by the Insured no later than 60 days after the determination of a war risk occurrence by the National Transportation Safety Board or other cognizant government entity for loss or damage, or expense for which the Insurer may become liable (unless such time is extended in writing by the Insurer), stating the place, time, and cause of the loss or damage, the interest of the Insured and of all others in the Equipment, the Sum Insured at the time of the loss thereof, the amount and nature of the loss or damage, all encumbrances on the Equipment, all changes in title, and all other valid and collectible War Risk hull insurance covering said Equipment.

V. Subrogation Rights

The Insurer shall be subrogated to all the rights which the Insured may have against any other person or entity, in respect of any payment made under this Policy, to the extent of such payment, and the Insured shall, upon the request of the Insurer, execute all documents necessary to secure to the Insurer such rights. The Insured shall do nothing after a loss covered by this Policy to the prejudice of such rights or defenses of the Insurer. The Insurer and Insured will cooperate fully in the investigation of any loss.

VI. Insured Aircraft and Property

The insurance provided hereunder covers only loss or damage to the Equipment described in the Schedule (as may be amended from time to time pursuant to Section II, above) while the Equipment is being operated by the Insured (or others approved by the Insured) which shall be deemed to include, but not be limited to stop-overs, ground time, and ferry flights to position or reposition the aircraft and/or maintenance or storage of Equipment.

VII. Payment of Claims

A. The FAA shall make prompt payment in full of any claim covered under this policy after confirmation of loss. Any subsequent post-incident losses, directly related to the incident shall be covered by this Policy as a loss directly related to the original subject loss incident.

B. The FAA may, at its sole discretion and at any time prior to the final settlement of any claim by the Insured, elect to make a partial payment to the Insured for any loss, damage, or expense covered by this Policy.

VIII. Premium Payment

A. The actual premium for this Policy of Insurance shall be $0.012 per hundred dollars of the total Sums Insured of the aircraft of the Insured as set forth in the Schedule as in effect of the date of this policy, per year, prorated on an aircraft day basis for the number of days the policy is in effect.
B. The Insured shall estimate a deposit premium as specified in VIII (A) above for each day the policy is in effect and in total for the entire duration of the policy. The Insurer reserves the right to increase or decrease the premium offered by the Insured based on the Insurer's analysis of expected operations by the insured.
C. The total deposit premium will be paid in a single installment representing the fraction of the total duration of coverage provided during the period October 1, 2010 to December 31, 2010. Insured shall pay the first estimated premium installment within 10 days of the beginning of the policy period.
D. Within 30 days of the expiration or termination of this Policy of Insurance, the insured shall calculate and submit data to reconcile the actual premium owed with the deposit premium estimated.

    1. Final reconciliation will be based on the calculation of aircraft day valuation based upon actual values reported by the Insured to the Insurer.
    2. If the premium owed is greater than the deposit premium paid by the Insured, the Insured shall pay the premium difference to the Insurer.
    3. If the premium owed is less than the deposit premium paid by the Insured, the Insurer will refund the premium difference.

THIS ENDS PART I OF THE POLICY OF INSURANCE

UNITED STATES OF AMERICA
DEPARTMENT OF TRANSPORTATION
FEDERAL AVIATION ADMINISTRATION
Policy No. ___________

Part II: Comprehensive

I. Coverage

A. The Insurer, represented by the Administrator, acting for the Secretary of Transportation, shall provide by this Policy of Insurance, in accordance with applicable provisions of law and subject to all limitations thereof, comprehensive liability insurance for, (i) the loss of property of others carried by the Insured (or others approved by the Insured) or in the care, custody or control of the Insured or for which the insured has agreed to be responsible (including but not limited to baggage and personal effects, cargo, mail and aircraft and/or aircraft spare parts and equipment), (ii) for the personal injury, bodily injury or death of Passengers or crewmembers of the Insured, and/or (iii) premises liability, products/completed operations liability, and hangarkeepers liability, in the limits shown herein for War Risk Occurrences arising from the Air Transportation Business of ___________ (hereinafter, the Insured).

B. Subject to the limits of liability, exclusions, conditions, and other terms of this Policy of Insurance, the Insurer hereby agrees to pay on behalf of the Insured (including Other Insured Parties) and/or its vendors, agents, and subcontractors (Additional Insureds) whose products and services are required for the operation of its aircraft for which the insured has entered into an indemnity agreement, all sums which the Insured shall be legally liable to pay, or by final judgment be adjudged to pay, to any person or persons, including damages for personal injuries, and/or bodily injuries sustained, including death at any time resulting therefrom, damages for care and loss of services, or by reason of loss or damage to or destruction of property resulting from the occurrence of loss resulting from War Risk Occurrences.

II. Amounts

A. The amount of Insurance provided under this Policy of Insurance shall not exceed US___________ (dollar amount) of liability per occurrence, per aircraft incurred by the Insured and/or the Additional Insureds for losses resulting from a War Risk Occurrence, which is the limit of liability in the Insured's commercial policy in effect on November 25, 2002, or for those who did not hold a commercial all risk insurance policy as of November 25, 2002, the amount equal to the limit contained in the Insured's previous FAA war risk policy, or for those who were not previously insured by the FAA, the limit in the Insured's current commercial all risk insurance policy.

B. The Insured agrees that, if the limits of liability contained in the Insured's commercial insurance policy carried against liabilities arising from risks other than war risks are voluntarily reduced to amounts of insurance less than the limits of liability stated by this Policy, the insurance under this Policy shall be considered to have been automatically amended to the new limits of liability on the Insured's commercial policies at the time of such amendment.

III. Defense and Settlement of Claims

A. The Insurer shall have the right and duty to defend any suit or claim against the Insured and/or the Additional Insureds seeking damages on account of any bodily injury, personal injury, or property damage covered under this policy, even if such suit is groundless, false or fraudulent and may make such investigation, negotiation, and settlement of any claim or suit as it deems proper and expedient, but the Insurer shall not be obligated to pay any claim or judgment or to defend any suit or claim after the applicable limit of the Insurer's liability has been exhausted by payment of judgments or settlements.

B. During such time as the Insurer is obligated to defend a claim or claims under the provisions of the preceding paragraph, the Insurer shall pay with respect to such claims:

1. Subject to the applicable limits of liability, all expenses incurred by the Insured and/or the Additional Insureds, all costs taxed against the Insured and/or the Additional Insureds in any suit or claim defended by the Insurer and all interest on the entire amount of any judgment thereon which accrues after entry of the judgment and before the Insurer has paid or tendered or deposited in court that part of the judgment which does not exceed the limit of the Insurer's liability thereon under this Policy; and
2. In addition to the applicable limits of liability, all reasonable expenses incurred by the Insured and/or the Additional Insureds at the Insurer's request, other than for loss of earnings or for wages or salaries of employees of the Insured and/or the Additional Insureds.

IV. Prompt Notice of Loss

A. In the event of any known or suspected War Risk Occurrence which may result in loss, damage, or expense for which the Insurer may become liable, prompt notice thereof, on being known to the Insured, shall be given by the Insured to the Administrator consistent with this section. Failure to give such prompt notice because of uncertainty of the event causation, the occasion of War Risk Occurrences, or intervening regulations shall not necessarily prejudice this insurance.

B. If a claim is made or suit is brought against the Insured and/or the Additional Insureds for which the insurer may become liable, the Insured shall immediately notify the Insurer and timely provide a copy of every demand, notice, summons, pleading, motion, document filed with a court, settlement offer, and other process received by the Insured or its representatives.

V. Assistance and Cooperation of the Insured

A. The Insured and/or the Additional Insureds shall not interfere in any negotiations of the Insurer for settlement of any legal proceedings in respect to any War Risk Occurrence for which the Insurer may be liable under this Policy of Insurance. Provided that, in respect to any War Risk Occurrence likely to give rise to a claim under this Policy of Insurance, the Insured is obligated to, and shall take such steps to, protect its and the Insurer's interests as would reasonably be taken in the absence of this or similar insurance. The Insurer shall consult in good faith, and adequately in advance, with the Insured and/or the Additional Insureds regarding its proceeding and settlement strategy and proposed settlements, and ensure that it develops in good faith with the Insured a litigation defense or settlement strategy. The Insured and/or the Additional Insureds shall do nothing after a loss covered by this Policy to the prejudice of such rights of the Insurer. The Insurer and Insured and/or the Additional Insureds will cooperate fully in the investigation of any loss.

B. Whenever required by the Insurer, the Insured and/or the Additional Insureds shall aid in securing information and evidence and in obtaining witnesses and shall cooperate with the Insurer in the defense of any claim or suit or in the appeal from any judgment, in respect of any War Risk Occurrence as herein provided.

VI. Action Against the Insurer

No action shall lie against the Insurer unless, as a condition precedent thereto, the Insured shall have fully complied with all of the terms of this Policy and until the amount of the Insured's obligations to pay, with respect to the specific legal action or claim in question, shall have been finally determined either by judgment against the Insured after actual trial or by written agreement of the Claimant and the Insurer. Any person or organization or the legal representative thereof who has secured such judgment or written agreement shall thereafter be entitled to recover under this Policy to the extent such judgment or written agreement is not in excess of the remaining insurance afforded by this Policy. Nothing contained in this Policy shall give any person or organization any right to join the Insurer as a codefendant in any action against the Insured and/or Additional Insureds to determine the Insured's liability. Neither the filing nor the adjudication of bankruptcy or insolvency of the Insured or Insured's Estate shall relieve the Insurer of any of its obligations hereunder.

VII. Subrogation Rights

The Insurer shall be subrogated to all the rights which the Insured and/or Additional Insureds may have against any other person or entity, in respect of any payment made under this Policy, to the extent of such payment, and the Insured shall, upon the request of the Insurer, execute all documents necessary to secure to the Insurer such rights. The Insured shall do nothing after a loss covered by this Policy to the prejudice of such rights or defenses of the Insurer. The Insurer and Insured will cooperate fully in the investigation of any loss.

VIII. Payment of Claims

A. The FAA shall make prompt payment in full, on behalf of the Insured, of any claim covered under this Policy after the Insured and/or the Additional Insureds shall become legally liable to pay, or by final judgment be adjudged to pay. Any subsequent post-incident losses, directly related to the incident, incurred shall be covered by this Policy as a loss directly related to the original subject loss incident.
B. The FAA may at its discretion, and at any time prior to the final settlement of any claim by the Insured and/or the Additional Insureds, elect to make a partial payment to the Insured for any loss, damage, or expense covered by this Policy.

IX. Premium Payment

A. The actual premium for this Part II of the Policy of Insurance shall be based upon whether the Insured conducts passenger or air freight operations, or a combination of the two. The premium calculations are set into four Classes based upon the amount of coverage set forth in Article II. Class I calculations address Article II coverage amounts that are less than Five Hundred Million Dollars ($500,000,000). Class II calculations address Article II coverage amounts that range from Five Hundred Million Dollars ($500,000,000) but less than One Billion US Dollars ($1,000,000,000). Class III calculations address Article II coverage amounts that range from One Billion US Dollars ($1,000,000,000) or more, but less than One and One-Half Billion US Dollars ($1,500,000,000). Class IV calculations address Article II coverage amounts that are One and One-Half Billion US Dollars ($1,500,000,000) or more. The premium for each Class shall be calculated as follows:

Class I. If the amount of coverage in Article II amounts to less than Five Hundred Million US Dollars ($500,000,000), the total premium shall be calculated as the sum of premiums for passenger and freight operations as set forth below:

Formulae for Class I

$$\text{Premium for Passenger Operations} = (\$0.14 \times \text{number of enplanements}) + (\$0.14 \times \text{RPM}/1{,}000)$$

$$\text{Premium for Freight Operations} = \$0.01 \times \text{RTM}/1{,}000$$

Class II. If the amount of coverage in Article II amounts to Five Hundred Million US Dollars ($500,000,000) or more, but less than One Billion US Dollars ($1,000,000,000), the total premium shall be calculated as the sum of premiums for passenger and freight operations as set forth below:

Formulae for Class II

$$\text{Premium for Passenger Operations} = (\$0.18 \times \text{number of enplanements}) + (\$0.18 \times \text{RPM}/1{,}000)$$

$$\text{Premium for Freight Operations} = \$0.01 \times \text{RTM}/1{,}000$$

Class III. If the amount of coverage in Article II amounts to One Billion US Dollars ($1,000,000,000) or more, but less than One and One-Half Billion US Dollars ($1,500,000,000), the total premium shall be calculated as the sum of premiums for passenger and freight operations as set forth below:

Formulae for Class III

$$\text{Premium for Passenger Operations} = (\$0.23 \times \text{number of enplanements}) + (\$0.23 \times \text{RPM}/1{,}000)$$

$$\text{Premium for Freight Operations} = \$0.02 \times \text{RTM}/1{,}000$$

Class IV. If the amount of coverage in Article II amounts to One and One-Half Billion US Dollars ($1,500,000,000) or more, the total premium shall be calculated as the sum of premiums for passenger and freight operations as set forth below:

Formulae for Class IV

$$\text{Premium for Passenger Operations} = (\$0.23 \times \text{number of enplanements}) + (\$0.23 \times \text{RPM}/1{,}000)$$

$$\text{Premium for Freight Operations} = \$0.02 \times \text{RTM}/1{,}000$$

B. The Insured shall estimate a deposit premium as specified in IX (A) above for each day the policy is in effect and in total for the entire duration of the policy. The Insurer reserves the right to increase or decrease the premium offered by the Insured based on its analysis of expected operations by the insured.
C. The total deposit premium will be paid in a single installment representing the fraction of the total duration of coverage provided during the period October 1, 2010 to December 31, 2010. Insured shall pay the first estimated premium installment within 10 days of the beginning of the policy period.
D. Within 30 days of the expiration or termination of this Policy of Insurance, the insured shall calculate and submit data to reconcile the actual premium owed with the deposit premium estimated.

   1. If the premium owed is greater than the deposit premium paid by the Insured, the Insured shall pay the premium difference to the Insurer.
   2. If the premium owed is less than the deposit premium paid by the Insured, the Insurer must will a refund the premium difference.

THIS ENDS PART II OF THE POLICY OF INSURANCE

UNITED STATES OF AMERICA
DEPARTMENT OF TRANSPORTATION
FEDERAL AVIATION ADMINISTRATION
Policy No. ___________

Part III: Third Party War Risk Liability Insurance

I. Coverage

A. The Insurer, represented by the Administrator, acting for the Secretary of Transportation, shall provide by this Policy of Insurance, in accordance with applicable provisions of law and subject to all limitations thereof, and upon the payment of a premium, pursuant to the provisions of chapter 443, Third Party War Risk Liability Insurance (hereinafter, the Insurance) of the type indicated and in the limits shown herein for War Risk Occurrences arising from the Air Transportation Business of ___________ (hereinafter, the Insured, including

Other Insured Parties), and, through indemnification agreements entered into by the Insured with its vendors, agents, and subcontractors for goods or services related to the Insured's Air Transportation Business.

B. Subject to the limits of liability, exclusions, conditions, and other terms of this Policy of Insurance, the Insurer hereby agrees to pay on behalf of the Insured all sums which the Insured (including Other Insured Parties) and/or its vendors, agents, and subcontractors whose products and services are required for the operation of its aircraft for which the insured has entered into an indemnity agreement shall be legally liable to pay to any person or persons who are not Passengers or employees who are on active duty in the course of their employment of the Insured, or by final judgment be adjudged to pay to any such person or persons, including damages for personal injuries and/or bodily injuries sustained, including death at any time resulting therefrom, damages for care and loss of services, or by reason of loss or damage to or destruction of property, including the loss of use thereof, resulting from a loss resulting from a War Risk Occurrence arising from the Insured's Air Transportation Business.

II. Amounts

The amount of Insurance provided under this Policy of Insurance shall not exceed US ____________ (dollar amount equal to the limit of third-party liability in the Insured's previous FAA war risk policy, or for those who were not previously insured by the FAA, two times the per-occurrence liability limit in the Insured's current commercial all risk insurance policy) incurred by the Insured and/or Additional Insureds for losses resulting from a War Risk Occurrence.

III. Defense and Settlement of Claims

A. The Insurer shall have the right and duty to defend any suit or claim against the Insured and/or Additional Insureds seeking damages on account of any bodily injury, personal injury, or property damage covered under this Policy of Insurance, even if such suit is groundless, false or fraudulent and may make such investigation, negotiation, and settlement of any claim or suit as it deems proper and expedient, but the Insurer shall not be obligated to pay any claim or judgment or to defend any suit or claim after the applicable limit of the Insurer's liability has been exhausted by payment of judgments or settlements.

B. During such time as the Insurer is obligated to defend a claim or claims under the provisions of the preceding paragraph, the Insurer shall pay with respect to such claims:

1. Subject to the applicable limits of liability, all expenses incurred by the Insured, all costs taxed against the Insured in any suit or claim defended by the Insurer and all interest on the entire amount of any judgment thereon which accrues after entry of the judgment and before the Insurer has paid or tendered or deposited in court that part of the judgment which does not exceed the limit of the Insurer's liability thereon under this Policy; and
2. In addition to the applicable limits of liability, all reasonable expenses incurred by the Insured at the Insurer's request, other than for loss of earnings or for wages or salaries of employees of the Insured.

IV. Prompt Notice of Loss

A. In the event of any known or suspected War Risk Occurrence which may result in loss, damage, or expense for which the Insurer may become liable, prompt notice thereof, on being known to the Insured, shall be given by the Insured to the Administrator consistent with this section. Failure to give such prompt notice because of uncertainty of the event causation, the occasion of War Risk Occurrences, or intervening regulations shall not necessarily prejudice this insurance.

B. If a claim is made or suit is brought against the Insured and/or the Additional Insureds for which the insurer may become liable, the Insured shall immediately notify the Insurer and timely provide a copy of every demand, notice, summons, pleading, motion, document filed with a court, settlement offer, and other process received by the Insured or its representatives.

V. Assistance and Cooperation of the Insured

A. The Insured shall not interfere in any negotiations by the Insurer for settlement of any legal proceedings in respect of any War Risk Occurrence for which the Insurer may be liable under this Policy of Insurance. Provided, that in respect of any War Risk Occurrence likely to give rise to a claim under this Policy of Insurance, the Insured is obligated to, and shall take such steps to protect its and the Insurer's interests as would reasonably be taken in the absence of this or similar insurance. The Insurer shall consult in good faith, and adequately in advance, with the Insured regarding its proceeding and settlement strategy and proposed settlements, and ensure that it develops in good faith with the Insured and/or Additional Insureds a litigation defense or settlement strategy.

B. Whenever required by the Insurer, the Insured shall aid in securing information and evidence and in obtaining witnesses and shall cooperate with the Insurer in the defense of any claim or suit or in the appeal from any judgment, in respect of any War Risk Occurrence as herein provided.

VI. Action Against the Insurer

No action shall lie against the Insurer unless, as a condition precedent thereto, the Insured shall have fully complied with all of the terms of this Policy of Insurance and until the amount of the Insured's obligations to pay, with respect to the specific legal action or claim in question, shall have been finally determined either by judgment against the Insured after actual trial or by written agreement of the claimant and the Insurer. Any person or organization or the legal representative thereof who has secured such judgment or written agreement shall thereafter be entitled to recover under this Policy of Insurance to the extent such judgment or written agreement is not in excess of the remaining insurance afforded by this Policy of Insurance. Nothing contained in this Policy of Insurance shall give any person or organization any right to join the Insurer as a co defendant in any action against the Insured and/or Additional Insureds to determine the liability of the Insured. Neither the filing nor the adjudication of bankruptcy or insolvency of the Insured or the Estate of the Insured shall relieve the Insurer of any of its obligations hereunder.

VII. Subrogation Rights

The Insurer shall be subrogated to all the rights which the Insured may have against any other person or entity, in respect of any payment made under this Policy of Insurance, to the extent of such payment, and the Insured shall, upon the request of the Insurer, execute all documents necessary to secure to the Insurer such rights. The Insured shall do nothing after a loss covered by this Policy to the prejudice of such rights or defenses of the Insurer. The Insurer and Insured will cooperate fully in the investigation of any loss.

VIII. Payment of Claims

A. The Insurer shall make prompt payment in full, on behalf of the Insured and/or Additional Insureds of any claim covered under this Policy of Insurance after the Insured and/or Additional Insureds becomes legally liable to pay, or by final judgment be adjudged to pay. Any subsequent post-incident losses incurred that are directly related to the incident shall be covered by this Policy of Insurance as a loss directly related to the original subject loss incident.
B. The Insurer may at its discretion, and at any time prior to final settlement of any claim by the Insured, elect to make a partial payment to the insured for any loss, damage, or expense covered by this Policy of Insurance.

IX. Premium Payment

A. The actual premium for this Part III of the Policy of Insurance shall be based upon whether the Insured conducts passenger or air freight operations, or a combination of the two. The premium calculations are set into four Classes based upon the amount of coverage set forth in Article II of this Part III. Class I calculations address Article II coverage amounts that are less than One Billion US Dollars ($1,000,000,000). Class II calculations address Article II coverage amounts that range from One Billion Dollars ($1,000,000,000) or more, to less than Two Billion US Dollars ($2,000,000,000). Class III calculations address Article II coverage amounts that range from Two Billion US Dollars ($2,000,000,000) or more, but less than Three Billion US Dollars ($3,000,000,000). Class IV calculations address Article II coverage amounts that range from Three Billion US Dollars ($3,000,000,000) or more. The premium for each Class shall be calculated as follows:
Class I. If the amount of coverage in Article II amounts to less than One Billion US Dollars ($1,000,000,000), the total premium shall be calculated as the sum of premiums for passenger and freight operations as set forth below:
Formulae for Class I

$$\text{Premium for Passenger Operations} = (\$0.03 \times \text{number of enplanements}) + (\$0.03 \times \text{RPM}/1{,}000)$$

$$\text{Premium for Freight Operations} = \$0.17 \times \text{RTM}/1{,}000$$

Class II. If the amount of coverage in Article II amounts to One Billion US Dollars ($1,000,000,000) or more, but less than Two Billion US Dollars ($2,000,000,000), the total premium shall be calculated as the sum of premiums for passenger and freight operations as set forth below:
Formulae for Class II

$$\text{Premium for Passenger Operations} = (\$0.04 \times \text{number of enplanements}) + (\$0.04 \times \text{RPM}/1{,}000)$$

$$\text{Premium for Freight Operations} = \$0.25 \times \text{RTM}/1{,}000$$

Class III. If the amount of coverage in Article II amounts to Two Billion US Dollars ($2,000,000,000) or more, but less than Three Billion US Dollars ($3,000,000,000), the total premium shall be calculated as the sum of premiums for passenger and freight operations as set forth below:
Formulae for Class III

$$\text{Premium for Passenger Operations} = (\$0.05 \times \text{number of enplanements}) + (\$0.05 \times \text{RPM}/1{,}000)$$

$$\text{Premium for Freight Operations} = \$0.30 \times \text{RTM}/1{,}000$$

Class IV. If the amount of coverage in Article II amounts to Three Billion US Dollars ($3,000,000,000) or more, the total premium shall be calculated as the sum of premiums for passenger and freight operations as set forth below:
Formulae for Class IV

$$\text{Premium for Passenger Operations} = (\$0.05 \times \text{number of enplanements}) + (\$0.05 \times \text{RPM}/1{,}000)$$

$$\text{Premium for Freight Operations} = \$0.33 \times \text{RTM}/1{,}000$$

B. The Insured shall estimate a deposit premium as specified in IX (A) above for each day the policy is in effect and in total for the entire duration of the policy. The Insurer reserves the right to increase or decrease the premium offered by the Insured based on its analysis of expected operations by the insured.
C. The total deposit premium will be paid in a single installment representing the fraction of the total duration of coverage provided during the period October 1, 2010 to December 31, 2010. Insured shall pay the first estimated premium installment within 10 days of the beginning of the policy period.
D. Within 30 days of the expiration or termination of this Policy of Insurance, the insured shall calculate and submit data to reconcile the actual premium owed with the deposit premium estimated.

1. If the premium owed is greater than the deposit premium paid by the Insured, the Insured shall pay the premium difference to the Insurer.
2. If the premium owed is less than the deposit premium paid by the Insured, the Insurer will refund the premium difference.

THIS ENDS PART III OF THE POLICY OF INSURANCE

Appendix B
The Government of Canada's Undertaking with Respect to War Risk Insurance

Undertaking with respect to Aviation War Risk Liability (2011-01-01)
Minister of Transport, Infrastructure and Communities

Undertaking

To: Every person covered referred to in the attached schedule

I, the undersigned, Minister of Transport, Infrastructure and Communities, acting on behalf of the Government of Canada, pursuant to Order-in-Council P.C. 2010-1608 of December 9, 2010, hereby agree to indemnify any person covered referred to in the Schedule attached, in accordance with the terms and conditions set out herein and the Schedule attached.

Acceptance of this undertaking on the part of any person covered is presumed without any formal communication by that person being necessary.

The liability of the Government of Canada under this undertaking is subject to the terms and conditions set out herein and in the Schedule attached. Notwithstanding anything herein or in the Schedule attached, such liability shall not exceed the

Y.O.M. Nyampong, *Insuring the Air Transport Industry Against Aviation War and Terrorism Risks and Allied Perils*, DOI 10.1007/978-3-642-32433-8,

limit of the amount covered for aviation liability under the insurance policy of the person covered.

All applicable terms and conditions of the insurance policies shall apply to this undertaking, with such modifications as may be required to give effect to this undertaking.

Words and expressions used herein shall have the same meaning as ascribed to them in the Schedule attached.

This Undertaking takes effect from January 1, 2011, and replaces the Undertaking dated April 23, 2009.

Dated at Ottawa, Ontario, this 20th day of December 2010.

(original signed by)

Honourable Chuck Strahl, M.P.

Minister of Transport, Infrastructure and Communities

Canada

Schedule
Terms and Conditions

Definitions

"airline" means an airline[1] that is Canadian as defined in the *Canada Transportation Act*.

"airport operator" means the operator of an airport in Canada.

"commercially available", in respect of aviation war risk liability coverage, means aviation war risk liability coverage that is available in the insurance market, but does not include coverage that the Minister of Transport, Infrastructure and Communities may, from time to time, in his sole discretion, declare in writing to be not commercially available on reasonable terms during any period specified in the declaration.

"person" means any individual, company, corporation, partnership, limited partnership, firm, trust, sole proprietorship, government or government agency, authority or entity however designated or constituted.

---

[1] For greater certainty, the word "airline" includes any person operating a commercial air service.

Persons Covered[2]

Any person covered under an insurance policy held by an airline, an airport operator, NAV CANADA, or any supplier of goods or services to an airport operator, an airline in Canada or NAV CANADA who is insured against general liability under an insurance policy.

Risk Covered

Risks listed in the clause headed "War, Hi jacking and Other Perils Exclusion Clause" in the standard aviation insurance policy to the extent that such risks have been included in a standard write-back endorsement[3] to a policy and any other such risk that is not included in the standard write-back endorsement that the Minister of Transport, Infrastructure and Communities may, from time to time, in his sole discretion, declare in writing to be subject to this Undertaking to the limit[4] of the amount covered for aviation liability under the insurance policy, less whatever coverage is commercially available during the period referred to below.

Period

From January 1, 2011, to December 31, 2013.

Contractual Terms

Same as in a write-back endorsement, except for the limit of coverage, the period and the renewal that are set out in this document.

---

[2] For greater certainty, "person covered" includes any person that an airline, an airport operator, NAV CANADA or any supplier of goods or services to an airline in Canada, an airport operator, or NAV CANADA is entitled to add as an "additional insured" under the insurance policy.

[3] Such clauses are commonly titled "Extended Coverage Endorsement".

[4] For greater certainty, the wording with respect to the limits of liability is intended to refer to the general limits within the aviation policy and is not intended to incorporate the sub-limits contained in an Extended Coverage Endorsement or any other sub-limit relating to aviation war risks.

Declaration (2011-01-01)
Minister of Transport, Infrastructure and Communities

Declaration

I, the undersigned, Minister of Transport, Infrastructure and Communities, acting on behalf of the Government of Canada, hereby declare, solely for the purposes of the definition of "commercially available" in the Undertaking respecting aviation war risk liability coverage given by me on December 9, 2010, pursuant to Order in Council P.C. 2010-1608, that the insurance products more particularly described in the Schedule attached hereto are deemed not to be commercially available on reasonable terms during the period while this declaration remains in effect.

This declaration replaces the declaration dated April 23, 2009, and takes effect from January 1, 2011, and shall remain in effect until 7 days after it has been rescinded or varied and notice of its rescission or variation has been posted on the TC web site at www.tc.gc.ca/programs/airports/liabilityprogram/menu.htm.

Dated at Ottawa, Ontario, this 20th day of December 2010.

(original signed by)

Honourable Chuck Strahl, M.P.

Minister of Transport, Infrastructure and Communities

Canada

Schedule

Any additional coverage in respect of aviation war risk liability for Third Party Bodily Injury and Property Damage in excess of the first US $150 million covered by insurance underwriters under AVN52E or other standard write-back endorsement in respect of an airline or in excess of US $50 million covered by insurance underwriters under AVN52G or other standard write-back endorsement in respect of all other persons covered or where a person covered by the Undertaking has purchased insurance covering war risk liability for Third Party Bodily Injury and Property Damage of more than US $150 million in respect of AVN52E or US $50 million in respect of AVN52G, any additional coverage in excess of the amount purchased.

Appendix C
Measures Planned or Taken by EU Member States to Assist Air Transport Operators Cover the Additional Costs of Insurance in the Immediate Aftermath of September 11, 2001[a]

Member State	Insurance—Own Airlines	Requirement—Foreign Airlines	Insurance—Service Providers	Duration	Premium
Belgium[b]	Up to former level	ECAC	Up to former level	30 days	Former level plus surcharge
Denmark[c]	Up to former level	Set out in air navigation act	Up to former level	1 Month	$0.25 for $50–750 m
					$0.50 for $750 m–$1 bn
Germany[d]	Up to former level	Former level	Up to former level	1 Month	Not yet decided
Greece[e]	Up to former level	–	Not yet decided	30 days	Not yet decided
Spain[f]	Up to former level	Rome Treaty	AENA included and other service providers not yet decided	30 days	$0.25 up to $750 m
		Air navigation act—royal decree no. 37/2001			$0.50 up to $2 bn
France[g]	Up to former level	No change	Up to former level	30 days	Not yet decided
Ireland[h]	Up to former level	Not covered by Ireland	Up to former level	30 days	Not yet decided
Italy[i]	Up to a maximum of €2.2 bn for each aircraft	Not covered	Not covered for the moment	30 days	Free (no premiums required)
Luxembourg[j]	Former level—up to $2 bn		No notification of cancellation received	1 Month	Waived
Netherlands[k]	Up to former level	ECAC	Up to former level	1 Month	Premium waived for first 30 days
Austria[l]	Up to $700 m	–	–	30 days	Market conditions—premiums not yet decided

(continued)

Y.O.M. Nyampong, *Insuring the Air Transport Industry Against Aviation War and Terrorism Risks and Allied Perils*, DOI 10.1007/978-3-642-32433-8,

Portugal[m]	Up to former level	Former level	Up to former level	1 Month	Not yet decided
Finland[n]	Up to $1 bn	–	–	Max 30 days, subject to cancellation at any time	Theoretically same as previous premium—waived initially for legal reasons
Sweden[o]	Up to former level	–	–	30 days	"Premium reflects as far as possible the risks associated with the guarantee"
United Kingdom[p]	Up to former level	Not covered	Up to former level for providers whose cover withdrawn	30 days (7 days notice of cancellation	$0.25 per passenger flight up to $750 m. $0.50 per passenger flight above $750 m (waived for first 30 days) 25 % of former premium for service providers

[a]EC COM (2001) 574 final (2001), Annex. The additional information provided in the footnotes does not form part of the original table

[b]Under and by virtue of *Décisions des Conseils des ministres du 5 octobre et du 26 octobre 2001* (Decisions of the Council of Ministers made on 5th and 26th October 2001), the Belgian government established a scheme of State-issued insurance coverage for airlines and airport service providers based in Belgium, similar to that which existed before September 11, 2001 relating to risks of war and terrorism. See EC State Aid No. NN 141/2001 O.J. C 3 (2002c)

[c]Under and by virtue of *Aktstykke nr. 285 af 24. September 2001*, the government of Denmark issued a State guarantee valid for an initial period of 30 days to ensure the continued provision of third-party liability insurance cover to air carriers and service providers in the aviation sector for certain war and terrorist related risks following the events in the USA on 11 September 2001. See EC State Aid No. NN 146/2001 O.J. C 13 (2002d)

[d]Under and by virtue of § *12 Nr. 2 Haushaltsgesetz 2001*, the government of the Federal Republic of Germany issued a State guarantee valid for an initial period of 30 days to ensure the continued provision of insurance cover to air carriers, airport managers and service providers in Germany for risks related to acts of war and terrorism, following the attacks in the USA on 11 September 2001. See EC State Aid No. NN 162/2001 O.J. C 23 (2002f)

[e]Under and by virtue of Article 16 of Law No 2892/2001 and Article 48 of Law No 2956/2001, the government of Greece issued a State guarantee valid for an initial period of 30 days to ensure the continued provision of insurance cover to air carriers in Greece for certain war and terrorist-related risks, following the attacks in the USA on 11 September 2001. See EC State Aid No. NN 145/01 O.J. C 20 (2003g)

[f]Under and by virtue of *Real Decreto Ley 14/2001, de 28 de septiembre, por el que se establece el régimen del reaseguro por cuenta del Estado de los riesgos de guerra y terrorismo que puedan afectar a la navegación aérea* and *Acuerdos de Consejo de Ministros de 5 y 19 de noviembre por los que se amplía el ré gimen del reaseguro por cuenta del Estado de los riesgos de guerra y terrorismo que puedan afectar a la navegación aérea, regulado en el Real Decreto Ley 14/2001 de 28 de septiembre*, the Spanish government established a State guarantee scheme valid for an initial period of 30 days to ensure the continued

provision of insurance cover to air carriers in Spain for certain war and terrorist-related risks, following the attacks in the USA on 11 September 2001. See EC State Aid No. NN143/2001 O.J. C 3 (2003a)

[g]Under and by virtue of *Décision du ministre de l'économie en date du 22 septembre 2001*, the French government established a State-issued insurance scheme for airlines and airport service providers based in France valid for an initial period of 30 days to provide insurance cover similar to that existing before 11 September 2001 relating to the risks of war and terrorism. See EC State Aid No. NN 157/2001 O.J. C 10 (2003h)

[h]Under and by virtue of the *Air Navigation and Transport (Indemnities) Act, 2001* (Act No. 48 of 2001), the Irish government established a government indemnities scheme for airlines and other aviation sector enterprises established in Ireland in the event of losses suffered as a result of their third-party liability in respect of risks of war and terrorism. The scheme was valid initially for a period of 30 days. See EC State Aid No. NN 34/02 O.J. C 32 (2003b)

[i]Under and by virtue of *Decreto legge n. 354 del 28 settembre 2001. Legge 27 novembre 2001, n. 413; legge 27 febbraio 2002 n. 14; legge 24 maggio 2002 n. 100; decreto del president del Consiglio dei ministri 2 ottobre 2002 (Gazzetta ufficiale dell'8 ottobre—Serie* Generale—n. 326), the Italian government established a State-issued insurance scheme for airlines and airport service providers based in Italy to provide insurance cover similar to that existing before 11 September 2001 relating to risks of war and terrorism. The scheme was valid for an initial period of 30 days. See EC State Aid No. NN 142/2001 O.J. C 15 (2003e)

[j]By *Règlement grand-ducal du 24 septembre 2001*, the government of Luxembourg issued a State guarantee valid for a period of 1 month to provide airlines based in Luxembourg with insurance cover similar to that existing before 11 September 2001 relating to risks of war and terrorism. See EC State Aid No. NN 140/2001 O.J. C 2 (2003d)

[k]Under and by virtue of *Verzekeringsovereenkomst luchtvaartuigen op basis van artikel 4 van de Zee- en luchtverzekeringswet van 1939* and *Garantieovereenkomst tussen de staat en dienstenleveranciers in de luchtvaartsector*, the Dutch government set up a State-issued insurance scheme for airlines and other aviation sector enterprises established in the Netherlands to provide insurance cover similar to that existing before 11 September 2001 relating to risks of war and terrorism. The scheme was initially valid for a period of 30 days. See O.J. C 24 (2004)

[l]Under and by virtue of *Bundesfinanzgesetz 2001, Artikel IX, § 1 Z 7, BGBl. I 117/2001*, the Austrian government issued a State guarantee valid for an initial period of 30 days to ensure the continued provision of insurance cover to air carriers, airport managers and service providers in Austria for risks related to acts of war and terrorism, following the attacks in the USA on 11 September 2001. See EC State Aid No. NN 153/2001 O.J. C 23 (2002e)

[m]Under and by virtue of two statements by the Portuguese Minister for Finance and for Social equipment and Resolution 153/2001 of the Portuguese Government of 27 September 2001, the government of Portugal issued a State guarantee valid for an initial period of 1 month to ensure the continued provision of insurance cover to air carriers and service providers in Portugal for certain war and terrorist-related risks following the attacks in the USA on 11 September 2001. See EC State Aid No. NN 144/2001 O.J. C 10 (2003f)

[n]Under and by virtue of *Valtioneuvoston päätös väliaikaisen valtiontakuun myöntämisestä suomalaisille lentoyhtiöille koskien kolmansille osapuolille sotariskitilanteissa aiheutuvia vahinkoja*, the government of Finland established a State-issued insurance scheme valid for an initial period of 30 days to provide Finnish airlines with third-party liability insurance cover similar to that existing before 11 September 2001 relating to risks of war and terrorism. See EC State Aid No. NN 45/2002 O.J. C 33 (2003c)

(continued)

[o]Under and by virtue of Swedish government decision of 27 September 2001 (decision I 20), the government of Sweden issued a State guarantee valid initially for a period of 30 days to ensure continued provision of insurance cover to air carriers and service providers in the aviation sector for certain war and terrorist-related risks, following the attacks in the USA on 11 September 2001. See EC State Aid No. NN 139/2001 O.J. C 3 (2002b)

[p]Under and by virtue of the "Relationship agreement" signed on 23 September 2001 between The Lords Commissioners of Her Majesty's Treasury, AON Limited, Willis Faber Limited, Global Aerospace Underwriting Limited and Alnery No. 2190 Limited, the government of the United Kingdom established a State-reinsured insurance company known as Troika to continued provision of insurance cover to air carriers and service providers in the UK for certain war and terrorist-related risks, following the attacks in the USA on 11 September 2001. The scheme was valid for an initial period of 30 days. See EC State Aid No. NN 90/2001 O.J. C 3 (2002a)

References

EC (2002a) Authorisation for State aid pursuant to Articles 87 and 88 of the EC Treaty – Cases where the Commission raises no objections: State Aid No. NN 90/2001 – United Kingdom – Airline insurance. O.J., vol C

EC (2002b) Authorisation for State aid pursuant to Articles 87 and 88 of the EC Treaty – Cases where the Commission raises no objections: State Aid No. NN 139/2001 – Sweden – Aviation insurance guarantee. O.J., vol C

EC (2002c) Authorisation for State aid pursuant to Articles 87 and 88 of the EC Treaty – Cases where the Commission raises no objections: State Aid No. NN 141/2001 – Belgium – Temporary Aviation Insurance. O.J., vol C

EC (2002d) Authorisation for State aid pursuant to Articles 87 and 88 of the EC Treaty – Cases where the Commission raises no objections: State Aid No. NN 146/2001 – Denmark – Temporary Insurance Cover for Third Party Liability on Danish Airplanes and Airports. O.J., vol C

EC (2002e) Authorisation for State aid pursuant to Articles 87 and 88 of the EC Treaty – Cases where the Commission raises no objections: State Aid No. NN 153/2001 – Austria – Système de garantie fédéral destiné à l'industrie aérienne. O.J., vol C

EC (2002f) Authorisation for State aid pursuant to Articles 87 and 88 of the EC Treaty – Cases where the Commission raises no objections: State Aid No. NN 162/2001 – Germany – State guarantee for the aviation sector. O.J., vol C

EC (2003a) Authorisation for State aid pursuant to Articles 87 and 88 of the EC Treaty – Cases where the Commission raises no objections: State Aid No. NN143/2001 – Spain – State Re-insurance for the risks linked to war and terrorism that may affect air navigation. O.J., vol C

EC (2003b) Authorisation for State aid pursuant to Articles 87 and 88 of the EC Treaty – Cases where the Commission raises no objections: State Aid No. NN 34/02 – Ireland – Aviation insurance scheme. O.J., vol C

EC (2003c) Authorisation for State aid pursuant to Articles 87 and 88 of the EC Treaty – Cases where the Commission raises no objections: State Aid No. NN 45/2002 – Finland – Temporary State guarantee in respect of third-party liability insurance for airlines relating to risks of war and terrorism. O.J., vol C

EC (2003d) Authorisation for State aid pursuant to Articles 87 and 88 of the EC Treaty – Cases where the Commission raises no objections: State Aid No. NN 140/2001 – Luxembourg – State guarantee to airlines. O.J., vol C

EC (2003e) Authorisation for State aid pursuant to Articles 87 and 88 of the EC Treaty – Cases where the Commission raises no objections: State Aid No. NN 142/2001 – Italy – Urgent measures concerning air transport. O.J., vol C

EC (2003f) Authorisation for State aid pursuant to Articles 87 and 88 of the EC Treaty – Cases where the Commission raises no objections: State Aid No. NN 144/2001 – Portugal – Transitory

Y.O.M. Nyampong, *Insuring the Air Transport Industry Against Aviation War and Terrorism Risks and Allied Perils*, DOI 10.1007/978-3-642-32433-8,

emergency measures adopted with the view of facing the exceptional consequences for air navigation sector caused by insurance companies. O.J., vol C

EC (2003g) Authorisation for State aid pursuant to Articles 87 and 88 of the EC Treaty – Cases where the Commission raises no objections: State Aid No. NN 145/01 – Greece – Airline Insurance. O.J., vol C

EC (2003h) Authorisation for State aid pursuant to Articles 87 and 88 of the EC Treaty – Cases where the Commission raises no objections: State Aid No. NN 157/2001 – France – Dispositif de couverture du risque aérien avec la garantie de l'État. O.J., vol C

EC (2004) Authorisation for State aid pursuant to Articles 87 and 88 of the EC Treaty – Cases where the Commission raises no objections: State Aid No. NN 35/2002 – Netherlands – Government insurance scheme against the risks of war for the aviation sector. O.J., vol C

European Commission (EC) (2001) Communication from the Commission to the European Parliament and the Council on the repercussions of the terrorist attacks in the United States on the air transport industry. EC, Brussels

Index

A

Adequate insurance coverage, xi, 4, 9, 59, 61, 65, 66, 107
Adverse selection, 55, 123, 126–130, 132, 134, 135, 168, 169, 173, 174, 196, 262
AEA. *See* Association of European Airlines (AEA)
AICG. *See* Aviation Insurance Clauses Group (AICG)
AIG financial products, 193
Air operators certificates, 59
Alternative carriers, 158
Alternative products, 158
Alternative risk financing (ARF), 170, 273
Alternative risk transfer (ART), 157, 175, 273
Ambiguity aversion, 137, 139
Appropriation, 86, 101, 102, 104
ARF. *See* Alternative risk financing (ARF)
ARPC. *See* Australian reinsurance pool corporation (ARPC)
ART. *See* Alternative risk transfer (ART)
Association of European Airlines (AEA), 7, 161, 258
Asymmetric information. *See* Imperfect information
Australian Reinsurance Pool Corporation (ARPC), 238
Availability heuristic, 142
Aviation insurance
  all risks insurance policy, 41
  conditions, 6, 29, 41, 45, 47, 53, 55, 86
  exclusions, 8, 13, 41, 47, 48, 53, 55, 56, 73, 76, 78, 80, 87, 89, 98, 111
  hull war risk coverage, 5, 108–109
  passenger liability coverage, 5
  third party liability war risk coverage, 5, 6, 108, 109
  warranties, 41, 47, 53, 55, 86
Aviation insurance clauses group (AICG), 2, 3, 44, 81, 84, 85, 105, 110
Aviation war and terrorism risks, xi, xii, 2, 4, 8–10, 13, 67, 71, 116, 142, 146, 150, 152, 157, 158, 165–168, 170, 174, 175, 179, 183–185, 187–189, 194, 196, 197, 200, 205, 207, 208, 228, 231, 235, 236, 244–247, 252, 258–260, 262, 265, 271–273, 275, 276

B

Basel Committee, 197–199
Basel II Accord, 198
Basis risk, 173, 174, 180, 184, 187
Behavioral law and economics, xii, 115, 116, 142

C

Capital market solutions, 169
Captive insurance, 7, 19, 159, 160, 203, 256
Captives. *See* Captive insurance
Catastrophe bonds, 133
CDS. *See* Credit default swap (CDS)
Channelling, 10, 229
Civil commotion, 62, 76, 89, 97
Civil war, 8, 75–78, 89–91, 94, 95, 97, 102, 213
Committed funding arrangements, 171
Competitive general equilibrium theory, 120

Y.O.M. Nyampong, *Insuring the Air Transport Industry Against Aviation War and Terrorism Risks and Allied Perils*, DOI 10.1007/978-3-642-32433-8,

Confiscation, 2, 83, 101, 102, 208
Consorcio de Compensacion de Seguros, 239
Contingent capital, 19, 146, 171–173, 273, 275
Contracts of indemnity. *See* Indemnity insurance
Contribution, doctrine of, 38
Cover note, 47
Credit default swap (CDS), 193
Credit risk, 173, 175, 176, 183, 191–193, 198
Credit Suisse First Boston (CSFB), 183
CSFB. *See* Credit Suisse First Boston (CSFB)

D
Detention, 86, 101, 102, 104
Direct insurance, 17, 43, 49
Drop-down mechanism, 218, 225

E
Electromagnetic pulse, 163
Equitime, 7, 160–162
EU. *See* European Union (EU)
EU Member States (EUMSs), 162, 257
EUMSs. *See* EU Member States (EUMSs)
EU partial market failure guarantee, 162
European Union (EU), 59, 61, 62, 225, 226, 256
Eurotime, 7, 161
EU state aid regulations, 256
EU total market failure guarantee, 162, 163
Externalities, 119–122, 262, 263, 265
Extremus Versicherungs AG, 238, 239

F
FAA. *See* Federal aviation administration (FAA)
FAA Aviation Insurance Program, 107, 248, 252
Facultative reinsurance. *See* Reinsurance
Fairness, 137, 139
Federal Aviation Administration (FAA), 6–7, 248, 279
Federal Home Loan Mortgage Corporation, 190
Federal National Mortgage Association, 190
Fédération Internationale de Football Association (FIFA's), 183
FIFA's. *See* Fédération Internationale de Football Association (FIFA's)
Fire Offices Committee (FOR), 77–78
FOR. *See* Fire Offices Committee (FOR)

G
GAREAT. *See* Gestion de l'Assurance et de la Réassurance des Risques Attentats et Actes de Terrorisme (GAREAT)
General risks convention (GRC), 11, 64–66, 204, 205
Gestion de l'Assurance et de la Réassurance des Risques Attentats et Actes de Terrorisme (GAREAT), 237–238
Global credit crisis, 190
Globaltime, 7, 162–167, 203, 227
  participation agreement, 165, 166
Government, reinsurer of last resort, 246, 247
GRC. *See* General risks convention (GRC)

H
Hijacking, 2, 83, 105, 208
Hindsight bias, 142
Hostile detonation, 3, 80, 82, 84–86, 95, 110

I
IAIS. *See* International Association of Insurance Supervisors (IAIS)
Imperfect information, 126
Indemnity insurance, 25–27, 37
Independent intermediaries, brokers, 44
Informational asymmetry. *See* Imperfect information
Insurability, 10, 13, 51, 52, 55, 67, 129, 146, 147, 152, 208, 211, 215, 216, 231, 275
Insurable interest, 28, 30–32, 35, 38, 186, 187, 193, 250
International Association of Insurance Supervisors (IAIS), 159, 199
International Civil Aviation Compensation Fund, 64, 217, 231, 275
International Civil Aviation Organization, 7, 42, 64, 203, 218
International Fund. *See* International Civil Aviation Compensation Fund
International Oil Pollution Compensation Fund (IOPC), 220, 242
IOPC. *See* International Oil Pollution Compensation Fund (IOPC)
Irrational abhorrence, 137, 142, 143

J
Joint Technical and Clauses Committee (JTCC), 2, 5, 81, 108
JTCC. *See* Joint Technical and Clauses Committee (JTCC)

L

Law of large numbers, 22, 41–43, 54, 272
Life insurance, 20, 25, 31, 32, 34, 39, 89, 148
Liquidity risk, 176
London market, xi, xii, 2, 8, 19, 44, 45, 47, 73, 76, 78, 79, 81, 82, 105, 106, 248

M

Malicious acts or acts of sabotage, 2, 83
Market-enhancing theory, 265
Market failure, 7, 12, 13, 71, 87, 106, 108, 112, 116, 118, 120–123, 125, 129–132, 134, 136, 143, 162, 163, 260, 262, 265
Microeconomic efficiency, 118–120
Minimum insurance requirements, xi, 40, 62, 63, 66, 67, 205
Montreal convention. *See* Montreal convention of 1999
Montreal convention of 1999, 10, 60, 205, 206, 208
Montreal protocol of 1978, 63
Moral hazard, 32, 52, 53, 55, 123–126, 129, 131–132, 136, 146, 173, 174, 180, 195, 196, 213, 253, 264
Mutualization schemes, 159

N

Nationalization, 8, 86, 101, 102
New Eurotime, 7, 161, 162
Non-premium insurance. *See* FAA Aviation Insurance Program
Nuclear weapons, 2, 83, 163

O

OECD. *See* Organization for Economic Cooperation and Development (OECD)
Organization for Economic Cooperation and Development (OECD), 145

P

Pareto-optimal. *See* Microeconomic efficiency
PFLP. *See* Popular Front for the Liberation of Palestine (PFLP)
Pool reinsurance scheme, 237
Popular front for the liberation of palestine (PFLP), 79, 106
Portfolio diversification, 181, 182
Portfolio theory, 181–183, 191
Pre-emption, 2, 83
Premium, 4–6, 8, 19, 22–24, 30, 42, 44–46, 50–54
Premium insurance. *See* FAA Aviation Insurance Program
Probable maximum loss, 272
Propitious selection, 135, 136
Public goods, 120, 121, 262, 263

R

Recharacterization risk, 186
Reinsurance, 6, 8, 12, 17, 27, 43, 48–51, 130, 133, 146, 148, 149, 157, 159, 162, 168–170, 173–175, 177–181, 183–189, 196, 200, 220, 231, 232, 237–239, 246, 248, 250, 274
Requisition for title or use, 82, 86, 101, 102, 104
Restraint, 86, 101, 102, 104
Retrocession, 17, 43, 50, 51, 130, 146, 148, 149, 185, 196, 200, 238
Retrocessionaires. *See* Retrocession
Riot, 90, 96–98
Risk-as-feelings hypothesis, 140
Risk management, xii, 12, 13, 18, 21, 67, 119, 151, 157, 158, 170, 213, 246, 271
Risk retention group (RRG), 7
Rome convention of 1952, 11, 63, 204–206
RRG. *See* Risk retention group (RRG)

S

Securitization, 50, 51, 148, 150, 151, 175–179, 181–188, 191–194, 196, 197, 199, 200, 273
Seizure, 62, 72, 73, 86, 89, 101–104
September 11, 2001, xi, 3, 4, 6–8, 10, 11, 13, 19, 67, 71, 83, 85, 98, 106, 107, 109, 111, 117, 131, 139, 143, 147–149, 151, 157, 160, 162, 163, 167, 179, 183, 203, 226, 228, 231, 232, 236, 239, 244, 247, 248, 253–257, 260, 263, 272, 275, 276
SGWI. *See* Special group on war risk insurance (SGWI)
Slips, 44, 46, 47
Spanish civil war of 1936, 76, 77
Special group on war risk insurance (SGWI), 229
Special purpose vehicle (SPV), 51
SPV. *See* Special purpose vehicle (SPV)
Strict liability, 64, 205, 211, 213–216, 221, 223, 240, 242
Strikes, 2, 76, 83, 96, 208

Subprime mortgages, 191–194
Subrogation, 36–38, 87, 225
Systemic risk, 12, 13, 112, 117, 143–145, 148–150, 184, 189

T
Terrorism Risk Insurance Act (TRIA), 98, 239
Terrorist acts, 2, 83, 236
TRIA. *See* Terrorism Risk Insurance Act (TRIA)

U
Uberrima fides, 29
UIC Convention. *See* Unlawful interference compensation convention
Underwriting risks, 177
Unlawful interference compensation convention (UIC) convention, 11, 64–66, 204, 207, 275
Unlawful seizure, 80, 82, 85, 229
Unlimited liability, 206, 223, 230, 232, 276
Utmost good faith, 29

V
Vertical placement, 46

W
War and Civil War Risks Exclusion Agreement, 76
Warlike operations, 74, 89, 94, 95
War risks waterborne agreement, 77
Warsaw convention, 59
Weapons of mass destruction (WMD), 20
WMD. *See* Weapons of mass destruction (WMD)
World Trade Center, 100, 104

MIX
Papier aus verantwortungsvollen Quellen
Paper from responsible sources
FSC® C105338

If you have any concerns about our products,
you can contact us on
ProductSafety@springernature.com

In case Publisher is established outside the EU,
the EU authorized representative is:
Springer Nature Customer Service Center GmbH
Europaplatz 3, 69115 Heidelberg, Germany

Printed by Libri Plureos GmbH
in Hamburg, Germany